Judaism

Judaism
The Evidence of the Mishnah

Jacob Neusner

The University of Chicago Press

Chicago and London

For

Suzanne Richter Neusner

The University of Chicago Press, Chicago 60637
The University of Chicago Press, Ltd., London

Library of Congress Cataloging in Publication Data

Neusner, Jacob, 1932–
  Judaism, the evidence of the Mishnah.

  Bibliography: p.
  Includes indexes.
  1. Mishnah—Criticism, interpretation, etc.
I. Title.
BM497.8.N474   296.1'2306   80–26080
ISBN 0–226–57617–5

JACOB NEUSNER is University Professor and Unger-
lieder Distinguished Scholar of Judaic Studies at
Brown University. He is the author and editor of
numerous works, including *Stranger at Home: "The
Holocaust," Zionism, and American Judaism,* published by the University of Chicago Press.

Contents

Preface

Come, weigh me the weight of the fire,
or measure me the measure of the wind,
or recall me the day that is past.
4 Ezra 4:5

Nowadays we can weigh fire and measure wind. But we still cannot recover a day which has gone. We do not even know what it would mean to recall it, if by recollection we wish more than memory. And memory is an exercise of deliberation and choice, an act of the shaping of the mortar, not of reconstruction out of available, already shaped, lumber and bricks. What we can do is try to compose an account of peoples' chosen memories, their recollection and their interpretation of what was happening to them. So the work is to reconstruct a frame of mind. It is to measure the consciousness of those who in mindful deliberation propose to reflect on what has happened on a day that is past and to say what it meant. Our task is to find out who people were from the evidence of what they said, to weigh the fire of their vision, to measure the weight and substance of their sigh.

This book is about the formation and social meaning of the ideas of a book which is not about a day that is past, but about a world sorely wanted in the future. Brought to closure about A.D. 200 in the Land of Israel, the Mishnah presents a grand design for the life of the house of Israel, the Jewish people, in all of its principal parts and requirements: time and space, both holy and profane, civil society and material economy, the cultic economy, making a secular living and shaping a holy life. In no way merely descriptive, the Mishnah's design for the Israelite household, or economy, was not realized in the time in which it came to closure and in the place in which it was framed. Indeed, it is not locative in either time or space. In context, the Mishnah is utopian and millenarian. Yet it also is the foundation for Judaism as we know it. Its shaping and closure mark the formative age of Judaism. The kind of Judaism of which the Mishnah is the first testimony ultimately drew into itself much else demonstrably in circulation in the time in which the Mishnah was taking shape and coming to closure. And the kind of Judaism inaugurated by the Mishnah ultimately went in directions not originally surveyed by the framers of the Mishnah.

For the Mishnah is the first document in the kind of Judaism of which the principal symbol is Torah; the primary rite, learning of Torah; the virtuoso, the rabbi; the emphasis, sanctifying the way of life of ordinary folk; and the point of central interest, the formation of a holy society of Israel. None of this is clearly to be found in the Mishnah, but all of it is adumbrated there. When the Mishnah was taking shape, in the main it contained a vision of how things might have been and should once more be. But, as it happened, both on its own and as mediator of Scripture, the Mishnah became the constitution of the Judaism which emerged in its aftermath. Along with the written Torah, the revelation of God to Moses at Mount Sinai, the Mishnah was set forth also as *Torah*, a coequal part of the Torah revealed to Moses. So in due course, what was a mere hope in some important ways became the practical design for everyday, material reality. There is no understanding of the kind of Judaism built, in some measure, upon the Mishnah's foundations, without a clear account of how the original document itself came into being and what it had to say in its own time and to its own circumstance. It is that kind of recollection of the day that is past—that is, of the day that would yet come—which I claim to present in this book.

But the Mishnah, in its own day, constituted only one among the many constitutive documents ultimately drawn into the formation of the kind of Judaism of which the Mishnah came to form the principal part. Clearly, the literary evidence for the formation of that kind of Judaism which begins with the Mishnah is not limited to the rabbinic writings collected in the two Talmuds. Everyone acknowledges that the same authorities (or cognate ones) who stand behind the Talmuds also sponsored the Midrashic compilations such as Genesis Rabbah, Leviticus Rabbah, and the Pesiqta-type Midrashim, not to mention the legal-exegetical compilations, Sifra, Sifré, and Mekhilta. No one doubts that the liturgy of the synagogue was received into and made normative for the Judaism of the rabbinic kind. Important bodies of religious experience and expression, surfacing only later on, moreover had their beginnings deep within the same formative period, if not amid the founding fathers of the Mishnah under study here. These include the mystical tradition first represented in writings from after the seventh century, e.g., in the Hekhalot visions. Not only do the Aramaic translations of the Scriptures, the Targums, clearly find a comfortable niche within the synagogue as it was shaped (or tolerated) by the rabbis of the Talmud. These same bodies of materials also contain important ideas which can be shown to have circulated in the time even before the turn of the Common Era, as well as after that date. True, we are not certain just who held those ideas or how they found their way into the larger rabbinic framework in which they are now located. Still, the diverse tributaries which flowed—water, mud, detritus and all—into the rabbinic mainstream are mighty and many.

An account of one important source in the formation of Judaism, together with the claim that ideas contained within that source tell us what some people were thinking in the first and second centuries, even before the closure of that source, by no means excludes other important evidence of the same period. On the contrary, once we have a reasonably reliable picture of what people had to say in the first century for the formation of a Judaism fully represented only in later writings, we have to bring that message into juxtaposition with the ideas of other people in that same time and place for the formation of the Judaism represented later on in that same corpus of religious writings. That is a problem to be dealt with a long time from now. In speaking of the evidence of the Mishnah about the formation of that kind of Judaism of which the Mishnah constitutes a principal, and the first, document, I clearly recognize the fragmentary character of the evidence under discussion, exhaustive only for itself, but flagrantly partial both for the Mishnah's period and for its kind of Judaism later on. The reader therefore must keep this fundamental fact in mind: the Mishnah is one source of evidence among many for the understanding of the formation in its day of its sort of Judaism. In this book I speak of what the Mishnah has to say and of the sources, in logic and in Scripture, of its thought, on the one side, and of the social perspectives of its thinkers, on the other. Under discussion is the evidence of the Mishnah for the formation of Judaism, hence my title.

The reason that I chose the Mishnah for the present exercise is that in earlier works of mine I have made possible the critical historical reconstruction which is undertaken here. No other document of earlier rabbinic Judaism is presently in that same condition of dissection and analysis as that in which I have placed the Mishnah. So here we take up not only a principal literary corpus. We speak also of the only one now ready for the work of reconstruction and restoration. My task is to reconstruct evidence which I already have translated, analyzed in its component parts, and laid out chronologically. My hope is to tell what that evidence allows us to report about the state of mind of people who flourished at diverse moments in the accumulation and agglutination of the document, the Mishnah, which now has been dissected and forced into decomposition. So from exegesis and analysis, I turn to reconstruction and interpretation.

This book thus is the natural successor to my history of Mishnaic law (see Neusner, *Purities, Holy Things, Women, Appointed Times, Damages*), forty-three books of translation and explanation, joined by my students' history of the Mishnaic law of agriculture. Other relevant, completed, and published writings are indicated in the bibliography under the names of Baruch M. Bokser, Joel Gereboff, Robert Goldenberg, David Goodblatt, Leonard Gordon, William Scott Green, Peter Haas, Abraham Havivi, Martin Jaffee, Shamai Kanter, Jack N. Lightstone, Irving Mandelbaum, Alan J. Peck, Gary G. Porton, Charles Primus, Richard S. Sarason, and Tzvee Zahavy. So the work of dissection is done and mostly in print. As indicated, the labor of reconstruction starts here.

The implications of the methods experimentally tested and first worked out in my *Development of a Legend: Studies on the Traditions Concerning Yohanan ben Zakkai, The Rabbinic Traditions about the Pharisees before 70,* and *Eliezer ben Hyrcanus: The Tradition and the Man,* then fully exploited in the aforelisted histories of the Mishnah's law, are now fully spelled out in this volume. There is nothing more to do along the path I set for myself in 1968–69 and I have followed from that time to this. That is not to say the work of the history of ancient Judaism is all done. It is to claim that, in both method and result, the foundations are now laid, the building's structure built; only the rooms are awaiting occupants and furniture.

The plan of this book is very simple. First, in the introduction, I shall place this work into the context of my previous work, telling how the appropriate sources were identified and characterized, and how the work of describing and interpreting the formation of something called Judaism was carried out. This methodological introduction is critical to all else, since, without understanding the scholarly traditions of the subject under study, the reader will not grasp the issues addressed in the substantive chapters which follow.

Second, in chapter 1, I shall briefly present an account of what we know of the issues confronted by all Jews in the period under study, and how others, equally claiming to be Israel, in the first and second centuries dealt with the questions facing the entire people of Israel. A simple typology would render the first century as an age of extreme hope, the second of extreme despair. The move from apocalyptic messianism and the fighting of holy wars to quiescent gnosticism and the making of fantastic imaginary systems and promising salvation through knowledge of such systems—the move is surely extreme.

Third, in chapters 2, 3, and 4, I shall describe the history of the state of the law and of the ideas embodied in the law before 70, that is, prior to the two wars against Rome, 66–73 and 132–35; in the interim between them; and in the period ca. 140–ca. 200, after the wars and up to the formation and closure of the Mishnah itself. The organization of these chapters is dictated by the organization of the Mishnah itself. In this way I make possible the comparison of the state of the law, through its parallel components, from one period to the next. This work is systematic and encompassing. The structure of the law is described in as clear a way as I can, with technical problems presented in their principal cognitive result. These chapters form the heart of the historical description presented in this book. As I have already said, they draw upon results printed elsewhere. The exercise undertaken here in putting together diverse and discrete results inevitably requires a review of vast stretches of the law. That is what is given, as clearly and simply as I can.

Then, in chapters 5 and 6, I shall interpret the history of the law in the social and intellectual context of the three periods of its unfolding. What is the Mishnah? What does the Mishnah mean? That is to say, given the vast amount of information taken by the Mishnah from Scripture and the clear evidence that the Mishnah speaks for several distinct groups in Israelite society, what is distinctively Mishnaic about the Mishnah? How is the Mishnah more than a composite of Scriptural information important to several identifiable social groups? Why, moreover, are we able to claim that the Mishnah constitutes a coherent, cogent, and distinct document and system of its own? These are the critical questions of interpretation. When we have answered them, we may claim to understand what the Mishnah is and what it means in its own context, that is, to answer the historical questions asked at the outset.

The claim was made in the behalf of the Mishnah by its earliest apologists that the document is part of the Torah of Moses, revealed by God at Mount Sinai. Now this claim, even in its mythic terms, yields two opinions on the character of the Mishnah: the Mishnah is essentially subordinate to the written Torah of Moses and is the construct of exegesis of the Pentateuchal law codes; the Mishnah is essentially autonomous of the written Torah of Moses. It is the *other* Torah, the other part of the "one whole Torah of Moses," formulated and transmitted orally from Moses's time to that of Judah the Patriarch, who is supposed to have formulated and closed the Mishnah and sponsored it as the law for Israel. Now while in a work in the history of religions, we hardly need to take up the exegesis of a theological and mythic interpretation of a principal document, in point of fact the examination of this claim concerning the definition and meaning of the Mishnah is fundamental to the problem of its interpretation. The reason is that, if the Mishnah does turn out to be essentially a secondary and contingent construct of the written Scripture, then the Mishnah cannot be placed squarely into the social context of its own time and asked to speak in particular to the political and theological crisis of the day. The Mishnah maybe expected to tell us only about how the Scriptures were mediated to that day, what the meaning of the Scriptures, autonomous of the age, dictated as a message (also) to that day. In other words, the position of the Mishnah vis-à-vis that document deemed to be definitive and determinative for the Mishnah's structure and contents turns out to be critical. My approach to the interpretation of the Mishnah as a social and intellectual document rests upon my examination of that claim which the framers of the Mishnah and their heirs laid upon it to begin with, I mean, the claim that this too is *Torah*.

I shall dispose of that claim by a detailed account of the facts of the relationship between Scripture and the six Divisions of the Mishnah and their various tractates. Three relationships are possible: the Mishnah depends completely on Scripture for not only facts but also basic issues; the Mishnah is completely independent of Scripture in regard to both facts and generative conceptions; and the Mishnah is partly dependent and partly independent. But since all three possible relationships can be shown to characterize the actual relationships of various tractates to the Scripture, it follows that the question has to be phrased in a different way. The matter of the relationship of the Mishnah to Scripture turns out not to be a possible point of differentiation, therefore, of definition. The taxonomic results permit no insight at all, when a document is shown to yield contradictory results. Since the Mishnah is dependent upon, and secondary to, some passages of Scripture, it is clear that close attention is paid by the Mishnah's framers to what some Scriptures have to say. But since the Mishnah is independent of other Scriptures, it is equally clear that an autonomous principle of selection of those Scriptures to receive close attention is in play. That is to say, the decision to choose one set of Scriptures and not some other is prior to the confrontation with any part of Scripture. The upshot is that the Mishnah is not simply a secondary expansion and extension of Scripture. The Mishnah is a construction, a system, formed out of an essentially independent and fresh perspective. Only after coming to full expression was it drawn to pertinent Scriptures. The Mishnah certainly can be shown to express the basic point of some passages of Scripture, to constitute an authoritative and accurate development of the meaning of selected verses in Scripture. But to understand the Mishnah we cannot turn to Scripture to begin with. The discovery and analysis of the principle of selection thus constitute a major point of differentiation, therefore of interpretation.

But the real issue is to explain the choice of those problems which determined the principle of selection in the first place. Whose problems are they? Whose questions are asked? Whose methods are used in the asking of those questions, and whose modes of thought determine the way in which problems will be phrased and solved? Thus the analysis of the substance and style, meaning and method in the document as a whole becomes the primary exercise in the interpretation of the history and structure of the Judaism framed by the Mishnah.

I shall point to what I believe to be three social groups which will have found urgent the information presented in the Mishnah or will have deemed self-evident and natural the mode of discourse through which that information is presented. These social groups are the priests, whose points of concern fill up the larger part of the document as a whole; the scribes, who contribute a concern for numerous matters of documentation of changes in status of people and property and also modes of discourse and rhetoric; and the householders, who will have taken special interest in those large tracts of the Mishnah which move beyond the particular concerns of the priests. The Mishnah thus bears the tribute of three distinct types of social groups: caste, profession, and class (to use these words in as neutral a way as I can). Yet the Mishnah as a document is fundamentally cogent, complete, and unitary in its basic concerns. Its aesthetic and intellectual traits are uniform throughout. So the question of how the contributions of the several social components are fused and joined together and of how the Mishnah may be shown to have transformed these tributaries and their gifts must be raised. This question will be dealt with from two perspectives: forms of discourse and modes of thought, on the one side; and distinctive intellectual program, or message, of the Mishnah, on the other. In these two aspects—style and substance—I claim that Mishnah is solely Mishnaic, distinct from its constituents, more, indeed, than the sum of its parts.

In order to facilitate the reader's work, I have supplied most of those biblical verses which are important in the formation of the law of the Mishnah. In appendix 4 these are presented in the order dictated by the unfolding of the law, therefore in the sequence of the allusions or direct references made to them in chapters 2, 3, and 4. That is, the Scriptural verses important in the Division of Agriculture as it took shape before the wars are given first, then come those important to the Division as it continued its development between the wars, and finally are those important only after the wars, and so for the other five Divisions. This form of presentation gives graphic evidence of the expansion and development of interest in Scripture.

Israelite survivors of the great wars of the first and second centuries, in the last decades of the second century, putting together an account of the house of Israel as they wished to see it, created the Mishnah. In this book I claim to describe what they had for bricks and mortar, and to explain the plan of the house they built. This, then, is the house of Israel, the Judaism revealed by the evidence of the Mishnah.

I need hardly point out that no one really could live in that house. Without a Temple, most of the laws of three of the six Divisions, as well as a fair part of those of yet a fourth, were simply not pertinent. Israelites living outside of the Land of Israel, under governments which

Acknowledgments

At three points my graduate students contributed to this book: first, an appendix of essays on the Division of Agriculture before 70; second, outlines of most of the tractates of the Division of Agriculture in Appendix 5; and, third, brief discussions of the relationship of those tractates to Scripture. I wish here to express my thanks and indebtedness to my students for their time and learning in my behalf. The specified contributions are found as follows:

Tractate	Author	Relationship to Scripture	Outline
Kilayim	Irving Mandelbaum	p. 174–76	p. 352
Shebiit	Leonard Gordon	p. 176–77	p. 352
Terumot	Alan Peck	p. 177–78	p. 355
Maaserot	Martin Jaffee	p. 178–80	p. 355
Maaser Sheni	Peter Haas	p. 180–81	p. 356
Hallah	Abraham Havivi	p. 181	p. 356

Richard Sarason's previously published writings are cited for Demai and for the introduction to the unit on the relationship of the Division of Agriculture to Scripture.

The manuscript of this book was typed by Mrs. Y. A. Marie-Louise Murray of Riverside, Rhode Island, and Miss Winifred C. Bell, Providence, Rhode Island. Both worked hard, promptly, and carefully, and I appreciate their dedication to the task. Mrs. Lee Haas served as research assistant in preparing the reference list.

The first parts of my *History of the Mishnaic Law of Purities* were written during my tenure as a Guggenheim fellow, and the last parts of the history as well as this book were composed during my tenure, five years later, as a Guggenheim fellow, 1974–75 and 1979–80, respectively. I am deeply grateful for the support and recognition twice

xvii

afforded by the John Simon Guggenheim Memorial Foundation, which greatly facilitated this history of the Mishnaic law and interpretation of it.

The principal critical reading of this book was contributed by my sometime student, oftentimes teacher, and always friend, Professor Jonathan Z. Smith, of the University of Chicago. He completely annotated the penultimate draft and especially called my attention to what was not immediately clear.

Everyday conversations with Wendell Dietrich and Ernest Frerichs provided an opportunity for attempting to state in a clear and simple way those chimeras of thought which, lacking a real audience, are nothing more than bright ideas, incommunicable, irrelevant, fantastic. I have learned over the years that, if I ever wrote a line I thought was a masterpiece, I should blot it out, as too personal and idiosyncratic to be of use. It is Wendell Dietrich and Ernest Frerichs who impart that astringent and healthy lesson.

Whatever little knowedge I have of the problems of study of the relevant Apocryphal and Pseudepigraphic documents I owe to James Charlesworth, whose generosity to colleagues knows no bounds. For our day, he is a major figure in the vigorous study of that part of ancient Israelite literature.

My sustained interest in the social description of ancient Judaism is only one of the many things I owe to Wayne A. Meeks. His criticism of my work, sympathetic, informed, constructive, and understanding as it is, more than occasionally leads me to recognize a blind alley and to start afresh.

Even though this book concerns literary evidence alone, I have benefited from the guidance and insight of Eric Meyers and A. Thomas Kraabel on the importance of archeological sources in the description of ancient Judaism. The probative value of material culture in making sense of the literary evidence to which it is relevant is beyond question. For its part, the Mishnah is here seen as a wholly intellectual construct. But while my interpretation of the context and meaning of the document does not pretend to take account of such archeological evidence as may prove relevant, it is not because I do not deem that evidence important. It is simply because it is not pertinent to the work undertaken here. That is why I am especially grateful for the counsel and friendship of these archeologists.

Correspondence with John Gager and Robert Kraft has kept me in touch with important streams of thought parallel to my own. I have benefited from the scholarly work of both colleagues.

During the period in which this book was composed, my former student, David Goodblatt, served as a visiting professor at Brown. Frequent conversations with him proved helpful to me in formulating problems and shaping ideas. My former students, William Green and Richard S. Sarason, are constant companions in my intellectual adventure. In letters and phone conversations there is a constant interchange of ideas and problems. Both read and criticized earlier drafts. Students in my graduate seminar in the period in which this work was taking shape, Leonard Gordon, Peter Haas, Abraham Havivi, Martin Jaffee, and Alan J. Peck, joined in these conversations and read the chapters as they came back from the typist. I found their interest encouraging, and their questions stimulating. Mr. Peck and Mr. Jaffee served as research assistants and greatly facilitated my progress. They read and criticized the manuscript as well.

There is a larger context for this work of mine, Brown University. No small number of colleagues in my department and in other departments, undergraduate students in courses of mine, graduate students in other programs in my department, and members of the administration of the university have played a large part in forming what is for us all a friendly and benign fellowship of learning. To name them all would be pointless. But I must make mention of Provost Maurice Glicksman, my friend and coworker, who for so many scholars on the Brown faculty makes the importance and progress of scholarly work a principal enterprise, a definitive activity, for this university. If, as many of us believe, we labor in an enviable circumstance, it is because of the success of our provost and dean of faculty. No tribute to what he has done over the past ten years, moreover, can omit reference both to his predecessor, Merton Stoltz, whose tradition is carried forward, and to our bright and shining president, Howard Swearer, who quickly has become part of this same tradition of seriousness and commitment to sustained projects of learning. At Brown we do not have to apologize for entertaining and fulfilling scholarly aspirations. Here it is understood that scholarship and teaching are one thing in two guises.

The person to whom this book is dedicated heard about its progress late at night and early in the morning, at intimate lunches and hectic suppers, and in diverse other circumstances. Since it comes as the climax of all I have done for over ten years, the book is appropriately dedicated to the person with whom, more than anyone else, I have done it.

J.N.

8 February 1980
21 Shebat 5740
The eve of the bar
mitzvah of my son
Eli Ephraim

Introduction

What Kind of Judaism

The kind of Judaism under discussion here, predominant from late antiquity to our own day, is represented principally, but not solely, in the Babylonian Talmud, and so is called *Talmudic*. Its religious virtuosi are called rabbis, so it is referred to as *rabbinic*. Theologians deem this kind of Judaism to be definitive, claim in its behalf the power of setting norms, and therefore call it *normative*. Among the simple the adjective *classical* suffices. That protean, distinctive, encompassing expression of Judaism, the kind claiming to inherit the whole revelation, written and oral, of God to Moses at Mount Sinai and so alleging its writings to constitute "the Torah," is called in all these ways: its name is legion.

But the period of its formation is not so difficult to specify as its rightful name. Whatever kinds of Judaism existed in the period before the turn of the first century, that kind represented in the Mishnah, the Talmuds, and other rabbinic writings of late antiquity did not. That is the fact. To be sure, much material deriving from these earlier kinds, beginning, after all, with the Hebrew Scriptures themselves, is taken over and amply exploited by the framers of Talmudic-rabbinic-normative-classical Judaism. Whatever kinds of Judaism continued to thrive in the period after the Moslem conquest of the Middle East, that kind represented in the Mishnah, the Talmud, and other rabbinic writings came clearly to predominate. So the formative period of the Judaism under discussion, that characteristic of most Jews who practiced Judaism from the seventh century to our day, is the first seven centuries of the Common Era.

The Purpose of This Book

This book describes the development of one important stream of materials flowing into the formation of the kind of Judaism which took shape

1

in the first few centuries of the Common Era and predominated thereafter. Those materials are the ones collected and expressed in the
Mishnah, attributed to Judah the Patriarch, ca. 200. In concentrating
on that singular corpus of ideas and how it takes shape, I do not wish to
suggest that there is no other important evidence from the period before 200 about the shaping of the kind of Judaism later on represented
all together by the Mishnah and its successors and continuators. The
contrary is the fact. There is apt to be pertinent information in a vast
corpus of relevant documents. These include two Talmuds, the compilations of biblical exegeses called midrashim made by rabbis of the
fourth, fifth, and later centuries, the synagogue liturgy (Siddur, Mah-
zor, earliest Piyyutim), the translations of the principal biblical writings
used in the synagogue and otherwise (the Targums), and the mystical
and magical writings represented in the extant Sefer Harazim, let alone
ideas held earlier but preserved only in such later collections as the
Hekhalot writings. All of these collections of evidence are apt to include materials deriving from the period before A.D. 200 and formative
afterward.

Nor do I wish to give the slightest credence to the conviction that
only the Mishnah contains ideas likely to have been in the minds of
those first- and second-century Israelites who stand behind the Mishnah and take part in the creation of the mode of Judaism expressed—in
what degree and measure we do not know—within the Mishnah, since
these important materials—Talmuds, Targums, Tosefta, and later Midrashic compilations—circulated earlier. To be sure, how they circulated we do not know. In what form, for what purpose, and among
what social circles they were formed in the first centuries of the Common Era and even earlier, we cannot say for sure. But we can say that
the Mishnah is not the only evidence for the character of its kind of
Judaism before 200, in "Tannaitic times."

This extended statement of qualification must be taken as the opening proposition of this book. Otherwise my claim and purpose simply
will not be understood, and, unhappily, the best once more will be
made into the enemy of the good and useful. What I do in this book is
one important task in the systematic description of the formation, earliest social context, and intellectual history of a kind of Judaism known
to us from a number of sources. These sources, later becoming one
encompassing Judaism, thus emerge as cognate to one another, each
presenting its distinctive perspectives (and, alas, methodological
problems). The ultimate, encompassing description of the Judaism of
which we speak in its earlier formation, in the first and second centuries, therefore will take account of much more than what the Mishnah has to tell us. But the Mishnah is the first document to be redacted
in something very like the character in which it now reaches us. It is a

vast and complex document. That is why on its own it deserves full and reverent attention. The results yielded here, based on over ten years of analytical work, in some measure will then have to be brought into juxtaposition with, and contrast to, parallel analyses—not as yet undertaken—into other documents. Then we shall know what is to be learned from them, too, about the same period from which Mishnah speaks. Here I describe the evidence of the Mishnah on Judaism in the "Tannaitic" age.

When, moreover, we claim to speak of one kind of Judaism at a given period, we must not be accused of neglecting other kinds of Judaism, the religious systems worked out by others, of the same time and place. These too claimed to be not merely a part of Israel but "the true Israel." The testimonies to these other kinds of Judaism are contained not only in the parts of the New Testament—for example, Matthew—produced in the later first century. They also persist in those massive and important compilations under the names of Baruch and Ezra. Like the Mishnah, these were prepared in the aftermath of the destruction of the Second Temple and in response to the crisis of the Israelite spirit precipitated by it.

Since, furthermore, the evidence of the Mishnah begins in the period before 70, a full account of the social and religious context in which the ideas ultimately brought to closure in the Mishnah take shape would have to pay attention to the literary legacy of the Essenes, contained in the library of Qumran and other places; the immense system of Philo, with its curious points of parallelism and intersection with ideas contained in much later rabbinic writings; the evidence on the state of Judaic consciousness, imagination, society, and institutions, preserved, for his own purposes, by Josephus; and indeed the bulk of those vast and diverse writings produced in the Land of Israel in the last two or three centuries before the Common Era and preserved, in the main, among circles other than those which succeeded and carried forward the ancient legacy into the Mishnah and its cognate writings—a very large domain.

In speaking of the unfolding of the ideas of the Mishnah, therefore, I stress at the very outset the simple fact that these ideas testify only partially to the inner life and world view of only one group among the many which ultimately coalesced and gave shape to that singular Judaism later called Talmudic or rabbinic, normative or classical. For there are other sources for what was happening in diverse circles contemporary to the Mishnah and also represented, later on, in that same kind of Judaism. But we do not yet know the relationship, before 200, of those circles and their ideas to the circles of thinkers who stand behind the Mishnah. We also do not know how or when the writings of the one group, those of the people behind the Mishnah, came to form part of a single kind of Judaism, and to intersect and fuse with the writings of another, for instance people behind the Targums, the synagogue liturgy, or the folk who created the Aggadic tales and Midrashic interpretations of Scripture, many of them demonstrably available in the same time in which the Mishnah was coming to full expression but only much later on written in the way in which we have them (see appendix 3, below). Perhaps the Targums and various fables and Scriptural twists and turns originated in circles other than those behind the Mishnah and only later on were taken over and deemed "rabbinic." Perhaps they came into being in the same groups as stand behind the earliest layers of Mishnaic thought. At this time we cannot be certain, having no controls or certain criteria. Not all problems are to be solved all at once.

A picture of Judaism based only on those materials later on utilized by the kind of Judaism which became normative obviously would be seriously inadequate for the description of the origins of that kind of Judaism in the period of which we speak.* Even the effort merely to contrast in the descriptive exercise the people whose writings we do employ and those whose writings we do not, such as those for whom 2 Baruch and 4 Ezra speak, requires attention to the character of that excluded group of Israelites and its concerns. Otherwise the points of comparison and contrast will hardly be amply charted.

Because all these points are definitive for the book as a whole, I wish now to go over them.

First, the Judaism represented by the group behind the Mishnah is apt to have been diverse before 200. That means that the Mishnah is only one body of evidence about the kind of Judaism for which the Mishnah (among other sources) is apt to speak.

Second, there is evidence in later rabbinic materials about ideas held in the period before 200, that is, in the time of the Mishnah.

Third, there were diverse kinds of Judaism before A.D. 200, of which the group behind the Mishnah represents only one kind.

Fourth, there are many other important components of the Judaism represented by the Mishnah but coming to full expression and closure only much later on. Some of these components are apt to have begun to take shape before 200. They may or may not have taken shape among the circles who at that time were working on the materials which ultimately became completed as the Mishnah. They certainly did find their place within the normative framework of rabbinic Judaism a century or two or even more after the formation of the Mishnah. So things important in later developments of the kind of Judaism called rabbinic, that kind for which the Mishnah is the first closed corpus of evidence, may

---

*This is a fault in Moore and Urbach.

well have begun to develop in the same time as the Mishnah, though not among circles congruent with those behind the Mishnah or even intersecting with them.

So the Judaism represented by the Mishnah here is not represented as normative, either in its formative period or thereafter. The Mishnah is not represented as the sole or even principal evidence of those participants in the formation of Judaism who were active in the time in which the Mishnah was under way, that is, before 200, or in the period conventionally called that of the Tannaim, that is, Mishnah repeaters. That is why this book is not about "the age of the Tannaim" in general, but about the description and interpretation of one important *book* generally supposed to have been made up by the Tannaim. This is a book not about "Judaism in the age of the Tannaim," but only about one important component of one kind of Judaism of the stated period. The evidence of the Mishnah is examined for an account of a kind of Judaism brought to expression in the Mishnah. So we speak of not an *age* but *evidence* of a single book; not all the things a given sort of Jewish religious authority may have made, but one book it made. Yet I claim that this too is a picture of *Judaism*.

What Is New Here

In this book, my program is both to provide an account of the stated topic—the history of the formation of a principal part of that distinctive kind of "Judaism," beginning in the period somewhat before the destruction of the Second Temple of Jerusalem in 70 and concluding with the formation and closure of the Mishnah itself, in about 200—and also to exemplify the way in which a topic comparable or equivalent to this one should be treated. Now there already is a justly famous work which does the same thing, that is, which purports to narrate the history of the same kind of Judaism as we examine, and also sets the example for others. It does so in a way which has served as the definitive model for continuators who wish to tell the same kind of history of the same kind of Judaism. I refer to George Foot Moore's *Judaism in the First Centuries of the Christian Era: The Age of the Tannaim* (1927).

I have at the outset to give a full account of why I propose to succeed Moore's *Judaism* with a different account of that same Judaism, worked out on the basis of an entirely different repertoire of evidence from Moore's, in accord with a wholly fresh principle of organization and a completely different set of questions and methods. For there is no point in merely replacing a treatment of a topic done rightly. But

from Moore's title onward, I think his book is wrong. This must be
explained.

In defining the task, Moore speaks for me: "The aim of these volumes is to represent Judaism in the centuries in which it assumed
definitive form as it presents itself in the tradition which it has always
regarded as authentic. These primary sources come to us as they were
compiled and set in order in the second century of the Christian era."
So Moore begins his masterpiece, part of the title of which I have
adapted in this work, and all of the intention of which I have made my
own. The Mishnah is the first relevant document for the representation
of Judaism "as it presents itself in the tradition it regards as authentic."
Whether, as I said, we call this kind of Judaism "rabbinic," "Talmudic," "normative," "classical," or even "Mishnaic" hardly matters. Under study is that part of the nascent stage as revealed in the
first-closed document of that expression of the religious world view and
way of life which, from its own day to ours, has shaped the consciousness and culture of the Jewish people and has defined what we mean
when we speak of "Judaism."

To be sure, there are two other writings which both indisputedly
derive from Israelite hands and also inform us about Israelite thinking
in the same period, from 70 to ca. 200. These are 2 Baruch and 4 Ezra.*
While some maintain that chapters in other Pseudepigraphic documents may derive from the times under discussion, all agree that these
two certainly come to full expression after 70 and provide a glimpse
into the mind of some people of that day. In addition, there are
allusions among Christian writers to the state of mind of Jews whom
they claim to have known but may have invented, as in the case of
Justin Martyr. But in so far as Moore's criterion governs the work of
presenting Judaism in the centuries in which it comes to its first full
expression, the Mishnah is the document which Judaism has always
regarded as authentic. The history of that kind of Judaic religion expressed in the Mishnah therefore is to be presented under Moore's
title, as I have adapted and revised it. So we speak not of all kinds of
Judaism in the age of the Tannaim who framed just one of those kinds,
as Moore's title suggests is his intention. We address only one kind of
Judaism and its history, that to which the principal and constitutive

* On Jewish Pseudepigraphic writings after 70, Professor James H. Charlesworth (personal letter, October 29, 1979) writes: "The major writings in the Pseudepigrapha in the
period after 70 but before 200 are 4 Ezra and 2 Baruch. Enoch and the Apocalypse are usually
dated to this period. The problem in working with them is that they are extant in the Old
Church Slavonic and with Slavic material we are faced with an exceedingly difficult problem
which is unparalleled in our work on the other documents. We know that the documents
extant in Slavonic have been preserved because of the Bogomiles. The Bogomiles,
however, created pseudepigrapha; they were both shaped and formed by older pseudepigrapha and also wrote new ones. The task is exceedingly difficult, therefore, to be certain
what is prior to the Bogomiles and, of course, that is our only interest."

document of the Tannaim, the Mishnah, first gives full expression and rich testimony.

The labor before us, specifically, is to take the strata of Mishnah's intellectual history, which I already have explained and analyzed in my history of Mishnaic law, and to put the parts together into that new and whole structure demanded for the purpose of historical reconstruction and interpretation. When that task has been accomplished, we shall have a picture of the beginnings and first major expression of the Judaism of which the Mishnah is the original flowering. What makes this account distinctively historical, however, will be its sustained effort to relate the unfolding of the ideas of the Mishnah to the historical setting of the philosophers of the document, to compare context and concept, to ask about the interplay between ideas and social, material reality. The historical purpose of this work, therefore, is identical to that of Moore's. This is so even though, in the nature of things, the evidence deemed relevant and the way in which the evidence is analyzed and brought together to form a reconstruction of the several stages in the formation of Judaism scarcely intersect with Moore's procedures at a single point. The difference is for two reasons.

First of all, as indicated, Moore's book is much too broad. That is to say, the evidence he adduces derives from, and therefore represents, altogether too wide a range of varieties of Judaism, over too long a period of time. Much of the evidence for "Judaism" in Moore comes from, and faithfully portrays, either the age long before 70 or the period four or five centuries after the formation of Mishnah in 200. More important: a vast amount of material derives from circles which cannot be deemed at all concentric with the social and intellectual group behind the Mishnah. So Moore describes many kinds of Judaism as if they formed a single, fully symmetrical construct. The claim of "normativity" for this Judaism is not merely wrong. It is confusing, for it specifies one "Judaism" where there are many.

Second, as I have already hinted, Moore's is to begin with not really a work in the history of religions at all, in this instance, the socially grounded, developmental, and formative history of a particular brand of Judaism. His research is into theology. It is organized in theological categories, not differentiated by historical periods at all. Moore presents a synthetic account of diverse materials (deriving from diverse, asymmetrical sources, as I said), focused upon a given topic of theological interest. There is nothing even rhetorically historical in the picture of opinions on these topics. Moore makes no pretense of accounting systematically for development and change. What is constructed is a static exercise in dogmatic theology, not an account of the history of religious ideas or—still more urgent—the society of people who held those ideas. So Moore in no way describes and interprets the

religious world view and way of life expressed, in part, through the
ideas under study. He does not explore the interplay between that
world view and the historical and political context of the community
that held it. In so far as history attends to the material context of ideas
and the social perspectives expressed by ideas and institutions alike, in
so far as ideas are deemed part of a larger social system, and systems
held to be pertinent to the given political and economic framework
which contains them, Moore's account of dogmatic theology has
nothing to do with religious history—the history of Judaism or of one
kind of Judaism in the first two centuries of the Common Era.

Let me now amplify this point so as to explain why I believe a fresh
account of the formation of Judaism out of the evidence of the Mishnah to
be necessary. The question to be answered has carefully to be spelled
out. Under a title reminiscent of Moore's, I present a book which
scarcely intersects with a single point of discourse or definitive category
deemed by Moore to be relevant to the topic at hand. His systematic
and dogmatic theology draws upon a vast range of evidence, ad-
ducing testimony for the character of the Judaism he purports to describe from documents deriving from diverse groups which, in their
own day, would not have understood one another, let alone accepted
one another as part of the same social group and cultic community.
When "Judaism" is made to refer to the exegetical compilations of the
rabbis of the fourth and fifth centuries—and much later—as well as the
writings of Philo, Pseudepigraphic authors, and the "sectaries at
Damascus" (as Moore calls them), then the term *Judaism* stretches so
far, covers so much diversity, as to lose all definitive form. Evidence
from the fifth century of the Common Era and from the first or second
century before it—six hundred years—serves to describe a single religion no more naturally (if also not less) than the poetry of the age of
Beowulf and that of our own day serves to describe a single language
(if also no less).

In proposing a completely different approach to the description of
Judaism in the first centuries of the Christian era, the age of the Tannaim, I wish now to take full account of the important and in many
ways prophetic criticism of Frank C. Porter (Porter, *Moore,* esp. pp.
41ff.). I believe that Porter's review of Moore's book should have led
to a fruitful debate and to a fresh approach to the work done so ele-
gantly, but with such major flaws, by Moore. As far as I know, from the
time of Porter's review of Moore to this date, there has been no effort
to take seriously the flaws pointed out by Porter, even though many
independently may have been aware of them. Indeed, the two principal
flaws pointed out by Porter—first, Moore's claim that the Judaism "of
the Tannaim" was normative, and, second, Moore's systematic aver-
sion to discussion of the Judaism revealed by the legal texts—were

self-evident from the start. Yet everyone who came after Moore continued the work of dogmatic theology, resorted to precisely the same undefined and undefended, essentially formless canon, and pretended that the Tannaim created everything and anything but the Mishnah.

It is time, therefore, for Porter to have that hearing denied him in his day, among the Jewish scholars of Judaism perhaps for one set of reasons, among the Christian scholars of Judaism perhaps for another set of reasons. I quote at length the principal paragraphs in which Porter sets forth the problem which I believe I have not neglected or sidestepped in this work, and in the rather sizable prior studies upon which this work is based.

First let us consider Porter's criticism of the matter of normativity:

The Judaism which Professor Moore describes with such wealth of learning is that of the end of the second century of our era, and the sources which he uses are those that embody the interpretations and formulations of the law by the rabbis, chiefly from the fall of Jerusalem, 70 A.D., to the promulgation of the Mishnah of the Patriarch Judah, about 200 A.D. When Moore speaks of the sources which Judaism has always regarded as authentic, he means "always" from the third century A.D. onward. It is a proper and needed task to exhibit the religious conceptions and moral principles, the observances, and the piety of the Judaism of the Tannaim. Perhaps it is the thing that most needed to be done of all the many labors that must contribute to our knowledge of that age. But Professor Moore calls this Judaism "normative"; and means by this, not only authoritative for Jews after the work of the Tannaim had reached its completion in the Mishnah, but normal or authentic in the sense that it is the only direct and natural outcome of the Old Testament religion. It seems, therefore, that the task here undertaken is not only, as it certainly is, a definite, single, and necessary one, but that other things hardly need doing, and do not signify much for the Judaism of the age of Christian beginnings. The book is not called, as it might have been, "The Judaism of the Tannaim," but *Judaism in the First Centuries of the Christian Era: The Age of the Tannaim.* Was there then no other type of Judaism in the time of Christ that may claim such names as "normative," "normal," "orthodox"? The time of Deuteronomy was also the time of Jeremiah. The religion of revelation in a divinely given written law stood over against the religion of revelation in the heart and living words of a prophet. The conviction was current after Ezra that the age of prophecy had ended; the Spirit of God had withdrawn itself from Israel (I, 237). But if prophecy should live again, could it not claim to be normal in Judaism? Where, in the centuries after Ezra, are we to look for the lines of development that go back, not to Ezra and Deuteronomy, but to Jeremiah and Isaiah? R. H. Charles claims the genuine succession for his loved Apocalypses. The Pharisees at least had the prophets in their canon, and it is claimed by many, and by Moore, that the rabbis were not less familiar with the prophets than with the Pentateuch, and even that they had "fully assimilated" the teaching of the prophets as to the value of the cultus (II, 14), and that their conception of revealed religion "resulted no less from the teaching of the prophets than from the possession of the Law" (I, 235). Christians see prophecy coming back to Judaism in John the Baptist and in Jesus, and find in Paul the new experience that revelation is given in a person, not in a book, and inwardly to each one through the indwelling Spirit of God, as Jeremiah had hoped (32:31–34). And now, finally, liberal Judaism claims to be authentic and normal Judaism because it takes up the lines that Jeremiah laid down.

It would require more proof than Professor Moore has given in his section on "History" to justify his claim that the only movements that need to be traced *as effecting religion* are those that lead from Ezra to Hillel and Johanan ben Zakkai and Akiba and Judah the Prince. Great events happened during the three centuries from Antiochus IV to Hadrian, events which deeply affected Judaism as a religion. But of these events and their influence Moore has little to say. It is of course in connection with these events that the Apocalypses were written.

It is to meet Porter's first point that I define this project as I do: Judaism as portrayed within a specific, socially circumscribed corpus of evidence. But I go a step beyond what Porter calls for. For I claim to speak not merely about the Judaism of the Tannaim, but the Judaism portrayed by a single document, the first one produced by, and attributed to, those authorities conventionally called "Tannaim." For reasons which I now have made quite clear, I make ample provision for the probability that there is much more evidence about the Judaism shaped by the authorities who stand behind the Mishnah than is contained solely within the framework of the Mishnah.

Porter's second criticism of Moore seems to me still more telling. He points out that Moore nearly wholly neglects the Tannaitic legal corpus—the Mishnah itself (!):

> In [Moore's] actual exposition of the normative, orthodox Judaism of the age of the Tannaim comparatively little place is given to Halakah. One of the seven parts of his exposition is on observances; and here cultus, circumcision, Sabbath, festivals, fasts, taxation, and interdictions are summarily dealt with; but the other six parts deal in detail with the religion and ethics, the piety and hopes, of Judaism, matters about which the Haggada supplies most of the material, and for which authority and finality are not claimed. The tannaite (halakic) Midrash (Mechilta, etc.) contains a good deal of Haggada together with its halakic exegesis, and these books Moore values as the most important of his sources (I, 135ff.; II, 80). The principles of religion and morals do indeed control the interpretation

of certain laws, so that Halakah is sometimes a source for such teachings, and "is in many instances of the highest value as evidence of the way and measure in which great ethical principles have been tacitly impressed on whole fields of the traditional law" (I, 134). This sounds as if the ethical implications constituted the chief value of the Mishnah for Moore's purposes. But these are not its chief contents. It is made up, as a whole, of opinions or decisions about the minutiae of law observance. It constructs a hedge of definitions and restrictions meant to protect the letter of the law from violation, to make its observance possible and practicable under all circumstances, and to bring all of life under its rule.

The Jewish scholar, Perles, in a pamphlet with which Moore is in sympathy, criticized Bousset, in *Die Religion des Judentums,* for using only books such as Bacher's, on the Haggada, and for expressing a preference for haggadic sources; whereas the Halakah in its unity, in its definitive and systematic form, and its deeper grasp upon life is much better fitted to supply the basis of the structure of a history of the Jewish religion. Moore agrees with Perles' criticism of Bousset's preference for the later, haggadic, Midrashim; but it is not because they are halakic that he gives the first place to the early Midrash. "It is this religious and moral element by the side of the interpretation of the laws, and pervading it as a principle, that gives these works [Mechilta, etc.] their chief value to us" (I, 135). Perles insists on the primary importance of the Halakah, not only because it shows here and there the influence of prophetic ethics, but because throughout, as it stands, it is the principal work of the rabbis, and the work which alone has the character of authority, and because, concerned as it is with ritual, cultus, and law *(Recht),* it has decisive influence upon the whole of life. This applies peculiarly to the religion of the Tannaim. The Haggada neither begins nor ends with them, so that Bousset ought not, Perles thinks, to have used exclusively Bacher's work on the Haggada of the Tannaim, but also his volumes on the Haggada of the Amoraim, as well as the anonymous Haggada which Bacher did not live to publish. It is only in the region of the Halakah that the Tannaim have a distinctive place and epoch-making significance, since the Mishnah, the fundamental text of the Talmud, was their creation.

Would Perles be satisfied, then, with Moore's procedure? Would he think it enough that Halakah proper, observances, should occupy one part in seven in an exposition of the Judaism of the Tannaim, considering that in their classical and distinctive work Halakah practically fills sixty-two out of sixty-three parts? Moore agrees with Perles that there is no essential distinction between earlier and later Haggada (I, 163), and that the teachings of the Tannaim about God and man, morals and piety, sin, repentance, and forgiveness are not only also the teachings of the later Amoraim, but run backward, too, without essential change into the Old Testament itself. There is no point at which freedom and variety of opinion and belief, within the bounds, to be sure, of certain fundamental principles, came to an end, and a proper orthodoxy of dogma was set up. But orthodoxy of conduct, of observance, did reach this stage of finality and authority in the Mishnah; and the tannaite rabbis were those who brought this about. It is in accordance with Moore's chief interest in haggadic teachings that he does not in fact confine himself to sayings of the Tannaim, but quotes freely from the Amoraim also; how freely may be seen by the list that ends Index IV.

Professor Moore's emphasis upon his purpose to present normative Judaism, definitive, authoritative, orthodox, would lead one to expect that he would give the chief place to those "juristic definitions and decisions of the Halakah" to which alone, as he himself sometimes says, these adjectives strictly apply. We should look for more about the Mishnah itself, about its systematic arrangement of the laws, its methods of argument and of bringing custom and tradition into connection with the written law, and more of its actual contents and total character, of those actual rules of life, that "uniformity of observance" which constituted the distinction of the Judaism of the rabbis.

How I have corrected this second, and principal, failing of Moore hardly needs specification beyond the title of this book. Curiously, in correcting Moore's failure to take account of the evidence of the Halakhah, that is, of the Mishnah, of the second-century authorities, I have been able to focus upon that other of Moore's errors of description which, as I said earlier, strikes me as critical, I mean, the omission of the social and political context of a religious structure and system. For the law of the Mishnah deals precisely with that—the construction of society, the formation of a rational, public, normative way of life.

The history of a religion tells about how a religion took shape and describes its concerns in relationship to the concrete historical context in which that religion comes to full expression. But these simply are not problems or even topics which form part of the hermeneutical framework of Moore's book. The critical, interesting issue in my view is the relationship between a religion, that is, the world view and way of life of a coherent social group, and history, that is, the material and political circumstance of that same social group. This elementary issue of history in Moore simply is not addressed. True, the history of a religion and the dogmatics of that religion are going to relate to one another. But a description of uniform dogmatics of seven centuries or more and an account of the contents thereof simply do not constitute, in addition, a history of the religion which, in a measure, comes to formal ideological expression in dogmatic theology. So Moore did not do what the title of his book and of his professorship (he was professor of the history of religion) promise, even though in his work are discussed numerous matters bearing historical implication. Since his aim, which is the right one for the description and interpretation of a religion, remains unmet, I here propose to begin to accomplish it.

The proposed account of the interplay between religious ideas and the social group that held those ideas takes its first step by asking about the sort of social group represented by the data we clearly have in hand. A further step is to propose a statement of the social perspective of that group whose viewpoint is documented before us. Moore did not attempt to extrapolate from the facts we have—that is, the ideas people clearly held at diverse times—to a picture of the questions people proposed to confront through those facts and the social perspectives which generated those questions. His successors then took for granted that Moore had defined the work to be done. He merely had not done it adequately. So each went over the same ground of dogmatic theology and called it history. But the history of a religion is the social relation of the world view and way of life of that religion to the material reality of the people who held those ideas. Self-evidently, we have first to trace and distinguish the layers of ideas welded together into a single, intellectually composite document. Merely telling which idea came first and which came later is not history. It (alas!) is not even much of a narrative.

To be sure, there is a further social history which must come, the actual history of the society in which the particular social group at hand formed a part. It is only in that larger, quite objective context that we can assess the character of a particular social perspective, a fantasy made concrete, such as is documented before us. True, I try to tell the story of how the things people in this document were saying actually related to the perspective, framed by them in particular, upon the encompassing context in which they lived, an age of wars and defeats. But then I say nothing about the facts of circumstance, economy, and society. The reason is that before us merely are the viewpoints, the fantasies, of a particular group in its own testimony and context. Describing the social perspective of a document does not carry us outside the framework of the document. It tells us who is apt to speak from within the document. It surely does not permit us to state the social facts to which the document constitutes a particular response, in this case, those upon which the thinkers of the Mishnah express their judgments. But describing a perspective or viewpoint, interpreting the ideas therein as addresses and responses to the world outside, does permit us to claim to move a small step beyond the limits of the document itself.

In this section I have tried to deal with what I believe are the two principal flaws in conception and method exhibited by Moore and his heirs and continuators, namely, (1) the false claim that the rabbinic literature describes "normative" Judaism, the inclusion into Judaism of the testimonies of diverse groups, with little in common, the presentation of a theological dogmatics; and (2) the neglect of the critical importance of the legal literature. The flaw consists in asking the wrong questions, of the wrong (because too much) evidence. Their work presents a formalistic and static account of a Judaism wholly divorced from material and social reality. It is not history, because there is no recognition of change and development, social context and political setting. It also is not an account of a religion, because there is no effort to show how theological ideas express a basic world view and explain a way of life.

Yet Moore's *Judaism* is a masterpiece, in portraying the state of mind of a scholar who, recognizing as few did the mortal danger posed to Jewry by Christian writers on Judaism in an age of gathering Jew-hatred, composed a splendid apologetic. Indeed, Moore's *Judaism* is a monument to Anglo-American and democratic goodwill, a monument constructed in an age in which for Jewry and for Judaism there was almost no goodwill at all among cultured people. We on the other side of the abyss of that dark age now are able to return to those questions. In claiming to do what Moore did, but asking different questions of different evidence, I gladly acknowledge my human debt to Moore. Had his apologetic not made a deep impression on successive generations of scholars of goodwill, there would be no interest in Judaism within the academic framework. I daresay, without Moore and people like him, perhaps even fewer of us Jews would have survived than did survive to do their share of the work.

The Mishnah's Evidence on Its Earliest Layers of Ideas

There is yet another major difficulty in the method and results of Moore and his continuators and imitators. It is a simple and obvious deficiency, one which would have made Moore's historical results untenable, had Moore even attempted a genuinely historical account to begin with. I refer to the matter of uncritically assigning sayings attributed to various authorities to the period in which the said authorities lived, and, among the still less critical, the prevalent assumption that if the rabbinic sources claim Mr. X said something, he really did say it, and if they tell a story about what Mr. Y did, he really did do it. This fundamental problem, occasionally recognized and sometimes called the matter of "dating sayings," was not taken seriously in a sustained and systematic way in ambitious work of a historical character on Talmudic materials prior to my history of Mishnaic law. That is the fact, even though, here and there, we do find people asking the question of how we know Mr. X really said what is attributed to him, or why we should believe Mr. Y really did what people tell about him. The recognition, for instance, that there is a difference between fable and fact is commonplace.

Yet Moore and all those who have worked on the present corpus of materials in no way take account of the central issue of justifying the location of a given saying in any given period before the time of the closure of, e.g., the Mishnah itself (not to mention still later redacted books). I have postponed this criticism until after my major critique of Moore, so that Moore's principal failures may be presented in terms of the state of historical thinking prevalent in his own day. That is why I lay such heavy stress on Porter's contemporary review. But now we cannot avoid yet another fundamental point of innovation of this book: using the criteria of my history of Mishnaic law, I systematically and consistently choose some sayings as valid evidence for what people were thinking at a given time prior to the closure of the Mishnah and exclude other sayings which lay claim to speak of the same period.

If we claim to relate ideas to a specific group of people and their social world, we have to justify the effort to correlate what is said with the historical period and society of that group. Now it is easy to justify doing so for the final generation of the redaction of the Mishnah. The people who have given us this document clearly propose to tell us about their view of the world as they see it or as they want to see it. Consequently, the Mishnah in its present condition does tell us a great deal about the perspective on the world of the people in the last half of the second century who are responsible for the present condition of the Mishnah. But the Mishnah claims far more than that. It is rich in attributions of sayings to authorities who are believed to have lived before the half-century of ultimate redaction, indeed, up to two hundred years before that time. The chronological organization of the present book, moreover, indicates that I take seriously the claim that we know something about the world of ideas held by people who stand both prior in time and in direct, traditional relationship to the people responsible for the closure and layout of the Mishnah. I must now explain the basis of that chronological organization. All of the results of this book for periods prior to the last half of the second century—the time of the closure of the Mishnah—rest upon a simple theory, developed in my history of Mishnaic law, of verifying or falsifying, or excluding as not subject to verification or falsification, the attributions of sayings to authorities who lived in the period before 70, or in the age between the two wars against Rome. A full account of how I developed the theory of historical knowledge operative in this book is now required.

Since the Mishnah was brought to closure in about 200, I first had to ask how we knew that anything in that document told us about times

prior to the moment of closure. For, after all, merely because the
Mishnah referred to the way things were, that is, used the past tense or
clearly wished us to believe that it spoke of a time before its own, that
did not mean that the philosophers of the document knew what they
were talking about, let alone that we had to believe what they told us.
True, the Mishnah placed sayings in the mouths of people who probably lived long before the completion of the Mishnah itself, for instance, before 70, or before the Second War against Rome. But to
compose my account of the ideas of contributors to the Mishnah who
flourished in times before the completion of the Mishnah, I had to have
more solid evidence than the mere assertion, on the part (after all)
merely of the Mishnah's final authorities themselves, that a given sentence was said (or an idea held) by an authority who flourished before
the time of those authorities. The claim that the final redactors "must
have had a reason" or "relied upon oral tradition" or "had solid foundations" I regarded as insufficient, unless it was substantiated item by
item and case by case.

It was not possible to prove that most of what is attributed to early
authorities really was true in the time in which they lived, since the
issues of the Mishnah's discourse rarely intersected with those concerns important to documents of the first century. True, the Temple
really was destroyed, so when a saying was assigned to someone,
taking for granted there was no Temple, that saying was likely to have
been formed after 70. But merely because a saying assumed there was a
Temple did not mean it was said before 70. Nearly the whole of the
Division of Holy Things, on how things are done in the cult, was
demonstrably put together after 140, when there was no possibility of
conducting a sacrificial cult in Jerusalem at all. So, in sum, I needed to
develop a theory of the literature before me and of the historical
knowledge to be derived from it.

First, a negative observation was in order. The literary and redactional traits of the Mishnah did not permit differentiation among the
layers of the document, because the governing literary traits of the
Mishnah were imposed within the processes of redaction, penultimate
and ultimate (see Neusner, *Purities* XXI). A single redactional theory
governed the formation both of the tractates and of their subunits. That
theory posited that the appropriate way for organizing and laying out
materials was to take up a theme and unpack its principal constituents,
then to· take up each of those constituents and unpack its generative
logic. So the principle of organization throughout, from the perspective
of ultimate redaction, was logical. Rejected principles of organization
were, first, according to the legal rule that all manner of topics might
have in common; second, according to the formulary trait, that all
manner of principles and topics might share; and, third, according to

the name of a single authority who touched on all manner of principles, topics, and formulary traits. All of these principles of organization could be shown to have been tried. But all were rejected in favor of the thematic and logical mode of organization for nearly the whole of the Mishnah. Excluded, among tractates, were only Eduyyot, which in general was organized not thematically but around the names of authorities, and Abot, the organizational principle of which fell totally outside of the Mishnaic framework.

What the chosen principle of organization—logical and topical—required was that I ignore the temporal sequence in which sayings were said. That is, I did not first expect redactors to give opinions of early authorities, then of later ones. They first gave fundamental propositions, then secondary ones, without regard to the temporal sequence of the names of the authorities who were claimed to hold, or discuss, said propositions. This mode of organization, moreover, logically precluded the possibility of preserving whatever form sayings may have had before they were brought together for their logical affinities. In fact, for logicoaesthetic reasons, everything on a given logical topic was presented within a single set of formal patterns (see below, pp. 241–48). If something was said long before some other thing and given its formal character only for the purposes of transmission, it did not matter to the redactors. That is why, as I said, the redactional and formal character of the Mishnah prevented differentiation among the Mishnah's materials by reference to differences in formal traits or in the literary sources of sayings. The exceptions to this rule were too few to matter.

I was left solely to make use of the traits of thought and the fact that particular ideas are given in the names of specific individuals or identifiable schools or "Houses." That is to say, I knew that there were no differentiating criteria emergent from the formulation, form, or redaction of the document. These had been shown to reflect the taste and judgment solely of the final editors. So I had to look elsewhere if I wished to claim that the Mishnah told us about an age prior to that of its own redaction alone. I turned to the contents of sayings and attributions attached to sayings. The pertinent evidence was in three parts.

First, there was the fact that most, though not all, individual units of thought in the Mishnah bore the names of specific authorities.

Second, there was the fact that all units of thought in the Mishnah made intelligible statements, exhibiting a logic coherent with the document as a whole. Thus I could attempt to correlate what was said in a given name with the place, in the unfolding logic of the document, of what that named authority was made to say.

This proposed system of correlation was possible thanks to a third piece of evidence, the fact that the named authorities came together in groups, which with a high degree of success could be differentiated by periods. That is to say, authorities A, B, C, and D always occurred in juxtaposition with sayings of one another, but rarely, if ever, occurred in juxtaposition with sayings in the names of authorities W, X, Y, and Z. Further, as I shall explain, evidence internal to the Mishnah itself, not adduced from other documents, showed that authorities A, B, C, and D generally said things which in logic stood prior to what was placed in the mouths of authorities W, X, Y, and Z. It seemed to me to follow that what I found in the names of authorities A, B, C, and D should tell me conceptions or principles or problems worked out prior to what I found in the names of authorities W, X, Y, and Z. The correlation between priority in the period in which an authority lived and anteriority in the logic of what was said by that authority forms the foundation for my claim that the Mishnah tells us something about the world before the period of its own closure, that is, the second half of the second century.

There were five important qualifications to this proposition. First, the verification of priority or posteriority on the basis of the correlation of attribution and logic was possible only when what was said by authority A, B, C, or D intersected with what was given in the name of authority W, X, Y, or Z. Where there was no continuity between a saying in the mouth of an earlier authority and one given in the name of a later one, I was not able to attempt an exercise of falsification, therefore, too, of verification. In such a case I do not adduce that saying in evidence at all in this book. In this book sayings not subject to a test of validation and falsification are treated as if they simply do not exist. Happily, they are a small sample of the whole.

Second, sayings in the names of authorities who lived after the Bar Kokhba War, that is, within forty or fifty years of the formation of the Mishnah itself, claimed far less antiquity than those in the names of authorities who lived two hundred years before the closure of the Mishnah. The mid-second-century authorities, moreover, generally were supposed to be the teachers of the (mostly anonymous) framers of the Mishnah. Where I was able to relate things in the names of those authorities to what was said by people who bore direct responsibility for the Mishnah, there was invariably a close correlation. For example, what was said in the name of the alleged principal of the Mishnah, Judah the Patriarch, invariably stood at the end of a sequence of logical steps attributed to his predecessors, never at the outset. So I took it as a matter of fact that what was in the names of authorities after the Bar Kokhba War did inform us about ideas held between ca. 140 and ca. 180, that is, the time in which that generation of Mishnah teachers was supposed to have flourished. Thus, in this book, I include all evidence bearing the names of authorities assumed to have flourished after the Second War against Rome in my account of the state of thought in the last half-century of the unfolding of ideas put together in the Mishnah (see chapter 4, below). The basis for that assumption is explained presently.

Third, there were some units of thought, to which I already have alluded, which bore no names at all. These, however, were easily brought into alignment with principles clearly to be located at a given point in the unfolding of ideas ultimately formed into the Mishnah. When they were, the anonymous sayings usually turned out to find a compendious place right where they should—in the history of ideas assigned to the authorities of the Mishnah. That is to say, they turned out to express the same principle as was in the name of a specific authority (usually an authority of the period after 140). For the fact is that the Mishnah's several tractates normally do more than provide information. They usually work out the internal logic of a given topic. Consequently, if I could locate a saying within the known, established pattern of the logical unfolding of a problem, I was on solid ground in maintaining that a saying lacking a name in fact fit into the thought of a given stage in the unfolding of the logical exposition of a tractate's problem. So in the main, though not always, sayings lacking names, in any case a very small proportion of the whole, did not present insuperable problems in the tracing of the history of the ideas of the Mishnah on a given subject. Unattributed sayings standing outside the logical framework of a tractate are ignored in this book; these, again, are very few indeed.

Fourth, it must be emphasized that I was able to differentiate only between "generations"—that is, groups of names, which commonly occur together, A, B, C, or D as against W, X, Y, or Z. I was not able to differentiate within a "generation," that is to say, among names of a single group. The reason was that within a given group of names, A, B, C, or D would occur in nearly all possible combinations. It followed that, while I was able to undertake a gross schematization in the history of the Mishnah's ideas, I was in no way able to speak of what was earlier and what was later within the sayings assigned to a given group of names, before 70, between the wars, after the Second War.

The internal evidence of the Mishnah on its own therefore permitted no more refined exercise of differentiation, temporal and logical, than that which I have described. So that is as far as I could go, which accounts for the three operative chapters (chapters 2, 3, and 4) within which I trace the history of the ideas of the Mishnah in the present book. For the groups break down, in general, into authorities assumed to have thrived before 70, with special reference to the Houses of Shammai and Hillel; those who we suppose lived from the time of the destruction of the Second Temple in 70 to before the Bar Kokhba War, ca. 120, that is, Yohanan b. Zakkai, Joshua, Eliezer, Gamaliel, Tarfon,

Aqiba, Yosé the Galilean, Ishmael, Yohanan b. Nuri, and others who
appear in units of thought along with them; and, finally, those who
flourished after Bar Kokhba's war, ca. 140–ca. 180, specifically, Judah,
Meir, Yosé, Simeon, Simeon b. Gamaliel, Eliezer, Eleazar, Joshua b.
Qorha, and the like. I see no possibility of differentiating between the
sayings in the names of authorities of the mid-second century and those
of the end of that same century, that is, Judah the Patriarch, Judah b.
R. Yosé, Simeon b. Eleazar, and others. Since Simeon b. Gamaliel and
Judah the Patriarch will occur in disputes within the same unit of
thought, there is no reason to attempt such a further differentiation.
Once more it is clear that the divisions within which our account flows
must be deemed gross and general. That is why, as I said just now, we
adduce in evidence only a few simple facts of the world outside of the
frame of the Mishnah's authorities: destruction of the Second Temple,
defeat in the Second War against Rome, and the closure of the Mishnah
itself.

The fifth and final qualification concerns the materials in the names
of authorities before 70, with special reference to the Houses of Shammai and Hillel. Where in my detailed survey of the whole of the Mishnah I did find a reason to doubt the validity of attributions, it consistently concerned what I had in the names of the Houses. The reason
was that it was not uncommon to find that the House of Shammai and
the House of Hillel took up positions on points profoundly rooted in
thought well attested to in the period after Bar Kokhba, that is, in the
names of authorities over a century after the Houses. Indeed, that
phenomenon was sufficiently common so that it came to appear likely
that the names of the Houses were often used for purposes other than
historical.

Where I could show that ideas or principles in the mouths of the
Houses were taken up and developed by people assumed to have lived
after that time, whether in the period following the destruction of the
Second Temple or in the period after Bar Kokhba's war, where the
Houses appeared to lay the foundations for an ongoing discussion, and
what was assigned to them appeared to come early in the unfolding of
that discussion, I use them to describe the state of mind of authorities
before 70 whose ideas are preserved—obviously, not in their own
words or even in their own frame of organization and reference—in the
Mishnah itself.

But in other instances, I found that ideas in the mouths of the Houses
expressed points at issue in lively disputes among authorities a hundred
years later. Of probative value, these disputes were on subjects or
principles otherwise developed also in the mid-second century and not
at all treated in sayings in the mouth of anybody prior to that time, up
to the period before 70 or even to 130. Specifically, authorities of the

long period between the time in which we assume the Houses flourished, before 70, and the period after Bar Kokhba's war, knew nothing not only of the specific opinions, but even of the problems or topics on which the Houses are supposed to have worked. This hardly suggested a continuous process of development and refinement. It certainly did not validate the claim that very early in the process of the formation of the Mishnah's principles and ideas, such issues as were assigned to the Houses actually came under discussion—and were really decided, one way or the other.

Here it appeared that the Houses were names assigned to sayings pseudepigraphically, for purposes which were not fully clear to us. The intent may have been merely mnemonic. It may have been polemical. The intent sometimes appeared to be to place both Houses in agreement on the position of one or another authority much later on. Or it was planned to put into the mouth of the House, which, in fact, was deemed on the wrong side of all arguments, the House of Shammai, the position which a later disputant rejected and wished to impute to the other side. In general, in this book, when I claim to know what was on people's minds before 70, I exclude all such doubtful cases and speak only of those which seem to me in accord with the stated criterion to be firmly and beyond doubt located in the period under discussion.

So, in sum, we deal with relative, sequential positions of ideas, some earlier, some later. We cannot be sure that the correlation of chronology and logic, of which I make so much, in fact is not merely the work of the final generation, wishing to impart to its document a claim of antiquity which, in fact, was spurious. To be sure, it is difficult for us to imagine why the framers of the Mishnah would have resorted to so infinitely complicated a device to secure credence that only some, but not all, of what they had to say derived from people living two hundred or a hundred years prior to their time. There were, after all, simpler ways at hand. The people who received the completed Mishnah chose one of those ways. They declared the entire document to be nothing less than ''Torah revealed by God to Moses at Mount Sinai'' (see appendix 2, below). They said the Mishnah had been transmitted from that time to modern days by a curious means of oral formulation and oral transmission, that is, they called the Mishnah, ''oral Torah.'' But that claim, in behalf of the Mishnah as a whole, is not attempted *within* the document, not for a single one of its sayings, even those allegedly *heard*. The state of affairs at the three periods under discussion shows a clear correlation with what the Mishnah's authorities appear to have been working on in that age. But that argument merely from content seems to me ultimately too flawed to be allowed to stand.

In the end, therefore, I simply must state at the outset that the facts upon which my picture of the history of the ideas of the Mishnah is based may be explained in ways other than that way composed by the picture which I present in this book. The correlations of chronological attribution and priority or posteriority in logic constitute facts I have discovered. These facts seem to me to be explained by the assumption that what appears to come earlier in the unfolding of a problem and also bears the name of an earlier authority is earlier in fact, not merely in its literary-logical traits. So I explain the facts as *history*. But, as I must emphasize, one may also claim that the framers of the document so planned matters that this is precisely how things would appear to be, and then the facts would have to be explained as *convention*. If I could make sense for myself of why people should have planned matters in such a way, I would offer a quite different account of the evidence of the Mishnah on the formation of Judaism in addition to the one I present here. That is, chapter 4 would be much longer, chapters 2 and 3 (alas) much shorter.

What We Study When We Study "Judaism"

The critical problem of definition in this project, and in others like it, is presented by the organizing category of the title of this book, "Judaism." Explaining *what* we propose to define when we speak about "Judaism" is the work of both contemporary philosophy of religion and history of religions. In general, historians of religions have tended altogether too rapidly to articulate that *phenomenon*, the history of which they claimed to describe. What generates this fairly widespread failure of definition and resort to undefended categories is the problem of dealing with a definitive category essentially asymmetrical to the evidence. That is, a deeply philosophical construct, "Juda-ism," is imposed upon wildly mythological or totally unphilosophical evidence, deriving from many kinds of social groups, and testifying to the state of mind and way of life of many sorts of Jews, who in their own day would scarcely have understood one another, let alone have known they all evidenced the same -ism, for instance, the Teacher of Righteousness and Aqiba, or Josephus and Bar Kokhba.

This now brings us to the definition of *what* we propose to describe and interpret through the Mishnaic evidence of the Tannaim, I mean, their kind of "Judaism." The problem of defining what sort of *thing* we study when we describe and interpret "Judaism" falls into two parts. First, what kind of an "-ism" is in hand? Second, what sort of sub-species of that "-ism," the "Juda-" kind of "-ism," do we treat?

If we declare that we study a religion, the Judaistic version of religion, we advance our discussion only a little bit. For precisely what we study when we study a religion, and what sorts of evidence we should examine and what kinds we may ignore when we do so, are not entirely clear. Indeed, if we reflect on the extant answers to those questions—what do we study when we study a religion? what kinds of data do we adduce for analysis in that connection?—we move far out toward the limits of imagination and the data of culture. People write the history of early Zoroastrianism on the basis of meanings of words not even strung out in sentences, for lack of other, better evidence. A complete version of a Judaism of late antiquity can be teased out of similar evidence, namely, symbols used in synagogue art and on gravestones. So all manner of evidence, from stones and single words on upward to wall frescoes and sentences, paragraphs and rooms, is found suitable for the description and interpretation of a religion.

The definition of religion, for its part, loses all promise of precision, when, in our own day, Marxism and psychoanalysis are termed religions. At the same time, traditional religion becomes an expression of something quite other than systems and convictions solely of a transcendental and supernatural content. For instance, religion is represented as a not-well-disguised social movement (Donatism), on the one side, or as a reponse to contextual dissonance of a structurally fundamental social order (a "cargo cult"), on the other.

So if we can use any evidence of any kind to study any phenomenon of any sort, what we do when we study religion, and how we do it, are not readily discerned. In this regard matters are admirably summed up in Arthur Darby Nock's inquiry about the matter of "Gnosticism." He wanted to know where are *the* Gnostic churches, who are *the* Gnostic priests, and what are *the* Gnostic church's books and doctrines (Nock 1:444–51). What he meant to point out, I believe, was that all we have are rather specific evidences, e.g., of Manichaeism or Mandaism, and now, of Nag Hammadi. Out of the agglutination and conglomeration of these diverse social groups and their writings scholars formed (I should say, invented) that higher idea, that "the"—the Gnostic religion. From a philosophical viewpoint the intellectual construct, Gnosticism, may bear scrutiny. From a historical viewpoint, it does not. The reason is that history, rightly done, must err on the side of radical nominalism, as against the philosophical tolerance of something close to pure realism. In invoking for analogical purposes these categories of ancient and medieval philosophy, I mean only to explain why, for the present purpose, "Juda-" and "-ism" do not constitute definitive categories.

What then is under discussion, stated quite simply, is the world view and way of life which speak of transcendent things and claim in this world to work out supernatural norms (hence, the religion) of a very small social group of Israelites in the later first and second centuries. Their creation, the Mishnah, is important because in time it came to define major elements of the world view and way of life of nearly the whole Jewish people. The second century Tannaim, therefore, laid the foundation for the religion of the Jews through almost the whole of the history of the Jewish people from the time of the formation of the Mishnah until nearly our own time, thus, for "Judaism." It goes without saying but bears repeating that in describing the seedtime of one kind of Judaism, I in no way claim to report on the character of the Judaism—the supernatural way of life and the transcendent world view—of nearly the whole of the Jewish people who expected the Messiah soon and who fought against Rome twice in the very time in which this (then) special kind of Judaism was aborning. That kind of prevalent Judaism is represented by 4 Ezra and 2 Baruch. In the end people will wish to ask whether our knowledge of how this kind of Judaism took shape, the particular set of circumstances to which, in the minds of some, it proved particularly relevant, gives us insight into how, in later centuries, the structures of Judaism resting on the constitution of Mishnah turned out to be strikingly pertinent to the historical condition of the Jewish people. But that engaging question lies far beyond the boundaries of this book.

To conclude: the subtitle, "evidence of the Mishnah," is meant to be severely limiting and restrictive. The kind of Judaism under historical analysis in this book is that attested to by a single important document, produced in what appears to have been a continuous and fairly coherent movement of men (there were no women) who knew one another and who claimed to have studied with the same great masters. The Mishnah fully expressed the world view and way of life of these men. That is not to suggest that the Mishnah exhausts the evidence about the group behind the Mishnah. But the Mishnah does exhaustively express a complete system—the fit of world view and way of life—fantasized by its framers. It is in theory a way of conducting the totality of life and constructing society, state, and cosmos. The Mishnah presents the Judaism which the Tannaim offered to the Jewish nation of the Land of Israel of their day—and which, in their day, in its wars against Rome, the Jewish nation rejected.

1

The Mishnah in Context: Ways Not Taken

The Questions of the Age

The kind of Judaism designed by, and fully expressed in, the Mishnah began to take shape in the middle of the first century, to be sure massively drawing upon ample materials of the centuries before that time, especially of Scripture. But in so far as ideas culminating in the Mishnah's full expression shaped a criterion for selection of what was useful in the old, and for the design of what was needed that was new, those ideas effectively shaped that principle of choice somewhat before, and somewhat after, the destruction of the Second Temple in 70. The nascent period of Mishnah's system, defined by its own attributions, runs back for two or three generations before the wars, and the age of closure is two or three generations after the wars. It follows that, to make sense of the issues confronted in the formative period of Mishnah's unfolding, we have at least briefly to listen to what other people, in the same times and places, had to say about the times. To begin with, let us briefly define the common agendum of them all, the historical events of the day.

The concrete historical facts which shaped the history of every particular kind of Judaism of the first century are few but beyond dispute. They are, first, that the Temple was destroyed in 70 in the midst of a major war against Rome; second, that three generations later, a second war against Rome produced the definitive exclusion of Israelites from Jerusalem and priests from the ruins of the Temple; leading, third, to the final recognition that, for some time to come, after over a thousand years there now would be no Temple and no cult. To the best of my ability, beyond the internal evidence of the Mishnah itself, I adduce, in evidence of any concern I impute to the framers of the Mishnah, or assign to their program, or invoke in explanation of things they wished to say, only these three facts. All my other statements about the history of Judaism of the particular kind under discus-

25

sion emerge only from an entirely inductive reading of the literary evidence itself.

Clearly, I do not claim to describe the state of mind and mode of life of the entire Jewish group ("people"), let alone of all those who, in the later first and second centuries, wished to call themselves "Israel." The reason is merely that we lack adequate evidence; it is not that such an encompassing account would not be interesting. It would be not only interesting but also decisive in making sense, also, of the particular corpus of evidence here under close examination. For in the end what the Mishnah redactors imagined must stand up against the reality, recorded independent of their fantasies, the objective political, social, and material reality in which they formed their dreams and designed their account of "Israel" and its life. This we cannot do, much as we want to. The probative evidence for how things actually were and how people were thinking is only in what they did and made. For the most part, literary materials, outside of the Mishnah, 4 Ezra, and 2 Baruch, are episodic and unrevealing for the large descriptive and interpretive labor which is ours. Knowing from archeology all that we know about the refugees associated with the war led by Bar Kokhba, whose household goods and documents have been recovered, as well as about the people buried in Beth Shearim and what they incised on their tombs, we are left with evidence just as random and—until demonstrated to be otherwise—just as unrepresentative as are the Mishnah, 2 Baruch and 4 Ezra. That is to say, we do not know for whom *else* the sherds of contracts and the incisions on sarcophagi speak, besides those who made them. And that is so of the Mishnah as well. So, until shown otherwise, the Mishnah speaks not only for itself, but also solely about itself and its framers' views.

Indeed, if we have to posit a large-scale social movement attested to in the evidence we do have, that is, the deeds of masses of people, we must take for granted it is not a movement shaped by the Mishnah but the movement of messianic hope represented by the successive generations of fighters for Israel's freedom from Rome. For two mass actions, about the program and concrete deeds of which we are exceedingly well informed in the main (if not in all desired detail), are the great movements culminating in wars against Rome. Now we have no evidence produced by the fighters themselves about what people were thinking who in 66–73 and again in 132–35 left their homes and fought, risking all and losing all. Incising on their coins, "The Freedom of Israel Year 1," they tell us something altogether too general. Further, our surmise, based on our own rough calculation that three generations—nearly seventy years—were allowed to pass from war to war, that the principal motive for the Second War had to do with the realization of the hopes for repeating the extraordinary pattern narrated in the biblical story of the first Temple's destruction and the people's suffering, atonement and restoration, also is too general. For despite Josephus' account of the First War we do not have first-hand documents which tell us what the participants in the mass movements of Israelite Palestine had in mind in doing what they did. So we cannot describe the world view and the way of life—that is, the "Judaism"—of the generality of Jews who really did shape the history of their nation and their part of the country in the period under study.

It nonetheless seems to me self-evident that their state of mind more nearly will have been expressed by the visionaries whose writings are assembled under the names of Baruch and Ezra (not to mention the vast literature of apocalypse and historiosophy of the period before 70) than it can be before us in the pericopes of the Mishnah. The reason is simple but compelling. Nothing in the Mishnah and its description of the Israelite world and way of life makes provision for, or leads us to expect, what the people really were doing in the first half of the period in which Mishnah took shape. Jews fought two massive wars against Roman armies in the Holy Land. So the Jewish people in the age of prologue to the Mishnah were making history. Nothing in the Mishnah explains why people should have made wars. So the framers of Mishnah were avoiding it. The Mishnah's is not a plan for that construction of the world which will make ample place for the kind of history that the Jews then wanted to make and did make. Its critical issues are elsewhere than on the battlefield.

The Mishnah's framers' deepest yearning is not for historical change but for ahistorical stasis (see below, pp. 119–21). Their notion of a holy deed does not encompass the battlefield as the normal setting for consecration. The principal lines of structure, the main beams of order, of the Mishnaic system follow the outlines of the village and the cult, two places in which, in the nature of things, world-shaking hsitorical events of politics and war are alien. Fur both are locations for an ongoing life, in which events are the uneventful: in the village, birth, marriage, childbearing, death; in the cult, the regular and routine, precise and orderly everyday offering of the produce of the field and the village. What is dangerous in the village is the moment at which, for instance, a woman leaves one status and enters some other. What is threatening in the village is change in the status of one person because of the violence or avarice of another. All things have their place; all produce has its price, no more, no less, than true value. In such a world where is there place for "the Freedom of Israel Year 1"? And what can such a concept of freedom have meant to people whose principal document was the Mishnah, where the word *freedom* does not appear even one time (excluding a single play on words)? So Mishnah is a document whose system cannot have impressed the mass of Israelites in the time in which the system was taking shape. There was then another normative—norm-setting—Judaism than "Mishnaic Judaism."

First-Century Apocalypse

The only extant documents originating in the decades immediately after the destruction of the Temple in A.D. 70 are 2 Baruch and 4 Ezra. We make better sense, as I said, out of what people did do when we know what they did not do, but what others among their contemporaries did, in response to the same crisis. That is why we must dwell on the writings of other Jews of the Land of Israel, besides those represented in the Mishnah. For if we ask how the character of the Mishnah's system for "Judaism" differs from that of the writings of other Jewish thinkers of the same general period, the first and second centuries after the destruction of the Temple, we have only 2 Baruch and 4 Ezra for comparison. Those writings give some perspective on the work of the framers of Mishnah, even though they have absolutely nothing in common with Mishnah. Still, it is in precisely the same period and under essentially common conditions that the authors of Baruch and Ezra choose one set of topics, which they treat in a particular way, and the earliest framers of Mishnah choose another set of topics, to be treated in a quite different way. If we wish to know what Mishnah does not discuss, all we need to do is to list the issues and concerns we have seen in writings in the names of Baruch and Ezra—and vice versa.

The crisis precipitated by the destruction of the Second Temple affected both the nation and the individual, since, in the nature of things, what happened in the metropolis of the country inevitably touched affairs of home and family. What made that continuity natural was the long-established Israelite conviction that the fate of the individual and the destiny of the Jewish nation depended upon the moral character both of the one and of the other. Disaster came about because of the people's sin, so went the message of biblical history and prophecy. The sins of individuals and of nation alike ran against the revealed will of God, the Torah. So reflection upon the meaning of the recent catastrophe inexorably followed paths laid out long ago, trod from one generation to the next. But there were two factors which at just this time made reflection on the question of sin and history, atonement and salvation, particularly urgent.

First, with the deep conviction of having sinned and the profound sense of guilt affecting community and individual alike, the established mode of expiation and guilt and of atonement for sin proved not inadequate but simply unavailable. The sacrificial system, which the priestly Torah describes as the means by which the sinner attains forgiveness for sin, lay in ruins. So when sacrifice turned out to be acutely needed for the restoration of psychological stability in the community at large, sacrifice no longer was possible—a crisis indeed.

Second, in the awful August of A.D. 70, minds naturally turned to August of 586 B.C. From the biblical histories and prophecies emerged the vivid expectation that, through the suffering of the day, sin would be atoned, expiation attained. So, people supposed, just as before, in three generations whatever guilt had weighed down the current generation and led to the catastrophe would be worked out through the sacrifice consisting of the anguish of a troubled time. It must follow that somewhere down the road lay renewal. The ruined Temple would yet be rebuilt, the lapsed cult restored, the silent Levites' song sung once more.

Now these several interrelated themes—suffering, sin, atonement, salvation—from of old had been paramount in the frame of the Israelite consciousness. A famous, widely known ancient literature of apocalyptic prophecy for a long time had explored them. The convictions that events carry preponderant weight, that Israelites could control what happened through their keeping, or not keeping, the Torah, that in the course of time matters will come to a resolution—these commonplaces were. given concrete mythic reality in the apocalyptic literature. Over many centuries in that vast sweep of apocalyptic-prophetic writings all of the changes had been rung for every possible variation on the theme of redemption in history. So it is hardly surprising that, in the aftermath of the burning of the Temple and cessation of the cult, people reflected in established modes of thought upon familiar themes. They had no choice, given the history of the country's consciousness and its Scriptural frame of reference, but to think of the beginning, middle, and coming end of time as it was known.

Before examining ways in which the question of the age came to be phrased in apocalyptic writings, let us rapidly review the following statement, by Morton Smith, of the world view represented in the common faith of Israelite culture and religion in the Land of Israel, in all its forms and expressions, down to the destruction of the Temple and for some time thereafter. This passage is important to our understanding of the setting in which the several types of Judaism came to expression, because it tells us the convictions common to them all, the world envisaged by each. It places into context, in particular, those reflections on the meaning of the destruction of the Temple which the apocalyptic prophets and poets left behind as testimony to the prevailing frame of mind of the common folk of the country, I mean, the people who fought the two major wars against Rome. So this is what

the world was like for that large part of Israel responsive to the vision
and poetry of apocalypse:

> The picture of the world common to Jesus and his Jewish Palesti-
> nian contemporaries is known to us from many surviving Jewish and
> Christian documents. It was wholly mythological. Above the earth
> were heavens inhabited by demons, angels, and gods of various
> sorts (the "many gods" whose existence Paul conceded in I Cor.
> 8:15, and among whom he counted "the god of this age," II Cor.
> 4:4). In the highest heaven was enthroned the supreme god,
> Yahweh, "God" *par excellence,* who long ago created the whole
> structure and was about to remodel, or destroy and replace it. Be-
> neath the earth was an underworld, to which most of the dead de-
> scended. There, too, were demons. Through underworld, earth, and
> heavens was a constant coming and going of supernatural beings
> who interfered in many ways with human affairs. Sickness, espe-
> cially insanity, plagues, famines, earthquakes, wars, and disasters of
> all sorts were commonly thought to be the work of demons. With
> these demons, as with evil men, particularly foreign oppressors, the
> peasants of Palestine lived in perpetual hostility and sporadic con-
> flict, but the relations were complex. As the Roman government had
> its Jewish agents, some of whom, notably the Herods, were local
> rulers, so the demons had their human agents who could do miracles
> so as to deceive many. The lower gods were the rulers of this age,
> and men who knew how to call on them could get their help for all
> sorts of purposes. So could women, whose favors they had re-
> warded by teaching them magic and other arts of civilized life. On
> the other hand, Yahweh, like the demons, was often the cause of
> disasters, sickness, etc., sent as punishments. He sometimes used
> angels, sometimes demons, as agents of his anger, and his human
> agents, his prophets, could also harm as well as help. Most Jews
> believed that in the end he would destroy or remodel the present
> world, and create a new order in which the Jews, or at least those
> who had followed his law, would have a better life. However, as to
> the course of events and the actors in the coming catastrophe, there
> was wide disagreement; any number of contradictory programs cir-
> culated, with various roles for one or more "messiahs"—special
> representatives of Yahweh—anti-messiahs, and assorted mytho-
> logical monsters.

This was the picture of the world *common* in first century Palestine. Even Herod Antipas, the Romans' puppet prince in Galilee, is
said to have thought Jesus was John the Baptist raised from the
dead. Even Josephus, a Jew of the priestly aristocracy who as a
young man was sent on a mission to Rome, held beliefs of this sort;
he was proud of the Jews' control of demons; he claimed to have
prophetic powers himself and to have prophesied that the Roman
general, Vespasian, would become emperor and rule all mankind;
and he saw Vespasian as a messiah foretold by at least some biblical
prophecies. His own prophecy was famous; the Roman historians

Suetonius and Dio Cassius reported it. Suetonius and Tacitus say that such messianic prophecies were common throughout the Near East. We should presume that almost all Palestinian Jews of Jesus' time thought themselves involved in the mythological cosmic drama. [Smith, *Jesus,* pp. 4–5]

Smith's general account of the frame of mind of the Jews of the Land of Israel provides ample justification for turning to the two Pseudepigraphic expressions of this "apocalyptic Judaism" which posited as mythic cosmic drama and which flourished both before and after 70. In a way entirely consistent with a general and prevailing drama, the visionaries before us tell us how, in particular, that ancient and pervasive mode of thought responded to the events of 70.

Thus do 4 Ezra and 2 Baruch introduce us to the mentality of the kind of Judaism predominant both before and in the encounter with the destruction of the Temple. The former Pseudepigraph records visions shown to Ezra in Babylonia (ca. 450 B.C.). The principal theme is how a righteous God causes Israel to fall by the hand of a pagan nation. Sin is the reason, and the theme produces reflection of a psychological character on the nature of human impulse to do evil. The writer sees a conflict between giving the Torah and the character of the people to whom it is given, since, it is clear, that people are unable to carry out the Torah. The destruction proves the impossibility of doing right. The tension is resolved in the belief that at the end of the present age, which is near, a new age—as Smith pointed out—will dawn in which the righteous will be able to keep the Torah. The seven visions of the book go over this same ground of history and its coming conclusion. The same familiar question is asked by 2 Baruch, phrased eloquently, about Israel's suffering and Israel's enemies' prospering. The answer is that the world to come is for the righteous. The recent destruction is a mark that the age is hastening to an end.

Because these two documents are cited merely for illustration and are not critical to the account, which is to come, of the evidence of the Mishnah on the formation of Judaism, I shall treat them very cursorily, first quoting current scholarship for a picture of what the apocalyptic prophets have to say about the events of 70, then simply citing passages in general illustrative of these prophets' overall frame of mind. A complete account of Judaism in the period under discussion would have to do much more here than what is needed for the modest picture of one kind of Judaism, yielded by the evidence under discussion in this book.

Charlesworth provides the following summary of 2 Baruch:

Most scholars have divided the book into seven sections, with some disagreement regarding borderline verses: an account of the destruction of Jerusalem (1–12); the impending judgment (13–20);

the time of retribution and the subsequent messianic era (21–34); Baruch's lament and an allegory of the vine and the cedar (35–46); terrors of the last time, nature of the resurrected body, and the features of Paradise and Sheol (47–52); Baruch's vision of a cloud (53–76); Baruch's letters to the nine and a half tribes and to the two and a half tribes (77–87). The pseudepigraphon is important for numerous theological concepts, e.g. the explanation that Jerusalem was destroyed not by enemies but by angels (7:1–8:5); the preoccupation with the origin of sin (15:5f., 23:4f., 48:42, 54:15, 19; 3 Ezra 7:116–31); pessimism for the present (85:10); the contention that the end will not come until the number of those to be born is fulfilled (23:4–7; cf. 4 Ezra 4:35–37); the description of the resurrected body (49:1–51:6); and the varied messianic concepts. [Charlesworth, *Research*, p. 84]

The following sizable excerpt from the vision attributed to Baruch, Jeremiah's disciple at the time of the first destruction, and generally attributed to a writer who lived in the decades after 70, will serve to portray the frame of mind of survivors. It expresses the perplexity of the age as it affects the destiny of the people of Israel:

Blessed is he who was not born,
Or he, who having been born, has died.
But as for us who live, woe unto us,
Because we see the afflictions of Zion,
And what has befallen Jerusalem.

I will call the Sirens from the sea,
And ye Lilin, come ye from the desert,
And ye Shedim and dragons from the forests:

Awake and gird up your loins unto mourning,
And take up with me the dirges,
And make lamentation with me.

Ye husbandmen, sow not again;
And, O earth, wherefore givest thou thy harvest fruits?
Keep within thee the sweets of thy sustenance.

And thou, vine, why further dost thou give thy wine;
For an offering will not again be made therefrom in Zion.
Nor will first-fruits again be offered.

And do ye, O heavens, withhold your dew,
And open not the treasuries of rain:
And do thou, O sun, withhold the light of thy rays.

And do thou, O moon, extinguish the multitude of thy light;
For why should light rise again
Where the light of Zion is darkened?

And you, ye bridegrooms, enter not in,
And let not the brides adorn themselves with garlands;
And, ye women, pray not that ye may bear.

For the barren shall above all rejoice,
And those who have no sons shall be glad,
For those who have sons shall have anguish.

For why should they bear in pain,
Only to bury in grief?
Or why, again, should mankind have sons?

Or why should the seed of their kind again be named,
Where this mother is desolate,
And her sons are led into captivity?

From this time forward speak not of beauty,
And discourse not of gracefulness.

Moreover, ye priests, take ye the keys of the sanctuary,
And cast them into the height of heaven,
And give them to the Lord and say:

"Guard Thy house Thyself,
For lo! we are found false stewards."

And you, ye virgins; who weave fine linen
And silk with gold of Ophir,
Take with haste all [these] things
And cast [them] into the fire,
That it may bear them to Him who made them,
And the flame send them to Him who created them,
Lest the enemy get possession of them.

Moreover, I, Baruch, say this against thee, Babylon:
"If thou hadst prospered,
And Zion had dwelt in her glory,
Yet the grief to us had been great
That thou shouldst be equal to Zion.

But now, lo! the grief is infinite,
And the lamentation measureless,
For lo! thou art prospered
And Zion desolate.

Who will be judge regarding these things?
Or to whom shall we complain regarding that which has befallen us?
O Lord, how hast Thou born [it]?

Our fathers went to rest without grief,
And lo! the righteous sleep in the earth in tranquility.
For they knew not this anguish,
Nor yet had they heard of that which had befallen us.

Would that thou hadst ears, O earth,
And that thou hadst a heart, O dust:
That ye might go and announce in Sheol,
And say to the dead:
"Blessed are ye more than we who live."

[2 Baruch 10:5–11:7 (Charles 2:485–87)]

A still more profound expression of the prevailing perplexity comes from 4 Ezra's reflection on the condition of the human being, now shown, in its awful, terrible essence, to be a mass of contradictions. Charlesworth introduces 4 Ezra as follows:

> The pseudepigraphon was composed in the last decades of the first century A.D., perhaps in Palestine. The original language is Semitic, but it is difficult to decide whether it is Hebrew or Aramaic. Most scholars now affirm the structural unity of the Jewish core, chapters 3–14.
>
> Eventually added to the core were two later Christian compositions in Greek, now sometimes called 5 (chaps. 1–2), and 6 Ezra (chaps. 15–16). The central section contains seven revelations to Ezra, called Salathiel, by Uriel, in which *inter alia* the writer confronts the problem of theodicy, and speculates about the coming of the Messiah and the end of this age. The prefixed chapters, probably added in the second century, delineate God's faithfulness and Israel's apostasy with subsequent exhortations. The suffixed chapters, probably added in the third century, contain prophecies of woe, followed by exhortations and promises of deliverance for the elect. [Charlesworth, *Research,* p. 112]

The complex of Pseudepigraphic writings in the name of Ezra affirms positions which the framers of the Mishnah may be assumed also to have maintained, for example, that God's ways are inscrutable, human intelligence is finite, and God loves Israel eternally (Box, in Charles 2:554–55). God is one, creator, judge, and redeemer of Israel and of the world. The Torah is the truth. These and also other positions, which Mishnah's philosophers may have received only with difficulty, if at all, are expressed in a series of colloquies and visions. Ezra speaks to God and engages in long discourses, as well as prayers. The angel talks back to Ezra so that the Pseudepigraph gives the impression of a philosophical dialogue, in mythic guise. Attention focuses upon the end which is coming, signs which precede the end. Subject to detailed attention is the divine plan for the world, the generations which follow one another under God's judgment. The earth now has grown old, and nature is degenerate. People are shorter than their parents. These are signs of the last time and the end. The road to future happiness is not going to be easy. There will be a Messiah, who will reign for four hundred years, then die. This catastrophe, however, will be followed by a general resurrection of the dead, final judgment, and the Day of Judgment. Only a few will make it through the suffering at the end. The Pseudepigraph is rich in prayers, visions, soliloquies and colloquies, conversations between angels and the speaker, and other dramatic artifices, but visions are what predominate, and conversations between the speaker and Heaven fill the work.

In 4 Ezra 7:62–74 the problem is phrased of human intelligence. The condition of the human being, of Adam, from creation to the age of destruction is natural. Catastrophe is the norm. For the very character of the human condition makes inevitable precisely what has happened even now. An extended quotation will serve us well when we consider what the framers of the Mishnah had to say in the same context:

> And I answered and said: O thou Earth, what has thou brought forth, if the mind is sprung from the dust as every other created thing! It had been better if the dust itself had even been unborn, that the mind might not have come into being from it.
>
> But, as it is, the mind grows with us, and on this account we are tormented, because we perish and know it.
>
> Let the human race lament,
>   but the beasts of the field be glad!
> Let all the earth-born mourn,
>   but let the cattle and flocks rejoice!
>
> For it is far better with them than with us; for they have no judgment to look for, neither do they know of any torture or of any salvation promised to them after death.
>
> For what doth it profit us that we shall be preserved alive, but yet suffer great torment?
>
> For all the earth-born
>   are defiled with iniquities,
>   full of sins,
>   laden with offences.
>
> And if after death we were not to come into judgment, it might, perchance, have been far better for us!
>
> And he answered me and said: When the Most High made the world, and Adam, and all that came of him, he first prepared the Judgement, and the things that pertain unto the Judgement.
>
> But, now, from thine own words understand: for thou hast said that the mind grows with us.
>
> For this reason, therefore, shall the sojourners in the earth suffer torture, because having understanding, they yet wrought iniquity, and receiving precepts, they yet kept them not, and having obtained the Law, they set at naught that which they received.
>
> What, then, will they have to say in the Judgement, or how shall they answer in the last times?
>
> For how long a time hath the Most High been longsuffering with the inhabitants of the world—not for their sakes, indeed, but for the

sake of the times which he has ordained!

[4 Ezra 7:62–74 (Box, in Charles 580)]

The materials of 4 Ezra (9:38–10:24) also encompass the recent events of Jerusalem and the Temple. The author phrases matters just as does the writer of 2 Baruch. This final, sizable quotation is apt because it asks the urgent questions of the age:

How is Sion, the mother of us all, in great grief and deep afflic-tion? It is right now to mourn, seeing that we all mourn, and to grieve, seeing that we are all grief-stricken; thou, however, art grief-stricken for one son. But ask the earth, and she shall tell thee, that it is she who ought to mourn the fall of so many that have sprung into being upon her. Yea, from the beginning all who have been born, and others who are to come—lo! they go almost all into perdi-tion, and the multitude of them comes to destruction. Who, then, should mourn the more? Ought not she that has lost so great a multitude? or thou who grievest but for one? But if thou sayest to me: my lamentation is not like the earth's, for I have lost the fruit of my womb
  which I bare with pains   .
    and brought forth with sorrows—
but as regards the earth, (it is) according to the course of nature; the multitude present in it is gone as it came: then I say to thee: Just as thou hast borne (offspring) with sorrow, even so also the earth has borne (given) her fruit, namely man, from the beginning unto him that made her.
  Now, therefore, keep they sorrow within
    and bear gallantly the misfortunes that have befallen thee
For if thou wilt acknowledge God's decree to be just, thou shalt receive thy son again in (due) time, and shalt be praised among women. Therefore go into the city to thy husband. And she said unto me: I will not do so: I will not enter the city, but here will I die. So I proceeded to speak further unto her, and said: No, woman! no, woman! do not do so;
    but suffer thyself to be prevailed upon by reason of
    Sion's misfortunes,
      be consoled by reason of Jerusalem's sorrow.
  For thou seest how
    our sanctuary is laid waste,
      our altar thrown down;
    our Temple destroyed,
      our harp laid low;
    our song is silenced,
      our rejoicing ceased;
    the light of our lamp is extinguished,
      the ark of our covenant spoiled;
    our holy things are defiled,

      the name that is called upon us is profaned;
      our nobles are dishonored,
         our priests burnt,
      our Levites gone into captivity;
      our virgins are defiled,
         our wives ravished;
      our righteous are seized,
      [our saints scattered,]
         our children are cast out,
         our heroes made powerless:
   and, what is more than all—
      Sion's seal now is sealed up dishonored,
      and given up into the hands of them that hate us.
 Do thou, then, shake off thy great grief,
    abandon thy much sorrow,
That the Mighty One may again forgive thee,
    and the Most High give thee rest,
    a respite from thy troubles!

               [4 Ezra 9:38–10:24 (Box, in Charles 2:603–5)]

The question of the age thus is framed in terms of Israel's condition. The Temple, the location and model of creation, had been Israel's heart and center. The world was made for the sake of Israel. Now Israel had lost the Temple, creation had been deprived of its model. The seven days of creation rehearsed, the apocalypse asks the inescapable and compelling question: How to bear it all, endure, and go on?

    These extended quotations from Baruch and Ezra serve to set the stage for what is to come: a document, formed in the same context, which resorts to a completely different mode of expression to express an utterly unrelated message. Indeed, without this sizable excursus into the poetry of the apocalyptic writers, we should not have a clear picture of how different the Mishnah is from other books of the same period. Nor should we perceive so clearly how remarkable is the Mishnah's utter silence on those tremendous issues of suffering and atonement, catastrophe and apocalypse, expressed with such power in the passages just now cited at length.

Second-Century Gnosticism

The second-century Church Fathers refer to Christian heretics called Gnostics, people who believed, among other things, that salvation came from insightful knowledge of a god beyond the creator-god, and of a fundamental flaw in creation revealed in the revealed Scriptures of Moses. The Gnostic understands "who we were, and what we have become; where we were . . . whither we are hastening; from what we are being released; what birth is, and what is rebirth'' (Pagels, p. xix). This insight into the true condition of the believer derives not from revelation but from self-knowledge, which is knowledge of God. Now in introducing the viewpoint of second-century Gnostics and juxtaposing their principal emphases with those of the Mishnah, I must emphasize that we know no writings of Gnostics who were Jews. We cannot claim that the viewpoint of Gnostic thinkers on two questions of fundamental importance to the Mishnah—creation, revelation—derives from Israelites of the Land of Israel. The only certainty is that the Mishnah takes up a position both specifically and totally at variance with the position framed, on identical issues, by people writing in exactly the same period. No one can claim that Gnostic and Mishnaic thinkers addressed, or even knew about, one another. But they did confront precisely the same issues, and when placed into juxtaposition with one another, they present a striking and suggestive contrast. It is that contrast which we now shall briefly contemplate.

If the apocalyptic prophets focused upon historical events and their meaning, the Gnostic writers of the second century sought to escape from the framework of history altogether. For Israel, Jerusalem had become a forbidden city. The Temple had long stood as the pinnacle of creation and now was destroyed. The Gnostic thinkers deemed creation, celebrated in the cult, to be a cosmic error. The destruction of the Temple had evoked the prophetic explanations of the earlier destruction and turned attention in the search for meaning in the destruction to the revealed Torah of God to Moses at Mount Sinai. The Gnostic thinkers declared the Torah to be a deceit, handed down by an evil creator. It is as if the cosmic issues vital to the first-century apocalyptic prophets were taken up one by one and declared closed, and closed in a negative decision, by the second-century Gnostics.

The thinkers of the Mishnah for their part addressed two principal issues also important to Gnostic thought, the worth of creation and the value of the Torah. They took a quite opposite position on both matters. The Mishnah's profoundly priestly celebration of creation and its slavishly literal repetition of what clearly is said in Scripture gain significance specifically in that very context in which, to others, these are subjected to a different, deeply negative, valuation. True, we have no evidence that Gnostics were in the Land of Israel and formed part of the people of Israel in the period in which the Mishnah reaches full expression and final closure. So we speak of a synchronic debate at best. In fact what we know in Gnostic writings is a frame of mind and a style of thought characteristic of others than Israelites, living in lands other than the Land of Israel. What justifies our invoking two ubiquitous and fundamental facts about Gnostic doctrine in the description of the context in which the Mishnah took shape is the simple fact that, at the critical points in its structure, the Mishnaic system counters what are in fact two fundamental and generative assertions of all Gnostic systems. Whether or not there were Gnostics known to Mishnah's philosophers, who, specifically in response to the destruction and permanent prohibition of the Temple, declared to be lies and deceit the creation celebrated in the Temple and the Torah governing there, we do not know. But these would be appropriate conclusions to draw from the undisputed facts of the hour in any case. The Temple designed by the Torah for celebrating the center and heart of creation was no more. Would this not have meant that the creator of the known creation and revealer of the Torah, the allegedly one God behind both, is either weak or evil? And should the elect not aspire to escape from the realm of creation and the power of the demiurge? And who will pay heed to what is written in the revelation of creation, Temple, and Torah? These seem to me conclusions distinctively suitable to be drawn from the ultimate end of the thousand-year-old cult: the final and total discrediting of the long-pursued, eternally fraudulent hope for messianic deliverance in this time, in this world, and in this life. So it would have been deemed wise for those who know to seek and celebrate a different salvation, coming from a god unknown in this world, unrevealed in this world's revelation, not responsible for the infelicitous condition of creation.

For our purposes, therefore, when we speak of Gnosticism as relevant, we refer, in Wilson's happy phrase to ''an atmosphere, not a system'' (Wilson, p. 261). In so far as Gnosticism incorporated a cosmic solution to the problem of evil, the Gnostic mode of thought had the power to confront the disaster of Israel's two wars against Rome and their metaphysical consequences. The Gnostic solution, if we may posit what someone might have been intelligent to conclude, is not difficult to discern. These events proved beyond doubt the flaw in creation, for the Temple had been the archetype of creation. The catastrophes demonstrated the evil character of the creator of this world. The catastrophes required the conclusion that there is another mode of being, another world beyond this one of creation and cult. So, whatever positive doctrines may or may not have found adherents among disappointed Israelites of the later first and second centuries, there are these two negative conclusions which anyone moving out of the framework of the cult, priesthood, and Temple, with its Torah, celebration of creation and the creator, and affirmation of this world and its creations, would have had to reach. First, the creator is not good. Second, the Torah, the record of creator and the will of the creator, is false.

Later Gnostic cosmogonies take as their primary problem the expla-

nation not of the creation of the world but of the origin of man and of
evil (Wilson, p. 172). A flaw in creation accounts for the condition of
the world, and this led to the conviction that the creator-god was evil.
Wilson states, "The Gnostic, convinced of the evil of matter and regarding this world as under the sway of powers hostile to man, considered the Creator as one of these powers and so introduced a distinction
between him and the supreme God" (Wilson, p. 184). The creator is a
hostile being, the supreme god is not. The evil of human existence
forces a dualism of a radical character (Wilson, p. 188). The created
world is only the lowest stage of being; there are numbers of heavens
above. Man really belongs not to this world but to a higher, heavenly
world (Wilson, p. 207): "The essential feature in the Gnostic view of
man is that he is really a divine being imprisoned in this material world
and separated by the barrier of the seven heavens from his true abode.
Salvation from fate, from body, from the bondage of matter, from the
changes and chances of this life, all the ills to which the flesh is heir, is
attained by gnosis, which may mean anything from knowledge imparted in a mystic initiation to a purely magical knowledge of names
and spells" (Wilson, p. 215).

Withdrawal to inwardness or despair of the world is a principal trait
of the Gnosticism of Nag Hammadi's library too. That accounts for the
Jewish contribution to Gnosticism: to designate the God of the Hebrew
Scriptures as "the malevolent force whose misguided blunder produced the world, a God who was ignorant of the hidden good God
beyond" (*Nag Hammadi,* p. 6). The Testimony of Truth states matters
very simply: "For no one who is under the Law will be able to look up
to the truth, for they will not be able to serve two masters. For the
defilement of the Law is manifest; but undefilement belongs to the
light" (*Nag Hammadi,* p. 18). When the Mishnah repeatedly resorts to
Scripture's facts to restate Scripture's opinion on virtually every important topic of the Mosaic law codes (see chapter 5, below), this
judgment of the character of the law becomes a powerful and affirmative statement of the rejected alternative. Knowing what the framers of
the Mishnah chose not to say and do, which is what others did do, we
begin to make sense of what the framers of Mishnah did have to say
and did choose to do.

In as much as the Mishnah reaches its systematic fullness after the
Second War against Rome, therefore, its framers have no choice but to
address and compose a response to the inescapable issues of the day.
These are defined by the facts that, first, Israelites no longer could even
enter Jerusalem; and, second, the Third Temple clearly would not be
restored in accord with the historical and mythic pattern of the Scriptural account of the destruction of the First and the building of the
Second. That is to say, three generations had passed from 70 to the war

led by Bar Kokhba. But instead of a restoration came war. And the road to war, through suffering and courage, in the end did not lead Israel back to Zion's mountain. People who wished to read Scripture as a set of accounts of how things should happen now could find little grounds for hope. Indeed, confidence in the veracity of the Mosaic revelation and in the goodness of God who had revealed the Torah to Moses can only have been severely shaken, as Ezra and Baruch have shown us. For fair numbers of people, it appears to have fallen to ruins. In the rubble of once-high hopes were buried the legacy of centuries of prophetic apocalypse. Misshapen stones formed themselves into patterns of despair, detritus signifying nothing but itself, ruins of hope, ruins of history.

As I said, we simply do not know that there even were Gnostics in the Land of Israel, let alone within the Israelite community known to the sages of the Mishnah. All we know is that, in the same time as the Mishnah's formation and promulgation, Christian communities from France to Egypt encompassed groups which took a position sharply at variance with that of the Hebrew Scriptures affirmed in the Church in general on precisely the questions of creation and revelation and redemption confronting the Israelite world of the second century. Among the many and diverse positions taken up in the systems reported by Christian writers or now documented through Christian-Gnostic writings found at Nag Hammadi there are three which, as I have emphasized, are remarkably pertinent. First, the creator-god is evil, because, second, creation is deeply flawed. Third, revelation as Torah is a lie. These conclusions yield, for one Gnostic-Christian thinker after another, the simple proposition that redemption is gained in escape; this world is to be abandoned, not constructed, affirmed, and faithfully tended in painstaking detail. It is in the context of this widespread negative judgment on the very matters on which, for their part, Mishnah's sages register a highly affirmative opinion, that the choices made by the framers of the Mishnah become fully accessible.

Characterizing the Mishnah's ultimate system as a whole, we may call it both locative and utopian, in that it focuses upon Temple but is serviceable anywhere. In comparison to the Gnostic systems, it is, similarly, profoundly Scriptural; but it also is deeply indifferent to Scripture, drawing heavily upon the information supplied by Scripture for the construction and expression of its own systemic construction, which in form and language is wholly independent of any earlier Israelite document (see chapter 5, below). It is, finally, a statement of affirmation of this world, of the realm of society, state, and commerce, and at the same time a vigorous denial that how things are is how things should be, or will be. For the Mishnaic system speaks of the building of a state, government, and civil and criminal system, of the conduct of transactions of property, commerce, trade, of forming the economic unit of a family through transfer of women and property and the ending of such a family-economic unit, and similar matters, touching all manner of dull details of ordinary and everyday life (see chapter 4, below).

So the Mishnah's framers deemed the conduct of ordinary life in this world to be the critical focus and central point of tension of all being. At the same time, their account of these matters drew more heavily upon Scripture than upon any more contemporary and practical source. The philosophers designed a government and a state utterly out of phase with the political realities of the day, speaking, as we shall see, of king and high priest, but never of sage, patriarch, and Roman official. They addressed a lost world of Temple cult as described by the Torah, of cleanness, support of priesthood, offerings on ordinary days and on appointed times in accord with Torah law, and so mapped out vast tracts of a territory whose only reality lay in people's imagination, shaped by Scripture. Mishnah's map is not territory.

Accordingly, for all its intense practicality and methodical application of the power of practical reason and logic to concrete and material things, the Mishnah presents a made-up system which, in its way, is no more practical or applicable in all ways to ordinary life than are the diverse systems of philosophy and myth, produced in its day in other parts of the world, which fall under the name, Gnostic.

What the framers of Mishnah have in common with the framers of the diverse world constructions of the Gnostic sort thus is, first, a system building, and, second, confrontation with two issues addressed in the diverse Gnostic systems of antiquity, the nature of creation and the creator and the character of the revelation of the creator-god. If in conclusion I may state in a few simple words the position of the Mishnah on these two burning issues of the day, it is that creation is good and worthy of man's best consideration, and that the creator of the world is good and worthy of man's deepest devotion. So out of creation and revelation will come redemption. The Torah is not only not false but the principal source of truth. A system which intersects with the rules of the Torah therefore will patiently and carefully restate, and, so, blatantly reaffirm, precisely what Scripture has to say about those same points in common. A structure coming in the aftermath of the Temple's destruction which doggedly restated rules governing the Temple so reaffirmed, in the most obvious possible way, the cult and the created world celebrated therein. For as soon as we speak of sacrifice and Temple, as 2 Baruch has shown us, we address the questions of creation and the value of the created world and of redemption. When, therefore, a document emerges rich in discourse on these matters and doggedly repetitive of precisely what Scripture says about exactly the same things, the meaning in context is clear.

Choices Made by Others

We make better sense of what people did do when we know what they chose not to do. This perspective on the people behind the Mishnah emerges from a consideration of the principal issues confronting all Israelites in the same place and time, the Land of Israel in the first and second centuries of the Common Era, and a review of the responses of people besides those represented in the Mishnah to those ubiquitous issues. For it is clear that the histories of several different kinds of Judaism run together through the period of time under discussion. But each of those histories follows its own course and its own path. This is natural, for the various people who made those histories, whose imagination and mode of being are expressed therein, all went their own way, ignoring one another, pretending to constitute, each for himself, the whole of the Israelite world—as indeed, in mind, was so.

The Mishnah represents one such world, an account of the world view and way of organizing and defining society, government and politics, time, space, the natural and sacred economy, the movement from birth to death, the formation of family and the dissolution of marriage—the entire way of life of the community to whom the document is addressed. What the Mishnah does not say, we shall see in ample detail, also contains a vivid statement on issues of the day. As a self-contained document, the Mishnah designs a whole world of meaning. But in its age were other such world-constructing systems for Israel.

Now when we turn to 2 Baruch and 4 Ezra, two other documents of this period, out of which an account of a different variety of a Judaism in the earlier part of the time under study may be framed, we confront a quite different set of concerns. While the Mishnah's framers wished to talk about constructing a world, with detailed attention to economy and cult, the interplay between the sacred and the ordinary, the visionaries represented in the two great post-70 apocalypses lament a world now in ruins. On the surface the philosophers of the Mishnah speak about different things to different people. Yet the philosophers of the Mishnah live in the same age as the poets of the apocalyptic writings. In that age none could for one minute avoid the definitive fact that the Temple had been destroyed. Since the mode of organizing life around the Temple and its cult was by then more than a thousand years old, the simple fact of its destruction drew attention and required response from whoever proposed to address the age beyond.

To be sure, there are important differences between the character of the Mishnah in its world, and the apocalyptic visions in theirs. While the Mishnah stands at the beginning of a movement of massive proportions and unlimited influence in the history of Judaism, 2 Baruch and 4 Ezra turn out to come at the end of another such movement. The Mishnah serves as a reference point to nearly all extant evidence in the succession to follow for many centuries. But the Mishnah on its part refers backward only to Scripture. It represents itself as an independent force in the history of Judaism. It demonstrably generates other forces. It is uncontingent in itself, but it makes other significant evidences and expressions of its variety of Judaism contingent upon it. For their part, 2 Baruch and 4 Ezra begin nothing and define nothing, but end much that is familiar. They find a comfortable position in a long sequence of equivalent documents. They take up long-explored and well-established themes. In response to the unprecedented events of their own day, they say no more and no less than had been said by others for a very long time, more than five hundred years. They serve to exemplify their type of Judaism. That is why our consideration of ''apocalyptic Judaism'' must be kept in mind as we turn to the Mishnah.

We move now from writings infused with spiritual power to touch us directly and move us deeply, to rules of which we can scarcely make sense. The transition, to be appropriate, must be abrupt. There is no bridge, none of common sense, none of sensibility, from the poetry of suffering, hope, and despair, to the filigreed work of a rigidly patterned way of life. The Mishnah may be shown to be a kind of philosophy. It is not poetry. It may be demonstrated to be a response to a common set of concerns for creation and revelation and redemption. But it does not speak of these things, or, indeed, about any thing to which, after two thousand years, we may gain ready access or convenient entry.

2

Divisions, Tractates, Principal Ideas before the Wars

Preliminary Observations

When the Mishnah is complete, then comes the time to describe it as a whole. Only after the two wars will it be appropriate for us to take up the work of description and interpretation of the total Mishnaic system for Israelite society. Before the wars and between them we cannot speak of the Mishnah as a whole, let alone the Mishnaic system. There are only bits and pieces of material, extant sherds of ideas which may have had a place in a larger structure in their own day, but which would find their place as we know it and entire meaning as we now interpret it only in systemic completion and closure. So for this chapter and the next the work is to take up discrete ideas. We examine rules and disputes out of any larger truly encompassing context. Then, for the ultimate part of systemic description and analysis, we shift our mode of discourse (see chapter 4, below). We shall speak of completed tractates and their generative conceptions, fully articulated systems and large-scale topics. At that point I shall describe the fantasy of the Mishnaic system and world as a whole, and express its principal statements to its day and age (see chapter 6, below). Since from the angle of redaction and formulation the Mishnah as a document, as literature, comes into being whole and complete (cf. Neusner, *Purities XXI*), it is only appropriate that this account of the evidence of the Mishnah concerning the several points in its unfolding should follow suit. The evidence and its condition at the several layers into which it is here sliced up are what must govern the description of the evidence and the organization of an account of its condition in the principal stages of its formation.

In so stating matters, I explain why what follows in chapters 2 and 3 must be disjointed and arcane: an account of opinions on scarcely coherent questions, a picture of random blips on a screen with asymmetrical and out of focus grids of depth and breadth. For the period under discussion the evidence of the Mishnah testifies to the state of opinion upon a few small matters. But from these few facts—that one group took an exactly opposed position from another on an issue no one else appears to have discussed at all—much can be learned. The handful of facts in our hands serve like stones and sherds in the hands of a dirt archeologist and like the report of marriage taboos in the mind of an anthropologist. To be sure, even a rapid survey of these fundamental data is apt to tax the reader's patience, and rightly so. There will be systematic reference to appendix 4. Without extended repetition of the facts of Scripture, particularly the Mosaic codes of Exodus, Leviticus, Numbers, and Deuteronomy, most of the issues of the Mishnah's law will be pure gibberish, and, consequently, we shall know opinions on matters of neither sense nor consequence (see below, pp. 69–71).

But even if we understand those traces of expansion and signs of fresh perspective yielded by a grasp of the details of the opinions held before the wars, our work has scarcely begun. For understanding the technical points of law hardly leads to a grasp of the state of people's thought: what they proposed to express through these details, the statement they wished to make. In this regard the contrast to the readily accessible works of imagination—the visions, symbols, invented transcendental discourse—of 2 Baruch and 4 Ezra is stunning. Without much mediation or explanation, just now we found ourselves able to grasp the sense of, and even respond to, the humanity of a cry to earth no longer to produce its fruit. That is why it made sense to quote at length. The world view centered upon coming redemption, with its imagery of swords and its sounds of the clashing of shields, fills the eye and ear with intelligible perception and even familiar emotion. And this is as it should be. The messianic fervor of the first century and the antimessianic despair of the second—the former expecting too much, the latter hoping too little and too late—affected the mass of Jews in the Israelite Land of the day. The Mishnah is ahistorical, unpictorial, atactile, aniconic, and unemotional. It is abstract and intellectual. The philosophical exercise of forming a sensible way of life in a stable, dependable community did not reach, let alone touch, many people. It took a long time before ordinary Jews accepted the measured, disciplined, and moderate system created in the centuries under study and collected and presented in the measured and disciplined language of the Mishnah itself. The framers of the Mishnah never lived to see that day.

So if the extreme sentiments of apocalypse and Gnosticism prove readily accessible to us, it is because in their own day they also reached and shaped the hearts of many. But then or now, how many minds are there, to begin with, to be shaped? And how many wish it? So, in sum, before us is the vision of philosophers, an intellectual minority in a society prepared to move and wanting to be moved. In their trivial discourse on questions the answer to which no one but them really pursued, that vision is hidden and revealed. Before us lie the beginnings of work which in its late day phrased in exquisitely trivial terms some of those old, perennial issues of philosophy contemplated by Aristotle and later considered by the Stoics, issues of potentiality and actuality, the physics of mixtures, and other odd and, from a practical viewpoint, empty questions, the answers to which, as I said, interested only those who asked the questions. In the end we shall confront a work of absolute fantasy: a nonexistent Temple, fully laid out, building, protocol, procedures; a society stretched out from the walls of the Temple, with its space and its regulation of time, its mode of establishing families and dissolving them, its economic life, all proportioned in relationship to that imagined Temple and its imaginary cult. Fantasy? Yes, for the Temple then lay in ruins, and Jerusalem was a forbidden city for Israelites.

Before us at the end will emerge a city of the mind, a particular place, framed in all due locative dimensions and requisite spatial descriptions, which, in fact, existed nowhere but in the mind, which by nature is utopian. Why therefore should we expect the concrete raw material of such a fantastic mental conjuration to prove of ready access to us, when it was not self-evident in the minds of the people before whom, to begin with, the materials were laid forth? And, given the extraordinary mastery of the Mosaic law exhibited by the philosophers of the Mishnah, from beginning to closure, we hardly may take for granted that what to them appeared obvious, indeed self-evident, to us will be possessed of even crude significance.

That is why, as I said at the beginning, what we now must do, which is rapidly to survey some details of the law, is apt to tax the reader's patience. I suppose the apt analogy is to sitting through the drilling of a tooth for the later pleasure of a healthy, painless bite. But before too long, I hope, the aptness of such an analogy of postponed pleasure will fall away. For the law exercises its own fascination. Its power is within itself. Once we enter its world, the law will appear self-evidently logical; its modes of thought obvious and necessary; its results inexorable; its points of conflict and dispute compelling and important; its results—I mean, the process, not the end thereof—exhilarating and stimulating. But to gain that entry—that is not so easy.

The shortest way is the most difficult, and that is the one we now shall take. We shall plunge head-on into the law and rapidly survey its main points in all their specificity. That is the purpose of this chapter and its companion. Chapter 4, which presents the full acount of the Mishnah's six complete subsystems, is much easier to follow and more readily accessible.

Just as we quickly surveyed some representative and suggestive writings of apocalypse in response to the two wars and some ideas of Gnostics on the other side of the wars, so now, equally quickly, in in somewhat greater differentiation of detail, we do the same. We now turn to that evidence which has awaited so long for this many-sided introduction and apology. We come to the Mishnah itself.

The Mishnah lays out its materials in six principal Divisions, each divided into tractates, arranged for the most part from largest in size to smallest. Even an account of the several stages in the unfolding of the Mishnah's law must survey that law in accord with the Mishnah's own mode of organizing it. This approach allows systematic attention to the several units of thought, in accord with their familiar setting and arrangement. It further permits allusion to the completed exegetical studies, rather than requiring restatement of materials in accord with some framework other than the established one, in which they already are known and available. At the same time, it would be seriously misleading to speak of "the Mishnah before 70," or "the Mishnah between the wars"—let alone the system of a given Division of Mishnah at these times in particular. If we were to do so, we should thereby suggest that that manner of collecting, dividing, and organizing materials known to us from the final document also governed the collection, division, and organization of the materials of the several Divisions and of the Mishnah as a whole at the several stages in their history prior to the formation and closure of the final document. This we do not know and cannot show. In fact, I shall try to demonstrate that, in the two principal periods prior to that in which the Mishnah comes into being as we know it, there are cogent traits and internally coherent formations of ideas. These formations indeed do differ in their fundamental interests and character from the ultimate one which the Mishnah now reveals. So they are not the same as the end product. But we cannot regard them as "earlier" Mishnahs or systems of a prior Mishnah.

The purposes of both accessible and accurate description therefore are best served by two distinct, if interrelated, procedures.

First, I shall rapidly survey the six Divisions and briefly relate the relevant rules and conceptions at each of the three periods at hand.

Second, I shall stand back and ask what sort of conglomerate of rules and conceptions we in fact have in hand at each period and how it may be described in relationship to those of the other periods.

In this way we shall have the benefit of a sequential, double vision of the sources, first, as they unfold in accord with the scheme of the final redaction, second, as they appear to coalesce outside of that scheme and in the two prior time frames of their formation.

In the end we shall see that the Mishnah takes shape in a twofold process. Once a theme is introduced early in the history of law, it will be taken up and refined later on. Also, in the second and third stages in the formation of the Mishnah, many new themes with their problems will emerge. These then are without precedent in the antecedent thematic heritage. The common foundations for the whole always are Scripture, of course (but see chapter 5, below), so that I may present a simple architectual simile. The Mishnah is like a completed construction of scaffolding. The foundation is a single plane, the Scriptures. The top platform also is a single plane, the Mishnah itself. But the infrastructure is differentiated. Underneath one part of the upper platform will be several lower platforms, so that the supporting poles and pillars reach down to intervening platforms; only the bottom platform rests upon pillars set in the foundation. Yet another part of the upper platform rests upon pillars and poles stretching straight down to the foundation, without intervening platforms at all. So viewed from above, the uppermost platform of the scaffolding forms a single, uniform, and even plane. That is the Mishnah as we have it, six Divisions, sixty-three tractates (and Abot), five hundred thirty-one chapters. But viewed from the side, that is, from the perspective of analysis, there is much differentiation, so that, from one side, the upper platform rises from a second, intermediate one, and, in places, from even a third, lowest one. And yet, as I said, some of the pillars reach directly down to the bedrock foundations.

To reveal the result at the outset: what is new in the period beyond the wars is that part of the ultimate plane—the Mishnah as a whole—which in fact rests upon the foundations not of antecedent thought but of Scripture alone. What is basic in the period before the two wars is the formation of that part of the Mishnah which sustains yet a second and even a third layer of platform construction. What emerges between the two wars, of course, will both form a plane with what comes before, that platform at the second level, and yet will also lay foundations for a level above itself. But this intermediate platform also will come to an end, yielding that space filled only by the pillars stretching from Scripture on upward to the ultimate plane of the Mishnah's completed and whole system. So let me now describe what I believe to be the state of the law as a whole before 70.

If my analysis of the history of Mishnaic law was correct, and the discrete laws we shall now survey do represent positions and principles adopted before 70 and continuously carried forward to the formation and closure of the Mishnah as a complete system, then the Mishnah as we know it originated in its Division of Purities. For the striking fact is that the Sixth Division is the only Division that yields a complete and whole statement of a topic dating from before the wars and its principal parts: (1) what imparts uncleanness; (2) which kinds of objects and substances may be unclean; and (3) how these objects or substances may regain the status of cleanness. Joined to episodic rulings else-where, the principal parts of the Sixth Division speak, in particular, of cleanness of meals, food and drink, pots and pans. It then would appear that the ideas ultimately expressed in the Mishnah began among people who had a special interest in observing cultic cleanness. There can be no doubt, moreover, that the context for such cleanness is the home, not solely the Temple. The issues of the law leave no doubt on that score. Since priests ate heave offering at home, and did so in a state of cleanness, it was a small step to apply the same taboos to food which was not a consecrated gift to the priests. It is less clear whether we hear ideas solely of radical priests, who wish to eat their home meals in the same conditions of cultic cleanness which pertain to their meals in the Temple, or whether in addition there were lay people who wished to pretend they were priests by adopting for their ordinary meals at home the priests' taboos, originating in the cultic setting. I believe that the system began among radical priests joined by lay people to form a holiness sect, but that is just a guess.

In either case what is said through the keeping of these laws is that the food eaten at home, not deriving from the altar and its provision for the priesthood of meat not burned up in the fire, was as holy as the meal offerings, meat offerings, and drink offerings, consecrated by being set aside for the altar and then, in due course, partly given to the priests and partly tossed on the altar and burned up. If food not consecrated for the altar, not protected in a state of cleanness (in the case of wheat), or carefully inspected for blemishes (in the case of beasts), and not eaten by priests in the Temple, was deemed subject to the same restrictions as food consecrated for the altar, this carries implications about the character of that food, those who were to eat it, and the conditions in which it was grown. First, all food, not only that for the altar, was to be protected in a state of holiness, that is, separateness. Second, the place, the Land, in which the food was grown and kept was holy, just like the Temple. Third, the people, Israel, who were to eat that food were holy, just like the priesthood, in rank behind the Temple's chief caste. Fourth, the act of eating food anywhere in the Holy Land was analogous to the act of eating food in the Temple, by the altar.

All of these obvious inferences from the repertoire of laws we are going to survey point to a profound conviction about the Land, people, produce, condition, and context of nourishment. The setting was holy. The actors were holy. And what, specifically, they did which had to be protected in holiness was eating. For when they ate their food at home, they ate it the way priests did in the Temple. And the way priests ate their food in the Temple, that is, the cultic rules and conditions observed in that setting, was like the way God ate his food in the Temple.

That is to say, God's food and locus of nourishment were to be protected from the same sources of danger and contamination, preserved in the same exalted condition of sanctification (see Levine). So by acting, that is, eating, like God, Israel became like God: a pure and perfect incarnation, on earth in the Land which was holy, of the model of heaven. Eating food was the critical act and occasion, just as the priestly authors of Leviticus and Numbers had maintained when they made laws governing slaughtering beasts and burning up their flesh, baking pancakes and cookies with and without olive oil and burning them on the altar, pressing grapes and making wine and pouring it out onto the altar. The nourishment of the Land—meat, grain, oil, and wine—was set before God and burned ("offered up") in conditions of perfect cultic antisepsis.

In context this antisepsis provided protection against things deemed the opposite of nourishment, the quintessence of death: corpse matter, people who looked like corpses (Lev. 13), dead creeping things, blood when not flowing in the veins of the living, such as menstrual blood (Lev. 15), other sorts of flux (semen in men, nonmenstrual blood in women) which yield not life but then its opposite, so death. What these excrescences have in common, of course, is that they are ambivalent. Why? Because they may be one thing or the other. Blood in the living is the soul; blood not in the living is the soul of contamination. The corpse was once a living person, like God; the person with skin like a corpse's and who looks dead was once a person who looked alive; the flux of the *zab* (Lev. 15) comes from the flaccid penis, which under the right circumstances, that is, properly erect, produces semen and makes life. What is at the margin between life and death and can go either way is what is the source of uncleanness. But, as we shall see, that is insufficient. For the opposite, in the priestly code, of *unclean* is not only *clean*, but also *holy*. The antonym is not to be missed: death or life, unclean or holy.

So the cult is the point of struggle between the forces of life and nourishment and the forces of death and extinction: meat, grain, oil, and wine, against corpse matter, dead creeping things, blood in the wrong setting, semen in the wrong context, and the like. Then, on the occasions when meat was eaten, mainly, at the time of festivals or other moments at which sin offerings and peace offerings were made, people who wished to live ate their meat, and at all times ate the staples of wine, oil, and bread, in a state of life and so generated life. They kept their food and themselves away from the state of death as much as possible. And this heightened reality pertained at home, as much as in the Temple, where most rarely went on ordinary days. The Temple was the font of life, the bulwark against death.

In this statement of the convictions of the priestly code about the metaphysical meaning of cultic cleanness and taboos relevant thereto, we see why Israelites interested in rules about meals will have thought such rules, in particular, to be important. It is hardly surprising, once the meal became a focus of attention, that the other two categories of the law which I believe yield principles or laws deriving from the period before the wars present precisely the same sorts of rules. Laws on growing and preparing food will attract attention as soon as people wish to speak, to begin with, about how meals are to be eaten (cf. Wächter; Dombrowski). That accounts for the obviously lively interest in the biblical taboos of agriculture. Since, further, meals are acts of society, they call together a group. Outside of the family, the natural unit, such a group will be special, cultic. If a group is going to get together, it will be on a Sabbath or festival, not on a workday. So laws governing the making of meals on those appointed times will inevitably receive attention. Nor is it surprising that, in so far as there are any rules pertinent to the cult, they will involve those aspects of the cult which apply also outside of the cult, that is, how a beast is slaughtered, rules governing the disposition of animals of a special status (e.g., firstborn), and the like.

That the rules for meals pertain not to isolated families but to a larger group is strongly suggested by the other area which evidently was subjected to sustained attention before the wars, I mean, laws governing who may marry whom. The context in which the sayings assigned to the authorities before the wars are shaped is the life of a small group of people, defining its life apart from the larger Israelite society while maintaining itself wholly within that society. Three points of ordinary life formed the focus for concrete, social differentiation: food, sex, and marriage. What people ate, how they conducted their sexual lives, and whom they married or to whom they gave their children in marriage would define the social parameters of their group. These facts indicate who was kept within the bounds, and who was excluded and systematically maintained at a distance. For these are the things—the only things—subject to the independent control of the small group. The people behind the laws, after all, could not tell other people than their associates what to eat or whom to marry. But they could make their own decisions on these important, but humble, matters. By making those decisions in one way and not in some other, they moreover could keep outsiders at a distance and those who to begin with adhered to the group within bounds. Without political control, they could not govern the transfer of property or other matters of public interest. But without political power, they could and did govern the transfer of their women. It was in that intimate aspect of life that they thereby firmly established the outer boundary of their collective existence. The very existence of the group and the concrete expression of its life, therefore, comes under discussion in the transfer of women.

The Division of Agriculture before the Wars

The rules of the Division of Agriculture affect the suitability of produce for Israelite consumption. Scripture specifies various agricultural tithes and offerings which are owing to the Temple and the priesthood and Levites. There are moreover diverse taboos governing the cultivation and disposition of the crops. The present Division takes up agricultural taboos pertinent not only to tithes and offerings to the priests and cult in tractates Terumot, Maaserot, Maaser Sheni, Hallah, and Bikkurim, but also those owing to the poor in tractate Peah. In addition, Scriptural taboos on crops, touching upon how they are to be planted, how they are to be disposed of at various points in the life of a plant, and their disposition and the conduct of labor in the sabbatical year are taken up and spelled out in tractate Kilayim, Shebiit, and Orlah. So, in sum, the Division deals with the condition under which a crop is raised and with its disposition in such wise as to allow Israelites to make use of the produce of the field and the vineyard. Since, as we shall see, the parts of the Mishnah that I have assigned to the time before the wars persistently treat the preparation and consumption of food under various special circumstances and in accord with diverse Scriptural restrictions, we are hardly surprised to find that whatever in the present Division probably goes back to that early period takes up the same set of themes on rules for food and meals.

The first tractate in which we find material from before the wars is Berakhot (for the place of all tractates in their divisions, see appendix 5, below). A point of interest among the Houses of Shammai and Hillel is legislation on how prayers are to be said, with special reference, first, to reciting the *Shema'*. The relevant Scripture (Deut. 6:4) speaks of lying down and rising up. The Shammaites interpret the Scripture to require lying down when one says the *Shema'* in the evening, standing up when one says it in the morning, and the Hillelites regard the verse as a reference to the time at which the prayer is to be said, evening and morning (M. Ber. 1:3). The bulk of the materials in Berakhot for the period before 70 however, deals with conduct of a meal. At issue are the particular blessings to be said over various kinds of food and in diverse circumstances, and the order of these blessings and of other rituals in connection with a common meal. Of special interest to the Houses is the blessing over wine and the prayer of santification for the Sabbath day (M. Ber. 6:5, 8:1–8). But while later authorities treat the same topics, they do not take up and develop the specific positions of the Houses (e.g., of the Hillelites), so we are not on solid ground in regarding as prewars any of this legislation for a common meal.

The requirement to leave the corner of the field for the poor and not to harvest its grain also attracts the attention of the Houses. Their interest is in the definition of a distinct area subject to the rule in a case in which there is reason to deem an area to be divided into two. For instance, if grain is sown among olive trees, there is the possibility of treating each plot individually, as the House of Shammai maintain, or as part of a single field, as the House of Hillel hold. The former position will be to the advantage of the poor (M. Pe. 3:1).

Ownerless produce is not subject to tithes. The House of Shammai rule that, if one declares his produce ownerless to the poor but not to the rich, that produce is free of tithes. The Hillelites insist that the crop must be totally beyond the control of the original farmer, thus ownerless to all comers (M. Pe. 6:1; M. Sheb. 4:2).

The Houses further deal with the definition of a forgotten sheaf, which must be left behind for the poor (M. Pe. 6:2–5).

Finally, the Houses take up a gray area of law, the status of the grapes of a fourth-year vineyard. Grapes produced in the fourth year after the planting of the vineyard are like the second tithe, in that they must be brought up to Jerusalem and eaten there. But they after all are not actually second tithe. The House of Shammai take that point to mean that only in the stated regard do said grapes fall under the rule governing disposition of food in the status of second tithe, and the House of Hillel impose all of the rules of second tithe because the principal one is shown to apply (M. Pe. 7:6).

The Houses provide the definition of some basic principles in the enforcement of the rules against planting diverse kinds of seeds in a vineyard. They specify the minimum size of an area which is to be deemed autonomous, that is, a field independent of adjacent fields. Such a field is regarded as available for planting one type of crop without reference to what is planted nearby (M. Kil. 2:6). They specify the minimum size of a vineyard along these same lines (M. Kil. 4:5). This conception of an autonomous field and the requirement to add to such a field an area of tillage, not to be sown with diverse kinds, go back to the period before the wars.

The Houses deal with the prohibition, in advance of the sabbatical year, of labor which will facilitate a crop's growth in the sabbatical year itself. They supply a date for the time at which it is no longer permitted to plow a tree-planted field in the sixth year (M. Sheb. 1:1). The Houses further know that one may not do fieldwork which during the Sabbath year benefits the growth of crops therein, and one also may not do fieldwork which even appears to benefit the crops (M. Sheb. 4:4, 5:4 for arum in particular).

Produce of the seventh year is to be eaten, not destroyed. The Houses supply a date for the application of that prohibition to a tree: once a tree has begun to produce a crop of fruit, it may not be cut down (M. Sheb. 4:10).

The strict prohibition against even appearing to violate the law of the seventh year leads the House of Shammai to prohibit selling a plowing heifer to one who is not reliable about keeping the law. The House of Hillel permit one to do so, since such a heifer may serve a purpose other than plowing (M. Sheb. 5:8).

The Houses decree that percentage of a crop which one must separate as a priestly gift. There is every reason to believe that that question goes back to the time before the wars (M. Ter. 4:3).

Dough which is baked in the normal way is deemed to be that kind of bread which is subject to the requirement of giving a dough offering to a priest. The Houses dispute about flour-paste and dumplings, presumably asking about whether or not these particular forms of dough are baked in the normal way (M. Hal. 1:6).

Although disjointed, these rulings add up to a fairly sizable corpus and cover fundamental issues of agricultural law. It is no exaggeration to say that biblical laws governing the production of food in the fields were subject to considerable work by early lawyers, and much was accomplished. As I said, that fact is congruent with the character of much else which I have found reliably assigned to the period before the wars, since, in general, what we have is a sizable corpus of rules on meals, including the way food is produced and prepared. The other half of the system of Agriculture, which focuses upon agricultural offerings—what is appropriate to be set aside and how it is to be delivered to the priest in a state of cultic cleanness—in the main had to await the attention of later lawyers.

The Division of Appointed Times before the Wars

The usable materials from before the wars in the Division of Appointed Times focus upon one significant issue, which is the preparation of meals on the festival day.

Apart from that matter, we have only routine treatment of the taboo against servile labor on the Sabbath. The Houses of Shammai and Hillel voted whether, while it is still light on Friday, it is forbidden to soak ink, dyestuffs, or vetches, unless the processing can be completed before sunset (M. Shab. 1:4–10). The defeated Hillelite position is that if an Israelite himself does not do labor, but the labor goes on naturally, then there is no violation of the Sabbath prohibition against work. The victorious Shammaites hold the Israelite responsible for what happens on its own, if the Israelite has begun the process. So in their view the prohibition of Sabbath labor applies to the person, not to the process of labor. The simple consideration here is that one not create a potential motive for violating the Sabbath, e.g., an occasion to intervene in an ongoing process. The present rule establishes a fence around the observance of the Sabbath taboo against servile labor.

To understand all the rules which follow, dealing with meal preparation for festival days, we must recall the Scriptural rule, stated with special reference to the opening and closing festival days of Passover, that while one must not work on the festival, just as on the Sabbath one must not work, on the festival one may prepare a meal. This act of cooking, by contrast, may not be done on the Sabbath. Ex. 12:16 states the matter as follows: "On the first day you shall hold a holy assembly, and on the seventh day a holy assembly; no work shall be done on those days; but what every one must eat, that only may be prepared by you." The implications and application of this rule occupy all the usable rulings before 70, all of them assigned to the Houses by the redactors of the Mishnah, in the Division of Appointed Times.

I shall first offer an explanation of how I believe this particular set of problems came to emerge from Scripture's rule. An egg laid on the festival day may be eaten that day, so the House of Shammai. The House of Hillel: It may not be eaten (M. Bes. 1:1–2; cf. M. Bes. 1:3–9, 2:1–5). At issue in this puzzling dispute between the Houses of Shammai and Hillel are the fundamental principles governing the preparation of meals on a festival day. As we just saw, Ex. 12:16 is clear that one may prepare food on the holy day. In this regard alone the holy day differs from the Sabbath, on which one may not prepare food. Now the generative question, on which the Houses are made by the Mishnah redactors to take up all possible positions in diverse pericopes, is whether the festival day is the same as the Sabbath except in this one regard. The implication is that, if so, then every effort is to be made to differentiate actions of food preparation, permitted on that day, from equivalent actions on an ordinary day. If not, that is, if the festival is different from the Sabbath and so comparable to a weekday, then there is no reason on the festival to differentiate the mode of doing an action connected with preparation of food from the mode of doing so on an ordinary day. so the egg laid on the day may be eaten that day.

Another expression of this difference in principle is whether or not one must do in advance of the holy day all actions which need not be done on that day itself. If we invoke the analogy of the Sabbath, then all actions which need not be done on the holy day must be done in advance. If we invoke the analogy of an ordinary, secular day, then actions which need not be done on the festival nonetheless may be done on that day. Now in the concrete disputes between the Houses, as I said, the two possible positions are attributed to the M. What is important is raising the question. The most lenient position will be that, by virtue of one's being permitted to prepare food on the festival day, one also may do all actions, however remotely related, which are pertinent to the preparation of food. In the classic formulation, one House prohibits doing acts only secondarily connected with food preparation, while the other permits one even to transport objects not used in cooking because one may transport objects which are used in cooking. Thus the two most extreme positions.

The House of Shammai say that on a festival people bring peace offerings (which yield food) but do not lay hands on them, and they do not bring whole offerings (which yield no food for the sacrifice) at all. The House of Hillel maintain that they may bring both and lay hands on them (M. Bes. 2:4–5; cf. M. Hag. 1:2, 2:2). The consideration here again is the familiar one that one may prepare food on the festival. At issue is actions indirectly related to cooking, or not related at all. The Shammaites are represented as allowing the sacrifice of peace offerings, from which the sacrificer—beneficiary of the rite—derives a good meat meal. But in that regard one need not lay hands on the beast. So that part of the rite is suspended. Whole offerings, which are completely burned up, are not offered at all. The House of Hillel now take up the most lenient possible position, permitting all actions of a given category because one of them is allowed, namely, the peace offerings which yield food.

The House of Shammai say, They take up bones and shells from the table (on the Sabbath). The House of Hillel say, One removes the entire table and shakes it out (M. Shab. 21:3). Since removing the bones and shells is incidental to the eating of the meal, which, obviously, *is* permitted on the Sabbath, one may also handle those things, which, when not incidental to a meal, serve no licit purpose and may not be handled on the Sabbath. The basic notion is that what serves a licit purpose is permitted, and what may not be used also may not be handled or touched. Subject to dispute now is whether one may handle what has served a permitted purpose but is no longer needed for said purpose, a refinement. The Shammaites here allow the person to continue to do so, the Hillelites allow only handling the table, which in any event is allowed.

On a festival which coincides with Friday, one may not cook for the following Sabbath day. But one may prepare food for the festival day

itself and leave some over for use on the Sabbath. One also may prepare food on Thursday and add to that food on Friday, using on the
Sabbath day what is left over on that account. The Houses differ on a
trivial detail: how many different dishes are to be prepared in that
regard (M. Bes. 2:1–3). The Sabbath and the festival are two distinct
and separate moments of sanctification. One may not do an act of
labor—cooking—which is permitted on the festival, for purposes extrinsic to the observance of that festival. With that basic conception in
mind this rule for "commingling of dishes" is not difficult to grasp. One
may undertake food preparation in advance of both the festival and the
following Sabbath, then continuing that ongoing process through the
festival, with the result that food is left over for the Sabbath.

If we now stand back from the several cases and principles before us,
we see that all take up a single problem, namely, the formation of
principles and rules for preparing a meal on a special day. That day, the
festival, is like the Sabbath in one way, and it is not like the Sabbath in
another, as I said at the outset. Consequently, the generative issue is
whether we spin out rules by analogy to the laws governing the Sabbath, in the theory that the festival is like the Sabbath; or whether we
shape laws in contrast with those of the Sabbath, in the theory that the
festival is not like the Sabbath. In this latter case we shall have to find
the outer limits of the contrastive laws. In sum, therefore, the specific
problems investigated in the discrete pericopes pursue a single line of
thought, namely, the contrastive-analogical mode of pursuing the implications of a Scriptural statement. That is, something is like something else, therefore follows the same rule, or it is unlike something
else, therefore follows the diametrically opposite rule (see also chapter
5, below). That fact is clear in the following sequence of propositions:

Scripture: One may prepare food on the festival day.

Houses: (1) One may do only what is directly connected with preparing food, *or* one may do even indirectly relevant actions. (2) What is
to be used on the festival must, *or* need not, be made ready for that
purpose beforehand. (3) What one does, by permission, on the festival
must be done in a way different from an ordinary day, *or* one does such
deeds in the normal way.

All three propositions naturally emerge as soon as one undertakes to
compile rules to amplify and apply the Scriptural law. (1) and (3) are
complementary, in both instances simply seeking to define the limits of
the Scriptural leniency. What (2) does is equally clear. Here is applied
to the permissible activities of the festival precisely the consideration
deemed urgent in connection with permissible actions and activities of
the Sabbath. Just as one in advance of the Sabbath must designate an
object which one plans to utilize on the Sabbath, so one must do the

same in regard to a festival, now with respect to food, which one may cook.

In sum, at issue in the entries in the names of the Houses before 70 are secondary questions, generated by the intention to analyze and apply what Scripture permits. The basic conceptions are, first, that the festival is analogous to the Sabbath in all regards except for the specified one, and, second, that what one is permitted to do on the festival is itself subject to qualification. In summary, rules in the Division of Appointed Times in fact deal with preparing meals, in this context, on the occasion of festivals. But the focus of interest is meals, and the advent of the issue of the festival merely precipitates an inquiry into what, in the case of the festival, we have to say about making food.

It would appear that, if someone had set out to organize a "Mishnah" before 70, his single operative category would have been making meals. He would have had a tractate on growing food in accord with certain biblical taboos, and another on preparing food on the festival. We shall now see that there is a quite separate definitive category, that is to say, a fresh "Division" within this imaginary Mishnah made before the advent of the great wars against Rome.

The Division of Women before the Wars

The rulings in the Division of women before 70 deal with two matters: first, marriages; second, vows. These laws do not coalesce around a single central and generative principle, as in the case of those in Appointed Times. But the ones for marriage do deal with a single theme, which is the cessation of marriage, so that a woman is free to remarry through the death of the husband; the infidelity of the wife; certain unusual nullifying conditions in the original formation of the marriage, e.g., in the case of a minor girl, or, especially, in the matter of the levirate connection and its abrogation.

The levirate marriage is required at Deut. 25:5–10. When a husband dies childless, his widow is supposed to marry a surviving brother or to undergo a rite of removing the shoe specified in Scripture. There are cases in which the levirate marriage brings a widow into conflict with the rules prohibiting marriage among close relatives (Lev. 18). The Houses take up a secondary problem involved in the recognition of that conflict, a case in which the woman was permitted to marry the man now deceased, but is now prohibited from marrying his brothers.

If a woman cannot enter into levirate marriage because the levir is prohibited by the rules of Lev. 18, then, in the view of the House of Hillel, all of her cowives also are prohibited from doing so and hence are entirely free of the levirate connection. The Shammaites do not deem the cowives to be exempted by reason of the consanguineous status of one of them (M. Yeb. 1:1–4). In the case in which the rule of levirate marriage conflicts with the prohibition of the marriage of blood relatives, in the Hillelite view there will be not only no levirate marriage but also no rite of removal of the shoe (Deut. 25:5–10). There is no connection whatsoever between these two Hillelite rulings.

In a case of levirate marriage, there is a prior rite, parallel to the rite of betrothal in the case of a natural marriage. It is the *declaration* that the levir intends to enter into levirate marriage with the childless brother's widow, called "bespeaking." Now when we consider the relationship of levirate marriage, effected at the hands of heaven, to normal marriage, effected by man's will and woman's consent, we want to know whether this act of bespeaking really is parallel in force to the fact of betrothal, and if so, how. The Shammaites deem the act of bespeaking in the case of a levirate marriage as the complete equivalent of an act of betrothal in an ordinary one. The Hillelites are not so sure of the matter and so treat the results as subject to doubt (M. Yeb. 3:5). The right of a woman awaiting levirate marriage is to dispose of property which accrues to her. The Houses concur that the woman who awaits levirate marriage is able to dispose of her property. It is in no way subject to the domain of the levir, even though she cannot marry anybody else. Once she is wed to the levir, he enjoys the full rights of the husband. In this matter the Shammaite view of the status of the bespoken widow does not come into play (M. Yeb. 4:3–4; M. Ket. 8:1–2).

We now come to three instances in which a marriage comes to an end other than through divorce, specifically, through the death of the husband; the coming to maturity of a minor girl previously married off by her mother or brothers; or the husband's suspicion of infidelity on the part of the wife. A woman may testify to her husband's death only in restricted situations, so the House of Hillel. The House of Shammai allow for such testimony under many conditions (M. Yeb. 15:2–3). The woman's testimony that her husband has died is sufficient not only to permit her to remarry but also to allow her to lay claim to property in settlement of her marriage contract.

The House of Shammai say that the right of refusal in the case of minor girls is given only to betrothed girls; the House of Hillel say that it also applies to married ones. The House of Shammai rule that it applies only to the husband; the House of Hillel extend it to the levir (M. Yeb. 13:1). While a father has an ironclad right to marry off his minor daughter, the mother or older brothers do not. If they choose to give the girl away as a minor, she has the right upon reaching maturity to reject their choice, through the right of refusal. The Houses work out elementary details on that matter. The House of Shammai permit the exercise of the right of refusal in restricted conditions. Essentially, they maintain, it applies where there are no permanent deeds, e.g., consummation of the marriage. They want a formal exercise in court, in the presence of the husband. They deny the right to a girl who, having been betrothed by her mother or brothers, then finds that her husband dies childless and so turns out to be subject to the marriage of a levir. The Hillelites treat the right of refusal as paramount and absolute, which means they deem the act of betrothal by the mother or brothers to be lacking in all legal effect.

In the case of a woman accused of infidelity by her husband, if the husband then dies and so does not impose the ordeal of drinking the bitter water (Num. 5:11–31), the House of Shammai say that the woman gets her marriage settlement and does not undergo the ordeal. The House of Hillel say there is no ordeal, but also no marriage settlement (M. Sot. 4:2). In a case of doubt the Shammaites will not deprive a woman of her marriage contract. Now when we do not know for sure that the wife accused of adultery has committed adultery, we are not, in their view, going to deprive the woman of her property rights. The Hillelites place the burden of proof on the woman. But since there is no rite of drinking the bitter water, there also is no chance for her to prove her innocence, and hence she loses her property rights.

Two rather miscellaneous rules on vows appear to derive from the period before 70. A vow null in part is wholly invalid, so the House of Hillel. The House of Shammai rule that the valid part of a vow is in force. Vows made under constraint are not valid. The Houses work out some minor details of this principle (M. Ned. 3:2, 4; M. Naz. 5:1–3, 5–7). Clearly, vows have no standing *ex opere operato*. On the contrary, where there is an error of fact or a consideration of constraint, the vow is treated as if it had not taken place. In general, therefore, a vow made in error, e.g., on the foundation of misapprehension of the facts, is deemed null. What comes under dispute is the case of a vow made in part in error, or made in part under constraint. The House of Shammai will maintain that that part of the vow not made in error or subject to constraint remains in force.

A vow made overseas to be a Nazirite (Num. 6:1–21) can be fulfilled only in the holy Land (M. Naz. 3:6). The Houses take for granted that land outside of the Land of Israel is cultically unclean, like a graveyard. At issue between the Houses is whether a vow covering many spells of thirty days is binding, or whether whatever vow has been said, only a minimum spell of thirty days as a Nazirite is owing. I shall explain later on how I think this set of rules relates to the ones on meals which survive in the Divisions of Agriculture and Appointed Times (see below, pp. 69–71).

The Division of Damages before the Wars

I found no available materials in the Divison of Damages for the period before the wars.

The Division of Holy Things before the Wars

The few available rules in the Division of Holy Things that date from before the wars deal mainly with food or preparing meals.

The House of Shammai hold that one may not slaughter a beast with a scythe. The House of Hillel permit doing so. This item bears no later indication of development, nor does it intersect with anything to follow (M. Hul. 1:1–2).

The House of Shammai prohibit an Israelite from eating the meat of a firstling. The House of Hillel permit (M. Bekh. 5:2). The status of the firstling, to be given to the priest, is worked out. The specific issue is whether or not the firstling is deemed a holy thing reserved for the priesthood.

Deut. 18:4 requires that the first fruits of grain, wine, and oil, and first fleece of sheep, be given to the levitical priest. The Houses work out the number of sheep one must own to constitute a flock. If one has two sheep, one is liable to make a gift of the first fleece, in the view of the House of Shammai. The House of Hillel deem a minimum flock to be five (M. Hul. 11:2).

None of these items hangs together with the others.

The reader may wonder why these materials do not find a place in the Division of Agriculture, rather than in the Division of Holy Things. The interests of the rulings, on animals given to a priest, surely conform to those of the Division of Agriculture, on produce given to a priest. In describing this stage in the creation of the materials ultimately brought together in the Mishnah, there is no good reason for adhering to the extant lines of splitting up and organizing the Mishnah's materials into Divisions. These lines were surveyed much later. That part of the work of redaction cannot be shown to have been under way so early. So the reader's question is a valid one, and there is no answer, for the period under discussion. Only long afterward, probably after a century or so, were the lines of organization laid down which made a distinction between animals owing to the priest, rules for which are given in the Division of Holy Things, and produce paid over to the priest, rules for which are presented in the Division of Agriculture. Indeed, the fact that both sets of rules have in common an interest in food preparation, not in the topics which, later on, would characterize the Divisions in which they appear, tells us something interesting. If any work of organization *had* been under way, one principal and organizing Division of the emergent document would have been on preparing food under various circumstances. But, as we know, that is not the way in which Mishnah ultimately would be organized.

The Division of Purities before the Wars

The laws in the Division of Purities pertinent to the age before the wars differ in one important way from those just now surveyed. While the other Divisions yield materials of an essentially random and episodic character, the Division of Purities presents us with laws which, in the aggregate, not only impart information but also tell a simple, whole story. That is, they form a complete system, and it is the one which persists into the final version of the Mishnah. The topic, Purities, is treated in a particular way, for a distinctive purpose. The story is about (1) how a source of uncleanness imparts uncleanness; (2) what sorts of objects are susceptible to uncleanness to begin with; and (3) how an unclean object may undergo a process of decontamination so as to return to its prior state of cleanness. What is important here is that the ultimate shape of the Division of Purities, as it will emerge in its final form in the Mishnah, is adumbrated by the materials before us, in primitive state and lacking detail to be sure. These laws tell us (1) sources of uncleanness; (2) principles definitive of objects which are susceptible to uncleanness (in addition to food and drink); and (3) modes of purification from uncleanness. The sources of uncleanness are those specified by Scripture. The Mishnah is able to add only substances analogous to the sources of uncleanness listed in Lev. 12–15, Num. 19, and other relevant passages. Scripture knows that food and drink, clothing and furniture, may be made unclean. The Mishnah provides criteria for distinguishing those sorts of objects which are susceptible from those which are not susceptible to uncleanness. Finally, what restores the cleanness of an object made unclean is the action of water in its natural state. The Mishnah's founders speak of water unaffected by the intervention of man. Only water which has collected naturally and not been drawn in utensils or brought into a pool is suitable to restore the natural condition of what has been affected by the designated sources of uncleanness. While the second and third stages in the unfolding of the law will greatly expand and complicate these simple principles, the system ultimately revealed in the closed document already is before us in these three formative and definitive categories of interest and in the principles which shape the concrete rules operative in the several categories.

When we draw together those rulings on the susceptibility of utensils which clearly belong to the Houses, we find three areas of concern (see

Neusner, *Purities* III, pp. 355–70). These are, first, the effort to explore the analogy between the tightly fitting cover which seals a clay utensil and prevents uncleanness from entering therein, specified by Num. 19:14–15, and objects of a similar character but not of clay, e.g., a metal utensil bearing a tightly fitting cover. The issue is whether, in the tent of a corpse, that object, tightly sealed too, is protected, as is a clay one. Second, all parties work out the definition of a utensil, agreeing that, when an object is autonomous, distinctive in character and use, it constitutes a utensil and is susceptible to uncleanness. Finally, when an object may be used for lying and sitting, it is susceptible to "pressure uncleanness" (*midras,* the uncleanness imparted to something used for lying or sitting by a *zab* [Lev. 15:1ff.] or an equivalently unclean person). When said object no longer is used for lying and sitting, it ceases to be susceptible in that way. At issue now is the definition of the cessation of that sort of susceptibility. The principal point, the notion of defining a utensil in terms of its suitability for use for a particular purpose, derives from the close reading of Lev. 11:32, which is clear that any utensil *used for any purpose* is susceptible to uncleanness. An object becomes a utensil when it is useful, and the rest follows (we see this more clearly below, pp. 106–7). The concomitant criteria of autonomy and distinctiveness simply fill out the picture. An insusceptible utensil is one which is useless, along the lines of the rule of Lev. 11:33, which holds that a broken oven is no longer unclean. The several governing principles therefore emerge from Scripture.

The discussion of sources of uncleanness focuses upon the principal one, corpse contamination. The Houses know that a tent spreads contamination when it overshadows a corpse, since Num. 19:14ff. is explicit on the subject. What they add is that things which are *like* a corpse also contaminate in a tent—a standard exercise in analogical-contrastive thinking. This then extends the category to things which contain corpse matter, e.g., a grave area. The really important development before 70 is the generative principle that, just as what is like a corpse produces corpse uncleanness, so what is like a tent spreads corpse uncleanness (see Neusner, *Purities* V, pp. 220–34). This step forward, also along the lines of established analogical-contrastive modes of thought, yields the stunning comparison and contrast, with rich and complex articulation, between a tent and a utensil, which may or may not function as a tent. A tent is defined as an enclosed cubic area of at least a handbreadth in breadth, depth, and height. This definition carries in its wake the notion that corpse uncleanness passes through an opening of more than a handbreath in two dimensions, or is contained by a closed cubic space of less than a handbreadth in three dimensions. Corpse uncleanness further is imagined as a kind of viscous mass which spurts up and down when under pressure, but does not move out to the sides. Finally, since if a space is enclosed to less than a handbreadth, corpse uncleanness will not pass through, an enclosed room with an entry of less than a handbreadth of open space may be comparable to a utensil, in that entry or egress is controlled by a space of the specified dimension. In sum, authorities before 70 know that corpses contaminate; when covering a corpse, tents spread contamination, or, when a corpse is outside of a tent, interpose against contamination. They simply make explicit what is stated at Num. 19:11, for the corpse, and Num. 19:14, for the tent. Num. 19:15, as we already have noted, is clear that the content of a sealed utensil is not affected by a corpse.

So the basic contribution of the authorities before 70 is the conception that a tent is a space measured by a handbreadth on each side, and that whatever is analogous to such a space—a utensil, along the lines of Num. 19:15, quite reasonably brought into juxtaposition with Num. 19:14—functions as does a tent, either to retain corpse contamination or to prevent the entry of corpse contamination. Corpse uncleanness is something which can be contained by a tent, and a tent is something which can contain or interpose against corpse uncleanness. This functional definition of what is at issue breaks down Scripture's specific and concrete understanding of the meaning of the word *tent,* opening the way to the superlatively sophisticated thought of the completed tractate Ohalot. It is the insight of authorities before 70 to treat the tent of Scripture as the foundation for an analogy; that is, a tent *or whatever is like a tent* (because it functions as does a tent) is subject to the law of the tent. Once more we see the working of the analogical-contrastive mode of thought, generating those principles upon which the towering intellectual structures of the final Mishnah are founded.

In the earliest consideration of the uncleanness of the menstruating woman, specified at Lev. 12:2 and 15:19, for a period of seven days, and the uncleanness of menstrual blood and of the woman who has a sustained discharge outside of her regular period—the *zabah* of Lev. 15:25, the established rules are taken up and complemented, but left essentially intact. Before 70 the proposition came under discussion that menstrual secretions other than blood which is red also may be unclean. The Houses assume that not all vaginal excretions mark the onset of the menstrual uncleanness. What that means is that the group subject to their tutelage will deem unclean a woman whom others, with a less differentiated conception of the matter, will regard as clean—and vice versa (M. Nid. 2:6–7).

Shammai and Hillel debated the retroactive imputation of uncleanness to things touched by a woman just before she produces menstrual blood (M. Nid. 1:1). Shammai maintained that if a woman has a regular period, we do not assume that her period began before the time at which it was expected, and at which blood actually did issue forth. We therefore should not impute uncleanness to things the woman has touched before her period. Hillel wanted a woman to examine herself regularly, even outside of her period. So they imputed uncleanness to things touched by the woman from the time of the actual appearance of blood back to the last examination prior to that time. Sages took up an intermediate position, in fact in line with Hillel's principle, that we impute uncleanness to things touched by the woman during the preceding twenty-four hours. So we do retroactively impose uncleanness, even by reason of doubt. In sum, the rules before 70 on menstrual uncleanness take up three topics: (1) unclean vaginal excretions; (2) the status of a woman in the days of her purifying (Lev. 12); and (3) the issue of retroactive contamination. These issues take the first step beyond the facts laid forth in Scripture and define the beginning of the law later on fully exposed in the Mishnah.

While the importance of determining when a woman is menstrually unclean principally concerns appropriate times for sexual relations, as Scripture says, there is a second, and, I think, generative consideration. When a woman is in her period, she imparts uncleanness to food and drink when she touches, as well as to beds and chairs on which she lies or sits. What this means, therefore, is that, if the family eats in a state of cultic cleanness, a woman cannot prepare meals for her family during the time of her period. Indeed, she would be best kept out of the house, in the Zoroastrian manner, if people proposed to eat their meals in a state of cleanness analogous to the cleanness of the cult. In any event the woman could not touch food or dishes to be used by those who ate in such a state. It follows that even in the present instance, we deal with an issue critical for the manner of preparation and consumption of ordinary meals.

The *zab*, the man who suffers a flux (Lev. 15:1ff.) is male, therefore in the status of one who has a seminal emission and subject to the law of Lev. 15:16; but he is subject to the same uncleanness as the *zabah*, the woman who suffers a flux, thus imposing a verbal analogy. Flux is like semen, hence comparable to uncleanness by reason of a seminal emission; but it is unclean as *zob*, the flux of the *zab* or *zabah*, so invoking the analogy to the *zabah*. The Houses take up the problem of negotiating among the operative analogies (M. Zab. 1:1). The House of Shammai compare the man who has had one flux *(zob)* to a woman who awaits day against day, that is, who has had a flow and watches out for another to confirm her status as a *zabah*, for she too has had a single flux. The House of Hillel compare the man to one who has had merely a seminal emission. Both Houses know that a man is confirmed as a *zab* if he has suffered three flows of flux but imparts uncleanness as a *zab* even if there were only two. A further exercise then will compare semen to flux (M. Zab. 1:2).

Two of the three principal components of the subsystem of Purities, the definition of sources of uncleanness and how they are spread, and the specification of things which are susceptible to uncleanness, with the concomitant notion that some things are not susceptible to uncleanness, thus relate closely to Scripture (see Neusner, *Purities* V, pp. 236–38). Yet the way in which these components are worked out, the definition of the exegetical program affecting them, is in no way to be predicted on the basis of what Scripture says in expressing its facts pertinent to those same matters. For tractate Kelim, on utensils, at issue is the susceptibility and insusceptibility to uncleanness of utensils in various conditions; for tractate Ohalot, on corpse uncleanness, the issue is the nature and function of tents and utensils in relationship to corpse uncleanness. In neither instance has Scripture contributed the Mishnah's formulation of the problem. The Mishnaic conception, that we must ask about whether or not a given object is susceptible to uncleanness, is alien to the few passages of Scripture which to begin with are relevant to the issue of susceptibility of utensils to uncleanness. The much-vexed question of tractate Ohalot, What is a tent and when does a utensil function like a tent? would be ludicrous to the authority behind Num. 19:11–22, who knows that, when we refer to a tent, we speak of an ordinary, everyday tent, with which everyone is familiar. The role of Scripture is to supply information to people who, with questions or interests of their own, have been motivated to turn to Scripture to find information. That is why the tent of which tractate Ohalot speaks bears no relationship to the real tent in which someone had died and which spreads uncleanness in the view of Num. 19:11ff.

When we come to the process of decontamination or purification of objects or persons which have become unclean and which can be made clean, we leave the realm of Scriptural information entirely. The reason is that at the outset the Mishnaic tractate on purification, Miqvaot ("Purification Pools"), knows that water in its natural condition, that is, unaffected by human intervention, possesses the power to effect decontamination and to restore the natural condition of cleanness. Scripture for its part knows that when water is used for washing an object which has become unclean, said object remains in its condition of uncleanness until sunset. Scripture likewise is well aware that water mixed with other substances, e.g., blood or ashes of a certain kind of cow which has been cremated, can effect purification. But water all by itself does not effect purification. But that is the absolute datum of the Mishnaic system. For tractate Miqvaot begins with the definition of water which has the power to undertake and complete the process of purification. Water which effects purification must be still and in the volume which will cover the body of a human being. The House of Shammai will accept a rain stream as a suitable purification pool, on the grounds that in the entire flow is the requisite volume of water. The House of Hillel want the requisite volume in one place (M. Miq. 5:6). The water must physically affect the whole body, hence must be in one place; the process is not merely symbolic.

If we have less than the requisite volume of still rainwater, it cannot be augmented by unsuitable water. We know that drawn water, that is, water subjected to human intervention, is not suitable. If a given volume of drawn water is poured into a pool containing an insufficient volume of valid water, the pool as a whole is invalidated. Shammai and Hillel dispute about the volume of drawn water which under the specified circumstances will suffice to invalidate the still rainwater (M. Ed. 1:3).

Their Houses, moreover, will concur that if one deliberately collects water, e. g., by placing utensils under a waterspout, that water is deemed invalid. Mere passage through the utensils which have been deliberately set out will invalidate the water for use in an immersion pool (M. Miq. 4:1). So the definition of drawn water is expanded, even at this early stage, to encompass water which collected on its own, but only by reason of what a human being has effectively done.

Ideas held before 70 include, first, the notion that drawn water, that is, water not in its natural state, cannot be used for purification. Second, gathering water in utensils is what makes it into drawn water. Mere passage through utensils suffices, if a person has intentionally collected the water by locating the utensils where he did. The Houses further know that the immersion pool is effective to restore the status of cleanness to water which has been made cultically unclean. They further take for granted that the immersion pool is effective for some substances but not for others. So, to summarize: rainwater purifies some things, but it must not be affected by human agency, e.g., drawn from a well or collected in utensils.

If we now stand back from what we have seen, we notice that the earliest stage in the unfolding of the law of Purities deals with domestic matters, not cultic ones. The points of special concern begin with the uncleanness of a woman in her menstrual period, at which point she may not prepare food which is to be kept in a state of cultic cleanness, or even sit on a chair and eat at a table at which a meal in a state of cultic cleanness is to be served. This matter brings us to the household and its hearth. The extensive early discourse of tractate Kelim on utensils susceptible to uncleanness is directed principally at domestic objects, used for sleeping and eating. The principles of tractate Miqvaot, on immersion pools, concern the restoration to cleanness of objects used in the home, exclusive of food and drink, which are beyond purification. These are the points to which much intellectual energy would later be drawn. They are what would remain fresh and interesting in the law. The expansion of sources of uncleanness rapidly reached limits imposed by the analogy to begin with utilized for that process. Indeed, the analogical limits were reached when we asked about the comparison of the *zab* to the *zabah,* on the one side, and to the one who has had a seminal emission, on the other; from there no movement is possible. The contaminating power of corpse matter, like that of a corpse, leads nowhere beyond the simple allegation that what is like a corpse contaminates like a corpse. But when we come to the definition of what is susceptible to uncleanness, on the one side, and what has the power to remove uncleanness, on the other, we shall see much work done in the future.

The Laws as a Whole

It seems to me no accident at all that those strata of Mishnaic law which appear to go back to the period before the wars deal specifically with the special laws of marriage (in Yebamot), distinctive rules on when sexual relations may and may not take place (in Niddah), and the laws covering the definition of sources of uncleanness and the attainment of cleanness, with specific reference to domestic meals (in certain parts of Chalot, Zabim, Kelim, and Miqvaot). Nor is it surprising that for the conduct of the cult and the sacrificial system, about which the group may have had its own doctrines but over which it neither exercised control nor even aspired to exercise control, there appears to be no systemic content or development whatsoever.

To recapitulate the argument: once the group takes shape around some distinctive, public issue or doctrine, as in odd taboos about eating, it also must take up the modes of social differentiation which will ensure the group's continued existence. For the group, once it comes into being, has to aspire to define and shape the ordinary lives of its adherents and to form a community expressive of its larger world view. The foundations of an enduring community will then be laid down through rules governing what food may be eaten, under what circumstances, and with what sort of people; whom one may marry and what families may be joined in marriage; and how sexual relationships are timed. Indeed, to the measure that these rules not only differ from those observed by others but in some aspect or other render the people who keep them unacceptable to those who do not, as much as, to the sect, those who do not keep them are unacceptable to those who do, the lines of difference and distinctive structure will be all the more inviolable.

The Mishnah before the wars begins its life among a group of people who are joined together by a common conviction about the eating of food under ordinary circumstances in accord with cultic rules to begin with applicable, in the mind of the priestly lawyers of Leviticus and Numbers, to the Temple alone. This group, moreover, had other rules which affected who might join and who might not. As I said, these laws formed a protective boundary, keeping in those who were in, keeping out those who were not. In accord with the inductive principles which have guided this account of the unfolding of the Mishnah, if we wish to identify the social group in which the Mishnah originated, it is at this point that discourse must come to a conclusion. The reason is that the Mishnah does not tell us the name of the group represented by the names of Shammai and Hillel and their Houses, Gamaliel, Simeon b. Gamaliel, his son, and others who appear in the Mishnah and who clearly form the earliest stratum of its named authorities. More important: the convictions of the named authorities deal with details. The vast territories of agreement have not been surveyed and marked out by them in particular. So, for all we know, the concrete matters subject to dispute represent the points at issue of no more than a tiny sector of a much larger group, which, in other ways, will have had still other points of discourse and contention.

The upshot is simple. We know of two particular groups in the period before the wars who held significant convictions about taboos governing meals and about marriage into their groups, the Essenes and the Pharisees. Because Gamaliel and his son, Simeon, appear in the Mishnah and, when they appear in other writings (Acts 5:34; Josephus, *Life*, 190–94), also are called Pharisees, people generally assume that the book which contains sayings in their names is their book, that is, a book originating among Pharisees. So it is assumed that the Mishnah is a Pharisaic book. While that may well be so, the internal evidence of the Mishnah itself does not direct our attention only to the Pharisees. As I just said, there were, after all, Essenes who can have kept these same laws within their social framework. And much which is written about the Pharisees does not appear to describe a holiness sect or an eating club at all. Nor does the Mishnah even mention Pharisees in those pericopes the ideas of which can securely be shown to belong to the period before the wars (see Lightstone, *Sadducees*). The Mishnah speaks mostly about the Houses of Shammai and Hillel. As I pointed out, we do not even know whether before us are the ideas only of radical priests, or only of lay people pretending to be priests, or of a mixture of the two. The information on the Essenes suggests the third of the three possibilities. But that does not settle the question for the group behind the stratum of the Mishnah set before the wars. And, it is clear, we are not even sure we can call the group by any name more specific and definitive than *group,* for instance, a *sect.* We use general language so as not to invoke the meanings associated with more particular categories.

What demands attention, rather, is a different question. Why should the Temple and the ideas of its priests have played so important a role in the mind of the people (whoever they were) who are represented by the earliest layer of ideas ultimately contained in the Mishnah? Since, as we shall see time and again, what the Mishnah presents is nothing other than what the Scripture says, and Scriptures that are chosen for representation time and again are those in the priestly code, we have to wonder why the priestly themes and repertoire of concerns should have so occupied the imagination and fantasy of the people who formed the group (or groups) represented in the laws before us. It is the continuity from the priestly code of the seventh through the fifth century B.C. to the beginnings of the Mishnaic code of the first and second centuries A.D., which requires explanation. For, end as much as beginning, the Mishnah is the formation of the priestly perspective on the condition of Israel (see below, pp. 248–50).

The Mishnah states what priests had long said, but in other language, in other documents. True, the Mishnah has its own perspective and method. These are drastically different from those of the priestly code (see below, pp. 211–17). As we shall see, the Mishnah employs the list-making method of the scribes. Indeed, the Mishnah takes up a remarkably unfriendly position on the priesthood, while acknowledging and affirming every single right and benefit owing to the priesthood. So, in sum, the Mishnah is not a merely contingent and secondary development of what is in the priestly code. Nonetheless, the continuity from the priestly code to the Mishnah is firm and impressive. If the founders of the Mishnaic code had something distinctive to say, it was in the vocabulary and images of the priestly code. The words were their own. But the deep syntax of the sacred, the metaphysical grammar, belonged to the priesthood from olden times. That is why it now becomes urgent to speculate on why the priestly code should have exercised so profound and formative an influence upon the founders and first framers of Mishnaic law.

From the Priestly Code to the Beginning of the Mishnaic Code

The reason that the priestly cope (P) (Lev. 1–15) exercised the forma-

tive power it did is that the problems addressed and (for some) solved
in the priestly code remained chronic long after the period of its formation, from the seventh century onward down to its closure in the time
of Ezra and Nehemiah. True, there were many ways to confront and
cope with the problems I shall specify. After all, third and fourth
Isaiahs flourished in the same time as did the philosophers, storytellers,
and lawyers whose ideas ultimately come to a single formation and to
closure in P. As Porter commented in a different context, Jeremiah and
the writers and editors of Deuteronomy were contemporaries too (see
above, pp. 10–12). But the priestly code states a powerful answer to a
pressing and urgent question. Since, as I shall now suggest, that question would remain a perplexity continuing to trouble Israelites for a
long time, it is not surprising that the priestly answer to it, so profound
and fundamental in its character, should for its part have continued to
attract and impress people too.

That is the argument I wish now to lay out. In order to follow it, we
have first to locate ourselves in the time of closure of the priestly code,
that is, in the late sixth and fifth centuries B.C., and to specify the
critical tensions of that period. Once we have seen the character of
these tensions, without needing much exposition we shall realize that
the same tensions persisted and confronted the thinkers whose reflection led to the conclusions, in resolution of those ongoing points of
dissonance, that the Temple's holiness enveloped and surrounded
Israel's Land and demarcated its people too (cf. Russell).

What marks ancient Israel as distinctive perenially is its preoccupation with defining itself. In one way or another Israel sought
means of declaring itself distinct from its neighbors. The stress on
exclusion of the neighbors from the group, and of the group from the
neighbors, runs contrary to the situation of ancient Israel, with unmarked frontiers of culture, the constant giving and receiving among
diverse groups, generally characteristic of ancient times. The persistent stress on differentiation, yielding a preoccupation with self-
definition, also contradicts the facts of the matter. In the time of the
formation of the priestly code, the people Israel was deeply affected by
the shifts and changes in social and cultural and political life and institutions captured by the word "Hellenization." That was the case
long before the conquest of Alexander. We may trace the ongoing
preoccupation with self-definition to the context which yielded the later
Scriptural legacy of the Pentateuchal redaction, for it was in that protracted moment of confusion and change that the priestly code came to
closure, and with it, the Pentateuchal heritage. As Morton Smith shows
(*Palestinian Parties*, pp. 57–81), the epoch of "Hellenization" began
long before Alexander and continued long afterward. Greek military
forces, Greek traders, Greek merchandise, and Greek ways penetrated

the Land of Israel. There were substantial Greek settlements before Alexander's conquest. Greek influence thereafter intensified. Now as we know, it is in the time of Nehemiah and Ezra that the priestly writers brought to completion and closure the collection of cultic traditions we now know as P. And, as Smith amply demonstrates, Nehemiah himself is the archetype of a Greek *tyrannos*, a type Smith describes as follows: "These new rulers were products of the economic and social change which was taking place all over the area.... Barbarian invasions had destroyed the order of the more ancient world, brought trade almost to a standstill, and reduced much of the New East to a culture of mere local subsistence." As civilization began to recover, "stabilization of society led to increase in population and foreign trade. Foreign trade increased venture capital and also produced a class of new rich.... Increases of capital, or population, and consequently, of need, produced successively borrowing..., default, confiscation, and enslavement. The resultant resentment and social instability were often used by ambitious political leaders to secure a following.... Such revolutionary leaders...were known as 'tyrants' (*Palestinian Parties*, p. 138). Nehemiah was one of these types. One of the characteristic parts of the program of such a political figure was to pass measures, again in Smith's words, "such as public works programs, cancellation of debts, release of persons enslaved for debt, confiscation of the property of their wealthy opponents, and redistribution of land" (*Palestinian Parties*, pp. 138–39). The program of the *tyrannos* included codification of laws of a society as a (somewhat later) response to social development. All of this political and legislative program therefore is part of the common inheritance of the modernization of the Middle East even prior to Alexander.

The upshot of the codification and closure of the law under Nehemiah was to produce a law code which laid heavy emphasis on the exclusivist character of the Israelite God and cult. "Judaism" gained the character of a cultically centered way of life and world view. Both rite and myth aimed at the continuing self-definition of Israel by separation from the rest of the world and exclusion of the rest of the world. Order against chaos meant holiness over uncleanness, life over death. The purpose was to define Israel against the background of the other peoples of the Near and Middle East, with whom Israel had much in common, and, especially, to differentiate Israel from its neighbors, e.g., Samaritans, in the same country. Acute differentiation was required in particular because the social and cultural facts were precisely to the contrary: common traits hardly bespeaking clear-cut points of difference, except of idiom. The mode of differentiation taken by the Torah literature in general, and the priestly sector of that literature in particular, was cultic. The meaning, however, also was social. The power of the Torah composed in this time lay in its control of the Temple. The Torah made that Temple the pivot and focus. The Torah literature, with its jealous God, who cares what people do about rather curious matters, and the Temple cult, with its total exclusion of the non-Israelite from participation, and (all the more so) from cultic comensality, raised high those walls of separation and underlined such distinctiveness as already existed. The life of Israel flowed from the altar; what made Israel Israel was the center, the altar.

Now we must consider that it was at just this time, from the seventh to the fifth century B.C, that the roads were opening to carry trade, culture, ideas, and, above all, to permit the mixing of peoples and races through what we may call direct personal encounter, that is, marriage (and parallel activities). So it was at just this time, long before the cultural reaction which expressed the oriental response to the political changes effected by Alexander and his successors (see Eddy), that groups had to take up and contemplate what made them different from one another. It also was clear at, or before, this time that a fair part of Israel would not live in "its own" Land at all. Israel also would preserve its distinctive group life and character somewhere else. That complicating fact also made all the more necessary a persistent exercise of self-definition—meaning, more accurately, self-differention—from the diverse people among whom, and essentially like whom, Israel lived out its life.

So long as Israel remained essentially within its own Land and frame of social reference, that is, before the conflagration of the sixth century B.C., the issue of separation from neighbors could be treated casually. When the very core and heart of what made Israel into Israel were penetrated by the doubly desolating and disorienting experiences of both losing the Land and then coming back, by the exercises in confusion in economic and social relationships to which I have alluded, and by the fact that the Land to which Israelites returned in no way permitted contiguous and isolated Israelite settlement, then the issue of self-definition clearly would emerge. It would remain on the surface and chronic. And it would persist for the rest of Israelite history, from the return to Zion and the formation of the Torah literature even down to our own day. The reason for the persistence is that the social forces which lent urgency to the issue of who is Israel (or, later, of who is a Jew) would remain. It is hardly an exaggeration to say that this confusion about the distinctive and ongoing identification to be assigned to Israel would define the very framework of the social and imaginative ecology of the Jewish people (see Neusner, *Way,* pp. xi–xiv). So long as memory remained, the conflicting claims of exclusivist Torah literature and universalist prophecy, of a people living in utopia, in no particular place, while framing its vision to itself in the deeply locative symbols of cult and center—these conflicting claims would make vivid the abiding issue of self-definition.

Now when we confront the matter of the Mishnah's place in the ongoing issue of who is Israel, we must place the beginnings of the Mishnah into historical context. Otherwise we shall lose sight of what is important in the Mishnah's version of Israel's definition and miss the reason for its continuity with the priestly one. For the Mishnah at its origins carries forward precisely those priestly and cultic motifs which proved important at the first encounter, in the time of Ezra and Nehemiah, between Israel and what would be Israel's enduring ecological framework. That was the encounter between the pressing claim to be exclusive and to serve an exclusivist God, on the one side, and the equally paramount facts of diffuse settlement in trivial numbers and diverse locations, on the other. These and related political and social factors making for the very opposite of an exclusive and closed society within high borders created a dissonance, not ever resolved, between social facts and the fantastic self-perceptions of Israel. Indeed, the very stress of the Torah literature on maintaining high and inviolable frontiers around Israel bespeaks the very opposite: a porous border, an unmarked boundary, an open road from group to group, down which, as I said, not only ideas but also unions of people could and did travel.

3

Divisions, Tractates, Principal Ideas between the Wars

Preliminary Observations

The principal initiatives and propositions of the law after 70 prove to be either predictable on the basis of what had just now happened or wholly continuous with what had gone before. The point of interest in the catastrophe of the First War against Rome, for the people whose ideas came down to the framers of the Mishnah, therefore lies in the stunning facts that, first, the Temple building had been destroyed, and, second, the cult had come to a halt. To them these points of total disorientation and sociocultic disorganization formed the problematic of the age. At issue were not tragedy and catastrophic history, but the shaking of the foundations of orderly life. Needed was not poetry but order. To the founders of the Mishnah the aftermath of the first defeat brought to an end the orderly life of the villages and the Land, the reliable relationship of calendar and crop with cult. The problematic of the age therefore was located in that middle range of life between the personal tragedy of individuals, who live and die, and the national catastrophe of the history of Israel. The pivot had wobbled; everything organized around it and in relationship to it had quaked. Left out were those two things at the extremes of this middle world: private suffering, and national catastrophe in the context of history, the encompassing history of Israel and of the world alike. That is why, when we contemplate how others of the same time framed the issues of the day, we are struck by the contrast.

The obvious and accessible dilemmas of Israel's suffering at the hand of gentiles, the deeper meaning of the age in which the Temple had been ruined and Israel defeated, the resort for expressing public sorrow to evocative symbols of private suffering and its mystery, the discourse on the meaning of human history in the light of this awful outcome for Israel—none of these (to us accessible and sympathetic) themes and modes of thought comes to the surface in those themes and topics which the precursors of the Mishnaic system deem the appropriate focus of discourse. It is as if before us in the Mishnah are bystanders, taken up with the result of the catastrophe and determined to make a quite distinctive statement about what was important in it. But the miserable world of the participants—the people who had fought, lost, and suffered—seems remote. It would stand to reason that before us is the framing of the issue of 70 by the priests, alongside people who, before the wars, had pretended to be priests and imitated their cultic routines. To such people as these, the paramount issues of 70 were issues of cult. The consequences demanding sustained attention, as I said, therefore were the effects of the wobbling of the pivot for the continued life of the cult in those vast stretches of the Israelite Land which remained holy, among those sizable Israelite populations of the country which remained vital. Israel had originally become Israel and sustained its perpetual vocation through its living on the holy Land and organizing all aspects of its holy life in relationship to the conduct of the holy Temple, eating like priests and farming in accord with the cultic taboos and obsessions with order and form, dividing up time between profane and holy in relationship to the cult's calendar and temporal division of its own rites. Now Israel remained Israel, loyal to its calling, through continuing to live in the mirror and under the aspect of that same cult. But these are matters which will require our attention to their own context. Let us now survey those laws which appear to have emerged in the age between the wars.

The sole fact to be adduced as definitive for the interpretation of materials attributed to authorities in the aftermath of the destruction of the Temple is that the Temple was destroyed. That fact by definition affected all else. But it also is general. There is no way to move from the self-evident facts that the Temple building was destroyed, the cult was no longer carried on, and the priesthood and Levites were now unemployed, to the specificities of the laws on these topics reliably assigned to the period under discussion. But there is no need to do so. For the main point of interest in an account of Judaism's unfolding is the expansion of the topics subject to discussion among precursors of the Mishnah's ultimate form, frame, and system. And, as we shall now see, the two new themes brought under systematic discourse directly relate to the destruction of the Temple, namely, laws affecting the taxes paid to the class of the poor and the caste of the priests, on the one side, and laws governing the conduct of the cult itself, on the other side. Since, moreover, the production of crops in accord with certain taboos was intimately related to the life of the cult, the sustained interest in the application of at least one significant taboo, that concerning mixed seeds, formed part of a larger statement about the way in which the country would respond to the loss of the Temple. Matters were to go forward as if the Temple still stood, because the Land retained its holiness, and God, his title to, and ownership of, the Land. Therefore the class of the poor, for its part, retained a right to a portion of crops prior to the completion of their harvest, and the priesthood, its claim to a part of them afterward. Sustained interest in the conduct of the cult, of course, represented a similar act of hope, an expression of the certainty that, just as God retained ownership of the Land, so too Israel remained responsible to maintain knowledge of the proper conduct of the sacrificial cult which returned to God part of what belonged to God out of the herds and crops of the holy Land and which so secured Israel's right to the rest. So far from the viewpoint of the Mishnah's precursors, what required sustained reflection in the aftermath of the destruction was the disorientation of the country's cultic life, both in its conduct of the agricultural—that is, the economic—affairs, governed as they were by laws emanating from the cult and meant to place economic life into relationship with the cult, and in its performance of the cult itself. The profound disorientation of defeat and destruction, the disorder brought about by the collapse of basic institutions of government, culture, and faith—these form the crisis defined in this particular way by these people.

Alongside these two fresh points of interest, the established one in the conduct of a meal in conditions of cleanness enjoyed continued interest. In addition to a close continuation of thinking already evidenced prior to the war, moreover, a number of new topics came up.

First, systematic attention was paid to sources of uncleanness which, prior to the war, seem in legal thought to have been neglected. That is, sources of uncleanness on which no work had been done in organizing and amplifying laws now received sustained attention. Important here is significant and rigorous work on the unclean persons and objects (houses, clothing) discussed at Lev. 13 and 14. These now join the unclean persons and objects of Lev. 11, 12, and 15, to which ample attention already had been paid.

Second, there was a quite original essay attempted on the one rite of the cult which was performed outside of the Temple building itself, namely, burning the red cow and mixing its ashes with spring water to make purification water for persons affected by corpse uncleanness (Num. 19:1ff.). What is said in this essay, as it is worked out between the wars, is that a place of true cleanness can be formed outside of the Temple. (Whether or not the rite itself was carried on is not information provided by the Mishnah; in fact, we do not know.) What had to be done was situating the conduct of the rite outside the Temple in an appropriate relationship to the Temple itself. That is, determining whether or not the rite should be done precisely as rites were done in the Temple, or, in a mirror image, precisely the opposite of the way

rites were done in the Temple, was the principal focus. This fundamental inquiry into the governing analogies generated ongoing
exegesis. Through imposing on participants in the rite perfect
attentiveness and perpetual concern for what they were doing while
they were engaged in the rite, the law would make possible that state of
cleanness appropriate to the conduct of a sacred rite in the otherwise
unclean secular world. It would follow that a state of cleanness still
higher than that of the Temple would be contemplated. The rules would
demand remarkable attentiveness. Why all of this should come under
discussion at just this time is obvious. For the underlying notion is
continuous with that of the laws of Purities prior to 70, that is to say,
cleanness outside of the Temple building *is* possible. A state of cleanness outside of the conduct of the Temple cult therefore may be required for certain purposes. What now is added thus is predictable,
given what had been said before 70. Just as a meal can and should be
eaten in a state of cultic cleanness by people not engaged in the eating
of bread and meat originating as priestly gifts in the Temple, so it is
possible even to conduct that one rite which Scripture itself deems
legitimate when performed outside the "tent of meeting," the Temple.
The laws remain valid; the relevant ones require study.

The Division of Agriculture between the Wars

Crops must be grown in accord with rules deemed to accord with and
express the holiness of the Land by assuring the orderly and regular
conduct of farming. Crops are to be utilized in conformity to the principle that God owns the Land and its produce, until a portion of the crop
has been paid over to sacred castes and classes, priests and poor,
respectively. Then the remainder of the crops enter into the domain of
the farmer. To the two matters expressive of the holiness of the Land is
appended a set of rules of liturgy. While biblical rules on taboos of
agriculture, on the one side, and disposition of the crops among the
holy classes and castes, on the other, presumably had long been observed, for the Mishnah the work of systematization and amplification
appears to have gotten under way only after the First War. The contrast between the paltry and random items which are apt to have originated before the wars and the full repertoire of rulings on a very wide
range of topics which we shall now survey surely suggests so. If that is
the case, then the important statement of the Mishnah upon the results
of the First War will have been that the Land retains its holiness, and,
as before, remains subject to God's ownership. In the aftermath of the
destruction of the Temple, in which the priesthood and Levites had
labored and which had from day to day celebrated and offered up the

produce of the Land, such a statement was weighty with meaning. It surely is no accident that, as we shall see, the other Division which appears to have begun its intellectual history at just this time is Holy Things, on the conduct of the sacrificial rites in particular. What is said is less important than *that* things were said on these two topics.

Of the various rules affecting the production of crops, two types attracted interest at the beginnings of the Mishnah's work on the topic. First, consideration was given to rules on planting crops, which stress, in particular, that each crop must be kept separate from all others, so that an orderly division among various kinds and species would prevail. Second, the conduct of farming during the orderly sequence of years of the septennial cycle, as well as that of the rhythm of a given crop's own cycle, received ample attention. There was, therefore, a grid composed of lines governing the layout of crops in a spatial framework as well as dimensions affecting the disposition of crops in a temporal one. As we shall see, it is Scripture which created the grid.

We come first to the matter of spatial order in the fields and vineyards of the country. Once discourse begins on the Scriptural prohibition (Lev. 19:19, Deut. 22:9–11) of planting diverse kinds of seeds together, one important question will be the determination of what sorts of seeds may not be planted in the same patch. The basic exercise in definition flows from the fact that there are various closely related, yet in fact distinct, species. To this exercise of definition contributions are made in the period under discussion. Specifically: species of the genus *Allium* of the lily family resemble each other and may be planted together (M. Kil. 1:3). If one wants to sow different kinds of vegetables among one another, in a case in which nearly all is of one kind, but one row will be a row of another kind, there are minimum measurements of the area which such a row must cover in order to create an autonomous field (M. Kil. 3:3). If a field is sown with onions and the farmer wants to plant rows of gourds in it, since the gourds will spread out and cover the onions, there is some opinion that the planting of the gourds should be restricted. This will avoid the appearance of diverse kinds, even though, in fact, there will not be a physical mixture of diverse kinds since the gourds are in separate rows (M. Kil. 3:6). This distinction between appearance and fact runs through discourse on the problem of diverse kinds. It expresses distinct theories of the basis for the expansion of the law and its application, that matters depend on the viewpoint of man or on the substance of material reality. If one sows diverse kinds in a vineyard—e.g., wheat and vines—one is penalized by having to destroy the seeds (M. Kil. 5:7). If one allows useless plants to grow, some opinion holds that even such plants cause the imposition of penalties, e.g., having to uproot the vines. Others maintain that vines are rendered invalid only if the diverse kinds sown among them are wanted

(M. Kil. 5:8). If a vine is supported by an espalier, there must be some distance set between the vines and a different species, and at this time opinion is expressed on how much space must be preserved (M. Kil. 6:1). Rules also were provided for the case of a vine trained over a fruit tree while at the same time putting seed underneath some other part of the fruit tree (M. Kil. 6:4).

The ordering of the years of a crop takes up two matters. First and by far the more important, there is the septennial cycle, affecting the use of the fields for all crops. The fields belong to God, and once in every seven years, God aserts ownership over them by insisting that they lie fallow. Effecting this principle involved taking up numerous concrete problems. For instance, since it is prohibited to work the fields in the sabbatical year, the law has to take account of the fact that some field labor performed in the sixth year of the septennial cycle in fact is of benefit to crops in the seventh year. Such labor is not to be done, even before the beginning of the seventh year itself. A field containing saplings may be plowed throughout the year prior to the seventh year, since it is not going to produce crops; by contrast, an orchard may be plowed only up to that point in the year at which plowing is beneficial to the same year's crop. Then it must stop. The definition of a sapling for the present purpose is provided at this time (M. Sheb. 1:8). On the other hand, during the sabbatical year, certain field labors are permitted. At issue is the predictable question of whether, since these acts are permitted, they may be performed in an ordinary way, or, whether, because it is, after all, the sabbatical year, there must be some change from routine practice. The main point is to do the permitted deed in such wise as not to prepare the field for cultivation (M. Sheb. 4:6). The applicability of the laws of the seventh year to Syria, deemed a gray area, not wholly Israelite, not wholly gentile, is worked out (M. Sheb. 6:2). Food produced in the seventh year must be treated with respect; what is for eating must be eaten, for drinking, must be drunk. If oil, which should be consumed, is used instead for rubbing on a hide, the consequence is waste of what should be eaten, and the one who has done so must make it up (M. Sheb. 8:9).

The other dimension of temporal rules concerns the first four years of a vine or other fruit-bearing plant or tree. The yield for three years is prohibited, and that of the fourth year is subject to special rules as well. The matter of the first three years appears to have been taken up, but only in one consequential ruling: Scripture prohibits use of the produce of a tree in the first three years of its growth (Lev. 19:23), so if one curdles milk with the sap of such a tree, use of the end product is prohibited (M. Orl. 1:7). The sap is deemed equivalent to the fruit.

We come now to the other half of the law of the present Division, the disposition of portions of the crop in accord with the wishes of the divine owner. Emphasized in the law before 70 were two basic matters, first, gifts to the poor, and, second, gifts to the priesthood. Both topics now underwent very substantial development and clarification. The basic notion at this time between the wars was that the priestly gifts remain required, even though the priesthood has momentarily lost its liturgical justification. The inevitable place of importance accorded to the poor taxes in this scheme is simple to explain. As Scriptural law makes clear, the poor get their share during the harvest, the priests afterward. The crops liable to the poor taxes are not yet liable to the priestly gifts. It must follow that consideration of the topics of priestly gifts would necessitate hard work on the topic of gifts to the poor. For the whole form a single and indivisible unit.

What topics could be and were left for later consideration were other kinds of agricultural taxes and offerings, for example, second tithe, which has to be brought to Jerusalem, as well as consideration of more general rules of tithing and the division of the holy part of the crop, such as are worked out at Maaserot, Demai, and other tractates. These topics appear not to have attracted much interest in the time between the wars. What apparently was urgent was the priests' income, there-fore and concomitantly, that of the poor. Other questions, equally important in the biblical system and in the ultimate Mishnaic one, were evidently not taken up until the Mishnaic system as a whole would be developed and filled out. The really pressing matter concerned support for the priests and the poor.

So, as I have explained, the two most important topics in the period under discussion were the poor taxes and the heave offering given to the priests at the moment at which the crop became liable to the priestly taxes. As I have explained, the law of leaving over a corner of the field for the poor and the requirement to set aside tithes are mutu-ally exclusive. The former applies up to that point at which the latter comes into force. The crop becomes liable to the giving of tithes once it is finally stacked, so, up to that point, householders are able to leave over the corner of the field to the poor without further taxes, that is, remaining exempt from tithes (M. Pe. 1:6).

Effort was made to define very basic matters, for instance, the limits of a given growing area subject to the leaving of the corner to the poor. A field reaped in patches is to be treated as a set of individual units, each of which, in the view of some, must yield a corner for the poor. Others maintain that the physical, not the functional, limits of the field apply, and a single corner for the whole suffices (M. Pe. 3:2). A similar interest in defining the smallest arable space liable to the leaving of the corner of the field to the poor produced a statement of minimum mea-sures of acreage subject to the law (M. Pe. 3:6). Equivalently funda-mental questions of definition involve the number of times per day that the poor were to be admitted to the field to collect their part of the crop (M. Pe. 4:5). Likewise, the authorities between the wars took up the definition of gleanings, the forgotten sheaf, and defective grape clusters, all of which were to be left for the poor (M. Pe. 4:10, 5:6, 7:7). The upshot was to lay the groundwork of fundamental definitions of poor relief and what householders had to do to provide it from their income in kind.

Heave offering must be separated from harvested produce and given to the priest. The gift was a modest proportion of the crop as a whole. At this time a fundamental question was raised, concerning the delineation of that crop from which heave offering is taken up. If one has a batch of produce which is clean, and another which is unclean, one may not deem the whole to constitute a single batch for purposes of the separation of heave offering. One has to give a portion to the priest from the clean batch, and another portion from the unclean (M. Ter. 2:1–3). A further basic question concerns the percentage of a batch of produce which has the potential, upon the householder's designation, to take on the status of heave offering. Some opinion holds that a small part of the batch or produce may be deemed heave offering, while others allow for much larger proportions (M. Ter. 4:5).

A complementary question deals with the mixture of produce in the status of heave offering with ordinary, secular produce. If there is a sufficient volume of the latter, it has the power to neutralize the former. Just as only a specified portion of a batch to begin with can become heave offering if so designated, so a specified portion of a batch, if heave offering, may cease to affect the entire batch when it is of a specified, negligible proportion of the whole (M. Ter. 4:7–11). Furthermore, if a given volume of unclean heave offering should fall into a hundred times larger volume of clean unconsecrated produce, some maintain that it is possible to remove that very volume of consecrated produce and burn it. The majority rule that the heave offering itself is neutralized. This matter of mixtures of heave offering and ordinary food is developed at some length (M. Ter. 5:2–4, 5–6).

Heave offering belongs to the priest. If, therefore, a person unintentionally disposes of it instead of giving it to the priest, the latter must be compensated for his loss. At issue at this time was what sort of restitution is to be paid, specifically, whether or not it had to be precisely what one had misappropriated. The alternative is to pay back something of the value, but not of the species, which one has used (M. Ter. 6:6, parallel to M. Ter. 2:1–3).

If grain in the status of heave offering should be used for seed, the crop retains the status of the seed. Yet, as we know, the poor have a claim on a portion of the crop. Whether or not all of the poor or only poor priests may glean (though, clearly, all of the poor have a claim on the gleanings) is to be worked out (M. Ter. 9:1–3). Likewise, the penalties for misappropriation of food in the status of heave offering had to be spelled out in detail (M. Ter. 11:2).

Discourse on the law of heave offering also is used to express in particular cases certain rather general notions. For example, if one does a deed which, at the outset, one had every right to do, but, at the end, one turns out not to be allowed to do, is one liable? May a person complete illicitly an act which he began licitly? Phrasing such philosophical questions in concrete terms proved suitable to thinkers between the wars (M. Ter. 8:1–3). We see nothing of the sort beforehand. Matters of the cult proved a suitable vehicle for parallel discourse, as we shall see. With reference to holy things, as with reference to heave offering, the issue of whether one should take effective action, which involves transgression, in order to prevent a still more severe transgression, or whether it is better to do nothing and let matters take their course, is raised (M. Ter. 8.8–12, and see above, p. 56). The matter of whether under certain conditions one is permitted to do what is usually prohibited may be phrased in any number of concrete cases.

Once the matter of heave offering came under discussion, it was natural to take up another priestly gift, also called a heave offering, namely the dough offering. Work on this topic not only was undertaken but appears to me at this time to have come nearly to its closure. The "heave offering unto the Lord" referred to at Num. 15:18–21 is understood to refer to an offering of dough to set aside for the priest. In the period under discussion, interest in the dough offering focused on the liability of dough made from grain which is to be taken out of the holy land. This is a gray area. What is grown abroad is not liable. Some opinion maintained that what is consumed abroad, even though grown in the Land, likewise is not liable. The operative ruling, therefore, is generated by the ultimate use of the dough. Other opinion was that the dough remained liable, even when used abroad, because the grain to begin with originated in the Land. So the source of the requirement to give the dough offering is the simple fact that the grain is the yield of the holy Land (M. Hal. 2:1).

Once more, in regard to the dough offering, we have a concrete expression of whether one should do an illicit deed in order to perform a more important licit one. Some maintained that one must in no way prepare dough in a state of uncleanness. If unclean, one should prepare the dough in portions smaller than the volume susceptible to uncleanness. Others ruled that one should prepare the dough in uncleanness, but not in tiny portions (M. Hal. 2:3).

Dough offering is owing from dough, not from the flour. If one prepares the dough offering from unkneaded flour, it is null, and the dough prepared from such flour itself is liable to dough offering (M. Hal. 2:5).

The rule that heave offering may not be taken from a batch of produce which is unclean to cover one which is clean applies to dough offering as well. One may not take dough offering from clean dough to provide for a batch of dough, some of which is unclean and some clean (M. Hal. 2:8).

The point at which the dough becomes liable, some maintained, is when it forms a crust in the oven, that is, when the enzyme which served for leaven has died (M. Hal. 1:6).

The status of grain produced in various regions adjacent to the holy Land received attention, with predictable interest, therefore, in what sorts of dough offering, if any, are called for from the dough made from such grain. It would be difficult to imagine that much work was left when these rulings had taken shape. Virtually all the principal questions generated by the theme of dough offering were taken up by the end of the period between the wars.

Produce in the status of second tithe is to be eaten in Jerusalem, so Deut. 14:22–27. If bringing the produce itself is difficult, the farmer may sell the produce and bring the proceeds in coin. At issue at this time was the conversion of the specie from one metal to another. The issue was whether the metal must be one in common circulation, such as copper, or whether it might also be one not commonly circulated, such as gold (M. M.S. 2:6–7). The more systematic analysis of this topic, as distinct from the rather episodic problem just now noted, would have to await another generation.

While the bulk of the general rules of tithing produce—for instance, rules specifying when the obligation to tithe applies to the crop and answers to similar fundamental questions—is taken up later on, at the period under discussion we do find evidence of consideration of a few minor matters of a general character. In particular, the established fact that produce becomes liable to tithing when it is brought into the courtyard produces a secondary question, which is, the disposition of produce grown in the courtyard itself. To be deemed liable to tithing, said produce must be harvested, e.g., like that which is grown in the field. If picked at random, for a nibble, it is not liable. Between the wars, the issue is raised concerning a piece of fruit which is divisible into smaller bits, such as a grape cluster or a pomegranate, and whether the stated concession—that one may make a random meal—applies to the whole of the grape cluster or only to bits and pieces thereof (M. Ma. 3:8–9).

Only food is deemed liable to tithes. Some crops may or may not serve as food. They will be liable if the farmer intends them to provide edible produce (M. Ma. 4:6).

The effort to define the authorized daily liturgy, which may have begun before the wars, produced important advances between them. Systematic work on when one is supposed to say the *Shema'*, evening and morning, the appropriate posture to assume while doing so, and even the requisite Scriptural pericopes to be recited, is spelled out (M. Ber. 1:1, 2, 3, 5). Qualifications of these requirements, produced in special circumstances, were further laid down. For example, a bridegroom need not recite the *Shema'* (M. Ber. 2:5–7). Whether or not the prayer, that is, a required number of blessings to be stated silently at specified times of worship, should be standardized came under discussion. A number of short prayers, specified as appropriate for the several occasions, as well as the consideration of variations for individual circumstance, strongly suggests a negative view, by contrast to the standardization of the *Shema'* (M. Ber. 4:4, 5:2). Still, the number of blessings in the prayer did come under discussion, as well as the order of certain fixed passages fore and aft (M. Ber. 4:3, 5:2). Overall, the tendency appears to have been not to attempt to standardize more than the principal outlines of worship. Not much value was placed upon a fixed wording or even structure (Zahavy, "Berakhot," p. 262).

There also was some work at defining appropriate blessings for various natural benefits. A formula was laid down for the blessing for water (M. Ber. 6:8). The protocol for reciting blessings was specified. If one's meal was made up of cooked vegetables, then after the meal one said a blessing for that sort of food. Whether or not eating certain food constitutes a meal, requiring an appropriate grace thereafter, depends upon the individual's views of what he is doing. If he thinks it is a meal, then a grace afterward is called for (M. Ber. 6:8). The appropriate "call to worship" for grace after meals in small and large groups also came under discussion (M. Ber. 7:3). A fully articulated system of blessings after the meal is not attested for the present period. The rulings are episodic and not integrated (Zahavy, "Berakhot," p. 277).

Since it is not possible to suppose that there were no liturgies before the war, the probable reason for work on this topic at just this time has to be located in an intention not to create liturgy but to legislate about it. And even in the matter of legislation and thus standardization, it would appear that only the most basic issues came up, for instance, rules governing the saying of the *Shema'* morning and night, for which, prior to the wars, we must assume there were established practices, as well as the sayings of blessings for various gifts of nature. What is important in this part of the law is that matters were discussed which aforetimes people would have done in accord merely with local custom. But that same observation applies to the other matters—obeying the agricultural taboos, giving out the taxes to class and caste—which were subjected to substantial work of amplification and expansion at just this time.

So what we see is that the method of the group which had taken shape before the war, which was to define itself through distinguishing and differentiating rules about eating and marrying, was carried forward. This same approach to confronting problems, namely, through making laws, now was taken over on a much larger scale, and for a broader range of purposes. Defining the way common practices were to be done then suggests that, in peoples' mind, was the intent to make even common practices into a mode of differentiation of an uncommon group. That, at any rate, is one possibility for interpreting both the continuation of an established mode of thought, namely, an obsession with rule making, and the expansion of the topics to which that mode of thought came to apply. But, then, it is difficult to imagine what sort of group will have carried forward the established procedures in this expansionary manner. To put matters differently, it is not self-evident to whom the law now addressed itself, and what sort of community the philosophers had in mind. Perhaps before the First War the social group was a sect. Certainly after the Second War, the social focus of the law was the nation as a whole (whether the nation listened is not our problem). But between the wars, in this most basic manner, things appear to me rather confusing. Many of the laws before us seem to me to take for granted that the locus of legislation is far more than a small group of people who ate together and intermarried. But none of them suggests that the locus now is the Jewish nation in its Land, that is, Israel. For, as we shall see in a moment, no provision is made for all of those transactions and institutions which a nation must govern, but to which a group assuming it is part of some larger social entity need not attend. That is why, time and again, we shall have to conclude that before us is an age of transition: growth but not fully realized expansion, a moment of change yet rich in confusion and ambiguity, an hour of decision which has not yet struck. If this unfulfilled character is clear where we do find clear evidence of expansion of the law towards its ultimate boundaries, it is even more obvious where we do not. In the Divisions of Appointed Times, Damages, and Women, in particular, little evidence suggests sustained effort or well-focused interest. Work on these topics would have to await another age, a different expectation, a fresh and unprecedented stimulus.

The Division of Appointed Times between the Wars

In the period after the destruction of the Temple and before the final rebellion against Rome, no material advance was made in formulating laws for the Division of Appointed Times. Rulings reliably situated in the period between the wars deal with the familiar matter of meals and the festival. In some instances, established issues of the period before 70, e.g., the question of whether the prohibition against cooking on the holy day is suspended for festival cooking alone, or for all sorts of deeds connected with preparing meals, are made to encompass other areas than the original one of festival meals. But the destruction of the Temple appears not to have stimulated much effort to rethink the matter of observance of the Sabbath and festivals. Certainly there appears to have been no fresh and creative impulse in this area, so important, as we shall see, in the system of the Mishnah as a whole.

One is supposed to prepare for the Sabbath by making ready in advance food, light, and clothing which are to be used on that day. The Sabbath lamp should be kindled with substances which burn smoothly and do not sputter (M. Shab. 2:1–3). A more important principle, fully articulated between the wars, stresses the distinctiveness of the Sabbath day. This principle is expressed in the notion that only what is designated for use on the Sabbath may be handled on that day. But what is not designated for use on the Sabbath may not be handled. Moreover, objects which may not be used on the Sabbath, e.g., implements of servile labor, also may not be handled at all. This, in general, is in line with the established notion that one must avoid entering into situations which may lead to Sabbath desecration. Just as one must not do a permitted deed which may lead to a prohibited one, so also one must not handle an object, use of which is going to violate the Sabbath (M. Shab. 4:2).

The recognition that there are distinct spatial domains, the reality of which is invoked by the advent of the holy day, is fully exposed in laws of the present period. Specifically, at this time sages knew that one is not supposed to transport an object from one domain, the private, to the other, the public. They dealt with the question of tossing an object from private to private domain, over intervening public domain (M. Shab. 11:1–2). That is assuredly a second-level problem, once the existence of distinct domains, between which transporting an object is prohibited, is established.

A further prohibition, already in place, is writing on the holy day. What now is defined is what constitutes an act of writing which is culpable. The principles at issue involve, first, the making of a lasting, intelligible mark, and, second, the completion of the action in the course of the single spell of one Sabbath. A much broader principle, covering many situations, takes up yet another second-level problem. It is known that certain religious requirements may be done on the Sabbath, even though doing them violates otherwise applicable prohibitions. For example, one must perform the rite of circumcision on the Sabbath, even though the operation involves a number of deeds which otherwise are not to be done on that day. What is subject to discussion now is whether secondary actions involved in that same rite also may be done on the Sabbath day. Aqiba takes the position that what must be done only at the moment of the required rite is permitted; but what may be done in advance must be taken care of before the Sabbath. Eliezer offers the more encompassing view that everything pertinent to the rite, however remote the connection, is permitted along with the actual rite itself (M. Shab. 19:1–3; M. Pes. 6:1–2). In point of fact, the principle under debate is familiar, but in a different area of law, namely, preparing a meal on the festival day. One may do so, we recall, but some hold that making the meal must be done in a manner different from that prevailing on an ordinary day, and others take the view that, because one may prepare the meal, one may do anything connected with that same act. Here we have in embryo precisely the principle at issue in this other area of law, an ongoing dispute through the layers of the Mishnah's history (see above, p. 17).

These few matters constitute the whole of the law of the Mishnah for the Sabbath. Since, as is both self-evident and demonstrable, long before the destruction of the Temple the Sabbath constituted a fully exposed set of observances and rites, it is clear that in the Mishnah we have only those matters subject to the attention of sages. We do not have a full repertoire of laws generally kept by the people, nor are we apt to have before us all the ideas of the Mishnah's progenitors on the subject of the Sabbath. What we do have is evidence or ideas selected, from what is surely a much larger corpus, for sustained examination. The principle of selection is not clear to me. The Mishnah's discourse for the present period expresses the following ideas. First, one takes precautions to avoid violating the Sabbath. That is why what is permissible for use on the Sabbath may be handled on that day, and what is not may not be handled. Second, there are two domains in respect to transporting objects. Third, an act of labor without lasting effect is null and produces no culpability. Fourth, if one is permitted for a special reason to do an action otherwise prohibited on the Sabbath, only that action, and not deeds associated with it but possible to do in advance, is permitted. What we have before us, as I said, is nothing like a complete account of how the Sabbath is observed. But out of the principles expressed in the concrete rules formulated between the wars a fair part of the ultimate tractate can have taken shape. We shall see later on, however, that the tractate as we now know it in fact is asymmetrical to the materials produced between the wars and follows a quite separate and fresh outline (see below, p. 132).

Since, as we already know, in the period under discussion the distinction of space between two domains, private and public, already was fully recognized, we may not be surprised to find that provision was then made for ambiguous space. Such space is neither entirely private, as is, e.g., a particular house, nor wholly public, as are, e.g., the streets or commons of a town. Clearly, one may not transport an object from

completely private to wholly public domain. The sages who created the
law ultimately put together into the Mishnah instinctively sought out
gray areas between established categories. There they invested their
finest speculative and theoretical powers. In the present context, sages
between the wars took up the matter of space, ownership of which is
ambiguous. They provided for definitively establishing that ownership
within private domain. They did so, in the case of courtyards closed to
the public but owned by a number of householders, by establishing the
rite of putting out a single, common meal, called an *erub*. This meal will
commingle the rights of ownership of all parties to a courtyard and so
establish common ownership among them. The same procedure comes
to bear, also, upon an alleyway which opens among a number of distinct courtyards. This too is defined as private property by a common
meal, symbolically available to the residents of the several courtyards.
Sages in the present period defined yet another mode of unifying ownership of an alleyway, specifically by setting up a symbolic gateway or
meal (M. Erub 1:2, 6:9–10, 7:10). They further asked about the status of
distinct areas within public domain, e.g., a cistern. Since this sort of
distinct area is private, it must be afforded a surrounding area, also
designated as private domain, so that on the Sabbath people may make
use of the cistern without transporting its contents forthwith from private to public domain. This is done by setting up some sort of flimsy
boundary, e.g., a fence of boards (M. Erub. 2:4–6).

There is a quite separate matter of importance in the definition of the
boundaries within which, on the Sabbath, a person may move about or
transport objects. This other, highly significant, matter has to do with
the Sabbath boundaries of a town. Scripture specifies, at Ex. 16:29,
that people are supposed to remain in their place on the Sabbath. The
framers of the law know that one's place is one's village. The limits of a
village are effective for all the residents thereof. Authorities of the
period between the wars were well aware that an individual's rights to
free movement come within a distance of two thousand cubits from a
given point, his "place" (M. Erub. 4:1–2, 5).

When we come to the matter of preparing meals on festivals, we find
that principles established before the wars tend in the time between
them to be carried forward and further illustrated. But it is difficult to
discover fresh aspects of those principles, only new applications of
what is familiar. We therefore find further discourse on whether to
allow a wide range of activities in connection with preparing food on
the festivals or whether to limit activity only to those things immediately pertinent to the making of food (M. Bes. 2:6–7). Likewise,
there is additional discussion on whether acts of preparing food are
done in the regular way or in some irregular way meant to take cogni-
zance of the holiness of the occasion (M. Bes. 2:8–10). There is the

clear restatement of established law in the rule that, if one cannot eat a beast on the festival, one also may not slaughter it on that day (M. Bes. 3:3). All of this is congruent with what had gone before. Since it had already been established that one must designate in advance of the festival things one plans to cook that day, it was a small step to the cognate rule that one may not cook on the festival food for use thereafter—that is, the other side of the holy day. So, in sum, where we had a set of established rules and principles, the succeeding authorities either added secondary applications to them or produced applications to new materials of ideas originally applied elsewhere.

We therefore see between the wars no fresh initiatives, either as to the formation of important principles or even as to the inclusion of fresh topics within established ones. In so far as there are rules pertinent to the Sabbath and festivals, they fit into the established scheme, which has to do with preparing meals on festivals. To be sure, there is some small beginning in the matter of rules governing the transport of objects from private domain to public domain and within property which is of an ambiguous status. But on further examination these rules too devolve upon the matter of preparing an appropriate meal, now with the purpose of establishing a symbolic residence for all of the partners to a courtyard or alleyway. The consequence of such a meal is that the parties are deemed then to constitute a single joint ownership, and property the status of which is ambiguous then is definitively deemed to be within private ownership. So the familiar matter of the interplay between food and holy days is further explored.

When, in the next chapter, we see the full shape and dimensions of the completed Division of Appointed Times, we shall understand how much was accomplished after the wars, and how wholly and drastically what had come down was revised to say something other than what had originally been the principal message of the law. In fact what now falls into the Division of Appointed Times essentially fits with ease into a different definitive Division, the one on Making Holy Meals, which we do not have.

The Division of Women between the Wars

The foci of the Division of Women as it ultimately reaches full expression are the beginning, middle, and end of a marital relationship, and the transfer of property at the beginning and the end thereof. There seems prior to the wars to have been a heritage of rulings on elements relevant to this larger scheme. But the main outlines of the scheme as a whole emerge only in the period under discussion, and then very unclearly. Still, now we find fairly well attested rulings covering the range of topics, with some attention, if slight, to how a marriage comes into being, with attendant documentation; a few measures—those specified by Scripture—on the power of the husband; and yet further attention to the issue of the end of a marriage. Ample interest in the issue of the transfer of property would have to await a still later generation. Between the wars the chief focus is located in the transfer of the person of the woman from the father's house to the husband's domain; only later would an extensive corpus of law on the concomitant movement of property come into being. That fact is congruent to our results for the Divison of Damages, on property cases in general.

When a woman claims that the absence of virginity is no fault of her own and the husband makes the contrary claim, some parties choose to accept the woman's claim, others, the man's. The latter seems to invoke the principle that we confirm the already-prevailing supposition (M. Ket. 1:6–9).

By the period between the wars the existence within the Mishnaic framework of a marriage contract of some sort certainly is well attested, though it is difficult to see important ideas about the marriage contract in the sayings belonging to this period (cf. M. Ket. 4:6, 5:1). When several wives of one man come to collect their marriage contracts from his estate, the claim bearing the earliest date is paramount (M. Ket. 10:5). None of these rulings indicates that important work on the topic of the documentation of the formation of a marriage through a settlement agreement was under way between the wars.

The rules covering the duration of the marriage pertain, in particular, to vows, which Scripture gives the husband the right to confirm or annul. Laws of an encompassing character are well attested to the period between the wars. The first of these is that euphemistic language is taken into account in the case of vowing, so that, if one uses langauge not wholly in accord with prevailing conventions, one is bound by that language (M. Ned. 1:1). At the same period the way of unloosing vows, e.g., suitable grounds, comes under significant and fundamental discussion (M. Ned. 9:1–5, 6–8). Refined, moreover, are various types of vows, e.g., those of incitement, exaggeration, those made in error, those imposed subject to constraint, which to begin with are invalid and do not require absolution at all (M. Ned. 3:1–3). A husband may not annul vows in advance (M. Ned. 10:5–7). It may be that a principal point of interest in vows later on, the notion that a vow covering a particular species leaves a person free to make use of the remainder of the genus of which the species is a part, is to be assigned to the period at hand (M. Ned. 7:1).

The main point in discourse on vows is that a vow is not valid merely because it is uttered. There are conditions which nullify the effect of a vow, so a vow is not effective *ex opere operato*, and language is more than a formula and has not got the power of an incantation. Reasons for nullification of vows and for their invalidity at the outset are specified. So in the period between the wars general principles on the making and abrogating of vows are worked out in ample detail.

The Nazirite vow, a special kind of vow, likewise is a subject of sustained interest at this time . A Nazirite is not supposed to go into a graveyard. If while standing in a graveyard a man takes the vow, it goes into effect only when he has left it (M. Naz. 3:5). A Nazirite vow taken in error is not binding (M. Naz. 5:4). There is discussion, also, on the offerings required of the Nazirite at the conclusion of his period of abstinence, or in the event of his being made unclean prior to that time, just as Scripture specifies (M. Naz. 4:5, 6:6, 11). A point of interest is that moment at which the sacrificial process becomes irreversible, so that the husband loses the right to nullify the wife's vow. There also are some special cases in connection with the cultic part of the process of making and carrying out the Nazirite vow. I think it probable, though it is not demonstrable, that in the same period the definition of the prohibitions to which the Nazir is subject was fully worked out (M. Naz. 6:1, 6:2–3, 7:1, 7:2–3, 8:1). Between the two wars, therefore, work on the vow to become a Nazir and conditions of its validity and duration appears to have been quite extensive. The distinctive contribution in the present period is to lay the foundations for discourse on the subject.

If the husband forms the opinion that his wife is unfaithful, he may require her to submit to the ordeal of the bitter water only if he provides suitable warning in advance (M. Sot. 1:1–2).

We come to the rules for ending a marriage. A writ of divorce must be properly delivered. If a writ comes from abroad, the messenger must give evidence that he personally has witnessed the writing and signing of the document (M. Git. 1:1–3). The writ must be written on substance which will last; it must be written in ink. Treatment of the topic begins with these rulings. The principle that the writ must be decisive and may not leave the woman encumbered, e.g., unable to marry any one she might choose, may begin at this time as well (M. Git. 9:1). If so, the fundamental character of such a ruling is well in line with the basic sorts of laws on the preparation and delivery of the document shaped at this time.

The rulings produced between the wars on the formation of a marriage and its cessation through abnormal means—levirate connection, the rite of *ḥaliṣah* (Deut. 25:10), for example—prove episodic. It seems likely that, at this time, there was attention to whether or not a eunuch performs such a rite under appropriate conditions (M. Yeb. 8:4–5). The manner in which the rite of removing the shoe was effected is subject to definition (M. Yeb. 12:1–3). The right of refusal by a girl married as a minor by her mother or brothers—another unusual way of ending a marriage—is treated as well; here, too, some basic points of definition are offered (M. Yeb. 13:2). Finally, the nullification of a marriage through the testimony that the husband has died is treated. Special attention is paid to the testimony of normally unacceptable witnesses, e.g., women about their own husbands or the husbands of their sisters-in-law or daughters-in-law. In general a woman is believed who testifies about her own status, but not about the status of some other party to the marriage (M. Yeb. 16:2, 7).

Assessing these rather paltry materials is not difficult. Clearly, Israelite society knew the answers to questions raised here for the first time, or at just this time. That is to say, there can be no doubt of the existence of conventions, a code of common practice, long before the destruction of the Temple. What is new here is only the consideration of familiar topics by people whose ideas would ultimately flow into the complete Mishnah. But while taking up the topic appears to have been an innovation, not much new or important seems to have been said about it. There is no predicting what would receive substantial attention, and what would receive little if any. Alongside absolutely fundamental conceptions in regard to vows in general and the Nazirite vow in particular, conceptions on which people might, and did, build entire tractates, we see random and episodic rulings. These latter sorts of rulings testify to interest in the theme of women and transferring them, along with property, from one man to another, but suggest no systematic and sustained work on that theme. In sum, the Division of Women appears in its main outlines perhaps to be adumbrated. We cannot claim the Division as we know it to have come into concrete existence. Still, if the formation of the Division as we know it is the work of the second-century authorities, they had in hand more than occasional materials. But they received from their predecessors less than balanced and fully articulated formations of rules.

The one aspect of the Division which does appear to reach its fullness is the matter of the effect of the spoken word: vows in general, the Nazirite vow in particular. Perhaps it is not farfetched to ask why, specifically after the destruction of the Temple, these kinds of expressions of the will to sanctify should come under particular scrutiny. When we recall that the way in which ordinary folk could join in the cult, beyond their paying the *sheqel* which formed their part of the daily community offering, was to declare a particular object to be holy, we may see what is at stake. What a person could do was to say that a given animal belonging to him or her was set aside and sanctified for the altar, e.g., as a thank offering, a peace offering, a pilgrim offering, or some other purpose. Holiness also could be invoked on objects, by dedicating them to the Temple (*qorban*); this rendered them forbidden for common use. Now with the Temple in ruins, people could, and evidently did, continue to make or at least contemplate such declarations. That the same applies to the vow to become a holy Nazirite is self-evident. So development of sustained interest in just these matters is part of that larger exercise in forming a law for the Temple and the cult. What does come forth, as we shall see in a moment, is a system with special emphasis upon the place and effect of the will of the human being in the conduct of the cult. This, in fact, we shall identify when we reach the Division of Holy Things.

This is a striking fact, for it indicates that a kind of "system" may have been aborning in the period between the wars, alongside, but distinct from, the system of meals and marriages which began before it. This separate system, dealing with the place of ordinary Israel in the cult to come, the force of people's intentions and attitudes upon the physical status of objects destined for the cult, the role of the human will in the metaphysical system of holiness resting upon the altar—this system did begin to take shape after the one war, and before the other. The conclusion we reached for the Appointed Times, which is that work done between the wars in fact contributes to a system other than the one ultimately revealed in the Mishnah's Division of Appointed Times as we now know it, applies once more. What we do find in the Division of Women need not have begun there. When we see the shape of the Division as a whole, we shall realize that it is out of place in its ultimate location. So had the Mishnah come to expression between the two wars, it would have looked quite different from the Mishnah we now know.

The Division of Damages between the Wars

What we find in the Division of Damages from between the wars is some random facts ultimately relevant to the Division of Damages as we know it. None of these facts has much impact upon what will emerge later on. The materials produced for the definition of the institutions of government and for the provision of civil law after the two wars in no way are congruent with what went before. Nothing lies before the Mishnah's ultimate system of civil law and government except Scripture.

Philosophers after 70 seem to have done some exegetical work on Scriptures relevant to the topics of the Division of Damages. Whether or not it was done with the aim of forming a systematic statement of rules of civil law and government is not clear. But it seems unlikely, given the episodic and random character of what assuredly goes back to the period under study. Topics treated include the matter of the ox which gores in the domain of the injured party, and the issue of whether, in

the case of a beast formerly deemed harmless, we assess full damages
(M. B.Q. 2:5). Another point of interest is whether or not one may
make use of the proceeds of the labor of a beast which one has found
and is keeping for return to the rightful owner. This is a step beyond the
basic assertions of Deut. 22:2 (M. B.Q. 2:7).

The principle of establishing title to land through a period of usucaption is well attested after 70. The theory is that, in allowing the squatter
to use the property for a period of years, the original owner has indicated he has given up hope of recovering it. If he had a valid and
enforceable claim against the squatter, the original owner would have
made it in the specified period (M. B.B. 3:1–2). Another detail of real
estate law securely located in the present period is the notion that if one
has sold a principal item, e.g., a house, one has sold what goes with
that item but not what is secondary to it, e.g., a cistern does not go
along, a door does (M. B.B. 4:2). This is an application to real estate
transactions of the principle well attested for, and primary to, vows:
that we differentiate, in language, between what is general and what is
subordinate. The same distinction of genus and species, moreover, is
commonplace in tractate Kilayim, in the Division of Agriculture.

Exegesis of Scripture yields the sole point on court procedure which
evidently belongs in the present period. The notion is that a third
witness is mentioned at Deut. 17:6 to impose on any number of perjur-
ers the penalties applicable to two of them (M. Mak. 1:7–8). General
principles of oaths, like those of vows including the Nazirite vow,
appear to have taken shape in the period between the wars. Whether or
not there is a minimum amount of food for which one is liable if one has
sworn not to eat or drink is specified. By way of exegesis of Lev. 5:4
there is discussion of whether an oath applies to what has happened in
the past or to what will happen in the future (M. Shebu. 3:1–4, 5).

There may have been some work on laws governing relationships to
appurtenances of idolatry. The basic idea, which is Scriptural, is that
what actually serves for idolatrous worship is prohibited for Israelite
use or enjoyment (M. A.Z. 3:5, 4:1–2). These ideas do not move far
beyond what Scripture itself has to say on the subject.

The Division of Damages would ultimately create a system of civil
law and government. It would provide a full account of rules for criminal and civil transactions, both in real estate and in commerce, as well
as of the institutions—courts, their authorities and procedures—by
which the law is enforced and conflict adjudicated. None of this
emerges in the period between the wars. Materials reliably situated at
that time yield no evidence whatsoever of sustained and systematic
thought about the topics of the present Division. At best there is interest in biblical verses which would ultimately prove relevant to the
Division. There is no reason to suppose those passages were selected

because of a broad inquiry into the requirements of civil law and government. Like Appointed Times and Women, the Division of Damages would have to wait for the end of the wars for its moment of pertinence. Before that time, no one involved in the formation of the Mishnah evidently imagined that there was need or call for work on civil law and government.

The Division of Holy Things between the Wars

With the Temple in ruins, the topic of sacrifice clearly attracted attention, and systematic work on some of the themes of Holy Things was undertaken. Of the two principal components of that theme—(1) sacrifice, and (2) the planning and upkeep of the Temple building—it is the former alone which received a fair amount of work. Under discussion, in particular, were overriding principles, for example, definitions of sacrilege, of the appropriate attitude toward the sacrificial act, of the disposition of animals set aside for one purpose but actually offered for some other, and of equivalently basic categories and questions. There is no evidence of effort at the description of the cult as it was generally carried on, with the various important rites and how they were prepared and effected, or at similar exercises in the organization and preservation of facts. These would come later. At the beginning lay a clear effort at answering a few comprehensive questions of definition and principle. Later on we shall see that topics seen to require definition were located, to begin with, in Scripture. The appropriate principle governing diverse issues was associated with Scripture. There is at this time slight claim to report how priests had actually thought things should be done in the real, material, earthly Temple which lay in ruins a few miles away. That was of no important concern to sages between the wars.

Evidence of the absolutely basic character of the issues at hand is seen in the definition of what sorts of sacrifices are required in various circumstances. Questions of this sort will hardly have been raised as they were, with quick reference to Scripture, had anyone wished to have recourse to the facts of how things had been done in the recent past. As it is, what we have are statements which, in the light of a living tradition of facts, will have been deemed not required at all. For instance, a suspensive guilt offering is required in a case in which we are not sure that a sin has been committed, or precisely what sin has been committed (M. Ker. 4:1, 2–3). A single action may or may not produce multiple liability for sin offerings, depending upon circumstance (M. Ker. 3:6). Once there is reason to distinguish one act of inadvertent sin from another, similar act, we impose liability to more than a single sin offering (M. Ker. 3:7–10). A suspensive guilt offering which is for a sin a person turns out not to have committed is offered anyhow, if not for that sin, then for some other (M. Ker. 6:1).

Of far greater sophistication is the character of rulings on the effect upon a beast of designation—that is, expressed intention—for use for a given sacrificial requirement. An animal designated for a particular purpose, e.g., meant to serve as a peace offering, may be slaughtered for some other purpose, e.g., as a guilt offering. But the owner has to bring another animal to fulfill his original obligation, which has not been carried out through the beast he originally designated. There are two exceptions to this rule. A beast set aside to serve as a Passover offering and one set aside to serve as a sin offering are indelibly marked for those purposes. If they are used for any other purpose, they do not constitute valid offerings for that other purpose (M. Zeb. 1:1). So the intention as to designation of an animal for a given purpose is of no effect upon the animal, except in the stated instances. If an animal is set aside for some other purpose and is offered as a Passover offering or a sin offering, some maintain that the Passover or sin offering also is invalid (M. Zeb. 1:2). In these rulings we see specified those improper intentions, designations, or motivations which invalidate the sacrifice of an animal. There also are improper actions which invalidate a rite. If a sacrifice is carried out by a nonpriest or an invalid one, the sacrifice is null (M. Zeb. 2:1). If people unfit to slaughter a beast do so, the act of slaughter is valid. An act of slaughter—as distinct from an act of sacrifice (e.g., collecting and tossing the blood)—is valid when done by nonpriests, women, slaves, unclean men, and so on. These also have the power to invalidate by improper intention, because their action is valid. But if they do a deed they may not do, such as receive the blood and toss it, their action is null. Therefore if they receive the blood with improper intention, that is of no consequence (M. Zeb. 3:1). Inappropriate intention concerning something itself invalid is null (M. Zeb. 3:3; M. Men. 3:1).

The ways to kill a bird for the altar are different from those used for slaughter for ordinary use. In the former instance one breaks the neck, in the latter, one makes a cut of the gullet. At issue now is whether we treat these two modes of killing the bird as different from one another. Some maintain that the rite of sacrifice is essentially distinct from the act of slaughter. The character of the bird is changed by a correct execution of a rite which is invalid to begin with. As spelled out, this matter carries forward the issue specified above (M. Zeb. 7:13).

When there is a confusion of limbs of a sin offering with those of a burnt offering, some would have all of them burned. The basic issue is whether we should take an action to prevent violation of the law, even though said action itself violates the law, or whether we should do nothing at all and allow matters to take their course (M. Zeb. 8:4–5). This issue of course is not particular to the matter of cultic sacrifice (M. Zeb. 8:6–10).

The power of the altar to sanctify what touches it is severely limited. It now is held that the altar imposes the status of sanctity only on what is appropriate for the altar. What is not to begin with suitable for a sacrifice is not made holy merely by touching the altar (M. Zeb. 9:1, 4; cf. also M. Men. 12:1). We take account only of what is regular and routine. There is some attention, also, to the penalties for sacrificing holy things outside of the Temple and for offering them up (M. Zeb. 13:1–2).

Anyone, including women and children, who issues a statement of substitution, saying that one beast is consecrated instead of another, already-consecrated beast, has the power to impose the status of consecration upon that beast of which he spoke. The other, already-consecrated beast, to be sure, remains consecrated as well, in line with Lev. 27:9–10 (M. Tem. 1:1). The analogues of consecrated animals are in their status, whether as offspring or as substitutes. They are to be offered just as if they were consecrated (M. Tem. 3:1).

If what is primary to an offering is invalidated, everything dependent thereon also is null. But if a secondary aspect of an offering is nullified, what is primary to the offering remains valid (M. Men. 4:3–4, 7:4). This notion, in tractate Menahot, is also expressed in regard to vows. It is a general principle, applicable everywhere and distinctive nowhere. The same is so of the rule which holds that if a person vows a certain kind of meal offering, he must carry out what he has specified, e.g., not one baked in a baking pan if he has pledged a cake made in a frying pan (M. Men. 5:8). There is, moreover, an extensive specification of the smallest quantity or volume of various things which one might pledge to the cult. Overall, not a single element of tractate Menahot clearly to be situated in the age between the wars is distinctive to the subject matter of that tractate.

Interest in the definition of sacrilege is expressed in the question of when the law of sacrilege ceases to apply to an animal sacrifice. Once the law of sacrilege is removed, the laws of refuse, remnant, and uncleanness do apply. That is, the meat must not be permitted to become unclean, to be left overnight, or otherwise in deed or in intention to suffer neglect. It must be eaten or burned. The main point of definition is that, so long as the blood of a sacrifice has not been properly tossed, that is, the act which permits the priests to possess the parts of the sacrifice reserved for them, the laws of sacrilege continue to apply. That tossing marks the end of the state of sanctification and so of possible sacrilege, in respect to a given beast. This status begins when the beast is designated as an offering for a particular purpose or of a particular character. The principal step forward in the period between the wars, apart from taking up the question, is the recognition that, so long as a piece of meat is sacred—subject to the laws of sacrilege—it cannot be subjected to the other taboos. One cannot do those things to a piece of meat which falls under the taboos of refuse, remnant, and uncleanness, until that piece of meat has become available for the use of the priests. For, in the nature of things, it is what priests may use for their own purposes which may be "allowed" to become refuse, left overnight, or be made unclean. What priests cannot use at all they must burn on the altar. And the rest follows (M. Me. 1:1). A concomitant, predictable issue, which is the status of a piece of meat only part of which has been rendered available to the priests, also will be worked out (M. Me. 1:2–3).

The firstborn of animals is subject to redemption from the priests, in line with Ex. 13:11–13 and other Scriptural verses. A predictable interest is in animals which are subject to doubt, on the one side, and the responsibility of the priest to establish his claim in a case of doubt, on the other. The basic principle is that the priest has to prove his claim that a beast is firstborn (M. Bekh. 2:9, 3:1, 1:3–4). A blemished firstling need not be redeemed. If a person deliberately blemished a beast, that beast may never then be slaughtered and eaten (M. Bekh. 5:3). But if an animal naturally is so blemished that it could not be used on the altar, it also is deemed sufficiently blemished so as not to require redemption; it may be slaughtered and eaten. So the same sorts of blemishes effective in the one case prove decisive in the other (M. Bekh. 6:1–8).

In slaughtering a beast for domestic use, the distinction—which makes no practical difference—between carrion and *terefah* meat ("torn") is spelled out (M. Hul. 2:4). A slaughtered animal must give some evidence at the point of death of continuing life for it to be deemed not to have died of natural causes (M. Hul. 2:6). Whether or not a foetus in process of being born requires slaughter if the dam is slaughtered is worked out (M. Hul. 4:1–3). On the domestic meal, the definition of what sort of meat may not be seethed in milk is worked out. Some maintain that fowl does not constitute meat for the present purpose.

When we compare these materials with the equivalent ones for the period before the wars, we realize how much work was accomplished after 70. Indeed, if the Division of Purities was under way before 70, then it appears now to have been joined by sustained work on something approaching a Division of Holy Things. The stimulus for such work hardly requires specification: plans for the ruined Temple would be preserved for the time of rebuilding.

What is interesting in the materials we have surveyed is two facts.

First of all, as noted, the source of information is Scripture. Second, there is a clear effort to supply basic principles and to specify conceptions applicable to a wide range of laws. What this means is that systematic work now appears to have gotten under way in the formation of a set of laws through specification of operative principles, then application of those principles to diverse areas of law. So out of a fresh reading of Scripture, on the one side, and a quite original effort to discover and apply valid principles, on the other, basic definitions for the cult and its conduct were to be forthcoming. This exercise then is aimed at the reform of the cult, when it would be restored to full activity, and the conduct of the cult along proper lines. We recall in this connection the priests' being made to say that they had not been faithful guardians of the Temple (see above, p. 33). The destruction of the Temple will have been seen by some as a sign that, when it stood, the Temple had been mismanaged by the priests. In general, the founders of the Mishnaic line of thought on Holy Things open Scripture, rather than claiming to report what had actually been done in the Temple. In doing so, they imply that Scripture alone is the reliable guide. So the way the priests had done things is not. Similarly, the Mishnah's thinkers formulate right and reasonable principles, based on logic and reason. Here, too, the exercise in regularizing and ordering matters contains an implication that formerly the rules had been irregular or inconsistent or simply wrong. In sum, the motive behind the nascent laws before us is one of reform. The method of reform would be sound reason and accurate exegesis of Scripture.

The Division of Purities between the Wars

The established framework of interest in the topic of Purities made a place for a full account of what imparted uncleanness to which sort of object or substance, with provision for remission of the consequence. After the First War and the destruction of the Temple this same framework sufficed to make a place for important new ideas as well as for the pursuit of remarkable refinements of established ones.

A significant source of uncleanness specified in Scripture but not treated in the first stage of the law is that sort of skin ailment described at Lev. 13 and 14. Fairly extensive work was done on those chapters. The principal results are these. First, anyone may inspect a spot of discolored skin, but the priest pronounces the decision. It must be the same priest throughout the sequence of inspections (M. Neg. 3:1). The important inspection is on the seventh day, on which the priest makes the decisive ruling, in the opinion of some. Others hold that what is important is what the sage sees, not the priest, and that it does not

matter when he sees it (M. Neg. 1:4, 10:5). Changes which take place
during the process of inspection are taken into account (M. Neg. 4:7–8,
11). Once the priest has announced the decision, we must wait for the
next inspection. No further changes in skin tone are taken into account
(M. Neg. 7:3). Gentiles are not susceptible to this form of uncleanness
(M. Neg. 3:1, 11:1, 12:1). Cases of doubt are resolved in favor of a
decision of cleanness (M. Neg. 4:11, 5:4). The sorts of discoloration of
the skin which denote uncleanness are spelled out (M. Neg. 1:1, 7:2,
11:4). The rites of purification described in Scripture are given some
minor embellishments (M. Neg. 14:6, 10). The interest in the relevant
Scriptural passages—Lev. 13 and 14—produces an extensive restatement and reorganization of the facts of the law stated by Scripture
itself. But most of the secondary problems developing out of the
exegesis of those available Scriptural facts are made up by authorities
after the wars. What is contributed between the wars thus is a detailed
review and restatement of Scripture's facts and some basic definitions
required for their application and interpretation.

A further, major step forward was to bring some order to laws of the
uncleanness of women, which may be of two types, first, that of the
woman in her period, the menstrual uncleanness, and, second, that of
the woman not in her period, the uncleanness specified at Lev. 15:1ff.,
the *zabah*'s uncleanness. Scripture provided the distinction just now
specified, and what had to be done was to explore some gray areas
between the two sorts of female uncleanness (with the male counterpart of the latter, the *zab*), once the topic emerged for vigorous inquiry.
The days between a woman's established menstrual periods are called
zibah days. The reason is that, should there be vaginal flow on those
days, the woman is declared unclean not as a menstruant but as zabah.
This is in line with the rules of Lev. 15. Now it clearly was recognized
that blood produced by a woman in labor, if it is not to be directly
attributed to the actual delivery of the baby, is attributed to the *zibah*
period. If, concomitantly, a woman while giving birth produces blood
at the time of her period, she is deemed unclean for that same reason,
within the same qualification (M. Nid. 4:4). If a woman goes into labor
within eighty days of cleanness following the birth of a female, e.g., by
reason of a second pregnancy and abortion, any blood she produces is
deemed clean as the "blood of purifying" referred to at Lev. 12 (M.
Nid. 4:6). Blood which appears during the days of purifying is clean
under all circumstances. A woman should examine herself very often
to be sure that her period has not begun (M. Nid. 2:1). If there are
bloodstains of unknown origin, a lenient ruling is to be handed down,
not a strict one. We attribute a bloodstain, for example, to a wound
which can open and bleed, rather than to menstrual uncleanness (M.
Nid. 8:3).

This brings us to yet another and parallel human source of uncleanness, the *zab*, an already-familiar topic. A person who produces flux for three days and so is a candidate for being declared a *zab* is examined as to seven possibilities of how the flux may have come forth. In this examination the possibility of some extraneous factor, which then would nullify the contaminating effects of the flux, is raised. For example, the candidate is asked whether he ate, drank, carried a heavy object, suffered an illness, had a sexual fantasy, or otherwise may have produced the flux for some other than an entirely "natural" reason, that is, through some source other than the body's own natural mechanism for generating unclean fluids. If the answer is affirmative, the man is not a *zab* at all (M. Zab. 2:2). If the *zab* or *zabah* sits or lies on an object, uncleanness is imparted to that object through the pressure exerted thereby. Now it is determined that said object need not be one on which the unclean person actually is sitting. If it is something which might be used for that purpose, and if the weight of the *zab* in some way comes to bear on that object, it is thereby made unclean (M. Zab. 4:1). This decision opens the way to the consideration of secondary or derivative pressure effected by the *zab*. That means that if a person sits on a stone, under which the finger of a *zab* is placed, that person is unclean. The *zab* has exerted pressure—even through the stone (M. Zab. 5:1–2).

The principal source of uncleanness, of course, is the corpse. What is important in regard to the corpse is the capacity to impart uncleanness under a tent or roof. In the period at hand, this familiar topic, already subjected to sophisticated reflection for some time, saw fresh and interesting initiatives. There was, for one thing, clarification of the matter of imparting uncleanness through overshadowing. An unclean person does not convey uncleanness by overshadowing, only by direct contact. It is solely the corpse which has the power to convey uncleanness through overshadowing (M. Oh. 15:10). Movables of the size, predictably, of a handbreadth or more convey uncleanness when they overshadow a corpse. But they become unclean if they overshadow a corpse no matter what size they are (M. Oh. 16:1–2). Some maintain that the power of the tent spread over a corpse to impart uncleanness to what is within its shadow is to be generalized. The tent which overshadows even scattered bits and pieces of a corpse "joins together" the contamination exuding from those bits and pieces and so imparts corpse uncleanness, just as it would if spread over a requisite volume of corpse matter, to whatever is in the shadow of said tent (M. Oh. 2:2). Others hold that divided unclean corpse matter does not impart uncleanness (M. Oh. 3:1). Again, to the contrary, some maintain that dirt from a graveyard, which is unclean, and dirt from abroad, which also is unclean, join together to form the requisite volume of unclean dirt to impart uncleanness (M. Oh. 17:5). So, in sum, theory on the functioning of the tent—whether it joins together distinct quantities of corpse matter which, not under its surface, individually are insufficient to impart uncleanness through overshadowing—is worked out. This marks an advance over the sorts of issues attributed to authorities before 70. For the shift is from stress on the source of uncleanness, the corpse, to the mode of conveying uncleanness, the action or functioning of the tent.

The established mode of expanding the law through analogy from the known to the unknown was carried forward in the designation of a grave area as unclean, not merely the corpse itself. A grave area produces uncleanness, because corpse matter may be pulverized within it (M. Oh. 16:4, 5). But this sort of source of uncleanness is less certain than a corpse itself and so produces cases of doubt. Limbs of a corpse are unclean, whatever their bulk. If they have sufficient flesh, they will contaminate as a corpse does, that is, through the overshadowing effect of a tent. Blood of a certain volume also imparts corpse contamination. So, as we know, what is like a corpse or derives therefrom contaminates in the same way (M. Oh. 1:7–8, 2:2, 3:5).

In the matter of overshadowing, finally, the familiar, if difficult, conception that a utensil is comparable to a tent generated further thought and an important new principle. The issue of the relationship of a utensil to a tent, surely one of the less accessible topics of the law, now yielded the notion that a utensil may be deemed to form part of the wall of a house (or tent). The result is that along with the wall it will afford protection against uncleanness at its outer surface. For instance, if there is a cistern covered by a basket, the basket is deemed part of the walls of the cistern—hence, its covering or roof. Then, if there is corpse uncleanness in the room served by the cistern, the cistern remains clean (M. Oh. 5:5–6). Likewise a board may form a "tent" to interpose over an oven or to keep corpse uncleanness's effect within the oven (M. Oh. 12:1–3). The comparison of the "tent" to the utensil further was carried forward in the discourse on the anomalous rule that a broken hive affords protection in the tent of a corpse while a whole utensil does not. It therefore was proposed that whatever will afford protection from the corpse, which is a severe source of contamination, also will afford protection from an unclean creeping thing, which is less severe than the corpse (M. Kel. 8:1; cf. also M. Kel. 10:1). Projections from a house (=tent) also come under discussion. If there is a projecting windowsill, for example, and a corpse passes underneath, then the sill will serve to convey the corpse uncleanness to the entire house of which it is a part. If there is a corpse in the house, such a projection will impart uncleanness to whatever passes beneath it, as if it passed beneath the roof of the house itself. So there is a simple and obvious step from the tent or house to projections and integral parts thereof (M. Oh. 12:3, 5, 8, 14:3–7).

The interplay between sources of uncleanness and substances or objects susceptible to uncleanness is most tightly worked out in the matter of removes of uncleanness, that is, (1) an original contact with a primary source of uncleanness, then (2) a contact of food with that substance which originally touched the source of uncleanness, then (3) a contact of other food with that food, and so on, thus uncleanness *once* removed from the source, *twice* removed from the source, and the like. I am fairly certain that this exceptionally difficult aspect of the law of Purities, namely that there are several removes from an original source of uncleanness, each with its associated power of contamination for a given sort of food in one or another state of sanctification, was worked out between the wars (see Neusner, *Purities* X, pp. 202–6). The basic notion is that there are four removes from the original source of uncleanness, which is to say, there has been a sequence of contacts, from the original source ("father of uncleanness") to the first party ("offspring of uncleanness"), from the first party to the second party, and so on down to four parties or removes. Unconsecrated food which touches a source of uncleanness is in the first remove and it is also unclean. What touches it is in the second remove and is "unfit" for eating, but does not then transmit uncleanness to food touching that food which is in the second remove. So what touches (1) food in an unconsecrated status which has touched (2) food in the same status is (3) itself *clean*. But when we come to food which is consecrated, e.g., in the status of heave offering, we deal with something which also is more sensitive to uncleanness. We therefore add a further remove of consideration. When we come to food in the status of holy things, by the same logic we expand to yet one more remove. All of this is handsomely worked out in the age between the wars (M. Toh. 2:3–6[+ 7]). The one who has immersed on the selfsame day is declared to be in the second remove of uncleanness (M. T.Y. 4:1–3). A further point of definition is that what such a one touches which is secondary to the mixture in which it is located is not going to affect the mixture as a whole (M. T.Y. 2:4, 5, 6).

In the matter of calculation of removes, yet another important issue concerns the effect of unclean food on the one who eats it. Some opinion places that person in the same remove as the food, that is, the first remove; others hold the person is unclean in the second remove, one less than the food (M. Toh. 2:2). The same range of issues is raised in regard to a house afflicted with that disease described at Lev. 14. Some hold that if one pokes hands into such a house, the hands are unclean in the first remove; others place them in the second remove (M. Yad. 3:1). The larger issue is whether the hands are deemed a domain, as to uncleanness, separate from the rest of a person's body. As to imparting uncleanness to hands, it is generally maintained that what is unclean in the first remove makes hands unclean, but what is made unclean in the second remove does not (M. Yad. 3:1–2).

Yet another brilliant essay on the topic of what is susceptible to uncleanness, with special reference to food, was developed at this same time. In the view of exegetes of Lev. 11:34, 37–38, food which is dry is not susceptible to uncleanness. They understood the simple meaning of those verses to be that what is not wet down will not be made unclean by a source of uncleanness. The issue raised now in an extensive essay on uncleanness of foods is in two parts. First, those liquids which impart susceptibility to uncleanness have to be defined. Scripture speaks of water, and at issue is the secondary expansion of the list of liquids deemed equivalent to water. The supposition then is that not merely wetting food down, but doing so by an appropriate liquid substance, is required to impart susceptibility to uncleanness. Second, and of still greater generative consequence, the circumstance in which food is wet down matters. The specific notion important at the beginning of the discourse on food's susceptibility to uncleanness through being wet down is simple but revolutionary. No power is imputed to water *ex opere operato* (or to analogous liquids). Why not? Because, predictably, we take account of context and circumstance. Specifically, if the owner of the produce deliberately wets down his produce, then it is made susceptible. But if the produce is wet down contrary to the owner's wishes or accidentally, we do not take that wetting down into account. The produce remains insusceptible. These two matters exhaust the ample intellectual accomplishment on the present topic. Seven liquids are listed, which have the capacity to impart susceptibility to uncleanness (M. Makh. 6:4). It is made explicit that if the person does not intentionally wet down his produce, the produce remains insusceptible (M. Makh. 1:3). The issue awaiting exegesis is secondary to that principle, for example, whether we make a distinction between liquid a person wished to apply to his produce, and liquid which is not wanted at all or which is not essential to the accomplishment of a person's purpose (M. Makh. 5:4, 5).

Domestic utensils as well as food, we recall, are subject to uncleanness. A fair amount of progress had already been made in taking up those relevant references of Scripture and working out the law implied by, or even contained within, them. Important new ideas were introduced between the wars as well. Now it was posited that not only is the use of an object determinative of its susceptiblity to uncleanness. The material of which an object is made likewise will affect its susceptibility. What is made of rock, dirt, and wood is not susceptible; what is made of metal or clay is susceptible (M. Kel. 17:14). A flat clay or wood object, lacking a receptacle, is not susceptible to uncleanness (M. Kel. 2:3, 7). A utensil which contains a receptacle will be susceptible (M. Kel. 2:8). A metal utensil which is autonomous is susceptible, except when it is made to be attached to the ground. A nail is susceptible when it is shaped for a particular purpose (M. Kel. 11:2, 3). Women's ornaments are susceptible, because they are individual and autonomous (M. Kel. 11:7–8). The operative principles of susceptibility in general are these: first, the presence of a receptacle; second, the permanence of the receptacle or of the object; third, the suitability of the object for a particular purpose or function, or its distinctiveness; fourth, the fully processed and complete character of the object. A susceptible object is one which is fully processed and available for routine, everyday use. The way in which it is used must be normal, and in its ultimate condition the object must function in a regular way. It also must have a distinctive and permanent character, shape or purpose, designated for that distinctive function, which involves human, not solely inanimate, needs. Between the wars the principle was fully explored that an object routinely used, for a fixed purpose, serving human beings, will be susceptible to uncleanness. Objects not fully processed, used in unusual or episodic ways, for random purposes, not part of the normal course of practical life, are insusceptible. So, in sum, a broken object is useless and therefore insusceptible, and a whole and useful object is susceptible to uncleanness.

The notion that a utensil in several parts is deemed divided, so that one part may be unclean while another part is still clean, was fully worked out between the wars, possibly on the basis of inherited speculation. The basic principle is that where there is an enclosed or partially enclosed space, that space is deemed a self-contained unit for purposes of contamination (M. Kel. 2:7). Utensils are deemed to be divided into an outer part, which is not made unclean by contact with a source of uncleanness, and an inner part, which is affected on its own as well. In some few objects, there is yet a third distinct space, relevant to the present purpose, a holding place (M. Kel. 25:7–8).

Matters of doubt concerning the uncleanness of food and drink or utensils, finally, were in general to be resolved in favor of a lenient decision. This is especially so when a matter of doubt involves public domain. When it involves private domain, some opinion will impose a more stringent decision (M. Toh. 6:2–3). It was further assumed that ordinary folk, who do not observe the cleanness taboos when eating ordinary food, will not deliberately contaminate the clean food of those who do observe those taboos (M. Toh. 7:7, 9). This assumption was embedded in numerous concrete laws.

We come now to the matter of purification of objects from uncleanness. There are two sides to this topic, breaking and immersion. An object ceases to be unclean when it is broken, we recall. But what has now to be clarified is another stage: repair or adaptation of the broken sherd for some new function. That is to say, an object which is damaged and no longer serves its original purpose is deemed both clean and insusceptible to uncleanness. If, however, it is adapted for some other purpose, and the adaptation is substantial and permanent, the object becomes susceptible to uncleanness once more, now within the rules of susceptibility governing that other purpose which it serves (M. Kel. 20:4, 22:9, 27:5). So, as to the process of purification through breaking susceptible objects, there are these three principles: breaking is purifying; changing the function of an object changes its status as to susceptibility, therefore also as to purification; the intent of the maker plays a part when we consider the effect of changing the function of an object (M. Kel. 20:6, 22:4, 7).

By far the more important of the two modes of purification, breaking and dunking, is immersion in suitable water. The principal established interest was in the definition of suitability, with special reference to the prohibition of drawn water. This principle now received the following concrete amplification. If jars are left on a roof and filled up with rainwater, that water is invalid for an immersion pool, having been deliberately collected. It falls into the category of drawn water (M. Miq. 2:7–9). If someone wrings out a garment into a pool containing insufficient valid water and this yields drawn water, the pool is invalidated. Drawn water spoils the pool cumulatively, if all the drawn water is poured in at one time or at a single spot (M. Miq. 3:3). If a cushion or mattress contains a collection of water, once one lifts up the lips out of the water in which the cushion or mattress is located, the water held within is deemed drawn water. It is better to immerse such an object by turning it upside down and to raise it by the bottom (M. Miq. 7:6). If wine changes the color of drawn water, it is no longer deemed drawn water at all (M. Miq. 7:5).

The clarification of definitions of water suitable for purification now turned to the question of a mixture of water and mud. Some opinion maintained that the immersion must take place only in the water, while others held that since the mud contains water, this too may be used (M. Miq. 2:10). What is soluble in water may be deemed to raise the level of water in a pool so as to complete the requisite volume, for instance, snow, hailstones, hoarfrost, and the like. If such as these fall into a pond of insufficient volume, they do not invalidate it as drawn water. By contrast, water in which food has been seethed or pressed and the like invalidates a pool of less than requisite volume, and does not serve to raise the volume to the required amount (M. Miq. 7:1–2). An invalid immersion pool may be rendered valid by joining its water together with the water of a valid pool (M. Miq. 3:1, 2).

When immersing something for purification, one's flesh must be in direct contact with the water. Nothing may be permitted to interpose (M. Miq. 9:2, 3, 10:1, 5). This principle is given abundant exemplification. What is important is a person's attitude or intention. How so? If there is something on one's body which is of no account in one's own eyes, that thing is not deemed to interpose. But if there is something about which one is fastidious, then that would be regarded as interposition. It is indeed sufficient to nullify the act of immersion for purposes of purification. Because one cares about a spot of dirt, the dirt interposes. If one had thought the spot nothing, the law would have deemed it null.

There is one last question pertinent to purification, which is the requirement of Num. 19:1ff. that a person made unclean by a corpse be sprinkled on the third and seventh days thereafter with a mixture of water and the ash of a red cow, especially burned to produce such purification water. This topic was taken up and systematically worked out at the time under discussion. In particular the way in which priests burn a red cow and prepare the ashes for mixture with water to form purification water required to remove corpse contamination (Num. 19:1ff.) was worked out. Scripture's requirements in defining the cow were restated and vastly augmented. The cow must not have been used for labor. In the opinion of some, it may be the hire of a harlot or the price of a dog, because it is to be used for a rite practiced *outside* of the cult, rather than in it, where such a beast may not be used (M. Par. 2:3). This approach to the law stressed that what is required for a sacrifice in the Temple is not done for a sacrifice outside of the Temple. The contrary approach, paramount between the wars, imposed upon a rite done outside of the Temple a much higher standard of cleanness and alertness than that which is needed within the protective walls of the Temple itself. The rite was thus compared to that on the Day of Atonement (M. Par. 4:1). The party which wanted a very high degree of cleanness will concur in that view. The water used for the rite must be pure and not adulterated with dirt or something unfit (M. Par. 8:11, 9:1, 3). Children who have never been affected by uncleanness are the ones who burn the cow (M. Par. 3:2). The basic conception once more is that the purity required for the rite is of the highest order, even higher than that required for the Day of Atonement.

Along these same lines, water collected for the rite must be guarded attentively. If one does an act of labor distinct from what is required to collect and transport the water to the ash for mixing, that water is invalid and may not be used. Only acts of labor intrinsic to collecting and transporting the water are permitted. In this regard the water is precisely the opposite of that used for purification in general. That is, of other-than-corpse-uncleanness. That water may not be subject to human intervention; the water in this case must be constantly subject to human concern and engagement (M. Par. 7:6–7, 10). Utensils used in the rite likewise must be in a high degree of cleanness (M. Par. 5:2, 3). Indeed, so high a measure of attentiveness is required to protect the water and utensils form uncleanness that the person who transports them may not lie or sit on any object. Whatever sort of object can be made unclean with *midras* uncleanness, that is to say, uncleanness imparted through lying or sitting by a person of sufficient uncleanness, is deemed already unclean so far as the purification rite is concerned. What this would mean practically is that the one who carries the water may not lie or sit but must continue to walk along and transport the water until it is mixed with the ashes (M. Par. 9:6, 10:1, 2, 6, 8:2, 11:1). Work completed in the present period therefore takes up every aspect of the rite of burning the cow to produce purification ashes: the definition of the red cow to be burned, how the cow is burned, the water; how the water is mixed with ash; purity rules applicable to the performance of the rite from beginning to end. In general the expectation of sages in the period under discussion was that this rite done outside of the Temple must be carried out in conditions of cleanness of an exceptionally stringent character. What will be done outside of the Temple must be done in accord with rules many times more strict than those applicable within the Temple. The analogy drawn to the Temple produces that one result: the rite outside the Temple is done in accord with the way in which rites are done within the Temple, but we must take account of the situation of the rite outside of the Temple walls.

The materials we have rapidly surveyed are both abundant and remarkably sophisticated. The conceptions of removes of uncleanness, the utensil and the tent, the creation of an enclave of cleanness outside of the Temple for both eating and burning the red cow, the obviously sustained and rigorous thought devoted to established themes and the discovery of related but essentially new problems and ideas—all of this stands in stark contrast to the state of the other Divisions. Much later, after the two wars, the other Divisions would reach an equivalent stage of full articulation, so that, when the whole would come to closure, the intellectual triumphs of the Division of Purities would appear as part of a serrated, yet essentially even, horizon. But for the moment the result of what was evidently a century of sustained reflection proved to be a Division approaching systemic fruition, rich in its intellectual initiatives, complete in its exploration of the potentialities of each of its themes. The fact that the Division takes up a world of obsession and compulsion may not be permitted to obscure what the philosophers between the wars, in sequence from those beforehand, in fact had achieved.

The Age of Transition

The destruction of the Temple is important, in the unfolding of the history of the Mishnah's laws and ideas, principally because of what it does not demarcate. It does not mark a significant turning in the history of the laws of Purities. These unfolded within the generative principles of their own logic. The inner tensions embedded from before 70 in the exercise of locating the unclean on a continuum with the holy and of situating ordinary food in place of that continuum account for what was said after 70. The loss of the Temple, enormous though it was, does not. The expectation that the rites governing agriculture and the disposition of the produce of the Land would remain valid accounts for the evidence we have surveyed, just as that same expectation, that people would eat in a state of cultic cleanness, clearly is in evidence in the character of the laws of Purities between the wars. True, the destruction of the Temple and the supposedly temporary cessation of the cult precipitated thought on laws governing the Temple altar and the priests in the act of sacrifice. That was a natural interest among people who, to begin with, thought that what happened in the Temple formed the center and focus of Israelite life. With the Temple gone, people will naturally have wondered whether some deep flaw in the conduct of its rites might explain the awful punishment Israel suffered in the destruction of the Temple and the holy city. So, in that same, essentially priestly, perspective of the world, it was entirely predictable that sustained thought on the right conduct of the cult should have gotten under way. So the themes and detailed principles collected in the Divisions of Agriculture, Holy Things, and Purities, the first and the third continuing from before the war, the second beginning in its aftermath, testify to a continuity of vision, a perpetuation of focus.

The people whose ideas come to full expression and closure in the Mishnah, as we shall see later on, were diverse. But in so far as the definition of the group is concerned, who, before and between the wars, contributed to the ultimate corpus of ideas contained in what was framed after the wars, that definition remains unchanged. They were priests and lay people who aspired to act like priests. These are the ones whose fantasy lies before us in the stratum of the laws of the Mishnah just now surveyed. Yet fresh elements in their thought turn out to have laid the foundations for what, in the end, is truly Mishnaic about the Mishnah, I mean, the Mishnah's message at its deepest structure about the interplay between sanctification, on the one side, and the human will, on the other. But that is something to which we shall return much later in this story (see below, pp. 270–83).

Instead we have to stand back from the laws we have surveyed and provide an overview of what was accomplished between the wars. That accomplishment may be stated very simply. The period between the wars marks a transition in the unfolding of the Mishnaic law and system. The law moved out of its narrow, sectarian framework. But it did not yet attain that full definition, serviceable for the governance of a whole society and the formation of a government for the nation as a whole, which would be realized in the aftermath of the wars. The marks of the former state remained. But those of the later character of the Mishnaic system began to make their appearance. Still, the systemic fulfillment of the law would be some time in coming. For, as I shall point out in the next section, the system as a whole in its ultimate shape would totally reframe the inherited vision. In the end the Mishnah's final framers would accomplish what was not done before or between the wars: make provision for the ordinary condition of Israelite men and women, living everyday lives under their own government. The laws suitable for a sect would remain, to be joined by others which, in the aggregate, would wholly revise the character of the whole.

The shift would be from a perspective formed upon the Temple mount, to a vision framed within the plane of Israel, from a cultic to a communal conception, and from a center at the locative pivot of the altar, to a system resting upon the utopian character of the nation as a whole. To be sure, this still would be what the cult-centered vision had perceived: a holy nation in a holy Land living out a holy life and deriving sustenance from the source of life, through sanctification set apart from death and uncleanness. But the shift is made. The orbit moved to a path other than what it was. Between the wars the shift is yet to be discerned. But if the orbit was the same as it had been for well over half a millennium, still, we see a wobble in the pivot.

When we take up the changes in this transitional period, we notice, first of all, continuity with the immediate past. What was taking place after 70 is encapsulated in the expansion, along predictable and familiar lines, of the laws of uncleanness, so to these we turn first.

If the destruction of Jerusalem and the Temple in 70 marks a watershed in the history of Judaism, the development of the system of uncleanness does not indicate it. The destruction of the Temple in no way interrupted the unfolding of those laws, consideration of which is well attested when the Temple was standing and the cult maintained. Development is continuous in a second aspect as well. We find that, in addition to carrying forward antecedent themes and supplying secondary and even tertiary conceptions, the authorities between the wars develop new areas and motifs of legislation. These turn out to be both wholly consonant with the familiar ones, and, while fresh, generated by logical tensions in what had gone before. If, therefore, the destruction of the Temple raised in some minds the question of whether the system of cleanness at home would collapse along with the cult, the rules and system before us in no way suggest so. To be sure, the destruction of the Temple does mark a new phase in the growth of the law. What now happens is an evidently rapid extension of the range of legislation, on the one side, and provision of specific and concrete rules for what matters of purity were apt to have been taken for granted but not given definition before 70, on the other. So the crisis of 70 in the system of uncleanness gives new impetus to movement along lines laid forth long before.

Let us first dwell upon the points of continuity, which are many and impressive. The development of the rules on the uncleanness of menstrual blood, the *zab*, and corpse uncleanness is wholly predictable on the basis of what has gone before. The principal conceptual traits carry forward established themes. For example, if we have in hand an interest in resolving matters of doubt, then, in the present age, further types of doubts will be investigated. Once we know that a valid birth is not accompanied by unclean blood, we ask about the definition of valid births. The present thought on the *zab* depends entirely on the materials assigned to the Houses, which, moreover, appear to be prior to, and independent of, what is attributed to the authorities after 70. The transfer of the *zab*'s uncleanness through pressure, forming so large and important a part of the tractate of Zabim, begins not with a reference to the *zab* at all, but to the menstruating woman. The fresh point in this regard is to be seen as a step beyond Scripture's own rule, a shift based on analogical thinking. Rulings on corpse contamination dwell upon secondary and derivative issues. One new idea is the interest in projections from a house and how they too overshadow and so bring corpse uncleanness. It is from this point that an important development begins. Once we treat the tent as in some way functional, it is natural to focus upon the process or function of overshadowing in general. A major innovation in regard to transfer of the contamination of corpse matter through the tent is the notion that the tent takes an active role, combining the diverse bits and pieces and corpse uncleanness into a volume sufficient to impart corpse uncleanness. What is done is to treat the overshadowing as a function, rather than the tent as a thing. Here the mode of thought is both contrastive and analogical.

What is new now requires attention. The comparison of the table in the home to the cult in the Temple is an old theme in the Mishnaic system. What is done at just this time appears to have been the recognition of two complementary sequences, the removes of uncleanness, the degrees of holiness. The former involves several steps of contamination from the original source of uncleanness. The latter speaks of several degrees of sanctification, ordinary food, heave offering, food deriving from the altar (holy things), and things involved in the preparation of purification water. Each of the latter is subject to the effects of contamination produced by each of the former, in an ascending ladder of sensitivity to uncleanness. Now this complex structure seems to me to result from the exceedingly difficult problem facing the Mishnaic system: what do do with the entire metaphor of domestic cleanness now that its cultic focus and center are (for the moment) no more. The answer is to treat the domestic table no longer as *like* the cult. The table now is a diminished cult, a lesser sanctuary, a place where the sacred abides, to be sure, not wholly as it did in the Temple. The metaphor of altar and hearth is shattered, but its pieces are put together into a not very different construction. When the table at home is deemed to be like the altar in the Temple, then we compare holy things to ordinary food and there is no reason to introduce the matter of heave offering. But when the table at home is placed into a continuum with the holy things of the cult, then what links the one to the other is precisely the continuing presence of the priesthood and its heave offering. So long as the priests preserve and eat heave offering in a state of cleanness, there is a way of relating the table at home to some higher sanctity, leading, moreover, to the highest. Once, therefore, the material and concrete continuum is worked out, it demands inclusion of attention to the one remaining material (nonmetaphorical) element of cultic sanctity, the priests' own food. That then completes the progression: the table of the ordinary Israelite, kept clean like the heave offering of the priesthood, points toward the ultimate sanctity inhering in the now-devastated altar. The steps in the ladder downward, to the corpse, then become possible, all forming a single continuum of death to life. This brilliant construction, created between the wars, is at its foundations continuous with what had gone before.

Treating as sufficient for the present purpose what was said above about the unfolding of agricultural laws between the wars (see p. 87), we turn directly to that other area of the law closely linked to the themes and conceptions which already were well established, and yet, an essentially new topic for intense analysis, Holy Things. At issue now is the formation, between the wars, of laws governing the cult. The principal statement of this new system is as follows: the Temple is holy. Its priests therefore are indispensable. But the governance of the Temple now is to be in accord with Torah, and it is the sage who knows Torah and therefore applies it. Since a literal reading of Scripture prevented anyone's maintaining that someone apart from the priest could be like a priest and do the things priests do, it was the next best thing to impose the pretense that priests must obey laymen in the conduct even of the priestly liturgies and services. This is a natural next step in the development of the law. A second paramount trait of the version of the system between the wars is its rationalization of those uncontrolled powers inherent in the sacred cult as laid forth by Leviticus. The lessons of Nadab and Abihu and numerous other accounts of the cult's or altar's intrinsic *mana* (inclusive of the *herem*) are quietly set aside. The altar sanctifies what is appropriate to it, not whatever comes into contact with its power. It is not too much to say that, in that principle, the sacred is forced to conform to simple conceptions of logic and sense, its power uncontrollably to strike out dramatically reduced. This same rationality extends to the definition of the effective range of intention. If one intends to do improperly what is not in any event done at all, one's intention is null. Third, attention is paid to defining the sorts of offerings required in various situations of sin or guilt. Here too the message is not to be missed. Sin still is to be expiated, when circumstances permit, through the sacrificial system. Nothing has changed. There is no surrogate for sacrifice, an exceedingly important affirmation of the cult's continuing validity among people burdened with sin and aching for a mode of atonement. Finally, we observe that the established habit of thinking about gifts to be paid to the priest accounts for the choices of topics on fees paid to maintain the cult. All pertain to priestly gifts analogous to tithes and heave offerings. Tithe of cattle is an important subject, and the rules of firstlings and other gifts to the priests are subject to considerable development. The upshot is that the principal concerns of the Division of Holy Things are defined by the end of the age between the wars.

The survey of the laws between the wars shows that episodic, but sometimes not unimportant, conceptions only later on to be ultimately fully developed in the Mishnah's other three Divisions, on Appointed Times, Women, and Damages, make an appearance. We shall now survey the state of thought on topics ultimately brought together in these three divisions of what was to be the system of the closed and completed Mishnah.

Systematic work on the formation of a Division of Appointed Times did not get under way in the aftermath of the destruction of the Temple. The established interest in rules governing meals, however, was carried forward in laws reliably assigned to the time between the wars. There is some small tendency to develop laws pertinent to the observance of the Sabbath; a few of these laws were important and generated later developments. But the age between the wars may be characterized as a period between important developments. Work on legislation for meals on Sabbaths and festivals had begun earlier. The effort systematically and thoroughly to legislate for the generality of festivals, with special attention to conduct in the Temple cult, would begin later on. In the intervening generations only a little work was done, and this was not systematic.

Certainly there was ample reason now to legislate for the festivals
and the Sabbath, since the destruction of the Temple raised some immediate questions. To Yohanan b. Zakkai is assigned a number of
ordinances on how to observe the Festival of Sukkot and the New Year
in the aftermath of the destruction of the Temple. These in context are
represented as temporary matters, allowing for keeping the Festival
in the interim before the Temple's reconstruction. The character of
what the postwar authorities actually did, that is to say, an extensive
corpus of legislation for the Temple and for rites closely associated
with the Temple, will show us the unimportance of what is attributed to
Yohanan b. Zakkai. For the critical issue was the Temple's place in the
observance of the pilgrim festivals, and that issue would not be faced at
this time. It had to be confronted only when it was clear that, for some
time to come, Jerusalem would no longer be accessible. Then provision
would be made for recording the way in which the pilgrim festivals had
been observed, a way of affirming the hope that they would once more
be kept. So the destruction of the Temple appears to have stimulated
little effort to rethink the matter of the observance of Sabbath and
festivals and brought about no creative impulse in this suggestive area
of the ancient religion.

When fully worked out, the Mishnah's Division of Women would
pay close attention to exchanges of property and documents attendant
upon the transfer of a woman from her father's to her husband's house.
Authorities between the wars provided only a little guidance for such
matters. For a very long time before 70 the national, prevailing law
must have defined and governed them. What is significant is that
broader and nonsectarian matters, surely subject to a long history of
accepted procedure, should have been raised at all. It means that, after
the destruction, attention turned to matters which sectarians had not
regarded as part of their realm of concern. This may have meant that
others who had carried responsibility for the administration of public
affairs, such as scribes, now made an appearance. And it also may have
meant that the vision of the sectarians themselves had begun to
broaden and to encompass the administration of the life of ordinary
folk, not within the sect. Both meanings are to be imputed to the fact of
interest in issues of public administration of property transfers along
with the transfer of women to and from the father's home. Concern for
definition of personal status devolves upon genealogical questions urgent to the priesthood, and, it follows, in the present stratum are contained matters of deep concern to yet a third constituency. But these
matters of interest to scribes and priests do not predominate. It is their
appearance, rather than their complete expression and articulation,
which is of special interest.

If we ask what the Mishnah wishes to say in particular about the general themes which it has chosen for its Division of Women, it is difficult to specify a distinctive and telling message. Much appears to be so commonsensical that, with Scripture in hand, anyone might have reached the same conclusions. Take, for example, that stipulation in writs of divorce or in betrothals must be carried out or the acts are null; women must be supported if their marriages end because of divorce or death; conflicting claims of property must be adjudicated by the principle that the claimant must prove the validity of his or her claim; a wife loses her property rights if she violates the law of Moses. While, as I said above, the laws of Holy Things seem to me to yield paramount traits which express important ideas, those of Women do not. They are discrete. There is no underlying and unifying conception to be discerned in any major segment of the laws, still less in the law as a whole.

And yet if we cannot characterize as a whole the components of the system, we can claim that before us we do see the shape of the system as it would ultimately emerge. The one important element to come after the wars, attention to property exchanges attendant upon betrothal, surely is predictable at this point in the unfolding of the system. For a law which defines property transfers at the end of a marriage in due course must provide the same sorts of definitions for transfers which come at the beginning of a marriage. It follows that, by the end of the interim period, the system of Women was pretty well in hand. The tendency of the system, moreover, to overcome and transcend its sectarian origins and to begin to make rules applicable to the community at large, laws in their substance in no way productive of social divisiveness upon which the sect would depend for its continuing existence, is established.

And that is the main point. The clearly implied aspiration of the laws was to apply to the Israelite world as a whole. That aspiration would not change. The context later on, moreover, would only confirm and intensify the original intention. For later on the authorities whose opinions find their way into the Mishnah would indeed take up a range of practical authority and receive a kind of power which, before that time, they appear not to have had. It follows that a system aiming at governance of the Israelite world at large is brought to fulfillment and perfectly natural closure at that point at which the social and political aspirations which underlay the earliest, directly antecedent legislation were realized. Sages now aspired to imagine the authority which their successors would enjoy: the right to make those concrete and everyday decisions of the administration of trivialities which, all together, constitute the effective government of the Jewish people. What is remarkable, therefore, was the power of the imagination of the legislators of the day to contemplate a world they did not then know.

Whoever before 70 had settled those disputes about real estate, working conditions, debts and loans, torts and damages, and other sorts of conflicts which naturally came up in a vital and stable society, the group represented in the Mishnah did not. That is why the Division of Damages, dealing with civil law and government, contains virtually nothing assigned to authorities before the wars. Scribes in Temple times served as judges and courts within the Temple government, holding positions in such system of administration of the Israelite part of Palestine as the Romans left within Jewish control. The Division of Damages is remarkably reticent on what after the destruction they might have contributed out of the heritage of their earlier traditions and established practices. Materials of this period yield little evidence of access to any tradition prior to 70, except (predictably) for Scripture. When people at this time did take up topics relevant to the larger system of Damages, they directed their attention to the exegesis of Scriptures and produced results which clarify what Moses laid down, or which carry forward problems or topics suggested by the Torah. That is not evidence that thinkers of this period had access (or wished to gain access) to any source of information other than that one, long since available to the country as a whole, provided by Moses. It follows that, in so far as any materials at all relevant to the later Mishnaic system of Damages did come forth between the wars, the work appears to have begun from scratch. And not much work can have been done to begin with. There is no evidence of sustained and systematic thought about the topics assembled in the Division of Damages. We find some effort devoted to the exegesis of Scriptures relevant to the Division. But whether or not those particular passages were selected because of a large-scale inquiry into the requirements of civil law and government, or because of an overriding interest in a given set of Scriptures provoked by some other set of questions entirely, we cannot say.

The net result of the stage in the law's unfolding demarcated by the two wars is that history—the world-shattering events of the day—is kept at a distance from the center of life. The system of sustaining life shaped essentially within an ahistorical, indeed antihistorical, view of reality, goes forward in its own path, a way above history. Yet the facts of history are otherwise. The people as a whole can hardly be said to have accepted the ahistorical ontology framed by the sages and in part expressed by the systems of Purities, Agriculture, and Holy Things. The people followed the path of Bar Kokhba and took the road to war once more. When the three generations had passed after the destruction and the historical occasion for restoration through historical—political and military—action came to fulfillment, the great war of 132 to 135 broke forth. A view of being in which people were seen to be moving toward some point within time, the fulfillment and the end of history as it was known, clearly shaped the consciousness of Israel after 70 just as had been the case in the decades before 70. So if to the sages of our system, history and the end of history were essentially beside the point and pivot, the construction of a world of cyclical eternities being the purpose and center, and the conduct of humble things like eating and drinking the paramount and decisive focus of the sacred, others saw things differently. To those who hoped and therefore fought, Israel's life had other meanings entirely.

The Second War proved still more calamitous than the First. In 70 the Temple was lost, in 135, even access to the city. In 70 the people, though suffering grievous losses, endured more or less intact. In 135 the land of Judah—surely the holiest part of the holy Land—evidently lost the bulk of its Jewish population. Temple, Land, people—all were gone in the forms in which they had been known. In the generation following the calamity of Bar Kokhba, what would be the effect upon the formation of the Mishnah? It is to that question that we now turn.

From Sectarian Fantasy to Social Vision:
After the Transition

Before the wars the people whose ideas come to full expression in the Mishnah formed a small group, perhaps to be categorized as a sect. If so, it was a cultic sect, a holiness order, expressing the aspirations of lay people to live as if they belonged to the caste of priests, and of priests to live as if the whole country were the Temple. It is no surprise that those definitive topics of the Mishnah which gain attention early on were the ones having to do with food and sex: how food is raised, the petty obsessions governing its preparation and consumption, and who may marry whom in the constrained circle of those who worried those small, compulsive worries. After the two wars, as we shall see in due course, the entire framework of the Mishnah would undergo revision. The range of topics so expanded that laws came to full expression to govern not merely the collective life of a small group but the political and social affairs of a whole nation. What had come from the then-distant past, from the preceding century, would be taken into caring hands and carefully nurtured, as if it mattered. But the fresh and the new challenge of an age of new beginnings would lead to daring choices: laws for real estate and commercial transactions, laws for the scribal profession and the documentation of changes in the status of people and property, laws, even, for the governance of the Temple, then in ruins, and the conduct of its rites throughout the cycle of appointed times and seasons, for the maintenance of the Temple and its caste of priests and Levites, and (of all things) for the design of the Temple when it would be rebuilt and for the conduct of its everyday offering. All of this would follow in that remarkable time of fulfillment and closure which came in the aftermath of the wars.

What was achieved between them? Small things, little steps—a bridge between that completed statement constituted by the sectarian fantasy framed before the wars, and that also-completed statement about everything and everyone: the political vision, the social policy, the economic program, in full and glorious detail, which would be the closed and ample Mishnah itself. Describing Moslem philosophical visions of the world of the Greek philosophers, Peter Brown comments, "Only a civilization of impressive density can cause the previous culture of a millennium to spin into so strange an orbit" (Brown, p. 31). When we consider the beginnings of it all in a narrowly priestly fantasy, acted out by a tight little circle of specialists in uncommon and egregious laws involving the contact of a loaf of bread of a specified status with a deceased reptile, we must wonder what swept the world out of the old and into the new orbit.

For, as I have just now stressed, the priestly vision, with its emphasis on the Temple as the pivot and the world as the periphery, the Temple as guarantor of life, the world as the threatening realm of death, the Temple as the security and strength of Israel, the world as its enemy, and, above all, the unreliable and perpetually threatening character of persons and substances on the borders between Temple and world—when we contemplate that vision, we must wonder that anyone could share it *and yet expand it.* That is just what happened. For the priestly component of the ultimate structure of the Mishnah remains paramount. Yet the Mishnah is not a priestly document. It is much more than that. As we know, had the Mishnah come to closure before the wars, it would have consisted of the system of uncleanness, fully exposed if lacking numerous details, a part of the system of agriculture, a system (quite its own) about food preparation, with emphasis upon doing so on special occasions (when the group presumably was able to come together), and, finally, a half-system on suitable marital candidates under special conditions, a set of laws calculated (if observed) to render members of the group unacceptable to non-members as marriage partners. Now, that version of the Mishnah spun about the Temple, in a stable orbit around the altar.

And the other Mishnah—the one we now have, pursues its predictable path in quite another orbit. It makes peripheral the Temple and its concerns, as they come to expression in everyday imitation of the priesthood. It treats as central other things entirely: civil and criminal law and political institutions and their power, in the Fourth Division; the conduct of the cult itself, not merely of people wishing to place themselves into relationship with a cult by setting their feet on a single continuous path to the altar, in the Second and Fifth Divisions; the web of documents which encase and protect transfers of persons and property, both in life and afterward, in the Third and Fourth Divisions; the full articulation of the rules governing the disposition of crops in accord with the holiness inhering in them, and the arrangement of relationships (hitherto remarkably ignored) between virtuosi of the law and outsiders so that all, all together, might constitute a single Israel, this in the First Division and in the Sixth. Now these changes, ultimately realized in the full expression and closure of the Mishnah itself, are no issue of small detail. They cut to the heart of the matter. They shift completely and ultimately the very center of focus of the document itself. They represent, as I said, a Mishnah wholly other than the Mishnah (if we may call it that) which would have taken shape before the wars, if anyone had thought to make one.

But, of course, so far as we know, no one did. So the truly stunning change effected after the wars was the formation of the book itself, the book which brought together the ideas and principles and laws in circulation before its time, and put them all together into something far more than the components, the paltry corpus of conceptions available to the framers of the document. Now we see with full clarity the ponderous movement from one orbit to the other, the shift of the previous culture of, if not a millennium, then at least nearly seven or eight hundred years (from the second century backward to the sixth). That old, reliable, priestly way of life and world view from the Temple mountain came to be subsumed by, and transformed into, a social vision, as I said, framed on the plane of Israel. What is stunning is the shift in perspective, not the change in what was to be seen. Merely seeing the Temple and its altar from a vantage point other than the Temple mount itself is a remarkable movement in perspective. Only framing a code of law framed in rules made of words in place of practice codified in gesture and studied act constitutes an astonishing shift in focus. From interests limited to the home and hearth the opening lens of social thought takes in a larger frame indeed: from home to court, from eating and drinking, beds and pots and pans, to exchanges of property and encounters of transactions in material power. What moved the world on its axis, the ball of earth in its majesty? The answer is self-evident: seventy years of wars and the tumult of wars. These shattered a hope which, to begin with, had little to do with the Temple at all. There was then a moment of utter despair about things which, from the perspective of the philosophers of the Mishnah, might as well have taken place on yet another planet (but, alas, things wholly within their experience). The previous culture of somewhat less than a millennium spun into another orbit, not because of the gravity of yet a new civilization of impressive density, though. The reason requires its own metaphor.

4

Divisions, Tractates, Principal Ideas after the Wars

Preliminary Observations

When we come to describe the state of Mishnaic discourse—laws and ideas—after the two wars, the situation radically changes from that which prevailed before and between them. For two reasons, both connected with the state of the evidence, our mode of inquiry also has to shift.

First, we no longer are able to differentiate between ideas of one generation of authorities and those of another, as we could, in general, between ideas held before and between the wars. It is generally supposed that the Mishnah comes to closure at about 200, that is, approximately sixty years, or two working generations, following the end of the Second War and consequent repression. In the Mishnah itself appear from time to time names of figures who do not belong to the generation immediately following the war, for instance, Yosé the son of R. Judah, that is to say, the child of one of the principal figures of the Mishnaic framework immediately after the war, not to mention Judah, later on called the Patriarch, son of Rabban Simeon b. Gamaliel.

So, it is clear, both chronological reasons and the evidence of attributions suggest we deal with two differentiated groups, hence should look for evidence of development and expansion of the law over two generations. But there is no way to do this work. If, as we suppose, there were two distinct generations, they appear not to have been so distinct from one another, so sharply set off, as the authorities between the wars surely were from those before and after them. The sayings immediately after the wars appear wholly intermingled with those belonging long afterward over the entire sweep of sixty years. We recall that it is rare indeed to find anyone from the group between the wars in the same literary unit as someone from before or after them. Aqiba is the sole figure who from time to time pops up with names of people who otherwise occur only with postwar names. But it is commonplace to find sayings attributed to Yosé b. R. Judah or Simeon b. Eleazar alongside, in the same pericope with, sayings assigned to the towering figures of the immediate postwar generation, e.g., Simeon, Judah, Meir, Yosé. Judah the Patriarch and Simeon b. Gamaliel, generally taken to be his father, do take opposite positions on mooted issues within a single literary unit. The literary evidence by itself therefore does not permit that inductive exercise, the results of which have been portrayed in the preceding parts of this study. Consequently, there is no way in which, on solely inductive grounds, we are able to effect the needed differentiation between one group and the next among the sequences of authorities who flourished after the wars and before the closure of the Mishnah itself.

The second reason that our mode of inquiry has to change is more important. When we speak of the situation before and between the wars, we ask about specific laws and underlying ideas apt to have originated in the specified periods. But now we bring into view the Mishnah as a completed document. The very fact that we cannot differentiate between ideas held right after the wars and those held by the following generation, the one responsible for the formation of the Mishnah as a whole, means that we can deal only with the latter phase of the evidence produced in the long period at hand. That is consistent with our procedure earlier. For what we did in chapters 2 and 3 was to provide an account of how things are apt to have looked at the end of the period before the wars, and, again, at the end of the period between them. We could not differentiate among the "generations" of authorities in the prior period, and so I had to claim to describe only the end product. This is what I did describe. Here too we must deal with the end product of an otherwise undifferentiated period. And that is the Mishnah itself. As I indicated earlier, when we confront the evidence beyond the wars, it is quite different in character. The evidence which requires description now is constituted by the whole, closed Mishnah. For that, as I said, is the net result of the sixty years of labor from the end of the wars to the closure of the document itself.

So now there is nothing to be gained by isolating a set of individual laws and assigning them to authorities beyond the wars, then, comparing them with what is reliably set in the mouths and minds of those between and before the wars, and, finally, showing what is new after the wars. For such a procedure (which, in fact, is worked out in great detail for the various tractates in my history of the Mishnaic law) would be seriously misleading. It would suggest that the labor beyond the wars is essentially analogous to that before and between them. But the facts speak for themselves: the result of the work from 140 onward is the creation of the Mishnah. By contrast the result of the work from long before 70 to the First War, and from the First War to the Second, is not the creation of the Mishnah, at least, not as we know it. So treating the laws item by item as we have done in chapters 2 and 3 would suggest the opposite of the fact. The fact is that beyond the wars there came into being something quite different from what there was before them. This new thing is the systematic, complete, integrated, cogent, and final statement constituted by the Mishnah itself.

To recapitulate the argument: the correct mode of description now takes up the whole, rather than first providing a further account of the formation of bits and pieces of the parts. We are constrained to skip a stage in the description. We might reasonably have asked ourselves to go through those many specific rulings in the name of authorities after the wars and to provide a further, detailed account of those matters which have become familiar from our earlier exercises. We might further have added a still more detailed account of those many matters which are fresh in the world beyond the wars—the centerpiece of three of six Divisions!—and given that same sort of description which was offered of the details of this law and that one before and between the wars. But, as is now clear, such a procedure would not be appropriate. The literary evidence does not permit the kind of differentiation required, between the end product—the completed system of the Mishnaic Divisions and the Mishnah as a whole—and the penultimate layer(s) of the end product, the vast corpus of details correctly assigned to the immediate postwar period or the later one. The true accomplishment of the sages beyond the wars is not going to be portrayed by such a detailed account. For what they did was to take up the whole antecedent heritage—including their own response to it—and to reshape and revise it into what it ultimately became, which is, I have now stressed, the Mishnah as we now know it. That is why we must see the whole as a whole, and not merely as the agglutination of an infinite number of all-too-clearly-differentiated parts.

In order to gain the desired perspective, we shall have to take up a position somewhat further from the ground of the Mishnah than that upon which up to now we have stood. Specifically, our work is no more to examine the Divisions as conglomerates of different rulings on diverse topics, but now as whole, working systems. We have further to look at the tractates not merely as efforts at organizing thematic units, but as essays, sometimes sustained and cogent, on their stated themes. So we shall not merely work out our way up and out from the parts to the whole. Now we shall take an essentially fresh picture of the whole beyond the parts. For the whole adds up, in the Mishnah, to more than the sum of the parts.

That missing step, from the parts created in the immediate generation beyond the two wars, to the whole formed by the ultimate generation of the Mishnah, not only cannot be taken. It also should not be taken. For the Mishnah's system as a system is the work of the whole sequence of authorities from 140 to 200. *The work on the parts now is part of the work on the whole.* That is the governing fact. It is only by seeing the whole as a whole that we shall understand and fully appreciate why that is so.

Up to now I have reviewed specific items. For abundantly clear reasons, we now turn to examine tractates as such, seeing them, moreover, from the pinnacle of the complete Divisions of which they form component parts. In order to do this, what we want to know is something new. It is the way in which the stated topic of a tractate is unpacked and spread out. What people wish to say about a given topic and how their ideas are ordered are the two critical points of interest in this part of the descriptive work. Knowing how they define the issues of a theme, what they wish to know about a given topic, as we take into account all the other things about which they do not ask, will lead us from the narrow frame of this rule and that, to the wide perspective of the Mishnah as a complete and intelligible statement. Once we have that statement clearly in mind, we shall be able to turn to the world in which, and upon which, the framers of the Mishnah and its philosophers made their comment.

In turning from isolated details of the law to an account of the generative problematic of the several tractates, we rely upon a simple device. If we want to know what people thought important about a topic, we have to begin with to examine the way in which they simply organize their ideas on that topic. This means two things. First, what aspects of the topic do they treat? Second, in what order do they treat them? A clear picture of how ideas are laid out tells us what people wish to know about those ideas. From knowing what people want to know about a given topic, it is a small step to ask what they think important. So sequence yields a picture of order. The fact of an orderly arrangement of ideas is the principal exegetical device in our hands. Since, as we shall see, it is feasible to outline every tractate and to present a clearly orderly account of each topic, the work is entirely suitable to the evidence, and the evidence—the Mishnah—is appropriate to the question raised about it. That is to say, what we shall see time and again is that the framers' mode of organization—the mere outline of a tractate—reveals very clearly, right on the surface, the blatant outline of precisely what the framers of that tractate deemed critical about the topic under discussion.

So the labor before us is in two parts. First, what is required is a simple statement of a topic and what the philosophers of the Mishnah tractate devoted to said topic thought important to say about it. This statement is given in the present chapter. Second, in order to substantiate that statement and, more important, in order to initiate the reader into the complete system and structure of the Mishnah as a whole, *seen whole,* I present an outline of the tractates under discussion, in sequence. The outline of the Mishnah as a whole is presented in appendix 5. In this way the topical unfolding of the Mishnah, tractate by tractate, Division by Division, and as a whole, will be fully and totally laid out before the reader. It is a tribute to the genius at form and order of the ultimate framers of the Mishnah that such a procedure is possible. It is a tribute to the genius at philosophy of the thinkers of the Mishnah that such a procedure actually can be, and I think is, interesting and compelling.

The Division of Agriculture after the Wars

The Division of Agriculture as it has come down to us treats two topics, first, producing crops in accord with the Scriptural rules on the subject, second, paying the required offerings and tithes to the priests, Levites, and poor. The principal point of the Division is that the Land is holy, because God has a claim both on it and upon what it produces. God's claim must be honored by setting aside a portion of the produce for those for whom God has designated it. God's ownership must be acknowledged by observing the rules God has laid down for use of the Land. In sum, the Division is divided along these lines: (1) Rules for producing crops in a state of holiness—tractates Kilayim, Shebiit, Orlah; (2) Rules for disposing of crops in accord with the rules of holiness—tractates Peah, Demai, Terumot, Maaserot, Maaser Sheni, Hallah, Bikkurim, Berakhot.

Let us first survey the topical scheme of the tractates and then take up the main ideas expressed in them.

Producing Crops in a State of Holiness

Kilayim. A genus and its species in regard to the prohibition of sowing diverse kinds; the minimum volume of seed which, when mixed with a different sort of seed, constitutes a violation of the rule against diverse kinds; how to sow different sorts of seeds in proximity to one another without violating the rules against diverse kinds. The definition of a vineyard, within which one may not sow grain; the space required for a vineyard's exclusive use, within which other kinds of seeds may not be sown. The prohibition against mating diverse kinds of animals. The prohibition against mixing wool and linen.

Shebiit. Preparation for the seventh year. Stopping labor in the sixth year, even before the advent of the seventh year, when that labor will benefit crops to be expected in the seventh year; definition of the end of the time in the sixth year in which it is permitted to perform various sorts of labor in the fields. Doing work in the seventh year which will benefit the crops of the eighth year; doing work in the seventh year which will not affect the crops of the seventh year. Gathering stones or wood from a field without thereby appearing to clear the field at a time at which such labor is prohibited. The status of diverse regions in regard to the seventh year. The disposition of crops produced in the seventh year.

Orlah. The fruit of trees in the first three years of their growth is not to be used: definition of the sorts of trees which are subject to the three-year rule; trees exempt from the three-year rule. Neutralization of produce prohibited as *orlah* which inadvertently is mixed with diverse other sorts of produce. Prohibition of all benefit from produce from a tree in the first three years of its growth, even indirect benefit.

Disposing of Crops in Accord with the Rules of Holiness

Peah. The amount of a field which must be left for the poor under the rule of leaving the corner of the field for the poor; the sorts of produce subject to the rule; the size and delineation of a field subject to the rule; special rules on leaving the corner of the field and produce subject to that rule. The rights of the poor to go into the field to search for leftover crops: gleanings and the rules governing the leaving of gleanings, the forgotten sheaf, and the corner of the field. The definition of gleanings; the disposition of crops received under the rule of gleanings, forgotten sheaf, and the corner of the field. The forgotten sheaf: definition and disposition. Grape gleanings: definition and disposition. The poor man's tithe.

Demai. The applicability of diverse tithing rules to *demai*, that is, produce about which there is doubt as to tithing. The uses of *demai* produce. How one tithes doubtfully tithed produce. What one may do with doubtfully tithed produce, to whom one may give it. Conduct with a person who does not faithfully tithe produce. How to tithe produce. Dividing produce and giving the tithes from it. Giving tithes in advance of a meal, by designating portions of the produce for various purposes.

Terumot. Who is allowed to designate a portion of produce as heave offering, and who may not validly do so; the sorts of produce which are liable for the designation of a part as heave offering. The specification of heave offering from several batches of produce at one time: what kinds of batches may be deemed to form a single batch for purposes of designating heave offering, and what kinds may not. Heave offering which turns out to be rotten or otherwise useless. The proper practice in designating produce as heave offering; how much heave offering must be set aside from a given volume of produce. Mixtures of heave offering with common produce and how they are disposed of. Misappropriating heave offering and paying compensation to the priests; penalties for misappropriating heave offering. Prohibitions against mixing food in the status of heave offering with unconsecrated produce. Consumption of heave offering by the priest.

Maaserot. General rules of tithing: what is liable to tithes. The point at which food becomes subject to tithing laws; diverse sorts of produce and their tithing seasons. The assumption that food has or has not been tithed and how one deals with commonplace cases of doubt. The point at which food becomes liable to tithing: special cases in which food is not liable to tithes. Making use of produce before it is liable to tithes and so imposing on it premature liability.

Maaser Sheni. Second tithe which is brought to Jerusalem. Uses to which produce in the status of second tithe may be put, and those to which it may not be put. The disposition of funds which have been received in payment for produce in the status of second tithe. Taking the money up to Jerusalem and spending it there; changing the money for coins of lower or higher denomination for the trip; disposition of the money in Jerusalem. Special cases of liability of crops to second tithe in Jerusalem. Establishing the price to be set upon produce which is to be redeemed for coins for transfer to Jerusalem. Produce of a fourth-year vineyard, which is subject to the same laws as apply to second tithe: relevant rules.

Hallah. The dough offering, to be set apart from all dough which is to be made into leavened bread. The sorts of grain which produce dough liable to the dough offering: the liability to dough offering applies to all sorts of bread, even to bread made from grain which otherwise is exempt from tithes. Special kinds of dough and whether or not they are subject to dough offering. The status of grain produced abroad and brought to the Land. Special cases and problems in connection with setting aside dough offering. The point at which the liability to dough offering applies to the dough.

Bikkurim. Bringing the first fruits and making the confession (Deut. 26:5): those who do both; those who bring the first fruits but do not make the confession; those who are not liable to bring the first fruits at all. The kinds of produce from which first fruits are brought. Diverse cases in which one may or may not be liable to bring first fruits. Comparison of first fruits and various other kinds of agricultural tithes and offerings: heave offering; second tithe; various other sorts of comparisons. Narrative of the bringing of first fruits to Jerusalem and presentation of them to the priesthood.

Berakhot. Reciting the *Shema‘* in the evening and in the morning: rules on the correct recitation of the *Shema‘*; people who do not have to recite it. The prayer and when it is said; appropriate behavior and attitude when one says the prayer. The blessings said over various kinds of produce before one eats them. The grace to be said after meals; rules for public recitation of grace after meals. Other rules about a meal, with special reference to opinions of the Houses of Shammai and Hillel. Other blessings.

The principal interests of the first group of tractates do not vastly differ from those of Scripture (cited below, pp. 329 ff.) on the same topics. On the main point of Kilayim, Mandelbaum writes:

> Mishnah Kilayim considers in turn plants, animals, and fibers. In each case Mishnah discusses permitted and prohibited ways of commingling different classes. The most important topic is the first, which develops the tractate's thesis that a mixture is prohibited only if it produces the appearance of a confusion of diverse kinds. The tractate's redactors, in fact, could have completed their treatise at the conclusion of this unit, for treatment of the second and third topics does not introduce into the tractate any major principles dealing with the laws of diverse kinds. These two topics serve only to include in the tractate Scripture's remaining two concerns, the commingling of animals or fibers of different kinds. It appears, then, that the primary interest of the tractate's redactors concerns issues relating to the commingling of different classes of plants alone. ["Kilayim"]

Shebiit takes up two principal matters, first, work in the fields in the year before the sabbatical year, which must not be allowed to benefit the crop of the sabbatical year itself, and the status of crops grown in the sixth year which mature in the seventh; and, second, the rules for the sabbatical year itself, with special reference, once more, to matters of labor and produce. Attention is paid to what may and may not be done in the sabbatical year, and how one may and may not dispose of crops during that year. So the interests of the tractate, in work and in produce in the sixth and seventh years of the cycle, clearly carry forward the basic biblical rule on the subject. There also is an appendix on the release of debts at the end of the sabbatical year.

Orlah deals with the status of produce fruit in the first three years after the planting of the tree, a period in which the fruit produced by the tree may not be utilized. The tractate defines what falls under the prohibition of *orlah* fruit, explains the prohibition of use of that fruit, and then asks about mixtures of forbidden and permitted produce, for instance, about mixtures of forbidden dyes in dyeing cloth and the use of fire made with coals from *orlah* fruit or trees. At the end it asks about cases of doubts involving the presence of *orlah* produce, produce subject to the *orlah* taboo.

The theory of the Division of Agriculture on the tithing laws is expressed by Richard S. Sarason. Since Sarason here has done the preliminary work of systematic description for this part of the Division, I shall quote his account at length.

> Mishnah's primary concern [in this portion of the Division of Agriculture] is with the process of sanctification of the various agricultural offerings, and, particularly, in the part which man plays in the process of sanctification. In this respect, I think it hardly coincidental that the lengthiest tractate in the Order of Seeds is Terumot, which deals with that offering regarded by Mishnah as holy *par excellence*. Nor is it coincidental that Mishnah devotes a tractate to second tithe, which is deemed holy, but not to the Levitical first tithe, which is not sanctified. The tractates on tithing give us a kind of geometry or logic of the sacred and sanctification in the realm of agricultural produce. A careful analysis of these tractates will show that Mishnah's theory of the holiness of produce which grows from the soil of the Land of Israel is transactional. That is to say, holiness does not naturally inhere in produce. Rather, God and man are the agents of sanctification. God, as owner of the Land, has a prior claim on its produce. But man must acknowledge God's ownership, and validate God's claim through actively designating and separating God's portion. Additionally, holiness is to be understood primarily in functional rather than substantive terms, i.e., that which is deemed holy belongs to God (and frequently is allotted by God to his priests), and must not be used by ordinary Israelites. Sacrilege thus is conceived as a violation of God's property rights.
>
> The authorities behind Mishnah primarily are interested in spelling out the role of human action and, particularly, intention in the process of sanctification. That role is determinative throughout the process. To begin with, the locus of susceptibility to sanctification is determined with reference to man's actions and intentions (cf. Tractate Maaserot). Not everything that grows in the soil of the Land of Israel is liable to the separation of heave-offering and tithes. Liability falls only on produce which is cultivated for human food (M. Ma. 1:1). This notion, of course, begins in Scripture, which requires Israelite farmers to offer to God, as owner of the Land, the best part of their grain, wine, and oil, and to feed the priests and Levites, who do not farm the land. Mishnah expands the liability to

include all edible produce. The tithing laws, then, are food laws. Only produce which can be human food enters the system of tithing and sanctification.

Similarly, the point at which produce becomes liable to the separation of *terumah* and tithes (i.e., becomes *tebel;* see below) is the point at which it becomes edible (M. Ma. 1:2). But man's actions and intentions further determine liability at this juncture. For before edible produce has been fully harvested or processed, it may be eaten randomly without incurring liability to tithing. Only if a man eats the produce as a regular meal before it is harvested must he tithe it. Furthermore, the point at which produce is considered to be fully harvested and liable to tithing also is determined by human intention regarding its ultimate disposition. If the farmer intends to bring his produce to market, it becomes liable to tithing when it is in that condition in which it will be brought to market—sifted, stacked, tied in bundles. If, on the other hand, he intends to bring the produce home to be eaten by his household, it does not become liable to tithing until it enters his private domain—the house or the courtyard.

Finally, produce becomes holy (i.e., God's property) only through man's act of consecration. This is made clear by considering the status of *ṭebel,* i.e., produce which has become liable to the separation of *terumah* and tithes, but from which these offerings have not yet been separated. Such produce must not be eaten by man, nor may benefit be derived from its use. But this is not because the produce now is deemed "holy," rather because it is now susceptible to sanctification, where previously it had not been. The whole is deemed "bonded" to God until his portion has been designated by the farmer's verbal declaration, and then separated. Even the priest, the ultimate recipient of the most holy portions (*terumah, terumat ma'aśer*) has no share in them until they actually have been separated. Before that time, these offerings exist only *in potentia.* For the same reason, *ṭebel* is treated as unconsecrated produce, rather than as *terumah,* regarding removes of uncleanness—the *terumah* does not come into being until it has been designated . . . .

To summarize: Mishnah's theory of holiness in *Seder Zera'im* is transactional rather than immanentist. Nothing (except perhaps for God) is inherently sacred. The Land of Israel is sanctified through its relationship to God. The produce of the Lord is sanctified by man, acting under God's commandment, through verbal designation and separation of the various offerings. Man, through his action and intention, additionally determines what is susceptible to sanctification (i.e., liable to tithing as human food), and the point at which it is susceptible (i.e., edible, at the point of completion of processing or harvesting, or the point of intention to make a fixed meal). Mishnah's primary concern in the tractates under investigation is that man should separate properly that which is due to God, so that non-priests will not inadvertently eat produce bonded to God or consecrated to him. Mishnah's authorities further wish to examine in detail man's role in the process of sanctification, and to specify the power of his will, word, and deed. ["Mishnah"]

This account of the main issues of the Division of Agriculture correlates with what we shall see when we turn to the succeeding Divisions.

The Division of Appointed Times after the Wars

The Mishnaic Division of Appointed Times forms a system in which the advent of a holy day, like the Sabbath of creation, sanctifies the life of the Israelite village through imposing on the village rules on the model of those of the Temple. The purpose of the system, therefore, is to bring into alignment the moment of sanctification of the village and the life of the home with the moment of sanctification of the Temple on those same occasions of appointed times. The underlying and generative theory of the system is that the village is the mirror image of the Temple. If things are done in one way in the Temple, they will be done in the opposite way in the village. Together the village and the Temple on the occasion of the holy day therefore form a single continuum, a completed creation, thus awaiting sanctification.

The village is made like the Temple in that on appointed times one may not freely cross the lines distinguishing the village from the rest of the world, just as one may not freely cross the lines distinguishing the Temple from the world. But the village is a mirror image of the Temple. The boundary lines prevent free entry into the Temple, so they restrict free egress from the village. On the holy day what one may do in the Temple is precisely what one may *not* do in the village. So the advent of the holy day affects the village by bringing it into sacred symmetry in such wise as to effect a system of opposites; each is holy, in a way precisely the opposite of the other. Because of the underlying conception of perfection attained through the union of opposites, the village is not represented as conforming to the model of the cult, but of constituting its antithesis.

The world thus regains perfection when on the holy day heaven and earth are united, the whole completed and done: the heaven, the earth, and all their hosts. This moment of perfection renders the events of ordinary time, of "history," essentially irrelevant. For what really matters in time is that moment in which sacred time intervenes and effects the perfection formed of the union of heaven and earth, of Temple, in the model of the former, and Israel, its complement. It is not a return to a perfect time but a recovery of perfect being, a fulfillment of creation, which explains the essentially ahistorical character of the Mishnah's Division on Appointed Times. Sanctification constitutes an ontological category and is effected by the creator.

This explains why the Division in its rich detail is composed of two quite distinct sets of materials. First, it addresses what one does in the sacred space of the Temple on the occasion of sacred time, as distinct from what one does in that same sacred space on ordinary, undifferentiated days, which is a subject worked out in Holy Things. Second, the Division defines how for the occasion of the holy day one creates a corresponding space in one's own circumstance, and what one does, within that space, during sacred time. The issue of the Temple and cult on the special occasion of festivals is treated in tractates Pesahim, Sheqalim, Yoma, Sukkah, and Hagigah. Three further tractates, Rosh Hashshanah, Taanit, and Megillah, are necessary to complete the discussion. The matter of the rigid definition of the outlines in the village, of a sacred space, delineated by the limits within which one may move on the Sabbath and festival, and of the specification of those things which one may and may not do within that space in sacred time, is specified in Shabbat, Erubin, Besah, and Moed Qatan.

While the twelve tractates of the Division appear to fall into two distinct groups, joined merely by a conmon theme, in fact they relate through a shared, generative metaphor. It is, as I said, the comparison, in the context of sacred time, of the spatial life of the Temple to the spatial life of the village, with activities and restrictions to be specified for each, upon the common occasion of the Sabbath or festival. The Mishnah's purpose therefore is to correlate the sanctity of the Temple, as defined by the holy day, with the restrictions of space and of action which make the life of the village different and holy, as defined by the holy day.

Appointed Times and the Village

Shabbat. General principles of Sabbath observance, with stress on the importance of avoiding situations which may produce violation of the laws of the Sabbath. What is to be done in preparation for the Sabbath in advance of the holy day: the lighting of the Sabbath light; the preparation of food for that day. The prohibition of transporting objects from private domain: clothing versus ornaments; minimum amounts of various substances which may not be transported across the Sabbath limit or from private to public domain. Other prohibited acts of labor. Further actions not to be done on the Sabbath: kindling a fire; merely handling objects which, in point of fact, may not be licitly utilized at all; circumcision on the Sabbath; preparation of food for humans and beasts on the Sabbath; seemly behavior in general.

Erubin. The delineation of a limited domain in which it is permitted to move about and to transport objects on the Sabbath: forming an alleyway into a single domain; forming an area occupied by a caravan into a single domain; creating a private domain around a well located in public domain; a large field. The *erub* (meal for commingling) and the Sabbath limit of a town: establishing a symbolic residence, other than one's home, for allowing a person to move two thousand cubits in one direction beyond one's normal limits, by setting a symbolic meal at the outer boundary of one's normally permitted range of movement. Violating the Sabbath limit; defining the normal Sabbath limit of a town, including extensions and outer areas. The *erub* and commingling ownership of a courtyard or an alleyway, permitting one to transport objects throughout the courtyard or alleyway; the *erub* as a symbolic common meal, joining the residents into a single household for the present purpose and so signifying common ownership of the alleyway or courtyard. The public domain in general, and carrying objects in and through the public domain on the Sabbath.

Besah. Preparing food on the festival day: doing deeds in that regard which are not essential for food preparation, but are tangential in the process; doing deeds in the way in which they are done on an ordinary day or doing them in some unusual way in recognition of the character of the holy day; designating food before the festival day for use on the festival day; other restrictions.

Moed Qatan. Conduct on the intermediate days of Passover and the Festival: labor in the fields; other acts of labor subject to restriction; cases of emergency and loss. Commercial activities. Burial of the dead and mourning on the intermediate days of a festival. In general: doing deeds in an ordinary way or doing them in some unusual way.

Appointed Times and the Cult

Pesahim. Preparation for Passover: removal of leaven from the household; avoidance of what is fermented; ceasing to work from the middle of the fourteenth of Nisan onward. The Passover offering: slaying and eating it; when the Passover offering is slaughtered. The special problems caused when the fourteenth of Nisan coincides with the Sabbath: doing only what cannot be done in advance, but preparing in advance so as to violate the Sabbath rules only when absolutely necessary. Roasting the Passover offering; uncleanness and the Passover offering; not breaking the bone of the Passover offering; eating the Passover offering in a household or other registered group. The second Passover. The Passover *seder*—a few rules.

Sheqalim. Collecting the *sheqel* in support of the public offerings of the

Temple and of the upkeep of the Temple building; transporting the *sheqel;* sacrilege and the *sheqel.* The use of the *sheqel* for Temple offerings for the altar; taking up the *sheqel* for the purchase of animals for public offerings; disposition of the *sheqel* for various offerings, daily whole offerings, additional offerings, drink offerings, wheat for the bread offerings; use of the surplus for wine, oil, fine flour, gold plate for decorating the house of the Holy of Holies, paying Temple employees. The Temple administration and procedures. Sale of the drink offering. Collecting other funds in the Temple. Disposing of coins and objects found in the Temple and in Jerusalem.

Yoma. The Temple rite on the Day of Atonement: preparing the high priest for his duties; clearing the ashes off the altar; the daily whole offering on the Day of Atonement; the high priest's personal offering. The two goats: the scapegoat and its rule. The sin offering for the priesthood, and the sin offering for the Temple. The conclusion of the sacrificial rite; the reading of the Torah and prayer. The laws of the Day of Atonement: not eating or drinking.

Sukkah. The appurtenances of the Festival: the *sukkah;* the *lulab.* The rites and offerings of the Festival: rites carried out on various days of Festival; the offerings on the Festival; the priestly courses and offerings on the eight days of the Festival.

Rosh Hashshanah. The designation of each new month through the year: receiving testimony that the new moon has appeared and declaring the advent of the new month. The horn *(shofar):* rules of the *shofar.* Liturgy for the New Year and sounding the *shofar* in that liturgy.

Taanit. Fasts called in order to bring rain: the sequences of fasts; liturgy of the community on a fast day; other rules about public fasts. Other uses of the *shofar* as an alarm. Israelite participation in the cult: the delegation *(ma'amad);* when the *ma'amad* says its prayer, the priests give a benediction four times in the day; definition of the delegation and its activities. Sad days in Israelite history.

Megillah. Laws of the reading of the Scroll of Esther. Laws of synagogue property and liturgy; the synagogal lections; proper conduct in the synagogue.

Hagigah. The appearance offering, festal offering, and peace offering of rejoicing, brought by ordinary folk on the festivals; liability; cost. The festal offering and the Sabbath: whether or not to lay on hands; whether or not to slaughter on the Sabbath a whole offering, which does not yield food for the sacrificer. At issue: whether one may do deeds only tangentially related to the preparation of food for the festival (as at M. Besah). Rules of uncleanness as they affect ordinary folk and holy things of the cult on festival days: ordinary folk are assumed to be in a state of cleanness on the festival. Consequences of that assumption.

This detailed outline shows how the Division of Appointed Times defines proper conduct both in the Temple and in the villages on the occasion of the Sabbath and festival, bringing into a single framework of definition the principles of permitted and forbidden conduct in both places. As we see clearly, the task is to establish the simile of the Temple for the village by raising high walls of restricted movement and behavior.

The Mishnah clearly has its notion of what is important about an occasion, "great day," "day of the Lord," or "holy day." In so far as it wishes to take up the meaning of "time," in the concrete framework in which the Mishnah carries on its discussion of any topic, it is in the present Division that the Mishnah makes its judgments. There are other ways in which philosophers of the same period as the Mishnah—the first and second centuries—formulate and work out the same general range of issues as are before us. To grasp the full weight and meaning of what the Mishnah chooses for its program of thought, we have to allude to the things the framers of the Mishnah, like others of their age, might have done, but clearly do not wish to do.

This is a very specific matter. The Mishnah does *not* propose an abstract essay on the nature of time, the meaning of history. It also does not draw the contrast between this age and the world to come, as we saw in Baruch and Ezra. This Division's framers do not reflect on any number of other mythic or philosophical conceptions which may be taken up and used to fill out with concrete substance the abstract conception of time. Indeed, when we consider the range of topics and themes—historical and messianic—available for inclusion in a Division devoted to the passage of seasons and sanctification of time, the festivals and, by extension, the meaning of this perpetual change and movement against the background of history, we must be astonished at the highly restricted agendum, cultic and ahistorical, laid forth by the Mishnah. The very conception of appointed time is allowed only one meaning. Unlike the recurrent emphasis of Deuteronomy, the Sabbath or festival is no longer a theme or topic available for referring to some moment in historical time, to something which happened to Israel. The theme does not speak of an occasion chosen and set forth long ago and now nearing realization—"next year at this time." Since "appointed time" may be used for diverse, one-time and deeply historical occasions, it is important to recognize what the Mishnah finds suitable or unsuitable as a reference. The Mishnah refers in Appointed Times solely to recurrent events, embedded in the regular lunar calendar, defined, in nature, by the movement of the seasons and the moon, and, in Scripture, in the main by the affairs of the cult. The festivals are important in the cult and its counterpart. What recurs is the perfection of creation through the reunion of opposites. That is what is expressed in the Mishnah's problems and laws.

When the Mishnah speaks of appointed times, it means not the end-time or the one-time fulfillment of time but recurrent Sabbaths and festivals, new moons and holy days. When the Mishnah asks what is to be done in response to those appointed times of nature and cult, it answers in terms of cooking and eating, working and resting, sleeping, celebrating, and rejoicing. The Mishnah's program for Sabbaths and festivals speaks not of a being other than the ordinary life of Israel, but of a heightened enjoyment of everyday pleasures. The reason is not a rejection of cosmic myth, such as Smith described (see above, pp. 29–31), but the compelling presence of a different myth of being. The Mishnah does not contemplate some age other than the present one. When it speaks of time, it does not mean history at all. (Indeed, in the Division of Damages the Mishnah finds it possible to design a complete political system without once referring to historical reality or making provision at any point whatsoever for time and for change.) The framers of the document, moreover, so lay out matters that the sole provision in the village is for comfort and relaxation. If there is interest in that realm of power and force in which the mythological cosmic drama is played out, that heightened reality of mythic being realized in the holy time of Sabbaths and festivals is not permitted to come to expression at all in the Mishnah's restrictive terms. The reason for the Mishnah's worldliness is its otherworldly conception of the this worldly life of Israel. What corresponds to heaven and complements heaven is heaven's projection onto earth, the Israelites in their villages. Here we have a different cosmic myth, which speaks of different things to different people.

The Division of Women after the Wars

The Mishnaic system of Women defines the position of women in the social economy of Israel's supernatural and natural reality. That position acquires definition wholly in relationship to men, who impart form to the Israelite social economy. It is effected through both supernatural and natural, this-worldly action. What man and woman do on earth provokes a response in heaven, and the correspondences are perfect. So the position of women is defined and secured both in heaven and here on earth, and that position is always and invariably relative to men.

The principal interest for the Mishnah is the point at which a woman becomes, and ceases to be, holy to a particular man, that is, enters and leaves the marital union. These transfers of women are the dangerous and disorderly points in the relationship of woman to man, therefore, as I said, to society as well. Five of the seven tractates of the Division of Women are devoted to the formation and dissolution of the marital bond. Of them, three treat what is done by man here on earth, that is, formation of a marital bond through betrothal and marriage contract and dissolution through divorce and its consequences: Qiddushin, Ketubot, and Gittin. One of them is devoted to what is done by woman here on earth: Sotah. And Yebamot, greatest of the seven in size and in formal and substantive brilliance, deals with the corresponding heavenly intervention into the formation and end of a marriage: the effect of death upon both forming the marital bond and dissolving it through death. The other two tractates, Nedarim and Nazir, draw into one the two realms of reality, heaven and earth, as they work out the effects of vows, perhaps because vows taken by women and subject to the confirmation or abrogation of the father or husband make a deep impact upon the marital life of the woman who has taken them. So, in sum, the Division and its system delineate the natural and supernatural character of the woman's role in the social economy framed by man: the beginning, end, and middle of the relationship.

The Mishnaic system of Women thus focuses upon the two crucial stages in the transfer of women and of property from one domain to another, the leaving of the father's house in the formation of a marriage, and the return to the father's house at its dissolution through divorce or the husband's death. There is yet a third point of interest, though, as is clear, it is much less important than these first two stages: the duration of the marriage. Finally, included within the Division and at a few points relevant to women in particular are rules of vows and of the special vow to be a Nazir. The former is included because, in the Scriptural treatment of the theme, the rights of the father or husband to annul the vows of a daughter or wife form the central problematic. The latter is included for no very clear reason except that it is a species of which the vow is the genus.

There is in the Division of Women a clearly defined and neatly conceived system of laws, not about women in general, but concerning what is important about women to the framers of the Mishnah. This is the transfer of women and property associated with that same transfer from one domain, the father's, to another, the husband's, and back. The whole constitutes a significant part of the Mishnah's encompassing system of sanctification, for the reason that heaven confirms what men do on earth. A correctly prepared writ of divorce on earth changes the status of the woman to whom it is given, so that in heaven she is available for sanctification to some other man, while, without that same writ, in heaven's view, should she go to some other man, she would be liable to be put to death. The earthly deed and the heavenly perspective correlate. That is indeed very much part of a larger system, which says the same thing over and over again.

The formation of the marriage comes under discussion in Qiddushin and Ketubot, as well as in Yebamot. The rules for the duration of the marriage are scattered throughout, but derive especially from parts of Ketubot, Nedarim, and Nazir, on the one side, and the paramount unit of Sotah, on the other. The dissolution of the marriage is dealt with in Gittin, as well as in Yebamot. We see very clearly, therefore, that important overall are issues of the transfer of property, along with women, covered in Ketubot and to some measure in Qiddushin, and the proper documentation of the transfer of women and property, treated in Ketubot and Gittin. The critical issues therefore turn upon legal documents—writs of divorce, for example—and legal recognition of changes in the ownership of property, e.g., through the collection of the settlement of a marriage contract by a widow, through the provision of a dowry, or through the disposition of the property of a woman during the period in which she is married. Within this orderly world of documentary and procedural concerns a place is made for the disorderly conception of the marriage not formed by human volition but decreed in heaven, the levirate connection. Yebamot states that supernature sanctifies a woman to a man (under the conditions of the levirate connection). What it says by indirection is that man sanctifies too: man, like God, can sanctify that relationship between a man and a woman, and can also effect the cessation of the sanctity of that same relationship.

To the message and the purpose of the system of Women, woman is essential and central. But she is not critical. She sets the stage for the processes of the sacred. It is she who can be made sacred to man. It is she who ceases to stand within a man's sacred circle. But God and man, the latter through the documentary expression of his will and intention, possess the active power of sanctification. Like the holy Land of Agriculture, the holy Temple of Holy Things, and the potentially holy realm of the clean of Purities, women for the Division of Women define a principal part of the Mishnah's orderly conception of reality. Women form a chief component of the six-part realm of the sacred. It is, as I said, their position in the social economy of the Israelite reality, natural and supernatural, which is the subject of the Division and its tractates. But the whole—the six-part realm— is always important in *relationship* to man on earth and God in

Heaven. Man and God effect the transaction. Sanctification is effected through process and through relationship. The center of logical tension is at critical relationships. The problematic of the subject is generated at the critical points of the relationship. The relationship—that is, the process or transaction—is what makes holy or marks as profane. God and man shape that process. Food grown from the earth, woman, cult, and the cultlike realm of the clean—these foci of the sacred form that inert matter made holy or marked as profane by the will and deed of God and of man, who is like God. Let us now consider the seven tractates of the Division of Women and rapidly survey their principal topics.

The Beginning of a Marriage

Qiddushin. Rules of acquisition of a woman in betrothal. Procedures of betrothal: agency; the token of betrothal; stipulations. Impaired betrothals. Stipulations, doubts in matters of betrothal. Appropriate candidates for betrothal; castes and outcastes; the status of the offspring of impaired marriages; castes and marriage among castes; miscellanies and homilies.

Ketubot. The material rights of the parties to the marital union; the wife; the father; the husband; conflicting claims. Fines paid to the father in the case of rape or seduction; the father's material rights; the husband's material rights. Rules for the duration of the marriage; the wife's duties to the husband; the husband's marital rights and duties; the dowry; property rights of the wife while she is married. Settlement of the marriage contract in the event of the husband's death; multiple claims on an estate; the support of the widow.

The Duration of a Marriage

Nedarim. The language of vows: euphemisms; language of no effect or of limited effect. The binding effects of vows: not to derive benefit in general; not to eat some specific kind of food in particular; not to use certain objects; temporal application of vows. The absolution of vows: grounds for absolution; annulling the vows of a daughter and of a wife; the husband's power to annul the wife's vows; vows of a woman who is not subject to abrogation.

Nazir. Becoming a Nazir, with special reference to the vow: the language of the vow; stipulations; the duration of the vow; annulling the Nazirite vow. The offerings required of the Nazir: designation and disposition. Prohibitions on the Nazir: the grape; contracting corpse uncleanness; cutting the hair.

Sotah. Invoking the ordeal of the bitter water. Narrative of the ordeal and its conduct. Rules of the ordeal: exemptions and applicability; testimony. Rites conducted in Hebrew; the annointed for battle and the draft exemptions; the rite of the heifer and the neglected corpse.

The End of a Marriage

Yebamot. The levirate connection is null in a case of consanguinity; *ḥaliṣah* but no levirate marriage; a normal levirate connection, worked out through *ḥaliṣah* or consummation of the marriage. Marriage into the priesthood and the right to eat heave offering. Severing the marital bond: marital ties subject to doubt; the rite of *ḥaliṣah;* the right of refusal; infirm marital bonds—the deaf-mute, the minor male. Severing the marital bond through death of the husband: the woman's testimony; identifying a corpse.

Gittin. Delivering a writ of divorce; preparing a writ of divorce. Irrelevant constructions: (1) confirming the prevailing supposition; (2) fifteen rulings make for the good order of society. The law of agency in writs of divorce: receiving the writ; appointing an agent to prepare and deliver a writ of divorce. Stipulations in writs of divorce. Invalid and impaired writs of divorce: improper delivery; improper preparation; improper stipulations; improper witnesses; grounds for divorce.

We see in this detailed account of the Division's repertoire of themes that we have an encompassing account of the formation, duration, and dissolution of marriages. The topic is worked out in a fairly systematic and orderly way.

From the Mishnah's perspective, women are abnormal; men are normal. The reason the framers of the Mishnah choose to work out a Division on women flows from that fact. Women are something out of the ordinary. That is why they form a focus of sanctification: restoration of the extraordinary to the ordinary and the normal. The Mishnah cannot declare a dead creeping thing clean. The Mishnah cannot make women into men. It can provide for the purification of what is made unclean. It can provide for a world in which it is normal for woman to be subject to man, father or husband, and a system which regularizes the transfer of women from the hand of the father to that of the husband. The regulation of the transfer of women is the Mishnah's way of effecting the sanctification of what, for the moment, disturbs and disorders the orderly world. The work of sanctification becomes necessary in particular at the point of danger and disorder. An order of women must be devoted, therefore, to just these things, so as to preserve the normal modes of creation ("how these things really are").

Maleness, that is, normality, thus may encompass all, even and especially at the critical point of transfer.

In this connection the process outlined, as we shall see, in the Division of Purities for the restoration of normality, meaning of cleanness, to what is abnormal, meaning uncleanness, is suggestive. What the Mishnah proposes is to restore the equilibrium disturbed by the encounter with the disruptive, disorganizing, and abnormal sources of uncleanness specified in the priestly writings. So the Division of Purities centers attention on the point of abnormality and its restoration to normality: sources of uncleanness, foci of uncleanness, modes of purification. Now, when we reflect on the view of women contained in the Mishnah, we observe a parallel interest in the point of abnormality and the restoration to normality of women: the moment at which a woman changes hands.

About woman as wife the Mishnah has little to say; about woman as mother, I cannot think of ten relevant lines in the Mishnah's Division of Woman. For these are not the topics to which the Mishnah will devote itself.The three systemically anomalous tractates from this perspective are not so far out of line. Sotah, of course, attends to the wife who is not a good wife. Nedarim, bearing Nazir in its wake, treats those moments specified by Scripture as especially important in the daughter's relationship to the father or the wife's to the husband. These are moments at which the father or the husband may intervene in the relationship of daughter or wife to God. In the present context, the relationship is unruly and dangerous, exactly like the relationship of daughter leaving father or of wife leaving husband, that is, at the critical moment of betrothal and consummation of the marriage, with attendant property settlement; or divorce or husband's death, at the critical moment of the dissolution of the marriage, with attendant property settlement.

An anomaly for the Mishnah is a situation requiring human intervention so that affairs may be brought into stasis, that is, made to conform with the heavenly projections of the created world. That quest for stasis, order, and regulation, which constitute wholeness and completeness, in the Division of Women leads the Mishnah to take up yet another circumstance of uncertainty. This it confronts at its most uncertain; just as the Division of Agriculture treats crops neither holy nor secular, so the system subjects the anomaly of woman to the capacity for ordering and regulating which is the gift and skill of priests and scribes.

The anomaly of woman therefore is addressed at its most anomalous. Yet the very essence of the anomaly, woman's sexuality, is scarcely mentioned. But it always is just beneath the surface. For what defines the woman's status—what is rarely made explicit in the Division of

Women—is not whether or not she may have sexual relations, but with whom she may have them and with what consequence. It is assumed that, from long before the advent of puberty, a girl may be married and in any event is a candidate for sexuality. From puberty onward she will be married. But what is selected for intense and continuing concern is with whom she may legitimately marry, and with what economic and social effect. There is no sexual deed without public consequence; and only rarely will a sexual deed not yield economic results, in the transfer of property from one hand to another. So, as I said, what is anomalous is the woman's sexuality, which is treated in a way wholly different from man's. And the goal and purpose of the Mishnah's Division of Women are to bring under control and force into stasis all of the wild and unruly potentialities of sexuality, with their dreadful threat of uncontrolled shifts in personal status and material possession alike.

The Mishnah thus invokes heaven's interest in the most critical moment—whether Appointed Times or harvest time or hymeneal season—for individual and society alike. Its conception is that what is rightly done on earth is confirmed in heaven. A married woman who has sexual relations with any man but her husband has not merely committed a crime on earth. She has sinned against heaven. It follows that when a married woman receives a writ of divorce and so is free to enter into relationships with any man of her choosing, heaven's perceptions of that woman are affected just as much as are those of man on earth. What was beforehand a crime and a sin afterward is holy. The woman may contract a new marriage on earth which heaven, for its part, will oversee and sanctify. What is stated in these simple propositions is that those crucial and critical turnings at which a woman changes hands produce concern and response in heaven above as much as on earth below. And the reason, as I suggested at the beginning, is that heaven is invoked specifically at those times, and in those circumstances, in which Mishnah confronts a situation of anomaly, changes or disorder and proposes to effect suitable regulation and besought order.

The Division of Damages after the Wars

The Division of Damages comprises two subsystems, which fit together in a logical way. One part presents rules for the normal conduct of civil society. These cover commerce, trade, real estate, and other matters of everyday intercourse, as well as mishaps, such as damages by chattels and persons, fraud, overcharge, interest, and the like, in that same context of everyday social life. The other part describes the institutions governing the normal conduct of civil society, that is, courts of administration, and the penalties at the disposal of the government for the enforcement of the law. The two subjects form a single tight and systematic dissertation on the nature of Israelite society and its economic, social, and political relationships, as the Mishnah envisages them.

The main point of the first of the two parts of the Division is expressed in the sustained unfolding of the three Babas, Baba Qamma, Baba Mesia, and Baba Batra. It is that the task of society is to maintain perfect stasis, to preserve the prevailing situation, and to secure the stability of all relationships. To this end, in the interchanges of buying and selling, giving and taking, borrowing and lending, it is important that there be an essential equality of exchange. No party in the end should have more than what he had at the outset, and none should be the victim of a sizable shift in fortune and circumstance. All parties' rights to, and in, this stable and unchanging economy of society are to be preserved. When the condition of a person is violated, so far as possible the law will secure the restoration of the antecedent status.

An appropriate appendix to the Babas is at Abodah Zarah, which deals wtih the orderly governance of transactions and relationships between Israelite society and the outside world, the realm of idolatry, relationships which are subject to certain special considerations. These are generated by the fact that Israelites may not derive benefit (e.g., through commercial transactions) from anything which has served in the worship of an idol. Consequently, commercial transactions suffer limitations on account of extrinsic considerations of cultic taboos. While these cover both special occasions, e.g., fairs and festivals of idolatry, and general matters, that is, what Israelites may buy and sell, the main practical illustrations of the principles of the matter pertain to wine. The Mishnah supposes that gentiles routinely make use, for a libation, of a drop of any sort of wine to which they have access. It therefore is taken for granted that wine over which gentiles have had control is forbidden for Israelite use, and also that such wine is prohibited for Israelites to buy and sell. This other matter—ordinary everyday relationships with the gentile world, with special reference to trade and commerce—concludes what the Mishnah has to say about all those matters of civil and criminal law which together define everyday relationships within the Israelite nation and between that nation and all others in the world among whom, in Palestine as abroad, they lived side by side.

The other part of the Division describes the institutions of Israelite government and politics. This is in two main aspects, first, the description of the institutions and their jurisdiction, with reference to courts, conceived as both judicial and administrative agencies, and, second, the extensive discussion of criminal penalties. The penalties are three: death, banishment, and flogging. There are four ways by which a person convicted of a capital crime may be put to death. The Mishnah organizes a vast amount of information on what sorts of capital crimes are punishable by which of the four modes of execution. That information is alleged to derive from Scripture. But the facts are many, and the relevant verses few. What the Mishnah clearly contributes to this exercise is a first-rate piece of organization and elucidation of available facts. Where the facts come from we do not know. The Mishnah tractate Sanhedrin further describes the way in which trials are conducted in both monetary and capital cases and pays attention to the possibilities of perjury. The matter of banishment brings the Mishnah to a rather routine restatement by flogging and application of that mode of punishment conclude the discussion.

These matters, worked out at Sanhedrin-Makkot, are supplemented in two tractates, Shebuot and Horayot, both emerging from Scripture. Lev. 5 and 6 refer to various oaths which apply mainly, though not exclusively, in courts. Lev. 4 deals with errors of judgment inadvertently made and carried out by the high priest, the ruler, and the people; the Mishnah knows that these considerations apply to Israelite courts too. What for Leviticus draws the chapters together is their common interest in the guilt offering, which is owing for violation of the rather diverse matters under discussion. Now in tractates Shebuot and Horayot the materials of Lev. 5–6 and 4, respectively, are worked out. But here it is from the viewpoint of the oath or erroneous instruction, rather than the cultic penalty. In Shebuot the discussion is intellectually imaginative and thorough, in Horayot, routine. The relevance of both to the issues of Sanhedrin and Makkot is obvious. For the matter of oaths in the main enriches the discussion of the conduct of the courts. The possibility of error is principally in the courts and other political institutions. So the four tractates on institutions and their functioning form a remarkably unified and cogent set.

Let us now turn to the full account of what is to be expected in the eight usable tractates of the Division. We ignore two miscellaneous ones, Abot and Eduyyot, tacked on but essentially outside of the framework of the Division of Damages (or any other Division of the Mishnah).

The Rules of Civil Society

Baba Qamma. Damages by chattels: assessing damages when the cause is one's property, animate or inanimate, the ox in particular; damages done in the public domain by the ox in particular; the ransom and death penalty for the ox; damages done by the pit, crop-destroying beast, and fire. Damages done by persons: theft; twofold, fourfold, and fivefold restitution in the case of theft; penalties for damages done to property; restitution of stolen goods.

Baba Mesia. The disposition of other people's possessions, with special reference to restoration of what someone has lost: conflicting claims on lost objects; returning an object to the original owner; rules of bailment in the case of conflicting claims. Commercial transactions of an illicit character: overcharge and misrepresentation; true value and fraud; usury and trading in futures; subterranean forms of usury. Licit commercial transactions: hiring workers; rentals and bailments; the mutual obligations of worker and employer; rentals; bailments. Licit transactions in real estate: landlord-tenant relationships; the landlord's relationships with a tenant farmer and sharecropper. Miscellanies: paying workers promptly; taking a pledge for a loan; jointholders of a common property and their reciprocal obligations and rights.

Baba Batra. Real estate: the mutual responsibilities and rights of jointholders of a common property (continued from Baba Mesia); not infringing upon the property rights of others; establishing title to a field through usucaption; transferring real estate and movables through sale (as distinct from usucaption). Licit commercial transactions: conditions of the irrevocable transfer of movables; unstated stipulations in commercial transactions. Inheritances and wills; other commercial and legal documents; the preparation and confirmation of commercial documents, writs of debt, and the like.

Abodah Zarah. Commercial relationships with gentiles; prohibitions precipitated by the advent of a gentile fair or festival; goods of gentiles prohibited even in ordinary commerce; goods prohibited for Israelite use but permitted in ordinary commerce. Idols: general principles; the *asherah; Merkolis* (Hermes); nullifying an idol. The prohibition of use and of commerce applying to libation wine, that is, to all wine of gentiles.

The Institutions of Civil Society

Sanhedrin. The Israelite court system: various kinds of courts and their jurisdictions; the court of three judges and commercial transactions; the court of twenty-three and criminal procedures; the court of seventy-one and political decisions; the heads of the Israelite nation and the court system—king and high priest; property cases—choosing the judges, examining the witnesses, making a decision; capital cases—the differences from property cases; the layout of the sanhedrin; examining the witnesses; making a decision. The death penalty: the four modes of execution and how they are administered—stoning, burning, decapitation, and strangulation; those liable to death through the four modes of execution, respectively.

Makkot. Perjury: how witnesses are penalized for perjury, e.g., flogging and receiving the penalty they planned to inflict on the accused. The penalty of banishment: those who are sent into exile; the cities of exile. Flogging: those who are flogged; the manner of flogging.

Shebuot. The considerations of Lev. 5: Uncleanness of the cult and its holy things and the guilt offering. Oaths: oaths in general; the rash oath; the vain oath; the oath of testimony; the oath of bailment; the oath imposed by the judges for use in trials. Oaths and bailments: a concluding conundrum.

Horayot. The offering brought because of an erroneous decision, inadvertently made by a court and inadvertently carried out by the community. The offering brought by the high priest who has unwittingly done what is contrary to the commandments of the Torah. That brought by the ruler under similar circumstances. Individual, anointed priest, community: the penalties thereof.

The goal of the system of civil law is the recovery of the prevailing order and balance, the preservation of the established wholeness of the social economy. This idea is powerfully expressed in the organization of the three Babas, which, as we shall see, treat first abnormal and then normal transactions. The framers deal with damages done by chattels and by human beings, thefts and other sorts of malfeasance against the property of others. The Babas in both aspects pay closest attention to how the property and person of the injured party so far as possible are restored to their prior condition, that is, a state of normality. So attention to torts focuses upon penalties paid by the malefactor to the victim, rather than upon penalties inflicted by the court on the malefactor for what he has done. When speaking of damages, the Mishnah thus takes as its principal concern the restoration of the fortune of victims of assault or robbery. Then the framers take up the complementary and corresponding set of topics, the regulation of normal transactions. When we rapidly survey the kinds of transactions of special interest, we see from the topics selected for discussion what we have already uncovered in the deepest structure of organization and articulation of the basic theme.

The other half of this same unit of three tractates presents laws governing normal and routine transactions, many of them of the same sort as those dealt with in the first half. Bailments, for example, occur in both wings of the triple tractate, first, bailments subjected to misappropriation, or accusation thereof, by the bailiff, then, bailments transacted under normal circumstances. Under the rubric of routine transactions are those of workers and householders, that is, the purchase and sale of labor; rentals and bailments; real estate transactions; and inheritances and estates. Of the lot, the one involving real estate transactions is the most fully articulated and covers the widest range of problems and topics. The Babas all together thus provide a complete account of the orderly governance of balanced transactions and unchanging civil relationships within Israelite society under ordinary conditions.

The character and interests of the Division of Damages present probative evidence of the larger program of the philosophers of the Mishnah. Their intention is to create nothing less than a full-scale Israelite government, subject to the administration of sages. This government is fully supplied with a constitution and bylaws (Sanhedrin, Makkot). It makes provision for a court system and procedures (Shebuot, Sanhedrin, Makkot), as well as a full set of laws governing civil society (Baba Qamma, Baba Mesia, Baba Batra) and criminal justice (Sanhedrin, Makkot). This government, moreover, mediates between its own community and the outside ("pagan") world. Through its system of laws it expresses its judgment of the others and at the same time defines, protects, and defends its own society and social frontiers (Abodah Zarah). It even makes provision for procedures of remission, to expiate its own errors (Horayot).

The (then-nonexistent) Israelite government imagined by the second-century philosophers centers upon the (then-nonexistent) Temple, and the (then-forbidden) city, Jerusalem. For the Temple is one principal focus. There the highest court is in session; there the high priest reigns. The penalties for law infringement are of three kinds, one of which involves sacrifice in the Temple. (The others are compensation, physical punishment, and death.) The basic conception of punishment, moreover, is that unintentional infringement of the rules of society, whether "religious" or otherwise, is not penalized but rather expiated through an offering in the Temple. If a member of the people of Israel intentionally infringes against the law, to be sure, that one must be removed from society and is put to death. And if there is a claim of one member of the people against another, that must be righted, so that the prior, prevailing status may be restored. So offerings in the Temple are given up to appease heaven and restore a whole bond between heaven and Israel, specifically on those occasions on which without malice or ill will an Israelite has disturbed the relationship. Israelite civil society without a Temple is not stable or normal, and not to be imagined. And the Mishnah is above all an act of imagination in defiance of reality.

The plan for the government involves a clear-cut philosophy of society, a philosophy which defines the purpose of the government and ensures that its task is not merely to perpetuate its own power. What the Israelite government, within the Mishnaic fantasy, is supposed to do is to preserve that state of perfection which, within the same fantasy, the society to begin everywhere attains and expresses. This is in at least five aspects. First of all, one of the ongoing principles of the law, expressed in one tractate after another, is that people are to follow and maintain the prevailing practice of their locale. Second, the purpose of civil penalties, as we have noted, is to restore the injured party to his prior condition, so far as this is possible, rather than merely to penalize the aggressor. Third, there is the conception of true value, meaning that a given object has an intrinsic worth, which, in the course of a transaction, must be paid. In this way the seller does not leave the transaction any richer than when he entered it, or the buyer any poorer (parallel to penalties for damages). Fourth, there can be no usury, a biblical prohibition adopted and vastly enriched in the Mishnaic thought, for money ("coins") is what it is. Any pretense that it has become more than what it was violates, in its way, the conception of true value. Fifth, when real estate is divided, it must be done with full attention to the rights of all concerned, so that, once more, one party does not gain at the expense of the other. In these and many other aspects the law expresses its obsession with the perfect stasis of Israelite society. Its paramount purpose is in preserving and ensuring that that perfection of the division of this world is kept inviolate or restored to its true status when violated.

The Mishnah's problems are the problems of the landowner, the householder, the division's basic and recurrent subject for nearly all predicates. The Mishnah's sense of what is just and fair expresses his sense of the givenness and cosmic rightness of the present condition of society. Earth matches heaven. The Mishnah's hope for heaven and its claim on earth, to earth, corresponding to the supernatural basis for the natural world, bespeak the imagination of the surviving Israelite landowners of the mid-second-century Land of Israel. These are people deeply tired of war and its dislocation, profoundly distrustful of messiahs and their dangerous promises. They are men of substance and means, however modest, aching for a stable and predictable world in which to tend their crops and herds, feed their families and workers, keep to the natural rhythms of the seasons and the lunar cycles, and, in sum, live out their lives within strong and secure boundaries, on earth and in heaven.

That is why the sense of landed place and its limits, the sharp lines drawn between village and world, between Israelite and world, and between Temple and world evoke metaphysical correspondences which we also notice in their full expression in the Division of Appointed Times. Israel, Temple, village form a trilogy, in perfect correspondence, a deep communion. The Mishnah's deepest boundaries are locative, not utopian. These are to be preserved and defended in all of their existent, fully realized perfection. Change above all is a threat to stability and thus to perfection, to the continuity of this world of perfect correspondences between heaven and earth.

The Division of Holy Things after the Wars

The Division of Holy Things presents a system of sacrifice and sanctuary: matters concerning the praxis of the altar and maintenance of the sanctuary. The praxis of the altar, specifically, involves sacrifice and things set aside for sacrifice and so deemed consecrated. The topic covers these among the eleven tractates of the present Division: Zebahim and part of Hullin, Menahot, Temurah, Keritot, part of Meilah, Tamid, and Qinnim. The maintenance of the sanctuary (inclusive of the personnel) is dealt with in Bekhorot, Arakhin, part of Meilah, Middot, and part of Hullin.

The Everyday Conduct of the Sacrificial Cult

Zebahim. The effect of attitude or intention upon the act of killing a designated (sanctified) beast or bird; rules for the offering up of the slaughtered beast or bird; the conduct of the altar.

Menahot. The effect of attitude or intention upon the taking of a handful of meal offering and offering it up; rules for the offering up of meal offerings; vows and meal offerings.

Hullin. Rules of slaughter of animals for use in the cult or at home: how an animal is killed; whether or not an animal is fit for Israelite consumption and for the altar. Application of scriptural rules about gifts to the priest: first fleece; priestly gifts of shoulder, two cheeks, and maw of animals slaughtered for secular purposes. Application of rules about preparation of food at home or in the cult: milk and meat; covering up the blood; prohibition of the sinew of the hip. Application of rules about what may be suitably eaten or offered: prohibition of taking the dam and the eggs; prohibition of slaughtering on the same day the dam and the young.

Keritot. Liability to sin offerings; liability to guilt offerings (Lev. 5:17–19); the possibility of liability to more than a single sin or guilt offering in the commission of a single act; a single sin offering multiple sins.

Tamid. The daily whole offering and how it is offered up. A narrative.

Qinnim. A set of fantastic conundrums on procedure at the altar when diverse sets of bird offerings are confused with one another.

*Rules for Providing Animals for the Daily Sacrifices
and for the Upkeep of the Altar and the Temple Buildings,
and Support of the Priestly Staff*

Bekhorot. Firstborn of animals which are either offered up or redeemed, with the priest receiving the benefit of the animal either way. Slaughtering a blemished firstling for the benefit of the priest: definition of blemishes; examination thereof. Firstborn sons, redeemed through gift of five *selas* to the priest. Tithe of cattle.

Arakhin. Valuations and vows for the benefit of the Temple and the altar (Lev. 27:1–8); the dedication and redemption of a field received as an inheritance; the devoted thing.

Temurah. A beast designated as a substitute for one already consecrated enters the status of that consecrated beast, but the latter remains holy (Lev. 27:9–10): the rules of substitution. The status of the offspring of substitutes. The language used in effecting an act of substitution.

Meilah. The definition of the sacrilege to which Scripture (Lev. 5:14–16) refers, with specific reference to what itself is consecrated for the altar and what in its value is consecrated; when laws of sacrifice cease to apply, but other taboos commence to apply; sacrilege against Temple property in general.

Middot. The layout of the Temple, a descriptive narrative.

Viewed from a distance, therefore, the Mishnah's tractates divide themselves up into the following groups (in parentheses are tractates containing relevant materials): (1) Rules for the altar and the praxis of the cult—Zebahim Menahot, Hullin, Keritot, Tamid, Qinnim (Bekhorot, Meilah); (2) Rules for the altar and the animals set aside for the cult—Arakhin, Temurah, Meilah (Bekhorot); and (3) Rules for the altar and support of the Temple staff and buildings—Bekhorot, Middot (Hullin, Arakhin, Meilah, Tamid). In a word, this Division speaks of the sacrificial cult and the sanctuary in which the cult is conducted. The law pays special attention to the matter of the status of the property of the altar and of the sanctuary, both materials to be utilized in the actual sacrificial rites, and property the value of which supports the cult and sanctuary in general. Both are deemed to be sanctified, that is: *qodoshim*, "holy things."

The basis of exclusion now is clear. Our Division prefers not to deal with the special offerings (e.g., those designated for particular days of the week or seasons of the year), which are treated in Appointed Times; with other than animal fees for the priesthood, specifically omitting reference to agricultural dues paid over in their support, dealt with in Agriculture; or with that matrix of cleanness in which the cult is to be carried on, expounded in Purities. Those three areas of the law pertinent to the cult will at best only be alluded to here.

The inclusive principle and interests, upon closer examination, prove to be equally clear-cut and carefully defined. The matter consists of much less than everything relevant to "cult." There are decisive and pointed choices. By "holy things" we refer specifically to the altar and animals and cereals offered on the altar or belonging to the altar, and to property and goods belonging to the altar or to the sanctuary. Within these two categories we find a place for the whole of the thematic repertoire of the Fifth Division or, at the very least, account for the inclusion of each and every one of its significant topics. The Division is content to leave over for use in other Divisions materials pertinent to the alter and the sanctuary.

The system of Holy Things centers upon the everyday and rules always applicable to the cult: the daily whole offering, the sin offering and guilt offering which one may bring any time under ordinary circumstances; the right sequence of diverse offerings; the way in which the rites of the whole, sin, and guilt offerings are carried out; what sorts of animals are acceptable; the accompanying cereal offerings; the support and provision of animals for the cult and of meat for the priesthood; the support and material maintenance of the cult and its building. We have a system before us: the system of the cult of the Jerusalem Temple, seen as an ordinary and everyday affair, a continuing and routine operation. That is why special rules for the cult, both in respect to the altar and in regard to the maintenance of the buildings, personnel, and even the holy city, will be elsewhere—in Appointed Times and Agriculture. But from the perspective of Holy Things, those Divisions intersect by supplying special rules and raising extraordinary (Agriculture: land-bound; Appointed Times: time-bound) considerations for that theme which Holy Things claims to set forth in its most general and unexceptional way: the cult as something permanent and everyday.

The order of Holy Things thus in a concrete way maps out the cosmology of the sanctuary and its sacrificial system, that is, the world of the Temple, which had been the cosmic center of Israelite life. A later saying states matters as follows: "Just as the navel is found at the center of a human being, so the land of Israel is found at the center of the world . . . and it is the foundation of the world. Jerusalem is at the center of the land of Israel, the Temple is at the center of Jerusalem, the Holy of Holies is at the center of the Temple, the Ark is at the center of the Holy of Holies, and the Foundation Stone is in front of the Ark, which spot is the foundation of the world." (Tanhuma Qedoshim 10, in Hertzberg, p. 143).

The Division of Purities after the Wars

The Division of Purities presents a very simply system of three principal parts: sources of uncleanness, objects and substances susceptible to uncleanness, and modes of purification from uncleanness. So it tells the story of what makes what unclean and what makes it clean. The tractates on these several topics are as follows: (1) Sources of uncleanness—Ohalot, Negaim, Niddah, Makhshirin, Zabim, Tebul Yom; (2) Objects and substances susceptible to uncleanness—Kelim, Tohorot, Uqsin; and (3) Modes of purification—Parah, Miqvaot, Yadayim.

Viewed as a whole, the Division of Purities treats the interplay of persons, food, and liquids. Dry inanimate objects or food are not susceptible to uncleanness. What is wet is susceptible. So liquids activate the system. What is unclean, moreover, emerges from uncleanness through the operation of liquids, specifically, through immersion in fit water of requisite volume and in natural condition. Liquids thus deactivate the system. Thus, water in its *natural* condition is what concludes the process by removing uncleanness. Water in its *unnatural* condition, that is, deliberately affected by human agency, is what imparts susceptibility to uncleanness to begin with. The uncleanness of persons, furthermore, is signified by body liquids or flux in the case of the menstruating woman (Niddah) and the *zab* (Zabim). Corpse uncleanness is conceived to be a kind of effluent, a viscous gas, which flows like a liquid. Utensils for their part receive uncleanness when they form receptacles able to contain liquid. In sum, we have a system in which the invisible flow of fluidlike substances or powers serves to put food, drink, and receptacles into the status of uncleanness and to remove those things from that status. Whether or not we call the system "metaphysical," it certainly has no material base but is conditioned upon highly abstract notions. Thus in material terms, the effect of liquid is upon food, drink, utensils; and man. The consequence has to do with who may eat and drink what food and liquid, and what

food and drink may be consumed in which pots and pans. These loci
are specified by tractates on utensils (Kelim) and on food and drink
(Tohorot and Uqsin).

The human being is ambivalent. That is to say, persons fall in the
middle, between sources and loci of uncleanness. They are both: they
serve as sources of uncleanness; they also become unclean. The *zab,*
the menstruating woman, the woman after childbirth, the *tebul yom,* and
the person afflicted with *nega'*—all are sources of uncleanness. But
being unclean, they fall within the system's loci, its program of consequences. So they make other things unclean and are subject to penalties because they *are* unclean. Unambiguous sources of uncleanness
never also constitute loci affected by uncleanness. They always are
unclean and never can become clean: the corpse, the dead creeping
thing, and things like them. Inanimate sources of uncleanness and inanimate objects are affected by uncleanness. Systemically unique,
man and liquids have the capacity to inaugurate the processes of uncleanness (as sources) and also are subject to those same processes (as
objects of uncleanness).

The Division of Purities, which presents the basically simple system
just now described, is not only the oldest in the Mishnah. It also is the
largest and contains by far the most complex laws and ideas. A mere
survey of the topics of the Division, such as I have offered for the
tractates of the preceding Divisions, will not suffice. If not explained
and given explication, the topics will prove inaccessible to readers,
therefore useless for a picture of the whole of the Mishnah's system.
Hence I shall devote somewhat more effort to the explanation of the
tractates and their themes than I have had to up to now.

Sources of Uncleanness

Ohalot. Tractate Ohalot is to be dealt with in two parts, its treatment of
sources of uncleanness and modes of their transfer, and its interest in
the theory of the tent.

The former segment develops the notion that things which are like a
principal source of uncleanness impart uncleanness as does that to
which they are likened. The definition of things which contaminate as
do corpses can go on indefinitely, since the potential for analogy is
unlimited. The matter of modes of the transfer of uncleanness is curiously undeveloped even in the completed tractate and does not take an
important place in the tractate as a whole; in point of fact, the sole really
fresh aspect of the problem after wars is the inquiry into whether
the tent is an active force, itself combining bits and pieces of corpse
matter subject to its overshadowing into the requisite volume, or
whether the tent is wholly a formal and passive thing. The limits of

overshadowing—through a tent, not through a man or a utensil—likewise lead nowhere. The one point of important expansion comes in the question of whether modes of the transfer of uncleanness have the capacity to "join together." This is secondary to the issue of combining sources of uncleanness. The unit as a whole, while rich in the definition of sources of uncleanness, devotes little space to secondary and tertiary movements out of primary allegations as to what is unclean and how uncleanness of a given sort is transferred. The structure of the tractate itself, which relegates these questions to preliminary and concluding units, while preserving the shank of the tractate for a more important and consequential issue, confirms the view that the definition and development of that which contaminates as does a corpse are not principal concerns.

Once a tent is defined as something so small as a handbreadth squared, by contrast, we confront the generative problematic of this tractate. The matter begins in the notion that corpse uncleanness flows through such a small space, or may be prevented from passing through such a small space. Conceived as a kind of fluid, corpse uncleanness then will be stopped up in such a way as to be forced to flow perpendicularly—that is, under pressure—or it will be so contained that it affects all the sides of its container—that is, not under pressure. These matters are not much developed, I think, because there is not much to be said about the physics of the flow of corpse matter, once the comparison to the flow of liquid has been made.

But the conception of the tent as an enclosed area so small as a handbreadth absolutely requires the comparison of the tent to that other enclosed area of very small volume, an ordinary utensil. If a tent and a utensil are analogous, then we must ask, first, can man make a tent? Second, since a utensil is like a tent, how does a utensil function when it serves as a tent? Does it afford protection as does a tent? Third, since a utensil is like a tent, can a utensil join with a tent, participate in its work of preventing the spread of uncleanness or facilitating its flow? Fourth, since a utensil is like a tent, can a utensil form a tent? Does a utensil serve as part, e.g., a base, of a tent? How does an object serve sometimes as a utensil, sometimes as a tent (M. Oh. 9)? How does a utensil (a pot) serve, like a tent, to block up the egress of uncleanness (M. Oh. 10)? What is the role of the human body in the passage of corpse uncleanness, which is to ask, if a utensil serves as a tent, does the body, which contains the belly, a kind of utensil, also serve as a tent?

The tractate's theorists carry to its logical conclusion the proposition that the squared handbreadth measures the space through which corpse uncleanness passes. When there is not adequate egress, then we have no tent. When there is adequate egress, then there is a domain separate and capable of containing uncleanness. They also develop the analogy of the tent and the conception of adequate egress. The entire structure begins in the standard measure, the square handbreadth, which itself expresses the generative problematic of the tractate, the notion that corpse matter conforms to the stated dimension. Everything else flows from that notion. The philosophers ask, as I said, when a utensil (a hive) is a utensil, and when it is a tent. They further wonder about the interrelationships between two tents, which is a closely correlated question. What is carefully omitted from the system of sources of uncleanness is human participation. Whether or not man can constitute a tent, man does nothing deliberately to create corpse matter and in no way inaugurates the working of the system. But the tent, as a human construction, is central to the transmission of corpse uncleanness. Things which man makes effect the transfer of that form of uncleanness, just as things which man makes are subject to uncleanness.

Negaim. Negaim, Niddah, and the part of Zabim devoted to the uncleanness of the *zab* and how that uncleanness is transferred, like the beginning and end of Ohalot, do not work out a problematic in connection with their respective themes, the uncleanness of the person with *nega'*, the menstruating woman, and the *zab*. There is nothing people want to know *about* these sources of uncleanness other than rules for their definition and application. An important notion is that we take account of changes in the condition of the sign of uncleanness because the sage, "expert in them and in their names," is always available to take account of said changes. Another is (M. Neg. 13) the issue of whether that which affords protection from uncleanness also is more susceptible to uncleanness than that which does not afford protection from uncleanness or than that which is not susceptible to uncleanness to begin with. We deal in Negaim with the following subjects: rules applying to all plagues, with special attention to the role of the priest, the process of inspection, the susceptibility of gentiles, the matter of doubts; the issues of colors and their definition and interrelationship; the character of bright spots and the signification that they are unclean; the boil and the burning; bald spots; clothing; houses; and, last, purification rites. Rulings are founded on the laws of Lev. 13 and 14.

Niddah. Niddah constitutes an extended commentary, not in exegetical form, to be sure, upon the basic law of Scriptures, in particular Lev. 12 and 15. I see no important idea which does not derive directly or derivatively from Scripture. At no point does the tractate raise questions not provoked by Scripture or the extension, by analogy or contrast, of Scripture's definitions and conceptions. Niddah presents a discourse on unclean body fluids and on doubts in reference to unclean body fluids, an exercise within the narrow conceptual framework of Negaim.

Makhshirin. The theme of Makhshirin is liquids which impart to dry produce susceptibility to uncleanness. The problematic is the role of human intention in the application of said liquids so that they function to render produce susceptible, and, secondarily, the role of human intention in the definition of effective liquids. The working out of the problematic is in terms of the interplay between what a person wants to do and what he actually does. One possible position is that we interpret the effects of what is done in terms of what is intended. A second and opposite position is that we define what is intended in terms of the ultimate result. These are the possible positions yielded by the logical requirements of the problematic. There are no others. The determinative problematic, whether or not liquids must be applied intentionally, thus is itself redefined in terms of a still more profound and fundamental question.

The process begins in the position that we take account only of water which has actually conformed to a person's original intent, ignoring the presence of water which is peripheral to the accomplishment of one's purpose. The process then is completed by the inquiry into this position, specifically the meaning of intent; the limitations upon the capacity of water to impart susceptibility imposed by one's original intent in drawing the water. The structure is articulated in terms of the view that water intrinsic to one's purpose is detached with approval, while that which is not essential to one's original intent is not able to impart susceptibility. If water applied with approval can impart susceptibility, then, as I said, only that *part* of the water which is essential to one's accomplishment of one's original intent imparts susceptibility. It is at this point that the question is raised about the relationship between intention and deed. There are three possibilities. First, one's action can produce a different effect from one's original intention. Or, second, what happens is retrospectively deemed to define what one wanted to happen. Or, third, what one wanted to happen affects the assessment of what actually *has* happened. There no other logical possibilities contained within the original problematic.

The place of Makhshirin, at the inauguration of the system of intention, raises the question of its relationship to Kelim. Both tractates wish in essence to say the same thing. For liquids and for food as for utensils (that is, for all constituents of the system's entire realm of susceptibility to uncleanness), man must deliberately do something to bring the system into operation. He must complete an object, regard it as a utensil. He must deem food to be edible (not a major point in the Division), liquid to be drawn with approval or otherwise useful, take dry, insusceptible produce and wet it down, with an eye to making use of the produce. Accordingly, no component of the multidimensional locus of uncleanness—utensils, food (produce), and drink—is exempt from the requirement that human deliberation play the principal and definitive role. It is man who creates the entire locus of uncleanness by introducing into that locus—rendering susceptible to uncleanness—the several materials which form its components. While Kelim, Makhshirin, and the relevant units of Tohorot fully work out their respective problematic, each one moreover finds completion and fulfillment in the provision of the corresponding and reciprocally pertinent tractate. Each says concerning its own topic what all of them say in common about the shared theme.

Zabim. Zabim is to be considered in two parts, first, its definitions of how a man becomes unclean as a *zab* and modes of transfer of his uncleanness in general, and, second, how a *zab* imparts uncleanness through pressure in particular. The former part, like Niddah and Negaim, presents a series of refinements and amplifications of Scripture's basic definition of the *zab*. The latter part in chapters 3 and 4, deals with the nature of pressure. The matter of pressure begins with the view that pressure need not be formal, in the sense that the *zab* exerts physical pressure upon a bed. If the *zab*'s weight is indirectly transferred to something which might be used for lying or sitting, even though that object is not utilized at present for that purpose, then the uncleanness has been transferred. After the definition of the problem of pressure in general, we find a full working out of the logical possibilities. Either (1) we hold that any pressure, even of both a *zab* and a clean person on one side of an object, involves the transfer of uncleanness. Or (2) only if the *zab* presses against a clean person or object is there such a transfer. That is to say, only if the clean person certainly has borne the weight of the unclean one are the person and his clothing unclean. For both positions we require the qualifications that, first, only if the object is capable of submitting to pressure, being infirm, is pressure uncleanness transferred; second, only if the pressure is exerted equally throughout the object is the transfer effected; and, third, only if the greater part of the *zab*'s weight is pressed against the object is the object unclean.

One view is that the only situation in which there is a transfer of uncleanness is when the clean person bears the weight of the unclean. But if the unclean bears the weight of the clean, then there is no carrying, no pressure. Another maintains that the *zab* imparts pressure (*midras*) uncleanness if he exerts pressure on something, and, also, the person who exerts pressure on the *zab* is equivalently unclean. A third opinion wants the unclean person to exert weight on the clean. We require the greater part of the weight of the *zab*'s body. All concur that mere vibration, not direct pressure, does not accomplish the transfer of uncleanness. So far, therefore, as Zabim deals with a source of uncleanness, it exhibits the same conceptual traits as Niddah, Negaim, and the opening and closing units of Ohalot.

Tebul Yom. The theme of Tebul Yom is the person or object which has immersed in an immersion pool on that selfsame day and must await sunset for the completion of the process of purification, hence, one who has immersed on that selfsame day. Its first element is whether the *tebul yom* is essentially clean or essentially unclean. If he is essentially unclean, then the matter is concluded. He functions to impart uncleanness as does any other source. But if he is essentially clean, then the next stage unfolds. We distinguish between what is primary and what is secondary in a mixture. If what is primary is affected, then what is secondary likewise is unclean. But if what is secondary is affected, what is primary remains clean. Now this distinction is distinctively related to the *tebul yom*, who, because of his own ambiguous status, is able to illuminate the ambiguities presented by the stated distinction as to connection. If the *tebul yom* touches what is secondary in a mixture, what is primary is unaffected and vice versa. Every possible position inherent in the twin problematic—the ambiguous status of the *tebul yom*, the ambivalent aspect of connection—is stated. The theme of the *tebul yom*, of course, is hardly exhausted, or even fully spelled out in the necessary detailed rules.

Utensils and Food Susceptible to Uncleanness

Kelim. What Kelim (utensils) wants to know about utensils in general is when they become unclean, the status of their parts in relationship to the uncleanness of the whole utensil, when they cease to be unclean, and the status of their sherds and remnants in relationship to the uncleanness of the whole. The uncleanness of a utensil depends upon two criteria: the form of the utensil and the materials of which the utensil is composed. A utensil which forms, or has, a receptacle can contain uncleanness. A utensil which is fully processed and available for normal use is susceptible to uncleanness. Full processing must impose on the utensil a distinctive function. The criterion is the human conception of function. An object which is fully manufactured, routinely used, for a fixed purpose, by man, is susceptible. Diverse materials, to be sure, exhibit different traits, but only within these criteria. The refinement of this view will deal with gray areas, e.g., imperfect receptacles, the status of parts of a utensil or of subsidiary functions, the distinction between the time at which a utensil serves

man and the time at which it does not, and the revision of the distinctive purpose, e.g., by a change in the form of an object. The assessment
of the status of parts of a utensil or of things affixed to a utensil represents a further refinement. A part must be firmly affixed. Parts which
are going to be removed, because they interfere with the functioning of
a utensil, are not taken into account as susceptible to uncleanness. A
part which is essential to the use of utensil is deemed integral to it.
Having completed the consideration of when a utensil is susceptible to
uncleanness, we turn to the point at which it ceases to be susceptible.
We simply state systematically the negative of the foregoing propositions. A utensil which is useless is insusceptible. One which is broken
is useless. One which no longer serves its original function is no longer
susceptible as it was before. When we assess uselessness, we focus
upon human intention in working with said utensil. Sherds and remnants are subject to the same criteria of uselessness. We determine
whether or not the utensil's sherd continues to be useful on its own. At
the end, we ask about the work of a skilled craftsman as against that of
an ordinary person, the intention of the rich as against that of the poor,
the actual accomplishment of a person's purpose, and changing the
status of a utensil in respect to its form or in respect to its function.

When Kelim asks about when a utensil becomes unclean, or when
a utensil becomes clean, what does the tractate really want to know?
It is, What is the relation of man—his purpose, intention, and convenience—to the susceptibility of the utensil or to the cessation of
susceptibility? The tractate's supposition is that it is human intention
which subjects an object to susceptibility, brings said object into the
system of uncleanness, and removes it from the system. Its themes,
utensils, and problems connected with its theme, catalogued above,
therefore are worked out within the problematic of the capacity of man
to introduce objects into, or remove them from, the process of contamination and purification.

The issue of Kelim therefore is the point at which human intention
and deliberate action introduce into, and remove from, the system of
contamination and purification diverse sorts of utensils, made from
various materials. Its specific interest is in the role of man. Its persuasive point is that human intention and action govern the introduction of
objects into the system of uncleanness.

Tohorot. The three paramount themes of Tohorot, on the uncleanness
of food, are to be treated separately. The first, the issue of removes of
uncleanness and levels of sanctification, is fully worked out in the
interplay between the one and the other. Once the levels of sanctification are defined, the structure demands completion through the
specification of corresponding, and opposite, removes of uncleanness.

It further will want to know how the two interrelate. At that point the system is complete. The secondary question of whether that which is unconsecrated may be raised, through appropriate deliberation and protection, to the level of sanctification not only of heave offering but of holy things, is further worked out.

The second theme, the relationship between the nonobservant Israelite and the observant one, begins in two conflicting principles. The former, the *'am ha'ares*, in general will act in such a way as to respect the cleanness of the property of the latter, the *haber*. Or the *'am ha'ares* is indifferent to the matter of cleanness. The problematic is to be stated in exactly those simple terms. It can be worked out in a myriad of cases, but no significant conceptual advance is possible or undertaken.

The third theme, the resolution of doubts, is open-ended. Once we postulate that matters of doubt are to be worked out through the application of diverse principles, then the number of potential principles is scarcely limited. There is no reason to suppose that those specified in Tohorot exhaust the potential.

Uqsin. Uqsin is coherent and exhibits traits of sophisticated formulary and redactional work. It treats, first, the status of inedible parts of food, whether they are susceptible because they are connected to edible parts, or insusceptible because they are inedible. The second aspect is joined to the first: How do we treat these inedible parts when we estimate the bulk or the volume of food? Accordingly, the issue is the status of what is joined to food but is not to be eaten. The logical possibilities, that these inedible parts are deemed (1) wholly part of the produce to which they are connected, (2) wholly separate from said produce, or (3) under some circumstances part, and under some circumstances not part, of the edible part of the food, are fully worked out.

Modes of Purification

Parah. Parah treats the conduct of a sacrifice outside of the Temple in a place of uncleanness, its requirements and limitations. The deep structure of the tractate is readily discerned, for at each point, the issue is how the requirements of a rite of sacrifice done in the Temple determine the necessities of burning the cow and mixing its ashes with suitable water, that is, a rite of sacrifice done outside of the Temple. Do we do outside the Temple exactly what we do inside? Do we do the opposite? Do the Temple's requirements of cleanness define those of the burning of the red cow? Do they stand lower or higher in the progression of strictness? The tractate also contains rules required by the theme, but not by the problematic, of the red cow, such as defining the water, spelling out how the purification water is used, and other prescriptions that hardly relate in detail to the overriding question. The principal foci of the tractate, the principle that labor extraneous to the rite spoils the rite of the burning of the cow and spoils the drawn water, and the conception that cleanness rules of unimagined strictness are to be observed, relate to that crucial point of interest, which is the analogy to the Temple.

The tractate centers upon the conception that human intervention in the process of preparing the purification water is absolutely essential. The utensil used for collecting the water and mixing the ashes must be a human construction. The act of drawing the water, by contrast to the act of forming an immersion pool, must be with full human deliberation. If at any point the human participant fails to devote his entire and complete attention to the work and so steps outside of the process, the whole process is spoiled. Once man is intruded, moreover, his attention is riveted to what he is doing by the omnipresent danger of contamination. If he touches any sort of object whatsoever—which is to say, if at any point he does anything at all which is not connected to the requirements of the rite—he automatically is made unclean. This is the rule for objects used for lying and sitting. The participant cannot cease from his labors in connection with the rite, for he cannot sit down on a chair. He cannot lie down on a bed. He must at all times be active, standing and alert, moving from the well from which he has drawn the water to the place at which he will mix it with the ash. It may also be the case that if he touches any sort of object which *can* become unclean, not only a bed or a chair, he is *eo ipse* unclean. Even though this is subject to dispute, the issue is secondary to the one on which all parties agree. Moreover, the assumption is that he will have burned the cow, and only then have gone off to collect the necessary water. So the process is continuous, from selecting the cow and burning it—which the tractate places first in its sequence of themes—to the gathering of the water and the mixing of the water with the ash. Only then do we take up the use of the water in the purification process.

Accordingly, the tractate commences its development with the principle that man is the key figure in the preparation of purification water. It follows that man must remain forever alert and conscious throughout the process. Utensils he is to use must be prepared by man, on the one side, and always protected until used for their ultimate purpose, on the other. Preparing the ash, then gathering the water, then mixing the two—these procedures require ultimate and complete devotion and attention. All analogies to the burning of the cow and the mixing of its ashes with the water are explored: to sacrifices, carried on outside the Temple; to holy things, done in a state of perfect cleanness; to the Passover, done outside the Temple, therefore in a locus of uncleanness; to the heifer whose neck is broken, outside the Temple; even to the *log* of oil of the leper and the blood of the guilt offering of the leper (Lev. 14), which are utilized outside the main locus of the cult. At each point the issue is, how does the law before us respond to the analogy of other sacrifices done outside the Temple or outside the inner court of the Temple? No further analogies are available for deeper inquiry than already has been accomplished.

It remains to observe that attention to the actual use of purification water is episodic and casual, just as Miqvaot has little to say about the practical use of the immersion pool, but a great deal to contribute to thought on the making of the immersion pool and the character of water used therein. Accordingly, both of the tractates on the modes of purification from uncleanness focus attention upon the creation of materials for purification—the right kind of water—to the near exclusion of utilization of said materials. The reason is that what is important to the two tractates is contained within the issue of purificatory substance, not purificatory procedure. Discussion of the latter is not spun out of the operative principles but tacked on at the end of Miqvaot and Parah (not to mention Negaim). This is a highly suggestive fact, illustrative of the principal point of interest of the system as a whole. The system asks not about such practical matters as how one immerses or the sort of hyssop with which one sprinkles purification water (though these are attended to), but about a quite separate range of issues.

Miqvaot. What Miqvaot wants to know about the immersion pool is the sort of water which is to be used. This issue carries in its wake the question of the role of man in the process of purification. Man is rigidly excluded from the process of making the pool. Water drawn by man is not to be used in the pool. It will follow that we must answer these questions: What sort of water is to be used? How much of such water is needed? What is the rule if acceptable water is mixed with unacceptable water? Can the former purify the latter? If so, in what volume? Does the latter render the former irreparably unfit, or is there a way to take an unfit pool and make it fit? This range of issues explores the deeper question of the role of suitable water in effecting purification. Once we say that a certain kind of water—specifically, that which man has not affected—is to be used, then we ask a range of questions dependent upon the workings of the suitable water, its relationship to unsuitable water, and its power to restore the suitability of unfit water. In asking these questions, moreover, we enter the inquiry into the actual workings of the immersion pool, for we want to know exactly what power the pool has even over its own constituent element, water, and, all the more so, over things which are different from its constituent element. The route to the analysis of the working of the pool, therefore, is the inquiry into the character of the water which is used in the pool and its power over all other things which enter therein. It follows that once we define the sort of water which is to be used, we must ask about its volume, the conditions of its collection, and the possibilities of its incapacitation. What is striking in Miqvaot is its focus upon exactly this range of issues, which are given full instantiation, and the tight way in which these issues draw together their negative aspects, spoiling the pool, ruining water for use in the pool, and restoring the power of a spoiled pool or of spoiled water.

The tractate works out rules on kinds of water suitable for purification, even showing that there are several sorts of such water, each with its own capacities in the larger structure. It then turns to water unsuitable for purification, showing under what conditions that water has the effect of impairing a pool, and further, how these effects upon a formerly suitable pool may be mitigated. In all of these inquiries the determinative role of man is carefully delineated. There are things man must not do, and, if he does them, he spoils the pool, the water of which furthermore itself then is held to impart uncleanness, an extreme statement of the matter. There are things which he may do. And there are aspects of the matter which man must do—that is to say, making use of the pool for purification. But there the matter, as we noted earlier, is left curiously undeveloped. The rules on how to use the pool for purification are few and incomplete. The principal concern is for interposition, and the reason is that that matter, in the large framework of use of the pool, allows us to restate our interest in the role of man. Things which man cares about interpose, and those of no concern to man do not. Accordingly, the primary concern in the use of the pool is tied—though rather loosely—to the principal interests of the tractate as a whole.

Miqvaot and Parah complement and complete one another. The one describes an aspect of purification from which man is excluded, while the other deals with an aspect of purification to which human deliberation is absolutely necessary. The interplay with Parah is still closer, when we recall that Parah treats a rite of sacrifice which takes place outside of the temple, and Miqvaot, it would seem, describes a rite of purification to begin with effective outside of the cult. As we noted, the rite lies beyond the imagination of the priestly legislators, who specify that things which are laundered, washed, or rinsed in ordinary water are unclean until the evening.

Parah and Miqvaot together deal with, on the one side, sacrifice in the system's principal locus of uncleanness, outside the cult, and, on the other, the mode of purification, outside the cult. The profound issue to be worked out by both is the definition of the role of man. What is accomplished by the two together is the balancing of the essential participation of man in the deliberate formation of the worldly locus to be protected from uncleanness on the one side, and his rigid exclusion in the formation of the mode of purification on the other.

Yadayim. The theme of Yadayim, the uncleanness of hands, is spelled out in the diverse rules. The principal issue has to do with cleaning hands in a way different from the way in which other parts of the body and other unclean things are cleaned, which is in an immersion pool. Once we determine that hands are unclean when the rest of the body remains unaffected, then we have to find an appropriate analogy for the mode of purification herein under discussion. It is in the law, not of Miqvaot, which concerns undifferentiated purification, but of Parah. The result is the strict requirement of the use of a utensil and of water drawn by man in a utensil, as against the conception of Miqvaot that we do not use water drawn in a utensil at all. The other aspect of the law is that two rinsings are required.

From Description to Interpretation

The results of this protracted description of the structure and contents of the Mishnah, completed at ca. A.D. 200, may now be stated briefly and simply. It is to a situation which is so fraught with danger as to threaten the order and regularity of the stable, sacred society in its perfection and at its point of stasis that the Mishnah will devote its principal cognitive and legislative efforts. For that situation, the Mishnah will invoke heaven and express its most vivid concern for sanctification. What breaks established routine or what is broken out of established routine is what is subject to the fully articulated and extensive reflections of a whole Division of the Mishnah.

To explore the meaning of this simple result requires us now to undertake the interpretation of that which has been so painstakingly described. For that purpose one question proves critical. Since the Mishnah stands in midstream in the history of Judaism, coming as it does about seven hundred years after the redaction of the Pentateuch, we must test the possibility that the Mishnah in no way constitutes what we have claimed, namely, a systematic construction in response to the critical issues of a particular age. It may be that the Mishnah should be viewed, when seen whole, in the context not of its own time in particular but of the unfolding of the history of Scripture. For a long time the Mishnah has been seen as the formation of an essentially exegetical process. In this process it is alleged, problems of a given day were brought to Scripture and investigated in the light of the imperatives of the law of Moses. So my insistence that the Mishnah be addressed as a document of its own day, rather than as a response of its day to a document of an earlier time, requires protracted testing. That is why in the next chapter we shall examine in ample detail the relationship of each tractate to Scripture, then of the Mishnah as a whole to the Torah of Moses. I can think of no more fundamental and urgent question dictated by the labor of interpretation. For only when that question is answered can we proceed to the analysis of the principal societal components revealed by the concerns of the Mishnah. I have pointed to many elements of the Mishnah which express concerns particular to priests, scribes, and householders. In chapter 6 we shall systematically ask what we may claim to be the contribution of these influential tributaries to the final document. The result is not going to bring surprises to those who have labored through the present chapter. The priests contribute a huge part of the whole. Scribes add much less to the program of topical interest, but, I shall explain, they define the way in which the Mishnah's propositions will be expressed. The householders, for their part, bring a small but critical set of concrete questions.

The final question can only be, Is the Mishnah only what has been put together in the agglutination of topics of special concern to a caste, profession, and class? Phrasing the question in a more general way, I inquire, in the second half of the last chapter, into those traits which make the Mishnah into something more than the sum of the interests of its social constituents. The argument is quite simple. When we want to know what makes the Mishnah Mishnaic, we have to examine those matters of style and substance, medium and message, mode of thought and result of reflection, which characterize the document as a whole and permeate each and every one of its parts. For, as indicated, the societal boundaries are delineated by topics. What is done with those topics, what is said about them, the problematic which makes the treatment of a subject not merely a compendium of information but also an essay into a theme and a structured argument—these are what make the Mishnah Mishnaic. They are those definitive traits of form and meaning which allow us to speak of a version of Judaism, that is, a way of seeing and thinking about the world. The Judaism presented by the Mishnah is a way of so living as to frame one's life to accord with a single vision of the world, above all, a claim that this way of life and world view represent God's perspective on all creation. So from this long labor of description, we systematically take up the exercises of interpretation which shape the facts into an account of the evidence of the Mishnah on Judaism.

5

Systems and Sources:
The Mishnah and the Torah
of Moses

Preliminary Observations

In the long unfolding of diverse versions of Judaism, one form of Judaism will take up and revise materials of another, existing one, dropping some available elements, adapting others, as well as inventing still others. But every sort of Judaism from the beginning to the present has had to make its peace with the Scriptures universally received as revealed by God to Moses at Mount Sinai or to the prophets, or by the "Holy Spirit" to the historians and chroniclers, psalmists and other writers. Insight into the modes and principles of selection among all these candidates for authoritative and generative status will therefore lead us far into the deepest structure and definitive tension of given kind of Judaism. From the formation of the Pentateuch onward, framers of various sorts of Judaism have had to take measure in particular of the Mosaic revelation and place themselves in relationship to it. Each version has found it necessary to lay claim in its own behalf to possess the sole valid interpretation of the Torah of Moses. All have alleged that they are the necessary and logical continuation of the revelation of Moses and the prophets. It is not surprising, therefore, that in behalf of the Mishnah an equivalent claim was laid down almost from the very moment of the Mishnah's completion and closure.

The diverse versions of that claim in behalf of the Mishnah indeed constitute one of the complex and interesting problems in the history of Judaism in the Mishnah's version both in the time in which the Mishnah was taking shape and afterward. But the analysis and historical evaluation of those efforts to lay down, in behalf of the Mishnah, a claim of the authority of revelation in the name of Moses and from the mouth of God just now need not detain us (see below, pp. 172–74). The reason is that these theological formations are post facto assertions. They are not data out of the inner history of the formation of the Mishnah itself and the unfolding of its ideas. Later

theologians dealt with later problems through assertions about the
Mishnah's origins and Scriptural foundations. A critical question in the
description and interpretation of the history of the Mishnah's version of
Judaism thus is badly framed. A survey of the main versions of the later
rabbinic theology of the status of the Mishnah as coequal revelation of
Moses ("oral Torah"), therefore, at the outset is not relevant to the analysis of the evidence of the Mishnah itself. No such articulated claim is
before us. Rather, it is necessary to frame the issue of the relationship
of the Mishnah to Scripture in such a way as to elicit insight into the character of the Mishnah's system itself. What we want to know is what we
learn about the Mishnah and the ideas of its philosophers from analysis
of the relationship of the Mishnah and its corpus of themes, ideas, and
facts, to the Scripture and its facts. After the facts are in hand, we may
use them to interpret the Mishnah's system.

At some time it may become possible to analyze that relationship in
stages, that is, the traits of the relationship between the Mishnah and
Scripture before the wars, between, and after them, in sequence. For
now, however, the first step in the framing of the issue is to come to the
decision to deal with only the final stage in the matter, the relationship
to Scripture of the Mishnah as a completed system. The reason is that,
at this stage of the analysis of the unfolding of the Mishnah's ideas, our
methods are not sufficiently precise and encompassing to permit us to
lay claim to detailed knowledge of how things were worked out before
and between the wars. The account I am able to present allows me to
summarize in two sentences the state of affairs before the latter half of
the second century. The framers of ideas ultimately to be located in the
Mishnaic system drew heavily and informedly upon what they found in
the Scriptures. But they drew upon materials they found relevant to
concerns already defined, framed essentially independent of issues and
themes paramount in Scripture itself. That is to say, once people had
chosen a subject, they knew full well how to develop their ideas about
that subject by examining and reflecting upon relevant verses of
Scripture. But what dictated the choice of subject awaiting amplification and expansion was hardly a necessary or ineluctable demand of
Scripture. Proof of that fact is the asymmetrical character of the interplay between the Mosaic codes and the topics developed in each of the
three periods in the unfolding of the ideas of the Mishnah.

Thus, a relationship of ambiguity—freedom of choice of topic, on the
one hand, disciplined literalism in working out what is to be said about
a stated topic, on the other—characterizes the final product of the long
period of interplay between Scripture and the philosophers of the Mishnah. That is to say, the relationship between the Mishnah and Scripture appears to be constant in the several periods of the unfolding of the
Mishnah. What the philosophers of the Mishnah's ultimate system will

say about any topic is, if not predictable, at least highly probable, upon the basis of what Scripture says about that same topic. But what topics the philosophers of the end product will choose for their reflection is not to be foretold on the basis of a mere reading of Scripture. At the same time, after all, that the priestly and holiness codes of Leviticus clearly appeared critical to the thinkers who lie in the remote past of the Mishnaic system of thought, to the religious imagination of the writers of the Gospels a wholly other repertoire of Scriptures obviously proved authoritative. And this is hardly surprising, for, as Porter points out (see above, p. 9), Deuteronomy and Jeremiah came out of the same age and social setting. They are related, yet essentially in conflict with one another. (To be sure, the same is to be said of Ezekiel and Leviticus. But that is another matter.) Certain passages of Israelite prophecy, therefore the prophetic writings of Scripture, proved critical to the mind of people attempting to frame an account of the world formed by their encounter with Jesus. The whole corpus of prophecy and history is neglected by the Mishnah. The priestly writings of Scripture took on that same self-evidence, that same critical importance, in the mind of people, early and late, who clearly had quite profound, equivalently powerful experiences, not through the encounter with a person, self-evidently, but in the transformation effected by a world-shaping vision of sanctification.

Nevertheless, we must not place too heavy a reliance upon the results of our description of the state of affairs before and between the wars, because there is a second ambiguity. As I said, if we were to describe the state of the relationship between Scripture and the ideas evidently circulating before 70 and between 70 and 140 which would ultimately flow into the completed system of the Mishnah, we should come up with an account of precisely the same relationship as we find at the end. Now when we realize that what we find at the end also characterizes what we find at the outset, we have to take account of the simple possibility that the picture at the end of the formation of the Mishnah has shaped the facts which we presumed testified to the state of affairs at the beginning and the middle of the process. On that basis I choose to present only the final and complete picture of the internal facts about how the philosophers of the Mishnah chose to relate to Scripture.

The second step in framing the issue of the relationship of the Mishnah to Scripture is to ask what the Mishnah had to say about the meaning of the parts of Scripture the founders of the Mishnah did choose. The fact that the Mishnah constitutes a vast and detailed account of what a group of men believed Scripture to say and to mean has not been fully appreciated. The contrary polemic, that they merely repeated what they found in Scripture, has obscured their fresh results.

That is to say, since it was important to apologists to show that the Mishnah constituted a contingent and dependent statement, attained through Scriptural exegesis, of what Scripture had long ago said, it has not been understood that, from a historical perspective, what we have is quite the opposite. Yet that fact is obvious and self-evident, as I shall prove. Whether or not the meaning imputed by the Mishnaic thinkers to the Scriptures is what the writers of that part of Scripture subject to exegesis wanted originally to say is not important in an understanding of the Mishnah. The fact that the Mishnaic thinkers not only selected a given topic but also framed their own ideas on that topic in response to what they found in Scripture tells us much about those ideas and that response. What we learn is how the philosophers evaluated various portions of Scripture and what they found important in them—a considerable statement.

It follows that we must not be taken in by the obvious links between Scripture and the Mishnah—links of theme, links of fact, links of conception. In no way may we now suppose that the Mishnah is the natural and obvious outcome of the purpose and message of Scripture. That claim on the surface is spurious, for the reasons stated by Porter. For all its complete dependence upon Scripture, by its selections of themes (let alone specific verses) for amplifications and augmentation in the Mishnah, the Mishnah effects a far-reaching choice. The Mishnah constitutes a statement on the meaning Scripture, not merely a statement *of* the meaning of Scripture. For the Mishnah tells us more than what its philosophers thought important in Scripture. It also tells us how they performed remarkably sophisticated acts of logical exegesis upon the verses chosen for inquiry. The modes of thought, the concrete results, the explanation and interpretation of those results, and the reframing and fresh statement and presentation of those results in language quite independent of the modes of expression and organization of Scripture itself—recognition in detail of these achievements of insight and independent thought constitutes the greatest contribution to be made in the study of the relationship between the Mishnah and the Mosaic codes.

But there also is the fact, demonstrated in this chapter, that much of the time the Mishnah's relationship to Scripture is not fresh and original, but subservient and literalist. The third step in the argument thus must be to point out that literalism too is not only a choice, but also a judgment upon both past and present. When the philosophers confronted the sizable heritage of Israel and made the choice to ignore most of what had been done since the time of the formation of the Mosaic codes (they would have said, at Sinai, and we know it was some six or seven hundred years before the closure of the Mishnah), they made a stunning comment. It was upon the worth and authority of what had been done in that long period separating themselves from the point in the past they chose to restate. Their judgment was that nothing of worth had happened from the time of Moses to their own day. That explains why they could ignore whatever was available in their own day and leap back to what was not. So from Scripture to their own day whatever custom or practice had come into common usage was treated as if it did not exist. This exercise in selectivity, alongside the parallel exercise in (merely) saying in their own words what already had been said in the verses chosen through the stated exercise of selectivity, constituted a program for theodicy and reform. It was more than literalism and mindless biblicism.

The point is that the Mishnah's Scriptural literalism is a response to the opening of an abyss: a bridge to the past. The Mishnah comes at the end of six or seven hundred years of history, from the time of the closure of the Torah literature at about 500 B.C. There is nothing traditional in leaping over so long a span of time. So the Mishnah's self-evident literalism when it comes to defining what is to be said about Scriptural facts is an act of reform—and therefore a disingenuous pretense. Parallel to the revival of Atticism and the idealization of the Greek past expressed in the second Sophistic, of the same time as the Mishnah, what the Mishnah does through its biblicism and literalism is to conduct a powerful polemic against folk in its own unhappy times. Its literalist traditionalism is an act of defiance, an initiative of willful consciousness.

Such a polemic, full of fresh initiatives in the utilization of ancient, but not stale, imperatives, thus is anything but traditional. It may be fairly seen as the trivialization of the past. It may not unjustly be accused of pedantry. It may reasonably be said at times to have wasted its (and our) best energies on externals. But these things, if done, were done by choice, for a purpose. The choice was not dictated by "tradition." The purpose was anything but trivial. All the minor, detailed teachings of the Mishnah, in context, address those same issues of mythological war, cosmos, and history which, in their way, others faced by going to war against the Romans and by searching for power over the rulers of this age or freedom from them. The pretense that "all we do and plan to do is merely what Scripture has said," the claim that "this time around, we shall do correctly everything the Scripture has said"—these constitute a powerful, reforming, and innovative polemic against the discredited way taken by most of their countrymen. They add up to a formidable, indeed a commanding, claim upon Israelites' attention and assent for the future.

To state the problem very simply: The superficial relationship of the Mishnah to Scripture is ambiguous only because the Mishnah never links its legal statements to Scripture or claims that it rules in accord with Scripture. On the surface, the Mishnah wishes to stand autonomous of Scripture and to claim that the source of its laws is other than Scripture. So, on first glance, the Mishnah, whatever it claims to be or to do, in no way links itself to Scripture. But, of course, hardly a second glance is needed to reveal the opposite, which is that the Mishnah depends in a deep way, for both thematic agendum and the facts of its topics and rules, upon Scripture. So, the real issue is: What are the nature of the dependence and the traits of the relationship?

The Division of Agriculture

Richard Sarason explains the relationship between the Division of Agriculture and Scripture as follows.

> With the exception of Tractates Berakhot and Demai, the topics of Mishnah's tractates in the division of Agriculture originate in Scripture. But the choice of topics also indicates Mishnah's interests. The tractates deal with the various agricultural gifts—to the priests, to the Levites, to the poor—which must be given from produce grown in the soil of the Holy Land of Israel, as well as with the various taboos which apply to such produce. Excepting Peah (gifts to the poor), each of these topics represents an aspect or a kind of holiness which can pertain to types of produce, grown in the Land, on which God has a claim.
>
> The Mishnah's primary interest in that half of the order dealing with the laws of tithing is in the process of sanctification, and the interaction in this process between human and divine will and action. Mishnah's system of tithes begins in a unitary, harmonistic reading of the Torah literature's diverse pericopae on tithing. These are as follows: Numbers 18; Deut. 12:17–79, 14:22–29, 18:4–5, 26:1–19; Lev. 27:30–33; Ex. 23:19, 34:26; cf. also Ez. 44:30, 45:13–17; Neh. 10:35–39, 12:44–47, 13:10–12. The tithes of grain, wine, and oil which Numbers 18 assigns to the Levites is juxtaposed by the Mishnah with the Deuteronomic tithe (Deut. 14:22ff.), which must be taken to Jerusalem and eaten there by the farmer and his family "before Yahweh your God." In the Mishnah, the Levitical and Deuteronomic tithes becomes first and second tithe, respectively, each a tenth part of the produce. Additionally, the Deuteronomic "welfare" tithe, which is stored up in the towns every three years for "the Levite, the resident alien, the fatherless, and the widow" (Deut. 14:28–29, 26:12ff.), becomes the Mishnah's poor man's tithe, separated in third and sixth years of each sabbatical cycle instead of second tithe, and given to the poor. Finally, the "tithe from the tithe," which Numbers 18 requires the Levites to give to "Aaron the priest" from the tithe which they receive, becomes Mishnah's "*terumah* from the tithe" (cf. Num. 18:28).

So far there is nothing unique in Mishnah's understanding of Scripture's "facts." A unitary reading of Scripture will yield the same information to any group or author. In fact, the same systemization of the scriptural tithes is found in the Books of Tobit and Jubilees, and in Josephus' *Antiquities,* the only differences being that Josephus and some versions of Tobit hold that the tithe for the poor is to be separated triennially as an additional third tithe.

In addition to these tithes, Mishnah knows three agricultural offerings which are given to the priest: the dough offering (*hallah*) of Numbers 15:17–21; the first fruits (*bikkurim*) of Numbers 18:13, Deut. 26, Ex. 23:19, 34:26, and Neh. 10:36; and the *terumah.* The derivation from Scripture of this last offering depends in part on the distinctive use of terminology at Num. 18:12–13, which assigns to the priest "all the best of the oil, and all the best of the wine and of the grain, the *first (or "best")* part of what they gave to the Lord . . . *The first ripe fruits* of all that is in their land, which they bring to the Lord . . ." The Mishnah distinguishes between the *re'šit* of v. 12 and the *bikkurim* of v. 13, and holds that these are two distinct offerings. In fact, the Numbers passage probably does bear this meaning originally. It is certain in any case that this is how Mishnah reads Scripture, since the heave-offering is referred to at M. Ter. 3:7 and T. Ter. 3:18 as *terumat re'šit.* It is also the case that Mishnah's usage of the term *terumah* to designate this particular offering to the priest is distinctive; to my knowledge the term does not occur with this meaning in any of the extant non-rabbinic sources from the Second Temple period. The Mishnahic usage of the term *terumah* (which in Scripture refers in general to a cultic offering or contribution) in this restricted technical sense is to be understood in light of such biblical passages as Num. 18:8, 11, 19, 26–29 (particularly the latter, where the priestly gift which the Levites separate from their tithe is referred to as *terumah,* parallel to that which the Israelites give to the priests from their grain, wine and oil), as well as Deut. 12:6, 11, 17, and Neh. 10:38–40. A harmonistic reading of Scripture can easily assimilate *terumah* in these passages to *re'šit* in contiguous verses (i.e., Num. 18:12) and other passages.

Mishnah and Tosefta depict a situation in which Israelite common folk scrupulously separate the priestly *terumah* (= the biblical *re'šit*), but cannot be relied upon to separate the Levitical tithe or the second tithe (*demai*). Thus the only offering separated is given to the priests. Against this practice, the rabbis behind Mishnah require the proper separation and distribution of *all* Scriptural tithes, according to their particular reading of Scripture, of course. While this requirement has the effect of supporting the otherwise neglected Levites, Tractate Demai makes it clear that the major concern of the authorities behind the Mishnah lies elsewhere. The problem with the tithing practice of common folk is that, by not separating the Levitical tithe, they also fail to separate the *terumat ma'aśer,* which is God's property and no less holy than the *terumah. Terumat ma'aśer,* like *terumah* is given to the priests by God. Produce from which *terumat maʿaśer* has not been separated is still holy to God and must not be eaten by man. Meticulousness therefore must designate all tithes in produce acquired from, or sold to, an *'am ha'areṣ* (cf. M. Dem. 2:2). This procedure insures the separation of *terumat maʿaśer* and prevents the inadvertent consumption of God's property by man.

These, then, are the scriptural data—the facts—with which Mishnah chooses to deal. But the important question, as I have indicated before, is: what does Mishnah propose to do with these facts? What does it want to know about tithes and *terumah?* What, in short, is its agendum? To begin with, it is not quite the same as Scripture's, although the basic tithing system remains the same. The various scriptural pericopae on tithing, of course, are not of a piece, and there are shifts of emphasis between them, particularly between those in Deuteronomy and those in the Priestly Code. Nonetheless, the following generalizations can be made:

Yahweh is conceived as the owner of the Land of Israel and as ruler of the people Israel. The people, as tenant farmers on Yahweh's Land (who also are concerned to insure the Land's on-going fertility), owe to Yahweh, through his priestly agents, the first ripe fruits of each year's harvest, and the first, or best, portion of their grain, wine, and oil and of their dough. The fruit of a newly-planted vineyard in its first year of harvesting (the fourth year of its growth) also is dedicated to Yahweh. The Deuteronomic tithe, while not given to the priests, is eaten by the farmer, his family, and the local Levites as a cultic meal "before Yahweh" in Jerusalem, and is designated as holy (Deut. 26). On the other hand, the triennial welfare tithe of Deuteronomy and the Priestly Code's Levitical tithe (Num. 18) are not offerings to Yahweh, but taxes paid to support the needy and the Levites. Scripture thus describes some offerings, but not others, as holy to Yahweh, and Mishnah closely adheres to the distinctions of Scripture. [Sarason, "Mishnah"]

In our consideration of the structure and program of the Division of Agriculture (see above, pp. 130–32), we have already reviewed Sarason's account of the differing emphases of Scripture and the Mishnah.

Producing Crops in a State of Holiness

Kilayim. Scripture deals with the topic of diverse kinds at Lev. 19:19 and Deut. 22:9–11. Both P (the priestly code, here the holiness code) and Deuteronomy (D) prohibit the commingling of different classes of plants, animals, or fibers, but the two sources differ with regard to the details of these prohibitions. While, for example, P prohibits the sowing of different classes of seeds with one another, D forbids only the sowing of seeds (e.g., of grains or vegetables) in a vineyard. Similarly, according to P it is forbidden to mate different kinds of animals with one another, while D prohibits only the yoking together of such animals to pull a plow. Finally, P maintains that one may not wear a garment composed of any two kinds of fibers which have been commingled, a rule which D applies only to garments composed of wool (an animal product) and linen (a plant product). On the whole, then, the two sources disagree either with regard to the types of items to which the prohibition in question applies (in the case of plants and fibers) or with respect to the act of commingling which is specifically prohibited (in the case of animals). In fact, D's prohibition against yoking together animals of different kinds refers only to the ox and the ass (Deut. 22:10), and so may be interpreted as forbidding the yoking together of these two animals alone. In this case too, then, D may differ with P as to the items to which the prohibition against commingling applies.

Taking the rules of P and D to be complementary, tractate Kilayim draws upon these two sources for its topical agendum. The tractate thus opens with a discussion of P's prohibition against sowing together different kinds of seeds (M. Kil. 1–3), followed by a treatment of D's rule against the sowing of seeds in a vineyard (M. Kil. 4–7). In its next unit (M. Kil. 8), the tractate deals with the commingling of different classes of animals both by mating them together (P) and by yoking them to one another (D). Finally, Kilayim deals in its last unit (M. Kil. 9) with the commingling of different classes of fibers. Here the Mishnah understands D as defining the fibers to which P's prohibition applies, thus discussing the commingling of wool and linen alone. The tractate thus closely follows Scripture in establishing the topics of its discussion.

Within this framework which it draws from Scripture, however, the Mishnah brings to its subject a conception of the law which is unknown to the earlier document. Scripture assumes that the different classes of plants, animals, and fibers were definitively established at creation, and that these categories must be kept absolutely separate from one another. By contrast, the Mishnah sets forth the view (specifically in its treatment of plants) that it is man who both defines what constitutes a class and determines how to keep different classes distinct from each other. This claim leads the tractate to examine issues which are wholly unknown to Scripture. For example, Scripture would maintain that wheat and barley may not be grown together in the same field, for the growth of two kinds in a single field would confuse the distinctions between these two kinds. According to the Mishnah, however, the commingling of different classes is prohibited only if the resultant mixture appears to man to contain a confusion of kinds, but not if the different kinds are arranged in an orderly manner. The Mishnah thus permits one to grow wheat and barley in the same field, provided that each kind is allowed a substantial amount of area, thus appearing to be sown in an area unto itself. Unlike Scripture, then, which is concerned with the absolute separation of different classes of items, the Mishnah attempts to determine how different kinds may be kept distinct from one another as they grow together. The Mishnah's views concerning the role of man in establishing order thus raise new and interesting issues in the law of diverse kinds.

IRVING MANDELBAUM

Shebiit. With regard to the law of the sabbatical year, Scripture specifies those field labors which are prohibited during the seventh year of the sabbatical cycle (Ex. 23:10–11; Lev. 25:1–7) and indicates that all debts are released at the end of the sabbatical year (Deut. 15:1–3, 9–10). Shebiit's topics are the same, though in the opening and closing units of the tractate introduce concerns not found in Scripture (M. Sheb. 1:1–2:10, 10:1–10). Because several kinds of fieldwork performed at the end of the sixth year benefit the crops of the following year (when cultivation is forbidden), the Mishnah prohibits those labors during the sixth year (M. Sheb. 1:1–2:10). Regarding the release of debts, the Mishnah introduces the concept of the *prozbul,* a document which allows a lender to collect debts beyond the sabbatical year (M. Sheb. 10:3–8). The discussion of how one actually releases debts is limited to M. Sheb. 10:1–2.

During the sabbatical year, land must lie fallow (Ex. 25:11; Lev. 25:4) and even crops which grow unaided may not be harvested (Lev. 25:5). Ex. 23:10–11 considers how Israelite society is to survive a full year without cultivating crops only insofar as it indicates that poor people and livestock may eat freely of produce that grows uncultivated in the field (Ex. 23:11). Lev. 25:20–22 adds that the sixth year will produce sufficient food for the community until the eighth year's crop may be harvested.

Deuteronomy introduces the second law, mandating the release of debts at the end of the sabbatical year (Deut. 15:1–3). Deut. 15:9–10 emphasizes that one may not withhold loans to the poor in the sixth year for fear that an unpaid loan will be cancelled.

The great bulk of Shebiit develops Scripture's concerns. M. Sheb. 3:1–6:6 elaborates upon P's rule forbidding field labor, adding that fieldwork of a nonagricultural character is permitted. M. Sheb. 7:1–9:9 goes on to specify how produce of the sabbatical year may or may not be used. Included among these rules are the ways in which one harvests, stores, and markets such produce. These activities, some of which are forbidden in Leviticus, are permitted with restrictions according to Shebiit. Thus, two laws related to the sabbatical year are defined by Scripture: Exodus and Leviticus deal with agricultural matters and Deuteronomy deals exclusively with the release of debts. While Shebiit begins with these subjects in the first case it expands upon Scripture's law, and in the second case it seeks primarily to circumvent the law through the use of the *prozbul.*

LEONARD GORDON

Orlah. Lev. 19:23 states that for three years the produce of a fruit tree is not to be used. Orlah defines the biblical requirement and explains the cases to which it does and does not apply; deals with situations in which produce subject to the prohibition is mixed with produce which is permitted; explains how to dispose of materials containing prohibited produce; and, finally, determines the rule for cases of doubt. Scripture thus has defined the theme. The Mishnah then has raised its questions, typical of, and distinctive to, the Mishnah: matters of mixture, cases of doubt. Here, therefore, the Mishnah tractate does more than provide complementary information to Scripture. But it obviously intends to amplify what Scripture says.

Disposing of Crops in Accordance with the Rules of Holiness

Peah. Tractate Peah has no program except in obvious ways to clarify and amplify Scripture's rules. Lev. 19:9–10 specifies the requirement to leave over a corner of the field for the poor, as well as to allow them gleanings and defective clusters. Lev. 23:22 goes over this same ground. Deut. 24:19–22 refers to the forgotten sheaf. The requirement to separate poor man's tithe is located at Deut. 14:28–29. Since the tractate does little more than explain how these requirements apply and are to be met, we must conclude that its sole effort is to complement Scripture. It has no essentially distinctive viewpoint on the topic or exercise of its own.

Demai. The status and disposition of doubtfully tithed produce are issues in no way generated by any verses or principles of Scripture.

Terumot. For the Mishnah, heave offering is a consecrated gift of produce made by Israelites to priests. The notion of such an offering has its source in the priestly code. Specifically, Num. 18:8–14 begins by discussing those parts of Temple sacrifices which belong to the Aaronide priests, and continues by referring to agricultural offerings. It states, "This also is yours, the offering of their gift, all the wave offerings of the people of Israel; I have given them to you, and to your sons and daughters with you, as a perpetual due; every one who is clean in your house may eat of it. All the best of the oil, and all the best of the wine and of the grain, the first fruits of what they give to the Lord

I give to you. The first ripe fruits of all that is their land, which they
bring to the Lord, shall be yours." It is unclear whether or not P's
"offering of their gift . . . the best of the oil, and all the best of the wine
and of the grain" in fact refers to an agricultural offering distinct from
the "first fruits" which which the continuation of the passage deals.
However that may be, the Mishnah clearly understands the passage as
referring to a separate offering, which it terms "heave offering." It
derives from Scripture basic facts about this offering. These are that it
is a holy offering, given by Israelites to priests, who, along with their
households, eat it in a state of levitical cleanness.

Outside of these basic facts, the Mishnah's discussion of heave offering is asymmetrical to what we might predict on the basis of Scripture. The central concern of the priestly code is the maintenance of the
Aaronide priesthood, which has "no inheritance in the land" (Num.
18:20). Tractate Terumot does not carry forward this theme. It does not
tell us, for instance, how the requirement that Israelites support the
priesthood is to be enforced. It has no interest in how heave offering is
to be conveyed to the priests, or, for that matter, in how one determines on the basis of need which priests may take the offering. The
tractate does not even detail which members of the priestly household
can join in eating heave offering. Unlike P, tractate Terumot's interest
lies in the fact that heave offering is holy. This moves matters in a
direction quite independent of anything stated in Scripture.The Mishnah takes as its task the description of the dynamics of the holy. That
is, it wants to know how by the power of his designation the householder is able to concentrate in a small quantity of produce the holiness
which previously was spread through all of the harvest, and how the
now-holy produce is maintained in his secular domain until it is returned to its rightful owner, the priest. Unlike in P, the priest plays thus
only a minor role in the Mishnah's schema, which is concerned for the
most part with the intentions and deeds of the Israelite householder.

ALAN PECK

Maaserot. Scripture's discussion of agricultural offerings informs that
of Maaserot at only a single point, in regard to the kind of produce from
which tithes need be removed. The Mishnah, with Scripture, assumes
that these offerings need be removed from agricultural produce only.
For the Mishnah, however, this fact has rather far-reaching consequences which Scripture never imagines. While Scripture, therefore,
serves Mishnah as a source of information, it in no way shapes what
the Mishnah will make of that information.

Scripture's discussion of tithes is scattered throughout the Pentateuch (Lev. 27:30–31; Num. 18:8–13, 19–32; Deut. 14:22–29,

26:12–15), and appears as well in the late work of the Chronicler (Neh. 10:35–39). In all sources, Scripture's chief interest in the topic is to ensure that these offerings, which it views as a tax upon the Land's produce, are properly conveyed to the people designated to receive them. Scripture points out that the offerings are to be removed from all the Land's produce (Lev. 27:30; Deut. 14:22) and are to be consumed by three categories of individuals: (1) Temple personnel, i.e., priests and Levites (Num. 18:8ff.); (2) those destitute of property or power, i.e., widows, orphans, sojourners (Deut. 26:12–15); (3) landowners, who eat the tithe as an offering before God in Jerusalem (Deut. 14:22ff.). Scripture is explicit that the tithes, which are deemed holy to God (Lev. 27:30–31), may be consumed only by those destined to receive them (Deut. 26:12ff.). In sum, then, Scripture's concern is that the required offerings are properly removed by landowners, and, after removal, are consumed by the designated individuals.

The Mishnah's only explicit contribution to Scripture's discussion is to define in greater detail the category of produce from which tithes must be removed. The tractate specifies that tithes be removed from all produce cultivated by human labor in the Land of Israel (M. Ma. 1:1, 5:5). This is a reasonable expansion of Scripture's notion that the tithes are a tax on the Land's produce. As a tax, tithes may be levied only upon property. Wild produce, it follows, or produce which is abandoned, cannot be taxed. The Mishnah's few forays beyond the plain sense of Scripture's discussion are not exegetically significant. The tractate argues that tithes need be removed only after the produce has ripened (M. Ma. 1:2–4, 5:3, 5:5). The point is obvious, for the tithes, which are to be eaten, must be removed from edible produce. Similarly, the tractate argues that produce taken from the field prior to the harvest need not be tithed (M. Ma. 5:1–2). This is a refinement of Scripture's view that the tithes are to be removed from each year's yield (Deut. 14:22). Mishnah points out that the tithe comes from the yield, but not from that which *precedes* the final yield.

Of the above conceptions only one is of any consequence in the unfolding of the Mishnah's discussion, i.e., M. Ma. 1:2–4's claim that tithes need be removed only after the produce has ripened and become suitable for human consumption. For the Mishnah the desire of the farmer to make use of the crop, a desire aroused only when the crop ripens, evokes as well a claim on the part of God, the owner of the Land, for his tithes. The task of adjudicating the claims of the farmer and God to the same batch of untithed produce is indeed the generative problematic of the entire tractate. While the bulk of the Mishnah's cases and rulings concern produce which has already ripened and been harvested, M. Ma. 1:2–5 is important in filling out the larger theory behind the Mishnah. It describes the earliest, point in the growth of a crop at which the law of tithes becomes potentially operative.

MARTIN JAFFEE

Maaser Sheni. The bulk of the tractate investigates the implications of facts given in Deut. 14:22–27. This passage requires the farmer to eat his tithe in Jerusalem. It goes on to say that if the farmer is unable to carry all of his tithe to the city, he may sell it and bring to Jerusalem instead the money he receives for the produce. This money is then used in Jerusalem to purchase food which is eaten in place of the original. The Mishnah carries forward three themes found in this passage. The first is that the tithe must be eaten in Jerusalem. The Mishnah explains that this means that the farmer may gain no other benefit from the consecrated produce. The tractate next considers the sale of consecrated produce. In particular, the Mishnah investigates how the selling price of the produce is established, declaring that the farmer may exchange the consecrated coins for other coins; that is, that he may make change. The coins must be spent only in Jerusalem and only on food. Finally, the Mishnah rules that once consecrated produce has been brought to Jerusalem, it may no longer be sold even if it is taken out of the city. This is so because the farmer now clearly is able to bring the consecrated food to Jerusalem.

In connection with the sale of consecrated produce, Scripture declares that if a farmer transfers the consecrated status of his produce to his own coins, he must pay an extra twenty-five percent of its value (Lev. 27:30–31). That is, if he is deconsecrating produce worth four *sela'im*, he consecrates five *sela'im* of his own money in its stead. M. M.S. 4:3–5 applies this rule to the deconsecration of second tithe.

M. M.S. 5:1–5 deals with produce of a tree's fourth year of growth. As regards such fruit, Scripture declares, "It shall be forbidden to you for three years and is not to be eaten, but in the fourth year its fruit is holy, dedicated to the Lord" (Lev. 19:23–25). From Scripture's language the Mishnah concludes that fruit of a tree's fourth year is like second tithe because it is holy yet is eaten by the farmer. M. M.S. 5:1–5 explores the implications of this analogy, claiming that in all regards such fruit is to be treated like second tithe.

The tractate concludes by considering the law of removal. The basic law comes from Deut. 26:12–15, which requires the farmer to clear his domain of consecrated produce which has accumulated there. He then must go to Jerusalem and aver that he has fulfilled this obligation. M. M.S. 5:6–9 describe first how the law is carried out as regards the various kinds of consecrated produce. The produce must either be given to its appropriate recipient or be destroyed. The discussion then moves on to consider how the law is applied in unusual cases: after the Temple's destruction, as regards produce still growing in the field and in connection with produce to which the farmer has no access. The text of the confession itself is the subject of a Midrashic interpretation at M. M.S. 5:10–14. This material reads into Scripture's text allusions to the various rabbinic laws of tithing.

PETER HAAS

Hallah. Scripture mandates the dough offering at Num. 15:17–21. The passage states that when the Israelites come to the promised land and eat of its bread, they are to separate a heave offering to Yahweh from the first of their bread dough. This offering is likened to the heave offering of produce. Tractate Hallah does little to advance this conception of the dough offering. The Mishnah basically defines aspects of the Scriptural command, fills in some questions not addressed by Scripture, and takes up one or two themes that are explored more fully elsewhere in the Mishnaic corpus. A good half of the tractate is concerned with defining what is bread dough, and what is Israelite bread dough. Topics absent in Scripture but taken up in the Mishnah are quantitative in nature—how much is to be separated? And, what is the minimum liable to the offering? Some attention is given to the issues of mixtures and intention, Mishnaic themes that we would expect to find in the tractate. The tractate largely is a well-ordered, carefully detailed restatement of Scripture.

ABRAHAM HAVIVI

Bikkurim. Deut. 26:1–11 specifies that one has to set aside first fruits and bring them to Jerusalem, and, further, in presenting the produce to the priest, one has to recite the "confession," assuring the priest that the crops conform to the rules of holiness. Tractate Bikkurim goes over this ground and is completely dependent upon the specified verses of Scripture for both its facts and its exegetical program.

Berakhot. While Berakhot refers to various biblical verses, e.g., those which comprise the *Shema'* (Deut. 6:4–9), its basic definitions of the three principal liturgies, the *Shema'*, the prayer, and the blessings before, and grace after, meals, are worked out essentially independent of Scripture, which provides no laws on these subjects. The tractate is associated with its Division because it provides a fitting conclusion to discourse on producing and consuming crops in accord with the sanctity of the Land: blessings to be said before and after eating the food, and, therefore, associated liturgies.

The Division of Appointed Times

The tractates which give rules for the village and the home on the occasion of appointed times tend in fresh ways to define the problem to be worked out in connection with the several subjects under discussion. Shabbat and Erubin take up one of the favorite themes of the several documents of the Mosaic codes in such a way as to ask a quite novel set of questions. True, the fundamental principles are Scriptural. But Scripture by itself cannot have permitted us to predict the particular points of interest and the principles under discussion and articulation in Shabbat and Erubin. On the contrary, it is the distance from Scripture, not the proximity to it, which is striking. Besah, for its part, approaches a problem presented by the rule that one may cook on the festival. But its analysis of the problem, its exploration of the limits and requirements of the analogy between the Sabbath and the festival, its inquiry into the rule of analogy and contrast or dissonance—these significant, suggestive approaches in no way emerge from Scripture. They derive from minds capable of original and independent thought on topics provided by Scripture, thought of a remarkably searching character into the weight and power of a simile. The analogical-contrastive mode of thought—something is like something else, therefore is bound within the limits of the laws governing that to which it is like, or it is different from something else, therefore is bound by laws totally opposite those governing that to which it is unlike—here spins out the engaging principles from which the concrete problems of the tractate take their form. The very basic supposition of Moed Qatan, finally, is unknown to Scripture, though, to be sure, it is invited by Scripture's provision of special offerings for the intermediate days of festivals, thus perhaps admitting to other special rules. These tractates begin quite early in the unfolding of Mishnaic law. It goes without saying that the four tractates are sufficiently rich in ideas and intellectual initiatives so that this claim of their conceptual autonomy is on solid, substantive ground. No one has decided to make a tractate on these four topics and then opened Scripture to see what information is there to be covered and developed. These tractates unfold through long and profound reflection. In so far as the Division as a whole contains deep thought, it is here. And, as we see, that thought reflects a world view at one and the same time engaged by and responsive to Scripture, and also essentially autonomous of Scripture and so able to see things fresh.

Most of the tractates which take up the cult in appointed times begin in Scripture, and whatever secondary layer of facts and ideas they build, it is without moving far from Scripture. None of them has a single important idea essentially independent of what Scripture has to say about the topic. Two of them, Pesahim and Yoma, slavishly follow the themes, and, in the case of Yoma, the exact order, provided by Scripture. They contribute nothing but some complementary facts, in the case of Pesahim, and a restatement, in Mishnaic language, of Scripture's picture of the occasion, in the case of Yoma. These same tractates begin after Bar Kokbha's war. As I said in other contexts, the evident intent is to provide a statement of how things are to be organized in time to come, when the Temple is rebuilt: "The next time around, things will be done right, so there will be no recurrence of what has just happened." For that purpose what is needed is what is given, which is a deeply literalist account of what everyone knows in Scripture anyhow. Let us now review the several tractates of our Division and examine the relationship of each to the corresponding materials on the same topic in Scripture.

Tractates of the Village and Home

Shabbat and *Erubin*. If the authors of the biblical texts could be asked to read this vast dual tractate and to respond to it, I think their first reaction would be not surprise, but satisfaction. For the principal themes of the various Scriptural passages which refer to the Sabbath and those of the double tractates are essentially the same: to refrain from cooking (Ex. 16:22–26), to remain at home and to rest on the seventh day (Ex. 6:29–30), to refrain from servile labor on the seventh day (Ex. 20:8–11, 31:12–17, 34:21, 35:2–3; Lev. 23:3; Deut. 5:12–15), and to provide the same rest for one's slaves and beasts (Ex. 23:12). One who deliberately violates the Sabbath by gathering wood on that day—deemed an act of labor—is put to death (Num. 15:32–36). Certainly no fact stated by the Mosaic code is omitted or treated as unimportant by the Mishnah's corresponding tractates. And yet, if these same legislators were to reflect some, they would surely recognize that their first reaction was wrong. For the Mishnah's version of the same subject does far more than supply necessary details for general principles laid down in Scripture.

First, where the Mishnah covers the same topics as Scripture, it is asymmetrical to Scripture. But, second, most of what is important to the Mishnah is not in Scripture at all. To be sure, important conceptions can have been teased out of Scripture, not merely read into it. True, the Mishnah tells how to prepare light and food for the Sabbath, and this theme is predictable on the basis of Ex. 16:22–26. And the Mishnah's introduction to its unit on prohibited acts of labor, M. Shab. 7:1ff., pretends to be interested in a wide range of prohibited actions.

But the Mishnah's principal interest, expressed at M. Shab. 1, 7–11, and 24, as well as in the entirety of Erubin, is not in servile labor in general. It is in the quite distinct conception of a domain in which it is permitted to transport objects, and a domain into and in which it is prohibited to do so. Ex. 16:29–30, which tells people to stay home on the Sabbath, may contain the distinction between private domain, where one has every right to move about, and what is not private domain ("one's place"), where one does not. But there is no way in which the great conceptions of (1) the distinctions among domains, (2) the recognition of the Sabbath limits of a village, (3) the preparation of a meal as the signification of where one will spend the Sabbath, (4) the provision of a common meal as a sign of common ownership of a courtyard or an alleyway, (5) the interest in the issue of how much of a given substance or material one must transport across the Sabbath limit to become liable for having violated the Sabbath—there is no way in which the encompassing conceptions of Erubin and the specified chapters of Shabbat will have emerged from that simple verse. The notion that on the Sabbath acts of labor are prohibited in the village if they are permitted on that same day in the Temple, on which, presumably, M. Shab. 12–14 is built, likewise is distinctive to the Mishnah. Then we come to the substantial discussion of not handling on the Sabbath objects of which to begin with one may not make use, and of the notion that for an object to be used on the Sabbath, in advance of that day, one must have formed the intention to make use of it. Here we find ourselves deep in the earliest layers of Mishnaic thought, and yet very far from anything Scripture has to say about the subject.

In sum, Scripture sets forth the great theme of the Sabbath and also presents one significant way in which that theme is to be explored, that is, in the prohibition of servile labor. But the Mishnah's definitive treatment of the theme, while obviously in complete accord with what Scripture has to say, treats as critical a range of problems and principles unknown to Scripture. On that basis we must declare Shabbat and Erubin to be essentially distinct from, though correlative with, Scripture.

Besah. Scripture lays down the basic fact which generates the problem of tractate Besah. Ex. 12:16 specifies that while one may not work on the festival day, one may prepare food on that day. In all other respects the festival is equivalent to the Sabbath. That conception precipitates thought on the limits and meaning of an analogy, and it is this analogical-contrastive problem—(1) unlike the Sabbath, therefore like an ordinary day in this regard, or (2) unlike the Sabbath *only* in this regard, therefore essentially like the Sabbath and therefore unlike an ordinary day *even* in this regard—which the Mishnah's original philosophers will have found engaging, indeed urgent. The exploration of the meaning of the analogy then generates the principles, illustration of which constitutes the sum and substance of this old tractate.

What Besah wishes to find out is whether preparing food on the festival day may be done in the way in which it is done on an ordinary day, because that work to begin with is permitted. Or must it be done in some unusual way, because of the character of the festival? Besah also asks whether only acts directly relevant to the preparation of food may be done, or whether even indirectly related sorts of labor may also be carried out. Besah further maintains that food for use on the festival must be available and subject to designation for use on the festival prior to that day. Besah works on the exploration of the applicability and limits of the analogy between the Sabbath and the festival. The festival is compared by Scripture to the Sabbath. The Mishnah then wants to know a great deal, as is clear, about the meaning of the generative-and-also-restrictive metaphor. These are questions to be asked by someone who proposes to encase the biblical rule in a sheath of secondary expansions and expositions. But the ideas themselves—the range of issues—are fresh and hardly flow inevitably from Scripture's simple declaration of the fact. It follows that Scripture presents the fact, but the Mishnah's framers—in the present instance, authorities early in the formation of Mishnaic law—take important fresh initiatives in their reflection upon those facts. Their mode of thought certainly is their own.

Moed Qatan. Discussing restrictions upon labor on the intermediate days of the festivals of Passover and the Festival, tractate Moed Qatan takes up a problem entirely unknown to Scripture, namely, the notion that there are such restrictions. Ex. 12:16, Lev. 23:7–8, 35–36, and Num. 28:18, 25, 29:12–15, know restrictions upon labor during the opening and closing sessions, but not on the intermediate days. But there are special offerings for the intermediate days. Someone may have come to the conclusion that, if there are special offerings, there also will be other sorts of special rules. That is, there is an analogy to be drawn between the intermediate days of a festival and the opening and closing days of the festival, rich in restrictions on labor, since on both sorts of days there are special cultic requirements. What then are the implications of that analogy?

The consequent theory, based on an analogical-contrastive inquiry, will have been that, just as in the cult, the intermediate days of a festival will be the occasion for offerings relevant to those days, so in the village, those intermediate days will be the occasion for the cessation of servile labor. Once that basic analogy is drawn, then the issues of the tractate may be addressed. The principles out of which the many discrete rulings are framed are, first, that one may do an act of labor to prevent substantial loss, but even then, it may not be an onerous act;

second, the work which ought to have been done prior to the festival may not be left over ("designated") to be done on the festival. In the background of such conceptions is the model of Besah. Scripture knows none of this, because it cannot imagine that there are rules for the intermediate days of festivals governing the village as well as the cult and thus linking the one to the other.

Tractates of the Cult

Pesahim. From beginning to end, tractate Pesahim simply takes up the themes of Scripture, specifically, Ex. 12:1–28, and provides some secondary amplification of them. Every fact in the tractate comes directly from that passage. All that is shifted is the order of topics. Scripture treats (1) setting aside and killing a lamb for the Passover offering; (2) unleavened bread and the taboo against leaven; (3) the disposition of the lamb. The Mishnah improves on this by first treating the prohibition of leaven and other preparations for the festival, then turning to the offering of the Passover sacrifice, roasting and eating it. Much of this tale is told through narrative style. Whether or not the Passover *seder,* which takes up the concluding chapter, constitutes a systematic response to the requirement to inform one's children of the events of the exodus from Egypt is not our problem. Pesahim as we know it simply restates and carries forward what is explicit in Scripture. It is repetitive in type.

Sheqalim. Ex. 30:11–16 requires the collection of a half *sheqel* for use in the support of the "tent of meeting." Tractate Sheqalim explains how the money is collected and utilized for the altar and goes on to other aspects of the financial administration of the Temple. There are some typical exercises on resolving cases of doubt, a mode by which the Mishnah not uncommonly fills out an otherwise rather thin tractate. Sheqalim has no independent stance vis-à-vis Scripture, but simply takes up and amplifies a matter introduced therein.

Yoma. It is not possible to understand the sequence of topics of tractate Yoma, let alone its exposition of their rules, without consulting Lev. 16. For all that Yoma offers is a restatement, in two modes of Mishnaic rhetoric, narrative and analytical, of the Levitical account of the cultic program for the Day of Atonement. Once that story is fully told, Yoma tacks on a perfunctory chapter on not eating and drinking on the holy day. So all we have is a narrative version of Scripture's own materials, with scarcely a pretense of doing more than telling, in the Mishnah's own words, Scripture's story—another repetitive tractate.

Sukkah. Lev. 23:33–43 specifies that the Festival is observed by making offerings, by taking the *etrog* and *lulab* ("the fruit of goodly trees, branches of palm trees, boughs of leafy trees, and willows of the brook"), rejoicing before the Lord, and dwelling in booths. Sukkah, for its part, provides rules for the building and use of the *sukkah* and for the preparation of the *lulab* and *etrog* and then deals with the rites and offerings of the Festival. Its special interest here is in the various observances carried out on different days of the Festival. So all Sukkah offers is a layer of secondary information on topics laid out in Scripture. It is completely dependent on Scripture, but complementary, not merely repetitive.

Rosh Hashshanah. Scripture speaks (Ex. 12:1–2) of a month which is at the head of the year, and, at Lev. 23:23–25, names the new moon of the seventh month as the day of sounding the *shofar,* a day observed by cessation of work as well. What is important about the New Year is the sounding of the *shofar,* so Num. 29:1–6. The two themes of tractate Rosh Hashshanah, the declaration of the new moon, the rules of the *shofar,* thus emerge from Scripture, the latter made more explicit than the former. The procedures for declaring the new month are worked out in mainly narrative style, those of the *shofar,* in analytical. But neither does much more than present some secondary explanations for how things are done. There is no important and sustainedly developed theme or idea which is essentially independent of Scripture. Even though there are many facts which do not emerge from Scripture, the tractate in its fundamental character depends upon Scripture, which it serves as a complement.

Taanit. The important ideas of tractate Taanit are, first, that fasts are called to bring rain; second, that there is a liturgy for that purpose, making extensive use of the *shofar;* and, third, that there are other uses of the *shofar* as an alarm. There is, finally, an appendix on the Israelite delegation associated with a particular group of priests. When the latter take up their duties in the cult, the former undertake certain liturgical tasks in their hometowns. Taanit follows in the wake of Rosh Hashshanah, because it is yet another tractate in which the use of the *shofar* receives considerable attention. But the tractate is distinct from Rosh Hashshanah. Since the Mosaic codes make no provision whatever for the fundamental procedures outlined in Taanit, the tractate must be declared entirely outside of the framework of Scripture and not generated by ideas, or even facts, important in Scripture's account of festivals and special occasions. It is a natural extension in general, but essentially independent in detail.

Megillah. Megillah is a negligible compilation setting forth the rules for reading the Scroll of Esther, as is required by Est. 9:16–32. The considerations important to the Mishnah are typically Mishnaic, e.g., the rule governing a person in one category who enters into another category. But the tractate cannot have come into being independent of the Scriptural requirement. It bears no significant ideas outside of what is needed to spell out what Scripture requires, e.g., who is a suitable person to read the Scroll, when it is to be done, and the like. The tractate therefore complements Scripture. The tractate's chapters on the laws of the synagogue property and liturgy flow from its basic theme, use of the synagogue for a cultic occasion, the lections for the synagogue on other occasions. While this part of the tractate is independent of Scripture, what is at issue is nothing other than the utilization of Scripture itself, that is, Scripture's role in the synagogue service. This tractate thus is complementary in both of its parts.

Hagigah. Speaking of three distinct offerings brought by ordinary folk on the occasion of the pilgrim festivals, tractate Hagigah has no information, other than that of Scripture, and bears no ideas generative of complex analytical pericopes, other than those borrowed from Besah. The appearance offering derives from Ex. 23:14–18, 34:23–24, which speak of not coming empty-handed to make an appearance before the Lord; the festal offering (*hagigah*) is understood to be required at Deut. 16:14; and the peace offering brought in the rejoicing of the feast is located by the exegetes at Deut. 27:7. Whether these offerings were in the minds of the authors of the several documents which refer to them is unimportant. What is significant for the tractate is that, once the conclusion is reached that there are such required pilgrim offerings, no important ideas, either independent of the stated requirement or flowing from it, come to expression. There is an effort to complement Scripture with some facts, e.g., who is liable to bring an appearance offering, how much it is to cost. It goes without saying that the special problem of the Sabbath will be introduced; that is, whether and how the festal offering, which yields meat for the sacrificer, is offered when the holy day and the Sabbath coincide. The other unit of the tractate, dealing with the principle that on the festival day ordinary people are assumed to be in a state of cultic cleanness, is independent of Scripture only in the sense that Scripture in any case cannot provide a merely descriptive statement of such a character. But since it is Scripture which imposes the duty of pilgrimage and cultic cleanness in the tent of meeting, one may hardly be surprised that the consequent issue of the presumed status of ordinary folk in the Temple and Jerusalem is addressed in that very tractate in which the pilgrim's offerings are explicated.

The Division of Women

The scribal focus of the Mishnah's system of Women, with its keen interest in regulation of the transfer of women from father to husband, along with appropriate documents, and the transfer of property from the father's domain to the husband's and back to the father's or to the divorcee's, has no counterpart in Scripture. The closest we come to an interest in legal documents is the casual reference at Deut. 24:1–4 to a writ of divorce. Here the contrast between Scripture's and the Mishnah's overall range of interest is blatant. The types of questions upon which the Mishnah concentrates simply do not arise in the Deuteronomic framework.

The fact that the program of the Mishnah is its own is still more obvious in those cases in which the Mishnah and Scripture share the same set of topics, that is, matters of vows in general and the Nazirite vow in particular, not to mention the generative conceptions of the great minds of Yebamot. The two priestly systems, that of the priestly code, with special reference to Lev. 12 and 15, and that of the holiness code, subordinate the topic of women to the paramount and critical theme of the codes themselves, which is cultic cleanness, and the purity of the Land preserved through avoidance of consanguineous marriages, respectively. The truncated system of Deut. 22, covering sexual relations of a betrothed virgin, a married woman, and a virgin who is not betrothed, simply has no counterpart in the Mishnah, although, of course, the facts of the matter are taken for granted and in no way controverted. The net result of a comparison among Scripture's several systems with the one of the Mishnah's Third Division is entirely negative. All we learn is that the Mishnah has its own points of critical tension. The Division of Women raises its own generative issues and constructs its world view, here as elsewhere, along lines dictated by its own most profound concerns, not those of any of the several Pentateuchal systems.

When, however, we ask about the rules and facts of Scripture and how they are utilized in the Mishnah, the picture changes completely. Here we see that Scripture has provided the Mishnah with a rich corpus of facts, many of them developed and augmented, all of them treated as fundamental data and received with respect. The relationship of the Division of Women to Scripture is superficially ambiguous. The reason is that the Mishnah rarely, if ever, links its legal statements to Scripture or claims that it rules in accord with Scripture, e.g., by saying, "as it is written in Scripture," or, "as it is stated in Scripture." It follows that, on the surface, the Mishnah pretends to stand autonomous of Scripture and wishes to claim that the source of its laws is other than Scripture. The language of Mishnah, it is obvious, in no way attempts to model itself after the syntax, morphology, word choices, or other salient traits of the language of Scripture. If, at first glance, the Mishnah pretends not to know Scripture, in fact the Mishanh depends upon Scripture in a deep way, in part for its thematic agendum, and in very large measure—wherever possible—for its basic facts. So the real issues are these: What is the nature of the dependence? What are the overall traits of the relationship? Above all, we want to point to those aspects in which the Mishnah does move beyond the range of facts and conceptions bearing Scriptural antecedents.

What we shall see is that the Division of Women is essentially distinct from Scripture at those points at which the Mishnah treats the topics critical to the Mishnah's own definition of the distinctive problematic of its theme. Specifically, tractates which discuss the transfer of women and of property associated therewith, Ketubot, Gittin, Qiddushin, and, above all, Yebamot, are either totally independent of Scripture, as in the case of the first three, or essentially autonomous of Scripture, though using Scripture's facts, as in the case of the fourth. Where the Division of Women goes over ground already treated in Scripture—vows, the Nazirite vow, and the rite of the accused wife—the Mishnah's repertoire of ideas complements those of Scripture. While not precisely complementary, other Mishnaic ideas raise issues required for a full account of the topic introduced by Scripture precisely as Scripture has chosen to define the problematic of that topic.

The Beginning of a Marriage

Qiddushin. When we come to Qiddushin, betrothals, we entirely leave the frame of topics known to Scripture in its discussion of the law of women. For its part, once it has determined to discuss the topic, the Mishnah has little to say about betrothals except what it already has said about marriage contracts (Ketubot) and writs of divorce (Gittin). When a woman is betrothed to a particular man, we come to a critical point in the transfer of women. That is why, given its larger problematic, the Mishnah simply has to produce a tractate on this subject. But unfortunately, at that point the Mishnah runs out of ideas, whether fresh, or used but at least merely generative, or even of any substance at all. The tractate presents some basic rules of betrothal. It spells out procedures of betrothal in terms of the salient issues of writs of divorce: agency, stipulations. Then it deals with impaired betrothals. At the end is a chapter corresponding in its interests to Lev. 18 and its parallels. But the topic—who may marry whom—now is phrased in terms of castes within the Israelite community, rather than consanguineous relationships within a given family. The principal interest of this unit is in the marriage of a priest to an appropriate woman and how women may be impaired for marriage to a priest. Here we have an entirely familiar conception.

In sum, Qiddushin merely repeats and augments a few Scriptural facts, when it does not merely repeat and augment a few Mishnaic facts. I am not inclined to see it as complementary to Scripture in any but the loosest sense, since its paramount topic, betrothals, is worked out in a scribal, rather than a priestly (genealogical), framework: documents, agency, stipulations. These receive more attention than castes and correct ancestry. Still, the tractate is so brief and flimsy that the opposite judgment, seeing the issue of caste as considerable, has much to recommend it.

Ketubot. The basic conception of Ketubot is that we provide a marriage settlement for a woman, functioning as alimony in the case of divorce and as an annuity in the case of the husband's death. This settlement is encapsulated in a document, the marriage contract, prepared with utmost care and enforceable in courts of law. This document is of such standing that it may enable a woman to seize possession even of real estate sold by the husband or placed under a lien or a mortgage to third parties. Consequently, that document must be regarded as one of the single most powerful instruments in the Israelite system as the Mishnah states it. And of all this the several Pentateuchal codes know absolutely nothing.

The tractate's choices of how the topic should be treated refer to the reciprocal and corresponding rights and obligations, principally of a material character, of all parties to the marriage at each point in its unfolding: the girl, the boy, the girl's father. At the outset the tractate tells us about the material agreement on the eve of a marriage, then, the reciprocal responsibilities of husband and wife, and, at the end, collection of the marriage contract upon the death of the husband. At three points, to be sure, a material right of the father derives from Scripture and is recognized and honored in Mishnaic law. Deut. 22:28–29 specifies that if a man seizes, and has sexual relations with, an unbetrothed virgin, the man pays the father fifty *sheqelim* and marries the girl. Ex 22:15–16 has the same general conception, that there is a marriage present paid over to the father. Deut. 22:13–21 reports a claim that the girl has not yielded tokens of virginity, which, if found false, means the husband has to pay a fine of a hundred *sheqelim* to the father. The rule of Deut. 21:22 is treated at M. Ket. 3 and 4. As is clear, the topic is subordinated to the larger construction about the unfolding of the discussion of the rights of all parties to the marriage. This account the tractate wishes to provide also on the rights of the father. So it is self-evident that the tractate draws on those facts of Scripture which even marginally are relevant to its interests. But the tractate does not begin in Scripture, nor does it derive from Scripture its problematic and its thesis about the orderly governance of property relations attendant upon the transfer of women. The subordination of those few items of Scripture which the tractate does find useful simply confirms the fact that Ketubot is wholly autonomous of Scripture.

The Duration of a Marriage

Nedarim. Nedarim, as well as Nazir and Sotah, relates to Scripture entirely differently from Yebamot and Ketubot, not to mention Gittin and Qiddushin. All three tractates on a marriage in being begin in Scriptural rules and accomplish important work of clarifying and augmenting what Scripture to begin with states without obscurity. Even though both Nedarim and, in its wake, Nazir, contain fresh and original conceptions, still the two tractates serve essentially to complement Scripture, not to build, alongside Scripture, structures meant to stand independent. What Scripture wishes to tells us about vows is (1) that they must be observed, but (2) that the father or husband of a woman has a right to abrogate the vows taken by the daughter or wife. A reading of Num. 30:1–16 leaves no doubt that that same conception forms the center of the priestly legislator's interest in the matter of vows. That, no doubt, is why the topic finds its way into our Division.

But, curiously, the congruity of the Division's principal interests—the transfer of women and other matters pertaining to the relationships of women to the men who are responsible for them—with Scripture's chief concern means little in the program of Nedarim on vows. This tractate unpacks the topic in ways we could never have predicted on the basis either of what Scripture says or of the very location of the tractate in its present Division. For what the Mishnah tells us is what Scripture ignores, yet invites: the definition of language which is so effective as to impose a vow, for instance; the matter of euphemism; language of no effect at all; and language of limited effect. Scripture ignores (or takes for granted the meaning of) the effects of vows. What the sorts of vows are which people take and how they restrict the everyday life of the person who takes them are matters carefully spelled out in the Mishnah's second unit. These include vows not to derive benefit in general as distinct from vows not to eat a particular kind of food. The Mishnah's important point, which is stated many times but amplified not at all, is that a vow to prohibit a species has no effect upon one's right to use other species of the same genus. But a vow to prohibit a genus obviously means that all species within the genus are prohibited. The third and closing unit of the tractate turns to grounds for the absolution of vows. While exegetes of the tractate locate diverse foundations in diverse Scriptural contexts for the absolution of vows by sages, in fact the locus classicus for vows knows nothing of their post facto absolution, only of their abrogation under decidedly limited circumstances. The tractate, by contrast, tells grounds for the absolution of vows; then, and only then, does it describe rules and procedures for the annulment of the vows of a daughter and of a wife. Finally, it lists the sorts of women whose vows cannot be annulled at all, since they are subject to neither a father nor a husband. In sum, Nedarim in the richest and fullest sense of the word complements Scripture.

Nazir. Nazir follows Scripture's portrayal of the shared topic of the Nazirite, at Num. 6:1–21. What Scripture wants to say about the Nazirite is that the Nazirite avoids wine, haircuts, the corpse contamination, and when the period of the vow is complete, brings certain offerings. If he or she is made unclean before completion of the vow, there is a sacrificial rite, described in detail, and if the vow is completed in a state of cleanness, there is another sort of rite. So what Scripture says is, first, what the Nazirite must not do, and, second, how the rites are conducted at the unsuccessful or successful completion of the vow, the two points obviously essential in the mind of the priestly legislator. Knowing how the Mishnah treats Nedarim, we should not find it surprising that, in addition to amplifying minor details of these same points, the Mishnah also will pay close attention to the vow of the Nazir, effective language, and to the abrogation of the vow.

The tractate treats the language of the Nazirite vow and stipulations and conditions introduced into it. A vow, for example, to observe only part of the rules is not valid, and a vow made in error is not valid. Further defined is the time limit of the vow, which Scripture has omitted to specify, and, finally, the abrogation or annulling of a vow. Here the right of the husband to abrogate the vow or to confirm it is taken for granted. Quite reasonably, the Mishnah reads the rules of Num. 30 into Num. 6. The second and third units of the tractate simply complement topics spelled out in Scripture, the offerings owed by the Nazirite, and the prohibitions observed by him or her, reversing Scripture's order but augmenting Scripture's sense with some decidedly secondary problems and issues. At the end, predictably, the Mishnah introduces some cases of doubt, e.g., about the applicability of the vow, or about the enforcement of its provisions. What makes the Mishnah distinctive and important is its inquiry into problems of the language, applicability, annulment, duration, conditions, and stipulations of the Nazirite vow. All of this simply complements a topic Scripture has spelled out in its way. The contrast between the priestly and Mishnaic conceptions of what one has to say about a given topic then is clear and self-evident.

The Mishnah takes up and asks its own questions about a topic introduced and treated in its own way by Scripture. But the Mishnah also provides further reflection on what Scripture says about that same topic.

Sotah. Sotah, for its part, shows us what a Mishnah tractate looks like when the Mishnah has nothing important to say about a chosen topic. The six chapters of the tractate devoted to the topic of the accused wife accomplish two things. First, the larger part provides a narrative of the rite of the bitter water and what is done in it. Num. 5:5–31 lays out the rule and rite of the accused wife. The bulk of the first three chapters of Sotah does the same. The Mishnah's other contribution is to spell out who is exempt from the rite, how testimony is received which imposes the rite upon a wife or may exempt her from it. Its main idea is that the rite is required only in a case of doubt. But if we have grounds to think the woman has done what the husband says she may have done, however flimsy these grounds may be, we do not impose the rite. Instead, we send the woman forth with a writ of divorce and with the settlement owing for her marriage contract. These are the sum and substance of Sotah's ideas on its topic: Scripture, and some minor clarifications of Scripture. It would not be accurate to say that Sotah substantially complements Scripture. At best the tractate adds some minor details and amplifications. Perhaps the fact that Num. 5 and 6 deal with the accused wife and the Nazir, respectively, played some part in joining them in our Division. If that is so, it would merely be yet another signification of the fact that the two tractates are utterly dependent upon Scripture.

The End of Marriage

Yebamot. Yebamot discusses three themes: establishing the marital bond through supernatural action; the priest's marriage; and severing the marital bond through supernatural action or under other unusual circumstances (thus excluding, in particular, the severing of the marital bond through a writ of divorce). The first and the second themes emerge directly from Scripture. Deut. 25:10–15 states that when a brother dies childless, his widow will marry the husband's brother, the levir. The first son will be named after the deceased. If the man does not wish to marry the widow, there is a rite of removing the shoe, *ḥaliṣah,* which severs the connection. On the basis of this statement, we should expect the tractate to devote attention to the *ḥaliṣah* ceremony, which is the center of interest to the Deuteronomic legislator. But that is not the case. For the opening, and principal, unit of Yebamot chooses to bring the levirate connection into relationship with the prohibitions of Lev. 18 (and related passages). If the surviving brother is married to the sister of the widow, then he cannot take the widow in levirate marriage. The reason is that, if he does, he will end up married to two sisters, which is not permitted. The critical tension of the Mishnah is located in the potential violation of the rules of Lev. 18 on account of the levirate connection and resolved in the notion that the woman in a consanguineous relationship to the levir is exempt from all levirate connection. Indeed, in the Hillelites' view, all of her cowives also are exempt—a step beyond the generative proposition. It will follow that there are women who are not subject to the levirate connection which circumstances have imposed on them. This will yield the second, and derivative, conception that some women are both subject and not subject to that connection, so sever it through a rite of *haliṣah*, and, of course, yet other women are fully subject to the connection. In so stating matters, we have given the main point of the opening unit, with its immense and attractive corpus of theoretical and imaginative cases. The Mishnah's comparison of *haliṣah* to an act of divorce, and its consequent comparison of levirate coition and betrothal, then account for the rest of the developments in M. Yeb. 1–5, which I believe to be one of the truly brilliant, perspicacious achievements of the Mishnah, the work, continuously, of a hundred-year sequence of thinkers.

The second unit of Yebamot is based on the facts, specified in Lev. 22:10–16, that the priest and his family, including his slaves, eat "holy things," which the Mishnah understands to refer to heave offering. If a priest's daughter marries an outsider, she no longer eats heave offering. If she is widowed or divorced without issue, and returns to her father's house, she eats heave offering. The problems of the second unit of Yebamot, M. Yeb. 6–9, simply take these simple facts and raise some routine secondary and tertiary questions arising from them. While the questions are thoughtful and original, none of them can be said to take up a perspective independent of the facts at hand. All of them depend, therefore, upon what, to begin with, Scripture states. They intend to amplify and augment the application of Scripture's facts.

The third Division of the tractate, in some measure, is a potpourri of diverse materials. The redactor did not wish to place any of these with Gittin, where they belong: severing marriage on every sort of basis but a writ of divorce. We begin with discussion of marital ties subject to doubt. Then we proceed to a brief account of the rite of *haliṣah*. We come, third, to the right of refusal, effected by a girl married off as minor by mother or brothers. When the girl reaches maturity, she has the right to reject the husband chosen for her by her brothers or mother. By contrast, Scripture is clear that if the father marries her off, the marriage is valid. Perhaps the conception of the right of refusal is a secondary development of the fact that the mother and brothers do not have the power that the father enjoys over the minor daughter. But I am inclined to see it as an essentially fresh and autonomous notion, not yielded by a close and specific exegesis of Scripture. The unit then turns to the infirm marital bonds of a deaf-mute, of a minor girl, and of a minor boy on the eve of puberty. Finally, the unit turns to severing the marital tie through the death of the husband. The important issue is testifying to the identity of a corpse. None of these topics seems to me to relate to any facts of Scripture.

Now when we line up the great tractate of Yebamot against Deut. 25:10–15, the latter appears rather small and unimpressive. The biblical pericope of the levirate connection merely states a few facts and contains not a single interesting and generative conception. The tractate, in fact, is not really about the levirate connection. It means to encompass all marital connections, effecting and severing them, which are subject to heavenly intervention or concern. The inclusion of the priest's daughter's right to eat heave offering is the key. The Mishnah does not innovate in this topic. But selecting this topic for inclusion at just this point constitutes a rather innovative view of the facts of the matter. Of greater consequence, the whole range of issues attending upon exceptional marital ties, inclusive of heaven's creation of new circumstances, e.g., through death, rather than through the deliberate action of man and woman, is simply separate and distinct from anything Scripture has to say.

What the tractate wishes to teach is that there is a correspondence, in the transfer of women, between heaven's work and the deeds of man. Both have the power to impose the marital bond. Both have the capacity to sever it. The modes of both of them of joining or of loosening the bond are equally holy. For the consequences of both are identical, despite the differences of their auspices and character. Heaven's bond (the levirate connection) and earthly union (betrothal, marriage-contract, and consummation), correspond to one another, as do death at heaven's hands and divorce. Each completes the possibilities opened by the other. A man's document effects sanctification of a woman for that particular man. So does the unfolding of Heaven's plan. A man's document removes the sanctity of a woman for that particular man. So does the fulfilment of the rite of *ḥaliṣah*.

When we ask about the relationship of Yebamot to Deut. 25:10–15 and other Scriptural passages which supply facts for the intellectual enterprise of the tractate, the question becomes rather difficult to interpret. Of course, we should have no tractate of Yebamot without Deut. 25:10–15, Lev. 18, and a few other verses. But the tractate of Yebamot does not emerge from those verses. It arises from deep, independent, and original reflection upon certain facts of Scripture. This reflection is precipitated by intellectual motivations in no way deriving from Scripture. On this basis, we must regard Yebamot as no less independent of Scripture, as we shall shortly see, than Kelim, Tohorot, and Makhshirin, on the one side, and, in their way, Arakhin and Meilah, on the other. The former scarcely know Scripture, although, when they can, they will use some its materials, presented in another connection entirely, for their own purposes. The latter do take up topics of Scripture. But they do so in such a fresh way as to make a statement Scripture's authors cannot have imagined to be important and required in connection with these same topics.

Gittin. This brings us to Gittin, writs of divorce. Deut. 24:1–4 refers rather tangentially to something which the Mishnaic authorities reasonably deem to be a writ of divorce: a woman who has been divorced and remarried may not then marry the husband who originally divorced her. It would be absurd to claim that the Mishnah then complements this passage by telling us a few minor rules concerning the writ of divorce. In fact, the Mishnah tells us what does not concern Scripture at all: the whole corpus of rules governing the preparation and transmission of a writ of divorce. Where it can draw upon Scripture for precedent, for example, Scripture's detail that the husband places the writ in the wife's hand, it does so. In this instance, the Mishnah then assumes that the writ of divorce is effective only when it reaches the wife's domain, whether this means her own hand, her property, or the hand of someone she has designated for the purpose of receiving the writ of divorce. So even here, where Scripture does supply a fact important to the Mishnah, the character of Scripture's fact in no way allows us to predict the importance which the Mishnah will assign to that same fact or the way in which the Mishnah will render complicated and subtle the character—the very facticity—of the fact.

Gittin therefore is wholly autonomous of Scripture, and everything in the tractate flows from a different conception of what is critical and generative in the theme of the writ of divorce. It tells about how a writ of divorce is delivered and prepared. It then treats laws of agency in the delivery and preparation of the document. Third, it asks about stipulations in a writ of divorce, on the theory that a valid stipulation must be carried out for the writ to be effective. Finally, the tractate turns to things done improperly: the invalidation of a writ of divorce because of improper delivery, preparation, stipulation, and—the one more or less new consideration—improper witnesses. The tractate thus takes up issues important to scribes. The Deuteronomic legislator has no interest in issues of this sort. The Mishnah expresses the concerns of people to whom documents are important. What it says about documents is that they are important because heaven will confirm what scribes do on earth, a message distinctive (in our context) to the Mishnah.

The Division of Damages

It is difficult in broad outline to compare the Mishnah's Division of Damages with equivalent materials of Scripture. The reason is that the Division draws together two distinct concerns, the substance of civil law, on the one side, and the institutions of civil law, on the other. Scripture tends to keep them apart. Thus the Book of the Covenant is rich in the former sort of rules, while omitting all reference to the latter, while Deuteronomy keeps its systematic discussion of the government of the levitical priesthood and the monarchy separate from its treatment of topics of civil law, e.g., damages, torts, and the like, which it associates rather with topics having nothing to do with civil law, e.g., religious crimes, laws governing women, and so on. So there is no possibility of a systematic description of civil law in Deuteronomy, or of civil government in the Book of the Covenant. A very brief review suffices to make that point.

When we ask about the biblical accounts of systems of law and political institutions, our attention first turns, naturally, to the Book of the Covenant, which, as we shall see in a moment, makes a definitive contribution to part of the Mishnah's system of Damages. Ex. 21–23 go over topics of property damages and other sorts of civil conflict. Clearly, we have something very much like the Babas (Baba Qamma, Baba Mesia, Baba Batra). Ex. 21:1–27 deals with relationships, property rights among human beings, with special reference to slaves (21:1–6) and women (21:7–11); then comes consideration of civil and criminal assault on persons (21:12–27). The second major topic is damages by and to chattels, worked out at Ex. 21:28–35, 22:1–15. First is the ox which gores or suffers damages (Ex. 21:28–36, 22:1–4a); then are miscellaneous damages, e.g., through a grazing flock, fire (Ex. 22:2b–6), and, at the end, damages in respect to bailments (Ex. 22:7–15). In fact, the systematic account of the Book of the Covenant appears to have provided the framer of Baba Qamma with his basic program. The only way we can make sense of the materials and organization of M. B.Q. 1–6 is to compare the order of topics and mode by which they are discussed with the equivalent materials in Ex. 21. To be sure, the order of the Mishnah is (damage by) chattels, then (damage by) persons. The Book of the Covenant, for its part, contains nothing either equivalent to the other tractates of our Division or even relevant to them.

The priestly books of Leviticus and Numbers make provision for the priestly government of Israel and provide the model accepted by the Division of Damages, that is, a joint rulership by a high priest and a "ruler" (for Sanhedrin: king; for Leviticus and Numbers: *nasi*). The work of the priesthood is to maintain the cult, make the offerings, bless the people, and the like. The priestly code has no interest in issues important in the present Division. The holiness code in Lev. 19 treats honoring mother and father and keeping the Sabbath; forbids worshiping idols; formulates rules for sacrifice, the harvest, provision for the poor; forbids stealing, lying, swearing falsely, and so on. None of this intersects with the Division of Damages, except in minor details (e.g., Lev. 19:13, not withholding the wages of a worker). The holiness code's system as a whole in no way is like the account of law and institutions of politics provided by the Mishnah. There is in fact no point of systematic comparison. That is despite the fact that two tractates of the Division of Damages, Shebuot and Horayot, wholly rest upon the foundations of Lev. 5–6 and 4, respectively, and the materials for inheritance at M. B.B. 10 similarly, draw heavily on Num. 36. There is no system of civil laws and institutions in the priestly and holiness codes, even though there are relevant facts.

As part of its account of Israelite life, Deuteronomy deals with the administration of justice and the establishment of a monarchy. These are joined at Deut. 17. Courts are to be set up in towns (Deut. 17:8–13), and the people are to accept the verdict. If someone does not obey the priest or the judge, he is to die. The recurrent interest of Deuteronomy in obedience to the Torah is expressed in this context too: "And all the people shall hear and fear and not act presumptuously again." There follows the rule for the king, which, predictably, stresses that the king is subject to the law. Deuteronomy proceeds to deal with the levitical priests. The account of civil law begins with the cities of refuge for the manslayer. There follows the rule for conducting a trial, two witnesses being required for conviction (Deut. 19:15–21). It is difficult to see any sort of system or order in the diverse laws of Deut. 21–25. Those relevant to the interests of the Division of Damages of course will make their appearance in the Mishnah. But the organizing principle of the topics when they occur in Deuteronomy bears nothing in common with the way in which the present Division is put together. Deuteronomy presents nothing like the Mishnah's system of civil laws and institutions.

When we come to the topics treated in the Division of Damages, we find it difficult to define a Scriptural system, or even to locate a systematic treatment in Scripture, of both of the two topical constituents of the present Division. Passages of Scripture which attend to institutions of government, amply cited in the Mishnah's Division, do not integrate

facts about the civil code of justice; those which do add up to something very much like a civil code of justice, particularly in the Book of
the Covenant, appear not to take a sustained interest in institutions of
government and the enforcement of the law. Even when we treat the
two topics severally, however, results still are meager. The civil laws
of Deuteronomy come to us in disorganized and unsystematized form.
There is no clear relationship between the larger polemic of Deuteronomy and either the substance or even the topical sequence of the
relevant laws of civil life. (see Kaufman). So what, if anything, the
framers of Deuteronomy wish to do or how they propose to lay out
these laws is not clear to me. The program of the Book of the Covenant, for its part, is still less accessible. Clearly here materials are well
organized. But the larger polemic of the code does not emerge from the
organization or even the substance of the laws. This must be found
elsewhere.

The Mishnah treats as fact everything Scripture has to say about the
topics of the present Division, even while taking no perceptible interest
in how Scripture organizes them. Once more we shall observe that the
framers of the Mishnah have their own very clearly perceived purposes
in doing their work. For them Scripture is a source of information, not
of modes of organizing or structuring information. But the facts of
Scripture invariably are made to serve the purposes of the Mishnah's
framers. Where the framers of the Mishnah are able to draw heavily on
Scripture for the purpose of working out the systematic plan, they
assuredly do so. But there is no predicting solely on the basis of Scripture the sorts of topics which will interest the framers of the Mishnah,
let alone how they will work them out.

For while Scripture is a rich resource for the Mishnah, at its foundation this Division is essentially independent of Scripture. That is so
even where Scripture plays a commanding role in what the Mishnah
will say about a given topic or in a given tractate. The reason is simple.
The plan of the Mishnah is prior. Its principles of selection are definitive. This fact becomes clear in the diverse relationships between
Scripture and the three Babas, assuredly a unitary exercise of remarkable cogency. Baba Qamma restates the main conceptions of Scripture
about its topic. The tractate proceeds to present what is merely a series
of immensely sophisticated exercises in the application of those available facts. The exercises, for their part, do generate second-level facts,
but, in the main, they are interesting as applications of the facts of
Scripture and explorations of their implications. Baba Mesia is much
less inventive in its presentation of what are essentially facts taken
straight from Scripture. Unpredictably, Baba Batra, which is integral
to the progam of the whole, turns out to bear almost no relationship to
Scripture at all. The reason is that the Mosaic codes have virtually

nothing to say about topics important in Baba Batra. The absence of biblical consideration of a topic self-evidently is not going to prevent the framers of the Mishnah from devoting sizable attention to that same topic. So, as I said, Scripture is a reference book, not a ground plan or architect's design for the edifice built by the Mishnah.

The work on the institutions of civil society is asymmetrical to Scripture, even where there is any contact at all with the biblical materials. Most of Sanhedrin derives from some source of information both independent of Scripture and prior to the Mishnah's work on that subject. Since the work of Sanhedrin as a tractate appears to be mainly that of second-century philosophers and legislators, there is no way to know how long before the time of the framing of the tractate, let alone where, the facts were made up. Some sections—for instance, on banishment—simply restate and exemplify in the Mishnah's language the facts and operative considerations of Scripture. Others—for example, the long discussion on which mode of execution applies to what sort of capital crime—only occasionally intersect with Scripture, even though the fact that the death penalty applies to many of the crimes listed by the Mishnah is stated by Scripture. When we come to ancillary tractates, Shebuot and Horayot, by contrast, all we have is a reframing of Scriptural ideas in the Mishnaic constructions.

The Rules of Civil Society

Baba Qamma. Baba Qamma draws nearly all of its facts from Scripture and cannot be understood in detail without constant reference to the Scriptural rules on the same topics. Its four generative causes of damages—pit, ox, crop-devastating flock, and fire—simply go over the ground of Ex. 21:33–36 and 22:5–6. Its conception that there is a distinction between an ox deemed harmless and one which is an attested danger, with consequent differences in the rates and limits of compensation, is explicit at Ex. 21:33–36. Its idea that, if an ox commits homicide, it is stoned, is stated by Ex. 21:28–32. Its extensive discussion of paying fivefold compensation for stealing and disposing of an ox, and fourfold for a sheep, and twofold compensation for other theft of beasts, is at Ex. 22:1–4. The notion that a thief pays twofold compensation is also at Ex. 22:7–8. The principle of penalties for mayhem and assault is explicit at Ex. 21:18–19, though all five categories of compensation are not specified. The liability for the bailee, inclusive of the requirement to make full restoration and other penalties, is specified at Lev. 5:20–26. This rapid catalogue has now exhausted the entire topical agendum of Baba Qamma. Yet—amazingly—it in no way suggests the originality and initiative exhibited in Baba Qamma's exercises, let alone the exquisite formal arrangement of the whole and the careful formalization of the various exercises and of the language used within them.

Baba Mesia. Baba Mesia in a measure reorganizes but, essentially, merely replicates facts of Scripture. The rules on returning lost objects go over the ground of Deut. 22:1–4. The idea of true value and fraud can be read into Lev. 25:14, 17. Not taking interest is explicit at Lev. 25:35–37 and Deut. 23:20–21. The right of workers to be fed is at Deut. 23:24–25. Restoring a bailment or compensating for its loss is at Ex. 7:15ff. Paying workers promptly is at Lev. 19:13 and Deut. 24:14–15, and these verses are thoroughly explained and applied. Taking a pledge but returning it evenings is at Ex. 22:25–27 and Deut. 24:10–13, 17–18, and 24:6 (to follow the order of the Mishnah's treatment of the verses). This list exhausts the topics of the tractate.

Baba Batra. Baba Batra receives from Scripture markedly fewer facts, and much less critical ones, than the earlier tractates of the trilogy in which it stands. The reason is that its topics deal with more sophisticated real estate and commercial relationships than to begin with enter into the Mosaic codes. The requirement of just weights and measures, which appears briefly, is at Lev. 19:35–36 and Deut. 25:13–16. Laws of inheritance are at Num. 27:8–11 and Deut. 21:15–17. By contrast the entire repertoire of laws on real estate, the rights of property owners, title to real estate, transactions in movables and licit commercial transactions, unstated stipulations, and so on—all of the numerous legal facts and conceptions which are illustrated and explored in the bulk of the present tractate derive from some source other then Scripture. So here Scripture simply does not provide the required information for the Mishnah's program in the tractate. The facts come, in general, from the common legal heritage of the ancient Near East.

Abodah Zarah. While the basic conception behind Abodah Zarah is explicit in Scripture, the problems of the tractate are independent, defined in response to contemporary realities. The principle is that Israelites are to have no dealings with idolators and idolatry (Ex. 23:13, 24, 32–33; Deut. 7:1–5, 25–26, 12:2–3; and so on). But the concrete problems, having to do with commerce with idolators on the occasion of fairs and festivals, items Israelites are prohibited even to sell to gentiles, items Israelites are prohibited to use but permitted to sell, and the like—all emerge from everyday transactions. The special interest is wine which has served for a libation to a gentile idol flows from the notion that an idolator will make such a libation on every possible occasion and is therefore assumed always to contaminate the wine through idolatry, if he gets the chance. None of this is even hinted at in

Scripture. So while the basic principle is Scriptural, the tractate's shape and interests are wholly Mishnaic.

The Institutions of Civil Society

Sanhedrin. Sanhedrin makes ample use of the facts of Scripture. But these are not only organized in a fresh way. They are also augmented with a sizable corpus of other facts, which do not in a direct manner emerge from a reading of Scripture. The framers of the tractate may learn the requirement of establishing courts from Deut. 16:18–20 (as if the need for such a thing were not self-evident). But their concrete ideas about the threefold institution of courts and administrative centers (commercial, criminal, political) in no way are announced in Scripture, though, obviously, these ideas may be, and in fact were, read into Scripture. Rules for appealing to a high court are at Deut. 17:8–13, as is the penalty for the disobedient person (for the Mishnah: the sage). Num. 35:30 requires two witnesses in a capital case, as does Deut. 17:6–7. Lev. 21:10–12 presents the rule for the high priest; Deut. 17:14–20, that for the king. Deut. 21:22–23 states that the one who is executed is to be hung on a tree but taken down before nightfall. The felony of being a stubborn and rebellious son is at Deut. 21:18–21; that of the two towns which have gone over to idolatry, at Deut. 13:12–18. There are numerous other points in Scripture which prohibit certain actions, and of course, the tractate will take all of them into account. But its fundamental interest—the shape of the court system, the four death penalties, and those felons who are subject to each of them—is essentially independent of Scripture and served only in relatively slight measure by Scripture.

Makkot. For tractate Makkot the prohibition of perjury (Ez. 20:16; Deut. 5:20) is less urgent than the mode of dealing with perjured witnesses, spelled out at Deut. 19:15–21. The treatment of this passage in the tractate is nearly entirely dependent upon the exegesis of Scripture. The penalty of banishment and the specification of cities of exile are fully described at Num. 35:9–28 and Deut. 19:1–13, and the Mishnah does little more than repeat what Scripture states, adding a few routine and predictable exercises. The penalty of flogging, finally, is specified at Deut. 25:1–3. But the main interest of the Mishnah, in those who are subjected to that penalty, is not to be located in Scripture, which is remarkably vague about what turns out, in fact, to be a principal mode of punishment for a wide variety of infractions of the law. The Mishnah's description of the mode of carrying out that penalty, by contract, essentially depends upon and expands what Scripture specifies.

Shebuot. Shebuot is an exercise in the elucidation of Lev. 5 and 6, that is, those who bring a guilt offering. The interest is in Lev. 5:1–13, those involved with uncleanness and those who take a rash oath, and in Lev. 6:1–7, the oath of bailment. The further interest in the oath imposed by the judges does not change the picture of a tractate completely dependent upon Scripture for its themes and principles.

Horayot. Horayot does for Lev. 4 what Shebuot does for Lev. 5 and 6. It takes as its task the explication of the meaning of Lev. 4:1–5, 13–21, 22–26, and Num. 15:22–26. Nothing in the tractate is comprehensible without reference to these passages. The Mishnah simply provides definitions and explanations for facts of Scripture, a complementary layer of information, enriched by some standard analytical exercises.

The Division of Holy Things

The survey will show that the Mishnah's Fifth Division repeats, amplifies, and organizes conceptions in Scripture. It may also raise questions not asked by Scripture about facts supplied therein. In a few instances the Division rests upon facts (assumptions) distinct from those of Scripture and in some cases even contrary to Scripture's ideas. But when that is so, the Mishnah has not created these facts and on the face of it knows them only as givens. Their origins lie before the foundations of our document or outside its framework. For their part these givens do not themselves precipitate the creation of even a single chapter of the Mishnah. To the contrary they are used in the generation of the Mishnah's problems.

If the Division of Holy Things wants to say something other than is found in Leviticus and Numbers, however, it is difficult to specify what that might be in detail. Although the Division does not depend entirely on the facts given in Scripture, its dependence is so nearly complete that we may say there can have been no Division of Holy Things without the specified passages of the Pentateuch. While this Division effects clear-cut choices in the selection of Scriptures and facts for its amplification and extension, these too seem to me to yield no important insight into the mind and conception out of which the Mishnah originates.

In truth the important choices come at the outset and are revealed on the surface of things: the decision to make a Division of Holy Things, consisting of eleven tractates, on the subjects we have now reviewed (see above, pp. 150–53). The principal consequence of this analysis is the simple fact that the Mishnah has chosen to amplify every theme of Scripture's laws on Holy Things except for the ones dealing with the priesthood. The chief message of our Division is that there should be a Division on Holy Things.

Rules for the Altar

Zebahim. Tractate Zebahim takes for granted the whole corpus of Scripture's facts on animal offerings and constantly alludes to them. It knows some other facts, as well, but these data clearly stand in the distant background of the tractate's own work. Zebahim refers only to the sacrifices listed in Scripture, and in principal conceptions, e.g., about the blood rite and its centrality in the act of sacrifice, the tractate depends entirely on what Scripture has stated. What makes Zebahim more than a restatement of old ideas in fresh language, therefore, is solely the character of its own repertoire of themes and problems. This repertoire consists of three encompassing propositions.

First is the proposition that the improper intention or attitude of the officiating priest is effective to invalidate the sacrifice only in respect to two considerations. If the priest at the moment of slaughter or carrying out the blood rite intends to offer the sacrifice outside of the Temple and the proper location therein, the sacrificial meat is invalid. If he intends to eat the meat which will accrue to him outside of the proper time allotted for the eating, the meat is deemed refuse. This latter point excludes from the category of refuse all burnt offerings, e.g., the daily whole offering, which are not going to yield meat for the priest in any case. This definition of refuse, translated abomination, differs from that at Lev. 7:18: "If any of the flesh of the sacrifice of his peace offering is eaten on the third day, he who offers it shall not be accepted, neither shall it be credited to him; it shall be an abomination, and he who eats of it shall bear his iniquity" (cf. Lev. 19:7–8). This verse knows nothing of the issue of intention. Furthermore, since its context is peace offerings, which yield meat for the owner as well as the priest, the verse hardly is to be limited to the priest's actions. It follows that, in its single most important conceptual initiative, Zebahim begins in an assumption entirely separate from what on the surface would appear to be Scripture's intent. It will not serve to speculate on the facts of the cult itself, that is, on whether or not in the Temple, when it stood, the interpretation of the fundamental character of refuse was in accord with the Mishnah's understanding of it. We have no evidence on the priests' conduct of the rite and their conceptions of the definition of diverse issues such as these. It is important to observe, however, that the paramount ideas in Zebahim and (as we shall see) Menahot, taken for granted at the foundations of the tractates, in no way are to be located on the surface of the Scriptural record. It follows that someone has imposed upon Scripture a meaning not clearly present therein.

The Mishnah uses the fact to limit the possibility of the priest's improper intentions' spoiling the sacrifice. In the present, fundamental regard, therefore, all we are able to say is that the Mishnah begins its work in a conception quite distinct from Scripture's statement. That conception cannot be adduced as evidence of a viewpoint distinctive to, and expressive of, the Mishnah's own perspective on its theme. So at this point, the Mishnah simply stands apart from Scripture. We do not know in the company of what other documents or groups it takes its position.

The second set of ideas in Zebahim concerns the comparison of the killing of a bird in the cult by wringing its neck and the killing of an animal, whether or not in the cult, by the slitting of its throat with a sharp knife. Here Scripture simply supplies facts for the Mishnah's reflection and presentation.

The third unit of Zebahim deals with rules for the altar. One fundamental point is that the altar sanctifies what is appropriate to it and does not sanctify what is not appropriate to it. This proposition deprives the altar of the power of sanctification *ex opere operato* and treats the altar as essentially neutral, its *mana* subject to logical and reasonable laws. If wine or cereal touches the top of the altar, it stays there. If on the other hand gold or pomegranates should reach the top of the altar, they simply are removed. Contact with the altar in no way has changed them. This neutralization of the altar's power to effect taboo through mere touch alone will have surprised the author of the pericope of Nadab and Abihu (Lev. 10:1–3), as well as of Ex. 29:37 among the many Scriptural passages in which the intrinsic and uncontrolled sanctity of the cult, the altar, things offered on the altar, and cultic or holy objects, is taken for granted. The principle is well established. Someone before the beginning of the tractate's intellectual history has reached a conclusion taken for granted later on among the framers of the tractate's program of inquiry.

So far, there is no close tie between the two significant, and in some ways generative, conceptions lying at the foundation of the tractate, because their propositions in my view simply do not relate. That is, I do not see, specifically, how the "secularization" of the altar (in the limited sense just now defined) and the revision of the meaning of refuse to encompass priestly intention, relate to one another in concrete ways.

We need hardly dwell on the long lists of Scriptural verses which provide important facts for Zebahim. Mere allusion to Lev. 6:27–28 and the M. Zeb. 11 suffices to indicate the extent of the matter. Nor is the extended consideration of the rule against making sacrifices outside of the Temple in Jerusalem important evidence of a profound reworking of Scriptural conceptions or laws. Rather, in the face of the prolonged crisis after A.D. 140, it is simply a reaffirmation of the continued validity of one of the long-established facts of Israelite cultic law. If that is so in regard to the centralization of the cult in Jerusalem, it is also so in respect to scouring the pot in which the sin offering is boiled.

Scripture's facts are facts. The Mishnah's choice, among those facts, of a few for careful consideration reveals more about the Mishnah than it does about the Mishnah's general relationship to Scripture. Since it is obvious that before the framers is the possibility of making sacrifices outside of Jerusalem, to which Jews no longer had access, and so continuing the cult elsewhere, the current importance of the Deuteronomic law is dictated by the decision not to set in abeyance for the time being the ancient law requiring the centralization of the cult in Jerusalem. The philosophers chose, rather, to abrogate the cult entirely. That decision may have roots in some current or other of scriptural thought. It does not constitute, however, a "link" between Scripture and the Mishnah, let alone an aspect of the relationship between the two documents. It is, therefore, a choice made by second-century sages and set forth in the Mishnah, an aspect of what is new in the Mishnah, not of what is borrowed from Scripture.

Menahot. Tractate Menahot, on meal offerings, goes over much the same ground as Zebahim and repeats in terms of meal offerings some of the major constructions located in the earlier tractate on animal offerings. The factual foundations of Menahot, so far as I can see, are wholly Scriptural. Leviticus and Numbers specify a great many kinds of meal offerings. Menahot proposes to systematize all of them within its formal linguistic structures, e.g., lists of rules and regulations. We need not go over the ground of the Mishnaic conceptions of the effect of improper attitude on meal offerings. What we have said before applies without variation here. Questions raised about the facts of Scripture, e.g., concerning the matter of precedence of one offering over another, or of the dependence of one offering upon the validity of another, in no way are generated by Scripture's interests and propositions. They are typical of one side of the Mishnah: secondary, derivative, and routine. They in no way express the creative impulses which give us the Mishnah as a whole, or even the Mishnah tractate Menahot. The tractate's interesting unit on the relationship of vows to meal offerings rests upon the self-evident principles that one must do what one has vowed to do, and, as a corollary, that, when one is not sure what one has vowed to do, one should cover as many possibilities as one can.

Hullin. Treating slaughter of animals for secular use, tractate Hullin is no different from Menahot. It systematically takes up the following verses: Deut. 14:21, not boiling a kid in its mother's milk; Lev. 22–28, not slaughtering an animal and its offspring in one day; Lev. 17:13–14, covering up the blood of an animal which is slaughtered; Gen. 32:33, not eating the sinew of the hip; Deut. 18:3–4, the gift to the priest of the shoulder, cheeks, and maw of animals which are slaughtered; Deut. 22:6–7, not taking the dam and the eggs; Deut. 18:3–4, giving the first fleece to the priest. While there is some difficulty in determining the limit of the taboo against cooking meat in milk, it is clear that the basic meaning imputed to the Scripture is settled before the framers of the tractate take up the matter. In all of these cases the Mishnah essentially repeats a single operation, asking one set of questions and coming up with a repetitious sequence of repetitious answers. The Mishnah contributes little more than the fact that the listed topics will be subjected to discussion. The Mishnah has nothing fresh to say about them.

The details, in Hullin, of proper slaughter of an animal, whether this is for the home or the cult, may not arise from Scripture. The conception that the rules for slaughter apply in both home and cult is in place long before the Mishnah's secondary definition of its particular rules on the matter. The conception that Israelites eat animals which are slaughtered and do not die of themselves is yet another fact supplied by Scripture (Ex. 22:30), to which, at best, the Mishnah provides minor refinements and amplications. The standard and routine treatment of the specified food laws shows graphically the relationship to Scripture present implicitly even in the chapters of Hullin in which Scripture is not clearly alluded to, let alone explicitly cited.

Keritot. Keritot, on those liable to sin offerings, guilt offerings, or extirpation, catalogues the sorts of reasons for which one brings a sin offering, a guilt offering, and suspensive guilt offering. The catalogues merely assemble scattered statements of Scripture. There are some interesting secondary questions. While fresh and interesting, these debates in no way augment the basic conceptions of Scripture, but at best make use of those conceptions of Scripture. It is still, however, a secondary and derivative framework of thought. The dispute on the grounds for liability for a guilt offering in a broad sense is essentially exegetical. The interesting units of thought on a single sin offering for multiple sins, or many sin offerings for a single action ("sin"), hardly constitute important intellectual initiatives on what Scripture has provided for the theme and problems of the tractate. They fall, rather, into the category of the Mishnaic conundrum, not much different from Qinnim. It follows that Keritot depends for its facts entirely on Scripture and only in small and unimportant ways takes up these facts and augments them. Keritot also does set up and solve its own problems, and in this second regard, it is distinct, if not wholly autonomous, from Scripture.

Tamid. Tamid, on the daily burnt offering, claims through its rhetoric and contents alike to provide a little "historical" narrative of how the daily burnt offering is prepared. In no way does the tale pretend to rely upon Scriptural rules. On the contrary, Tamid purports to be an eyewitness account of the way things are really done in the Temple.

Qinnim. In so far as Qinnim weaves its little filigree of problems out of facts, they are (a) that birds which fulfill an obligation comprise a sin offering and a burnt offering, but birds which fulfill a vow are offered wholly as burnt offerings (Lev. 1:14) and (b) the blood of the sin offering is sprinkled below the red line around the altar, that of the burnt offering, above. On the basis of these two established facts, the unbelievably difficult conundrums of the tractate are spun out. There is no way that a statement of the facts can have led us to imagine the character or range of issues of the tractate. In this sense Qinnim is independent of Scripture—but only in this sense.

*Rules Providing Animals for the Daily Sacrifices
and for the Upkeep of the Altar and the Temple Buildings,
and Support of the Priestly Staff*

Bekhorot. We need hardly be detained by Bekhorot, on firstlings, which does little more than elaborate and amplify (uncited) Scriptural laws. With Scripture in hand, we are told what firstborn are subject to redemption, cases of uncertainty as to the status of the animal (e.g., one born of Caesarean section), the sorts of blemishes which remove the firstborn from the altar and allow it to be slaughtered and eaten under secular conditions, and the like.

Arakhin. If, by contrast, we had in hand only Lev. 27:1–8, we should not so readily have been able to predict the principal interests of Arakhin, on vows of a person's value to the Temple. Leviticus specifies the amounts of money to be paid in consequence of a vow of valuation. The Mishnah's interest is in a separate, though, of course, related question: the difference between a vow of valuation, which involves a fixed payment to the Temple of funds specified in Scripture, and a vow of one's worth, which requires payment in true market value. But, interestingly, the other topics of Arakhin are drawn from Lev. 27:16–25 and 28–29, so the tractate is assembled around Scripture's redactional plan (!). Where the Mishnah takes a position at variance with that of Scripture—on the notion that the *herem* goes to the priest and is not destroyed, as against the explicit sense of Lev. 27:28–29—there is nothing fresh or controversial expressed in the Mishnah's conception, which, it seems to me, is simply part of the factual foundation of the document. We do not know the point of origination of the revision of the rule for the *herem*, though on the face of it, it would seem likely to have come from the priesthood. Overall, however, Arakhin is an effort to amplify and augment the basic rules of Scripture. It does not say anything essentially distinct from Scripture, and it certainly does not take up an initiative on matters relevant to the topic but in no way adumbrated by Scripture.

Temurah. Carrying forward the redactional plan of Arakhin (Lev. 27), Temurah begins in the fact, stated by Lev. 27:9–10, that if someone attempts to substitute or exchange something for an animal set aside as an offering to the Lord, then that thing set up as a substitute or exchange is holy, and the original animal remains holy. For its part Temurah then explains (a) who may effect an act of substitution; (b) the sort of beast subject to the law (excluding meal offerings and drink offerings, for example; (c) animals exempt from the law; (d) the status of offspring of substitutes; and (e) the language used in effecting an act of substitution. All of these matters serve to augment Scripture's basic rule, and at no point in the tractate do we find anything other than secondary or tertiary conceptions arising out of Scripture's obvious implications.

Meilah. Meilah, on sacrilege, is reminiscent of Arakhin, in that its consideration of basic Scriptural fact—Lev. 5:14–16—provides important additional information. Just as Scripture specifies the penalty for making a pledge of valuation, so in the case of sacrilege its interest is in the penalty for an act of sacrilege committed "against any of the holy things of the Lord." The guilt offering and restitution as well as the added fifth constitute the penalty. The Mishnah now has its own range of questions, relevant to, but essentially distinct from, those selected for answer by Scripture. The Mishnah asks fundamental questions about the point at which the laws of sacrilege apply and cease to apply to an animal sacrifice. It will specify (as does Arakhin) the conception that one may consecrate for the altar something which may be used on the altar, or one may consecrate for the upkeep of the altar and the Temple the value of something which may or may not be used on the altar. In the latter case sacrilege pertains to aspects of the thing which in the former case will not be subject to sacrilege at all. The parts of a beast which cannot be used for the altar, the eggs of a turtledove, for instance, are subject to sacrilege if the value of the turtledove has been sanctified. The Mishnah also will contribute the notion that if something is not liable to the laws of sacrilege, this does not necessarily mean that it is to be treated as totally secular. In sum, the central issues of Meilah do not flow from Scripture, even though they are generated, to begin with, by Scripture's facts.

Middot. The same is so of Middot, which, in point of fact, presents a mixture of measurements, not all of them Pentateuchal or even Scriptural. It forms a pair with Tamid. The standpoint of both tractates is remarkable, in that each wants to supply not Scriptural facts and amplifications and extensions thereof, but a statement of the way things really were in "historical" time, in the immediate past. "I forget how things were" occurs a few times, as if to underline the purported source of facts and frame of reference.

The Division of Purities

The Division of Purities is autonomous and distinct from Scripture in respect to the second and third of the three parts of the system of Purities: objects of uncleanness (including food and drink), and means for the removal of uncleanness. It is entirely dependent for its principles upon Scripture in regard to sources of uncleanness (including modes of transfer of uncleanness). The Division of Purities does not contain a single new source of major uncleanness. Apart from adding analogous substances and the idol, it scarcely specifies any object or substance or person or status which generates major uncleanness.

A single fact explains why some tractates of the Division begin in exegesis of Scripture and others, in autonomous and original conceptions. The reason that the Division of Purities does not innovate in respect to major sources of uncleanness is that its primary focus lies elsewhere. The Mishnah's new ideas are elsewhere; it has no need to say anything new in this regard. It is the notion that the table at home must be clean as the altar in the Temple must be clean which is the Mishnah's generative and fresh idea. Domestic utensils have therefore in principle to be divided between those susceptible, and those insusceptible to uncleanness. The utensils subject to corpse uncleanness (Num. 19:15) are distinguished from the tent of the corpse. Means of attaining cleanness outside the cult (water) and a locus of cleanness even for sacrifice outside the cult (the place in which the rite of the red cow is conducted) are beautifully constructed. The complex rules governing food and drink are worked out at Tohorot and Makhshirin. Scripture's system of uncleanness and cleanness is augmented and enriched, not revised or overturned. Nothing declared by Scripture to be a source of uncleanness is held to be clean in the Mishnah. To the sources of uncleanness, as I said, specified in Scripture are added only

analogous substances. We shall now observe a difference in the relationship to Scripture of the two groups of tractates, Negaim-
Niddah-Zabim, on the one side, Kelim, the shank of Ohalot, Parah,
Tohorot, Miqvaot, Makhshirin, on the other. This difference begins in
a distinctive and fresh perspective of the authorities who brought to the
priestly code a peculiarly priestly interest in the analogy between sacred and secular, Temple and world, cultic altar and domestic table.

Sources of Uncleanness

Ohalot. The prologue of Ohalot (M. Oh. 1:1–3:5) deals with things
which contaminate in the tent, or through overshadowing; the epilogue
(M. Oh. 16:3–18:10), with graveyards, thus grounds or substances
which contaminate as does the corpse. Nothing in these sections on
sources of uncleanness equivalent to the corpse does more than extend
and fill out the Scriptural rule of corpse uncleanness itself. Accordingly, laws on sources of corpse uncleanness in the opening and closing
parts of Ohalot stand upon the foundation of Scripture, with remarkably little exegesis.

When, however, we deal with the shank of the tractate, M. Oh.
3:6–16:2, and turn to the subtle interplay between the tent and the
utensil, we leave the Scriptural domain entirely. Not a single concept
or presupposition derives directly or indirectly from the exegesis of
Scripture. The proposition that corpse uncleanness passes through a
handbreadth of open space and that its passage may be prevented by a
handbreadth of closed space, which stands behind every major formative conception of the shank of Ohalot, is autonomous. The obvious
difference is that the prologue and epilogue deal with sources of uncleanness, and the body of the tractate, with the locus, the definition of
the tent affected by the corpse.

Negaim, Niddah, Zabim. We now come to three further tractates
which give laws of sources of uncleanness. Negaim contains not a
single generative idea except for the distinction between the skin dis-
eases called *nega‘* and *sara‘at,* which, once drawn, makes no difference whatsoever in the articulation of the law. The tractate, which
provides an account of one source of uncleanness, follows, except
where it improves upon, the thematic agendum of Lev. 13 and 14. No
primary theme or supposition of Negaim diverges from what is explicit
in Scripture.

The laws of Niddah and Zabim begin in Scripture and rise in necessarily sequential and logical stages therefrom. It is easy to show that
every significant fact in the tractates represents either a simple restatement of what Scripture says, or a secondary development of the

clear implications of what Scripture says. All that the Mishnah adds is an account of the disposition of matters of doubt—a fairly typical, wholly contingent contribution.

Accordingly, the three tractates, Negaim, Niddah, and Zabim, devoted to the materials of Lev. 12, 14, and 15, those chapters of the priestly code which specify sources of uncleanness apart from unclean creatures, and M. Oh. 1–3 and 16–18 bear a single relationship to Scripture. All begin in the Scriptural conceptions as to the uncleanness of the *mesora'*, the menstrating woman, the *zabah*, the *zab*, the woman after childbirth, and the corpse. Among the sources of major uncleanness mentioned in priestly code, the Mishnah treats these at great length and in much detail. What the tractates have in common is that none of them innovates in any regard. All of them draw out tendencies and implications of Scripture. In their fundamental and generative conceptions, they constitute little more than secondary and derivative developments of the conceptions of the priestly code. By contrast, the tractates which define objects susceptible to uncleanness, areas in which, and processes by which, uncleanness takes place, and modes of purification from uncleanness contracted by such objects and in such areas all have in common the simple fact that Scripture contributes little of generative effect, that is, only a few ideas of consequence.

Makhshirin. While Makhshirin depends upon the datum of Scripture (Lev. 11:24, 38) that produce is susceptible to uncleanness only when it is wet, that tractate begins in an interest absent in Scripture, which is in the character of the liquid which imparts wetness, therefore susceptibility to uncleanness, and in the way in which the liquid happens to come upon produce. In fact, the tractate's first principle is its distinction between liquids which do and do not impart susceptibility to uncleanness. The tractate as a whole begins its major conceptual development with thought on the principal role of human intention in activating the supernatural forces of uncleanness, a view which does not begin in, and is not produced by exegesis of, Scripture.

Tebul Yom. The basic conception of tractate Tebul Yom so far as sources of uncleanness are concerned is that until sunset one who has immersed remains unclean. This notion derives from Scripture. Lev. 11:32 and 22:6–7 are explicit that the one who has immersed in water remains unclean until evening. But in the dim past of the tractate is the conception, which Scripture certainly does not know, that the person is unclean in a diminished state of uncleanness. That idea surely comes in the wake of the notion that, to begin with, water by itself, of an appropriate natural character, has the power to effect purification. Once that fact has registered, it will be natural to accommodate the Scriptural

passages to the known power of immersion in water by declaring the
one who has immersed to be unclean until sunset—but in a diminished
state of uncleanness. Yet even knowing that fact, we should not be able
to predict the principal interest of the tractate itself. That is in the
matter of the effect of one unclean in the stated status upon firm and
infirm connections, that is, on two substances, tightly or loosely joined
to one another. The secondary interest, in the character of this diminished state of uncleanness, to be sure, depends upon the fact upon
which the tractate rests. So, in sum, Tebul Yom is a tractate with a
tenuous relationship to Scripture. The tractate emerges from the interplay between a biblical rule and a fact of life known long before work
on the tractate got underway.

Loci of Uncleanness

Kelim. Kelim, a long and diffuse tractate, finds ample information in
Scripture for some of its basic propositions. Moreover, I shall show
how, through simple exegesis, Scripture can be made to yield further
important principles, on which the tractate is based. The notion that
utensils become unclean is at Lev. 11:29:35. If a dead creeping thing
falls upon an object of wood, a garment, a skin, or sacking, "any vessel
that is used for any purpose," the object is unclean. Once immersed in
water, it remains unclean until evening, so Lev. 11:32. Lev. 11:33 deals
with clay utensils, Lev. 11:34 with food and drink. These are the main
references, and they are important. Lev. 15:4–6 further deals with the
bed or chair on which a *zab* lies or sits; Lev. 15:9–12, a saddle on which
such a person rides; Lev. 15:19–24, the same for the menstruating
woman, and so on. Nor should we omit a reference to the fact that
utensils not tightly sealed, located in a tent which overshadows a
corpse, also are unclean. Among the established facts of the tractate
are the notions that, first, pressure uncleanness exerted by a *zab* or one
of his fellows imparts uncleanness to something used for sitting or
lying; second, the effects of the tent over a corpse are nullified by a
tightly sealed cover; third, breaking a clay utensil cleans it. All of these
facts are explicitly stated by Scripture.

When we seek the generative problematic of the tractate, it is not to
be found in these facts, but in the matter of an object's susceptibility to
uncleanness, specifically the principle that an object can become unclean when man deems it useful. In order to see where the tractate may
have found its conceptual core, we take a moment to see how the legal
philosophers and exegetes may have located that notion in Scripture.
For this purpose, we review what has been stated (see Neusner,
Purities III, pp. 368–69). How would a legal philosopher have come to
the conception that a random object becomes a utensil, therefore is

susceptible, at the point at which it is useful, and ceases to be a utensil, therefore becomes insusceptible, when it is useless? The answer is simply that, opening Scripture, he will have found the following at Lev. 11:32: "Any vessel that is used for any purpose." So there are some objects, also referred to as vessels, which are not "used for any purpose." After listing various materials, therefore, Scripture adds, "every utensil." This must function as an inclusionary phrase, followed by "used for any purpose," a limiting one—and the rest follows. That very simple process of reasoning, governing the answer to the question, When is a utensil a utensil? begins in a not very close reading of Scripture. So much for an object as utensil, that is, as something useful.

Now let us ask about autonomy and distinctiveness. These, I think, are the clear intent of the construction in inclusionary, then exclusionary, clauses: "Every utensil made of any material" will include any object whatsoever. Then, "any utensil used for any purpose" excludes the just-stated proposition, for we no longer have in mind any utensil, meaning any object, but now refer explicitly to any utensil meaning, any *useful* object. In other words, as soon as we refer to use, autonomy and distinctiveness will, in the nature of the Scripture, follow in its wake. Indeed, it is entirely possible that the categories of autonomy and distinctiveness ("having a name of its own") are Mishnaic ways of rephrasing the primary Scriptural statement, "with which work is done."

Add to this the view that an insusceptible utensil is one which is broken, and the matter of usefulness is reinforced. Restatements of the same matter will include the issue of permanence, on the one side, or perforation and breaking, on the other. In this matter we then include the oven. Everyone will agree breaking an oven purifies it, since Lev. 11:30 says so. The only question is: What is breaking? One conception of it is that breaking the oven and then reconstructing it so that it is useful, but not in its former form, does not constitute breaking. So "breaking" means "rendering useless," with stress on function, and not merely altering the primary form. If the oven still functions as before, despite the alteration of its form, it will be susceptible. What is important in this instance is the primary and unmediated resort to Scripture, the spelling out of matters directly consequent upon the open-endedness of the Scriptural statement.

Let us now ask about the matter of receptacles and the closely related issue of the division of a utensil into inner and outer parts. Lev. 11:33 speaks of "falling into its midst." The exegetical result: that which has a "midst" is contrasted against that which does not. Clearly, the interpretation of that which has a midst as, "that which has an inside, a receptacle," is not going to require a great many intervening stages of reasoning. From there, it is going to be a short step indeed to a negative formulation: what has no "midst" is not going to be subject to the susceptibility of an insect in contained air space. So we are in close accord with the simple meaning of the verse. In sum, the Scriptures can easily be shown to yield answers to the questions of Kelim—once we ask them.

Tohorot. Tohorot bears no close tie to Scripture at all. True, an effort is made to ground rules about removes of uncleanness, in particular about unconsecrated food, in Scriptural exegesis. But the exegesis is blatantly post facto and eisegetical. It looks to me as though the primary contribution of Scripture to Tohorot is the general notion that cleanness applies to foods and liquids. In the matter of removes of uncleanness as related to degrees of sanctification of such food, the clear evidence is that these notions in no way are rooted in a simple reading of Scripture. With respect to how people who keep cleanness deal with those who do not, we may suppose that some sort of corpus of principles may have existed. For the problem begins as soon as a few people undertake to keep the laws among many who do not. But Scripture does not know the problem.

Uqsin. Tractate Uqsin in no way relates to Scripture.

Modes of Purification

Miqvaot. When we turn to Miqvaot and the process of purification, we recall that the main point of the priestly code is that for cultic purposes purification is attained through the application of blood, or through immersion in living water, or through sunset. But for purification Miqvaot speaks only of immersion in an appropriate pool, or, self-evidently, a flowing stream. Miqvaot accepts immersion in a pool of water, the natural properties of which have not been affected by human agency. Since the purpose of immersion is the attainment of cultic purity, this tractate takes a position quite outside that imagined in Scripture. In Parah, too, we create a place for a sacrifice outside of the Temple, yet, though outside the Temple, a place of cleanness and holiness. In Miqvaot we call into being a means of attaining cleanness outside of the Temple, a kind of water not used for the Temple described in the priestly code. Spring water (which serves as well) is different from rainwater. The one is exceptional, the other ordinary, the one flows with force, the other stands still, the one (Miqvaot says) cleans in any amount, the other serves the body or the utensil only in the volume of forty *seot*. The spring water, which can purify for the cult and for the table alike, therefore has traits quite distinct from the sort of water which serves for the table. That is as it should be, for the difference between the altar of the Temple and the table of the home, both of which must be clean, is not to be obscured. None of this flows from Scripture.

Parah. Parah presents a noteworthy contrast to Scripture. Num. 19:1–20 takes for granted that the rite of burning the red cow is conducted in a state of uncleanness, since it is not performed in the tent of meeting. Participating in the rite makes a person unclean. Parah for its part assumes that a high degree of cleanness characterizes all those who participate in the rite as well as utensils used therein. The tractate spells out the requirements of cleanness in preparing the ash, drawing the water, and participating in the cult. Parah deals not with sources of uncleanness, but with the locus of cleanness. The cleanness rules of Parah thus create in the world outside the cult a place of cleanness analogous to the cult.

Yadayim. The notion that there are special rules governing the uncleanness of hands and their process of purification is unknown to Scripture.

Conclusion

On the surface, as we have seen a number of times, Scripture plays little role in the Mishnaic system. The Mishnah rarely cites a verse of Scripture, refers to Scripture as an entity, links its own ideas to those of Scripture, or lays claim to originate in what Scripture has said, even by indirect or remote allusion to a Scriptural verse of teaching. So, superficially, the Mishnah is totally indifferent to Scripture. That impression, moreover, is reinforced by the traits of the language of the Mishnah. The framers of Mishnaic discourse never attempt to imitate the language of Scripture, as do those of the Essene writings at Qumran. The very redactional structure of Scripture, found so serviceable by the writer of the Temple scroll, is of no interest whatever to the organizers of the Mishnah and its tractates, except in a few cases (Yoma, Pesahim).

I wish now to dwell on these facts. Formally, redactionally, and linguistically the Mishnah stands in splendid isolation from Scripture. This is something which had to be confronted as soon as the Mishnah came to closure and was presented as authoritative to the Jewish community of the holy Land and of Babylonia. It is not possible to point to many parallels, that is, cases of anonymous books, received as holy, in which the forms and formulations (specific verses) of Scripture play so slight a role. People who wrote holy books commonly imitated the Scripture's language; they cited concrete verses, or they claimed (at the very least) that direct revelation has come to them, as in the angelic discourses of Ezra and Baruch, so that what they say stands on an equal plane with Scripture. The internal evidence of the Mishnah's sixty-two usable tractates (excluding Abot), by contrast, in no way suggest that anyone pretended to talk like Moses and write like Moses, claimed to cite and correctly interpret things that Moses had said, or even alleged himself to have had a revelation like that of Moses and so to stand on the mountain with Moses. There is none of this. So the claim of Scriptural authority for the Mishnah's doctrines and institutions is difficult to locate within the internal evidence of the Mishnah itself.

We cannot be surprised that, in consequence of this amazing position of autonomous autocephalic authority implicit in the character of Mishnaic discourse, the Mishnah should have demanded in its own behalf some sort of apologetic. Nor are we surprised that the Mishnah attracted its share of quite hostile criticism. The issue, in the third century, would be precisely the issue phrased when we ask in general about the authority of tradition in Judaism: Why should we listen to this mostly anonymous document, which makes statements on the nature of institutions and social conduct, statements we obviously are expected to keep? Who are Meir, Yosé, Judah, Simeon, and Eleazar—people who from the perspective of the recipients of the document, lived fifty or a hundred years ago—that we should listen to what they have to say? God revealed the Torah. Is this Mishnah too part of the Torah? If so, how? What, in other words, is the relationship of the Mishnah to Scripture, and how does the Mishnah claim authority over us such as we accord to the revelation to Moses by God at Mount Sinai? There are two important responses to the question of the place of Scripture in the Mishnaic tradition.

First and most radical: the Mishnah constitutes *Torah*. It too is a statement of revelation, "Torah revealed to Moses at Sinai." But this part of revelation has come down in a form different from the well-known, written part, the Scripture. This tradition truly deserves the name "tradition," because for a long time it was handed down orally, not in writing, until given the written formulation now before us in the Mishnah. This sort of apologetic for the Mishnah appears, to begin with, in Abot, with its stunning opening chapter, linking Moses on Sinai through the ages to the earliest-named authorities of the Mishnah itself, the five pairs, on down to Shammai and Hillel. Since some of the named authorities in the chain of tradition appear throughout the materials of the Mishnah, the claim is that what these people say comes to them from Sinai through the processes of *qabbalah* and *massoret*—handing down, traditioning.

So the reason (from the perspective of the Torah myth of the Mishnah) that the Mishnah does not cite Scripture is that it does not have to. It stands on the same plane as Scripture. It enjoys the same authority as Scripture. This radical position is still more extreme than that taken by Pseudepigraphic writers, who imitate the style of Scripture, or who claim to speak within that same gift of revelation as Moses. It is one thing to say one's holy book is Scripture because it is like Scripture, or to claim that the author of the holy book has a revelation independent of that of Moses. These two positions concede to the Torah of Moses priority over their own holy books. The Mishnah's apologists make no such concession, when they allege that the Mishnah is part of the Torah of Moses. They appeal to the highest possible authority in the Israelite framework, claiming the most one can claim in behalf of the book which, in fact, bears the names of men who lived fifty years before the apologists themselves. That seems to me remarkable courage.

So that takes care of this matter of the Mishnah's not citing Scripture. When we consider the rich corpus of allusions to Scripture in other holy books, both those bearing the names of authors and those presented anonymously, we realize that the Mishnah claims its authority to be coequal with that of Scripture, while so many other holy books are made to lay claim to authority only because they depend upon the authority of Scripture and state the true meaning of Scripture. That fact brings us to the second answer to the question of the place of Scripture in the Mishnaic tradition.

The two Talmuds and the legal-exegetical writings produced in the two hundred years after the closure of the Mishnah take the position that the Mishnah is wholly dependent upon Scripture. Whatever is of worth in the Mishnah can be shown to derive directly from Scripture. So the Mishnah—tradition—is deemed distinct from, and subordinate to, Scripture. This position is expressed in an obvious way. Once the Talmuds cite a Mishnah pericope, they commonly ask, What is the source of these words? And the answer invariably is, As it is said in Scripture. This constitutes not only a powerful defense for the revealed truth of the Mishnah. For when the exegetes find themselves constrained to add proof texts from the Mishnah, they admit the need to improve and correct an existing flaw in Scripture itself.

That the search for the Scriptural bases for the Mishnah's laws constitutes both an apologetic for, and a critique of, the Mishnah is shown in the character of a correlative response to the Mishnah, namely, the Sifra and its exegesis of Leviticus (see Neusner, *Purities* VII). This rhetorical exegesis follows a standard syntactical-redactional form. Scripture will be cited. Then a statement will be made about its meaning, or a statement of law correlative to that Scripture will be given. Finally, the author of Sifra invariably states, Now is that not (merely) logical? And the point of that statement will be, Can this position not be gained through the working of mere logic, based upon facts supplied (to be sure) by Scripture? The polemical power of Sifra lies in its repetitive demonstration that the stated position—commonly, though not always, a verbatim or near-verbatim citation of a Mishnah pericope—is not only *not* the product of logic, but is, and can only be, the product of exegesis of Scripture.

What is still more to the point, that exegesis in Sifra's and the Talmud's view is formal in its character. That is, it is based upon some established mode of exegesis of the formal traits of Scriptural grammar and syntax, assigned to the remote antiquity represented by the names of Ishmael or Aqiba. So the polemic of Sifra and the Talmuds is against the positions that, first, what the Mishnah says (in the Mishnah's own words) is merely logical; and that, second, the position taken by the Mishnah can have been reached in any way other than through grammatical-syntactical exegesis of Scripture. That other way, the way of reading the Scripture through philosophical logic or practical reason, is explicitly rejected time and again. Philosophical logic is inadequate. Formal exegesis is shown to be not only adequate but necessary and indeed inexorable. It follows that Sifra undertakes to demonstrate precisely what the framers of the opening pericopes of the Talmuds' treatment of the Mishnah's successive units of thought also wish to show. The Mishnah is not autonomous. It is not independent. It is not correlative, that is, separate but equal. It is contingent, secondary, derivative, resting wholly on the foundations of the (written) revelation of God to Moses at Mount Sinai. Therein, too, lies the authority of the Mishnah as tradition.

So, there are two positions which would take shape. First, tradition in the form of the Mishnah is deemed autonomous of Scripture and enjoys the same authority as that of Scripture. The reason is that Scripture and ("oral") tradition are merely two media for conveying a single corpus of revealed law and doctrine. *Or,* tradition in the form of the Mishnah is true because it is not autonomous of Scripture. Tradition is secondary and dependent upon Scripture.

The authority of the Mishnah is the authority of Moses. That authority comes to the Mishnah directly and in an unmediated way, because the Mishnah's words were said by God to Moses at Mount Sinai and faithfully transmitted through a process of oral formulation and oral transmission from that time until those words were written down by Judah the Patriarch at the end of the second century. *Or,* that authority comes to the Mishnah indirectly, in a way mediated through the written Scriptures.

What the Mishnah says is what the Scripture says, rightly interpreted. The authority of tradition lies in its correct interpretation of the Scripture. Tradition bears no autonomous authority, is not an independent entity, and correlative with Scripture. A technology of exegesis of grammar and syntax is needed to build the bridge between tradition as contained in the Mishnah and Scripture, the original utensil shaped by God and revealed to Moses to convey the truth of revelation to the community of Israel. *Or* matters are otherwise. I hardly need to make them explicit.

The facts we have in some detail examined in the preceding exercises now permit us to make a quite independent statement of the relationship of the Mishnah to Scripture, of that of the third-century apologist-critics of the Mishnah.

First, there are tractates which simply repeat in their own words precisely what Scripture has to say, and at best serve to amplify and complete the basic ideas of Scripture. For example, all of the cultic tractates of the Second Division, the one on Appointed Times, which tell what one is supposed to do in the Temple on the various special days of the year, and the bulk of the cultic tractates of the Fifth Division, which deals with Holy Things, simply restate facts of Scripture. For another example all of those tractates of the Sixth Division, on Purities, which specify sources of uncleanness, depend completely on information supplied by Scripture. I have demonstrated in detail that every important statement in Niddah, on menstrual uncleanness, and the most fundamental notions of Zabim, on the uncleanness of the person with flux referred to in Lev. 15, as well as every detail in Negaim, on the uncleanness of the person or house suffering the uncleanness described at Lev. 13 and 14—all of these tractates serve only to restate the basic facts of Scripture and to complement those facts with other important ones (see Neusner, *Method and Meaning* II, chapters 11, 12).

There are, second, tractates which take up facts of Scripture but work them out in a way in which those Scriptural facts cannot have led us to predict. A supposition concerning what is important *about* the facts, utterly remote from the supposition of Scripture, will explain why the Mishnah tractates under discussion say the original things they say in confronting those Scripturally provided facts. For one example, Scripture takes for granted that the red cow will be burned in a state of uncleanness, because it is burned outside the camp = Temple. The priestly writers cannot have imagined that a state of cultic cleanness was to be attained outside of the cult. The absolute datum of tractate Parah, by contrast, is that cultic cleanness not only can be attained outside of the "tent of meeting." The red cow was to be burned in a state of cleanness exceeding even that cultic cleanness required in the Temple itself. The problematic which generates the intellectual agendum of Parah, therefore, is how to work out the conduct of the rite of burning the cow in relationship to the Temple: Is it to be done in exactly the same way, or inexactly the opposite way? This mode of contrastive and analogical thinking helps us to understand the generative problematic of such tractates as Erubin and Besah, to mention only two.

And third, there are, predictably, many tractates which either take up problems in no way suggested by Scripture, or begin from facts at best merely relevant to facts of Scripture. In the former category are Tohorot, on the cleanness of foods, with its companion, Uqsin; Demai, on doubtfully tithed produce; Tamid, on the conduct of the daily whole offering; Baba Batra, on rules of real estate transactions and certain other commercial and property relationships, and so on. In the latter category are Ohalot, which spins out its strange problems with the theory that a tent and a utensil are to be compared to one another (!); Kelim, on the susceptibility to uncleanness of various sorts of utensils; Miqvaot, on the sorts of water which effect purification from uncleanness, and many others. These tractates draw on facts of Scripture. But the problems confronted in these tractates in no way respond to problems important to Scripture. What we have here is a prior program of inquiry, which will make ample provision for facts of Scripture in an inquiry to begin with generated essentially outside of the framework of Scripture.

So there we have it: some tractates merely repeat what we find in Scripture; some are totally independent of Scripture; and some fall in between. Clearly, we are no closer to a definitive answer to the question of the relationship of Scripture to the Mishnah than we were when we described the state of thought on the very same questions in the third and fourth centuries. We find everything and its opposite. But to offer a final answer to the question of Scripture-Mishnah relationships, we have to take that fact seriously. The Mishnah in no way is so remote from Scripture as its formal omission of citations of verses of Scripture suggests. In no way can it be described as contingent upon, and secondary to Scripture, as its third-century apologists claimed. But the right answer is not that it is somewhere in between. Scripture confronts the framers of the Mishnah as revelation, not merely as a source of facts. But the framers of the Mishnah had their own world with which to deal. They made statements in the framework and fellowship of their own age and generation. They were bound, therefore, to come to Scripture with a set of questions generated other than in Scripture. They brought their own ideas about what was going to be important in Scripture. This is perfectly natural.

The philosophers of the Mishnah conceded to Scripture the highest authority. At the same time what they chose to hear, within the authoritative statements of Scripture, will in the end form a statement of its own. To state matters simply: all of Scripture is authoritative. But only some of Scripture is relevant. And what happened is that the framers and philosophers of the tradition of the Mishnah came to Scripture when they had reason to. That is to say, they brought to Scripture a program of questions and inquiries framed essentially among themselves. So they were highly selective. Their program itself constituted a statement *upon* the meaning of Scripture. They and their apologists of one sort hastened to add, their program consisted of a statement *of* and upon the meaning of Scripture.

In part, we must affirm the truth of that claim. When the framers of the Mishnah speak about the priestly passages of the Mosaic law codes, with deep insight they perceive profound layers of meaning embedded ("to begin with") in those codes. What they have done with P, moreover, they also have done, though I think less coherently, with the bulk of the Deuteronomic laws and with some of those of the Covenant Code. But their exegetical triumph—exetetical, not merely eisegetical—lies in their handling of the complex corpus of materials of the priestly code.

True, others will have selected totally different passages of Scripture, not in the Mosaic Codes to begin with. Surely we must concede that, in reading those passages, they displayed that same perspicacity as did the framers of the Mishnaic tradition who interpreted the priestly code as they did. It is in the nature of Scripture itself that such should be the case. The same Scripture which gives us the prophets gives us the Pentateuch as well—and gives priority to the Pentateuchal codes as the revelation of God to Moses.

The authority of Scripture therefore for the Mishnah is simply stated. Scripture provides indisputable facts. It is wholly authoritative—once we have made our choice of which part of Scripture we shall read. Scripture generated important and authoritative structures of the community, including disciplinary and doctrinal statements, decisions, and interpretations—once people had determined which part of Scripture to ask to provide those statements and decisions. Community structures envisaged by the Mishnah were wholly based on Scripture—when Scripture had anything to lay down. But Scripture is not wholly and exhaustively expressed in those structures which the Mishnah does borrow. Scripture has dictated the character of formative structures of the Mishnah. But the Mishnah's system is not the result of the dictation of close exegesis of Scripture—except after the fact.

These conclusions raise at the end of my description of the Mishnah precisely the question asked at the outset: How shall we account for the striking continuity from the priestly code to the Mishnah, or, to phrase matters in the current context, how shall we interpret the selections of Scriptures for exegesis made by the framers of the Mishnah? It now is appropriate to answer this question by recapitulating the principal argument offered above. The reason is that the main conclusions of the chapter to follow, and therefore of the book as a whole, about the suggestive correspondence of the social condition of Israel and the intellectual exercises of the Mishnah, rest upon the foundations outlined in the present argument. The mode of thought is the same here and in the next chapter, namely, pointing to the congruence between people's ideas and their social circumstance. The remarkable relevance to be discerned of abstract problems of thought they wished to solve to Israel's material situation of society and culture is the center of the interpretive exercise at the climax of this account of Judaism.

That is why once more we dwell on the continuity from P to the Mishnah. We see that the Mishnah takes up the perspectives of the work of the priests and Levites. We wish to account for this fact. That is, the Mishnah systematically and amply complements the priests' part of the Torah literature. It carries forward the great themes and theses of the priestly code. In theme and focus it is mainly, though not solely, a priestly document. That is why, to begin with, the Mishnah's principal themes and motifs, borrowed from the work of people of a much earlier age, have to be placed into continuity with the priestly code.

The Mishnah presents a way of organizing the world which only the priestly and other Temple castes and professions could have imagined. To point to obvious traits, we note that the document begins, in its First Division, with the claim that God owns the Land. The Land, therefore, must be used in a way consonant with the Land's holiness. More important, what the Land yields must be treated as belonging to God, until the claims of God, the landlord, have been satisfied. These claims require that the calender of the soil be set by the conduct of the cult in Jerusalem, on the one side, and that the produce of the Land be set aside for the support of the cultic castes, priests, Levites, and their dependents on the other. The document proceeds to specify the appointed times of the year, those days which are out of the ordinary. This it does by focusing upon two matters. First, the relevant appointed times, as we shall see later on, are treated principally, or solely, in terms of what is done in the cult in celebration of those special days. Second, rules governing conduct on appointed times in the towns and villages are so shaped as to bring into a single continuum of sanctification the village and the Temple. These are made into mirror images and complements of one another, so that what may be done in the Temple may not be done in the village, and vice versa. Just as the Temple is surrounded by its boundary, so the advent of the holy day causes the raising on the perimeters of the village of an invisible wall of sanctification as well. Third and fourth, two further principal Divisions of the Mishnaic system take up the matter of the conduct of the cult on ordinary days (Holy Things) and the protection of the cult from dangerous forces, understood by the Mishnaic philosophers as forces of disruption and death (Purities). All of this holds together. Uncleanness, which above all endangers the cult and must be kept away from the Temple, is what characterizes all lands but the holy Land (see Levine). The lands of the gentiles are unclean with corpse uncleanness. So death lies outside of the holy Land, with consequent uncleanness. And life lies within the holy Land, with consequent uncleanness. And life lies within the holy Land, with its locus and its apogee in the Temple and at the cult.

These statements, ultimately made in the final versions of four of the six Divisions of the Mishnah, of course would not have surprised the framers of the priestly code. Indeed, as we analyzed the substantive character of the Mishnaic laws by their tractates, we found time and again that they constitute important statements not only *upon* Scripture, but also *of* what Scripture already has said. The tendency of the later Mishnaic thinkers is to amplify, expand, and extend the principles they find in the priestly code, even while these same thinkers make an original and remarkably fresh statement upon what is in the priestly code. So, in sum, there is a close continuity at the deepest layers of sentiment and opinion between the priestly code and the Mishnah. Why is it that the framers of the Mishnah chose just these cultic and priestly matters for their painstaking and detailed study? Two significant factors come into play. First, we again take account of the beginnings of the Mishnaic system. Second, we rehearse what we have already said about the fundamental ecological facts which, to begin with, are confronted by the priestly system, and which, in later times, down to the closure of the Mishnah, remained definitive of the situation of Israel. Because of the centrality of this proposition to the thesis of the book as a whole, I recapitulate the entire argument in full (see also above, pp. 71–75).

Beginnings: As we now have seen, the Mishnaic system originates, in the century or so before 70, among either lay people who pretended to be priests, or priests who took so seriously the laws governing their cultic activity that they concluded these same laws applied even outside of the cult, or both (as in the Essene community of Qumran). When we reach the earliest possible suppositions of the earliest laws of

Purities in particular, the givens of discourse turn out to maintain a closely related set of positions. First, cleanness, with special reference to food and drink, pots and pans, is possible outside of the cult. Second, cleanness is required outside of the cult. Third, the cultic taboos governing the protection and disposition of parts of the sacrificial meat which are to be given to the priests apply to other sorts of food as well. They apply, specifically, to ordinary food, not food deriving from, or related to, the altar; that is, not food directed to the priesthood. Fourth, the levitical taboos on sources of uncleanness therefore apply to ordinary food, and, it follows, fifth, one must be careful to avoid these sources of uncleanness, or to undergo a rite of purification if one has had contact with said contaminating sources. Finally, the direction and purpose of the system as a whole, in its earliest formulation, clearly are to preserve the cleanness of the people of Israel, of the produce of the Land of Israel, of the sexual life of Israel, of the hearth and home of Israel. So the beginnings of the Mishnaic system lie, as I said, among lay people pretending to be priests by eating their food at home as if they were priests in the Temple, and also among priests with so intense a sense for cultic cleanness that they do the same. So, in sum, at the foundations were people who wished to act at home as if they were in the Temple, or to pretend that they must keep purity laws at home because their home and its life lay within the enchanted circle of the cult.

Now this position, invoking the cultic taboos for the Israelite home and table, in fact carries forward and brings to fulfillment that priestly position outlined in the priestly code. The social and cultural continuity of the priestly perspective from Scripture to the Mishnah is illustrated when its founders maintain, as they do, that the cultic laws of Leviticus govern the Israelite table at home as much as the altar in the Temple of Jerusalem. So I want to dwell on the matter, with special reference to what I take to be a principal and generative rule, the taboos about the menstruating woman's uncleanness.

When someone with the problematic of purity at home in mind opens Scripture, his attention is drawn to the conception that cleanness in respect to unclean bodily discharges must be kept so that the tabernacle will be clean: "Thus you shall keep the people of Israel separate from their uncleanness, lest they die in their uncleanness by defiling my tabernacle that is in their midst" (Lev. 15:31). But the menstruant, *zab*, *zabah*, and woman after childbirth do not go to the Temple. The priestly code is explicit that a rite of purification must be undertaken by the last three named (Lev. 15:13–15 for the *zab*, Lev. 15:28–30 for the *zabah*, and Lev. 12:6–8 for the woman after childbirth). Accordingly, someone reading the Scripture will have asked himself, How are the unclean people going to make the Temple unclean, when, in point of fact, before they are able to enter its precincts, they undergo the rite of purification Scripture itself specifies? And, he will have answered, The people of Israel itself, *in whose midst is the tabernacle,* is to be kept clean, so that the tabernacle, which is in their midst, will be in a clean setting. It will follow that the rules of cleanness in general pertaining to the Temple must apply as well to the people outside of the Temple.

The rules of menstrual uncleanness and comparable uncleanness in the beginning, before the revision accomplished by P in the sixth or fifth century, had nothing to do with the cult. Menstrual taboos are not associated with the cult even in the very pericopes of the priestly code which refer to them. It is only in the subscription (Lev. 15:31) that the priestly code naturally insists upon an integral and necessary relationship between menstrual taboos and the cult, and this, as I said, is even redactionally claimed only after the fact. We assume that everyone avoided having sexual relations with menstruating women, without regard to whether or not he intended to go to the Temple, indeed to whether or not he even lived in the Land of Israel. Land, people, Temple—all form an integrated and whole realm of being, to be kept clean so as to serve as the locus of the sacred. Israel must be clean because of the tabernacle in their midst. Because the tabernacle is in their midst, Israel must be clean, even when not in the tabernacle, which is exactly what Lev. 15:31 says—to someone who to begin with thought so.

Ecology: The exclusiveness which constituted the response of priests and the followers of Ezra and Nehemiah to the critical problems of Israelite self-definition in the sixth and fifth centuries because of continuing political and social changes remained a pressing problem for the next six or seven hundred years. When we find that a formative group in Israelite society retained the fundamental perspectives and even the detailed laws which took shape to make a statement upon the definition of Israel in that one situation, we are on solid ground in asking whether the reason may be that the situation remained essentially the same. The perennial dilemmas endured fundamentally unchanged, long afterward. Obviously, much that was new entered the Israelite social and political framework. Yet what we are constrained to call "Hellenization," meaning an epoch of internationalization and open borders, a cosmopolitan age of swiftly flowing currents in culture and thought, an era in which a common cosmopolitan culture spread throughout the great empire of the Mediterranean basin, expressed, to be sure, in an idiom distinctive to one group or some other—that "Hellenization" (I should prefer: *modernization*) remained a fact of life.

For from the moment at which trade and commerce in goods and ideas broke down walls of isolation of one group from another, one region from another, the issue of who each group was, and what each group might claim for its own self-definition in order to explain its distinctive existence, proved pressing. What was now needed was walls of another sort. No one now had to ask about what one group shared in common with all others. That was no issue. The answers in the cosmopolitan culture and economy were obvious. In the special case of Israel in the Land of Israel, moreover, the dispersion among gentiles within the holy Land, the absence of contiguous settlement, the constant confrontation with other languages and other ways of life along with the preposterous claims of Scripture that Israel alone owned the Land, and Israel's God alone owned the world—these dissonances between social reality and imaginative fantasy raised to a point of acute concern what was in other settings a merely chronic and ongoing perplexity.

Now when we ask why the Temple with its cult enduringly proved central in the imagination of the Israelites in the country, as indeed it was, we have only to repeat the statements which the priests of the Temple and their imitators in the sects were prepared to make. These explain the critical importance of cult and rite. The altar was the center of life, the conduit of life from heaven to earth and from earth to heaven. All things are to be arrayed in relationship to the altar. The movement of the heavens demarcated and celebrated at the cult marked out the divisions of time in relationship to the altar. The spatial dimension of the Land was likewise demarcated and celebrated in relationship to the altar. The natural life of Israel's fields and corrals, the social life of its hierarchical caste-system, the political life (this was not only in theory by any means) centered on the Temple as the locus of ongoing government—all things in order and in place expressed the single message. The natural order of the world corresponded to, reinforced, and was reinforced by, the social order of Israel. Both were fully realized in the cult, the nexus between those opposite and corresponding forces, the heavens and the earth.

The lines of structure emanated from the altar. And it was these lines of structure which constituted these high and impenetrable frontiers which separated from the gentiles Israel, which was holy, ate holy food, reproduced itself in accord with the laws of holiness, and conducted all of its affairs, both affairs of state and the business of the table and the bed, in accord with the demands of holiness. So the cult defined holiness. Holiness meant separateness. Separateness meant life. Why? Because outside of the Land, the realm of the holy, lay the domain of death. The lands are unclean. The Land is holy. For the Scriptural vocabulary, one antonym for *holy* is *unclean*, and one opposite of unclean is holy. The synonym of holy is life. The principal force and symbol of uncleanness and its highest expression are death.

That is why cult plays so critical a role in the self-definition of Israel, as both the priestly and holiness codes and the Mishnah at its beginnings wish to express what makes Israel distinct and distinctive. Their message is one of metaphysics. But it can be stated as a judgment upon society as well: if the people is to live, it must be as a holy people. Imitating the holy God it must be wholly other, wholly different, set apart from the unclean lands of death on earth, just as God is set apart from the no-gods in heaven. What has been said renders vivid the issue confronting the continuators of the Mishnaic work: the people who had witnessed the destruction of the Temple. It is one thing when the Temple is standing to pretend to be priests and to eat like the priests and like God in the cult. It is quite another to do so amid the Temple's rubble and ruins, and in the certainty that those who did the work would not live to see the Temple they were planning and to celebrate the perfection of creation at the altar.

6

Judaism:
The Evidence of the Mishnah

Preliminary Observations:
The Social Description of the Mishnah

The Judaism shaped by the Mishnah consists of a coherent world view and comprehensive way of living. It is a world view which speaks of transcendent things, a way of life in response to the supernatural meaning of what is done, a heightened and deepened perception of the sanctification of Israel in deed and in deliberation. Sanctification means two things, first, distinguishing Israel in all its dimensions from the world in all its ways; second, establishing the stability, order, regularity, predictability, and reliability of Israel at moments and in contexts of danger. Danger means instability, disorder, irregularity, uncertainty, and betrayal. Each topic of the system as a whole takes up a critical and indispensable moment or context of social being. Through what is said in regard to each of the Mishnah's principal topics, what the system as a whole wishes to declare is fully expressed. Yet if the parts severally and jointly give the message of the whole, the whole cannot exist without all of the parts, so well joined and carefully crafted are they all.

The critical issue in economic life, which means, in farming, is in two parts. First, Israel, as tenant on God's holy land, maintains the property in the ways God requires, keeping the rules which mark the Land and its crops as holy. Next, the hour at which the sanctification of the Land comes to form a critical mass, namely, in the ripened crops, is the moment ponderous with danger and heightened holiness. Israel's will so affects the crops as to mark a part of them as holy, the rest of them as available from common use. The human will is determinative in the process of sanctification. Second, what happens in the Land at certain times, at "appointed times," marks off spaces of the Land as holy in yet another way. The center of the Land and the focus of its sanctification is the Temple. There the produce of the Land is received and given back to God, the one who created and sanctified the Land. At these unusual moments of sanctification, the inhabitants of the Land in their social being in villages enter a state of spatial sanctification. That is to say, the village boundaries mark off holy space. This is expressed in two ways. First, the Temple itself observes and expresses the special, recurring holy time. Second, the villages of the Land are brought into alignment with the Temple, forming a complement and completion to the Temple's sacred being. The advent of the appointed times precipitates a spatial reordering of the Land, so that the boundaries of the sacred are matched and mirrored in village and in Temple. At the heightened holiness marked by these moments of appointed times, therefore, the occasion for an effective sanctification is worked out. Like the harvest, the advent of an appointed time such as a pilgrim festival is also a sacred season and is made to express that regular, orderly, and predictable sort of sanctification for Israel which the system as a whole seeks.

If we now leap over the next two divisions, we come to the counterpart of the Divisions of Agriculture and Appointed Times, Holy Things and Purities, namely, dealing with the everyday and the ordinary, as against the special moments of harvest, on the one side, and special time or season, on the other. Here what is to be said hardly needs specification. The Temple, the locus of sanctification, is conducted in a wholly routine and trustworthy, punctilious manner. The one thing which may unsettle matters is the intention and will of the human actor. This is subjected to carefully prescribed limitations and remedies. The Division of Holy Things generates its companion, the one on cultic cleanness, Purities. The relationship between the two is like that between Agriculture and Appointed Times, the former locative, the latter utopian, the former dealing with the fields, the latter with the interplay between fields and altar. Here, too, once we speak of the one place of the Temple, we address, too, the cleanness which pertains to every place. A system of cleanness, taking into account what imparts uncleanness and how this is done, what is subject to uncleanness, and how that state is overcome—that system is fully expressed, once more, in response to the participation of the human will. Without the wish and act of a human being, the system does not function. It is inert. Sources of uncleanness, which come naturally and not by volition, and modes of purification, which work naturally and not by human intervention, remain inert until human will has imparted susceptibility to uncleanness, that is, introduced into the system food and drink, bed, pot, chair, and pan, which to begin with form the focus of the system. The movement from sanctification to uncleanness takes place when human will and work precipitate it.

The middle Divisions, the Third and Fourth, on Women and Dam-

ages, finally, take their place in the structure of the whole by showing
the congruence, within the larger framework of regularity and order, of
human concerns of family and farm, politics and workaday transactions among ordinary people. For without attending to these matters,
the Mishnah's system does not encompass what, at its foundations, it is
meant to comprehend and order. So what is at issue is fully cogent with
the rest. In the case of Women, attention focuses upon the point of
disorder marked by the transfer of that disordering anomaly, woman,
from the regular status provided by one man, to the equally trustworthy status provided by another. That is the point at which the Mishnah's interests are aroused: once more, predictably, the moment of
disorder. In the case of Damages, there are two important concerns.
First, there is the paramount interest in preventing, so far as possible,
the disorderly rise of one person and fall of another, and in sustaining
the status quo of the economy of Israel, the holy society in stasis.
Second, there is the necessary concomitant in the provision of a system
of political institutions to carry out the laws which preserve the balance
and steady state of persons.

The two Divisions which take up topics of concrete and material
concern, the formation and dissolution of families and the transfer of
property in that connection, the transactions, both through torts and
through commerce, which lead to exchanges of property and the potential dislocation of the state of families in society, are locative and
utopian at the same time. They deal with the concrete locations in
which people make their lives, household and street and field, the
sexual and commercial exchanges of a given village. But they pertain to
the life of all Israel, both in the Land and otherwise. These two Divisions, together with the household ones of Appointed Times, constitute the sole opening outward toward the life of utopian Israel, that
diaspora in the far reaches of the ancient world, in the endless span of
time. This community from the Mishnah's perspective is not only in
exile but unaccounted for, outside the system, for the Mishnah declines
to recognize and take into account. Israelites who dwell in the land of
(unclean) death instead of in the Land simply fall outside of the range of
(holy) life.

Now if we ask ourselves about the sponsorship and source of special
interest in the topics just now reviewed, we shall come up with obvious
answers.

In so far as the Mishnah is a document about the holiness of Israel in
its Land, it expresses that conception of sanctification and theory of
its modes which will have been shaped among those to whom the
Temple and its technology of joining heaven and holy Land through the
sacred place defined the core of being, I mean, the caste of the priests.

In so far as the Mishnah takes up the way in which transactions are conducted among ordinary folk and takes the position that it is through documents that transactions are embodied and expressed (surely the position of the relevant tractates on both Women and Damages), the Mishnah expresses what is self-evident to scribes. Just as, to the priest, there is a correspondence between the table of the Lord in the Temple and the locus of the divinity in the heavens, so, to the scribe, there is a correspondence between the documentary expression of the human will on earth, in writs of all sorts, in the orderly provision of courts for the predictable and just disposition of exchanges of persons and property, and heaven's judgment of these same matters. When a woman becomes sanctified to a particular man on earth, through the appropriate document governing the transfer of her person and property, in heaven as well, the woman is deemed truly sanctified to that man. A violation of the writ therefore is not merely a crime. It is a sin. That is why the Temple rite involving the wife accused of adultery is integral to the system of the Division of Women.

So there are these two social groups, not categorically symmetrical with one another, the priestly caste and the scribal profession, for whom the Mishnah makes self-evident statements. We know, moreover, that in time to come, the scribal profession would become a focus of sanctification too. The scribe would be transformed into the rabbi, locus of the holy through what he knew, just as the priest had been, and would remain locus of the holy through what he could claim for genealogy. The tractates of special interest to scribes-become-rabbis and to their governance of Israelite society, those of Women and Damages, together with certain others particularly relevant to utopian Israel beyond the system of the Land—those tractates would grow and grow. Others would remain essentially as they were with the closure of the Mishnah. So we must notice that the Mishnah, for its part, speaks for the program of topics important to the priests. It takes up the persona of the scribes, speaking through their voice and in their manner.

Now what we do not find, which becomes astonishing in the light of these observations, is sustained and serious attention to the matter of the caste of the priests and of the profession of the scribes. True, scattered through the tractates are exercises, occasionally sustained and important exercises, on the genealogy of the priestly caste, upon their marital obligations and duties, as well as on the things priests do and do not do in the cult, in collecting and eating their sanctified food, and in other topics of keen interest to priests. Indeed, it would be no exaggeration to say that the Mishnah's system seen whole is not a great deal more than a handbook of how the priestly caste wished to design its life in Israel and the world. And yet in the fundamental structure of the document, its organization into Divisions and tractates, there is no place for a Division of the Priesthood, no room even for a complete tractate on the rules of the priesthood, except, as we have seen, for the pervasive way of life of the priestly caste, which is everywhere. This absence of sustained attention to the priesthood is striking, when we compare the way in which the priestly code at Lev. 1–15 spells out its concerns: the priesthood, the cult, the matter of cultic cleanness. Since we have Divisions for the cult and for cleanness at Holy Things and Purities, we are struck that we do not have this Third Division.

We must, moreover, be equally surprised that, for a document so rich in the importance lent to petty matters of how a writ is folded and where the witnesses sign, so obsessed with the making of long lists and the organization of all knowledge into neat piles of symmetrically arranged words, the scribes who know how to make lists and match words nowhere come to the fore. They speak through the document. But they stand behind the curtains. They write the script, arrange the sets, design the costumes, situate the players in their place on the stage, raise the curtain—and play no role at all. We have no Division or tractate on such matters as how a person becomes a scribe, how a scribe conducts his work, who forms the center of the scribal profession and how authority is gained therein, the rights and place of the scribe in the system of governance through courts, the organization and conduct of schools or circles of masters and disciples through which the scribal arts are taught and perpetuated. This absence of even minimal information on the way in which the scribal profession takes shape and does its work is stunning when we realize that, within a brief generation, the Mishnah as a whole would fall into the hands of scribes, to be called rabbis, both in the Land of Israel and in Babylonia. These rabbis would make of the Mishnah exactly what they wished. Construed from the perspective of the makers of the Mishnah, the priests and the scribes who provide contents and form, substance and style, therefore, the Mishnah turns out to omit all reference to actors, when laying out the world which is their play.

The metaphor of the theater for the economy of Israel, the household of holy Land and people, space and time, cult and home, leads to yet another perspective. When we look out upon the vast drama portrayed by the Mishnah, lacking as it does an account of the one who wrote the book, and the one about whom the book was written, we notice yet one more missing component. In the fundamental and generative structure of the Mishnah, we find no account of that other necessary constituent: the audience. To whom the document speaks is never specified. What group ("class") generates the Mishnah's problems is not at issue. True, it is taken for granted that the world of the Mishnah expresses the sanctified being of Israel in general. So the Mishnah speaks about the generality of Israel, the people. But to whom, within Israel, the Mishnah addresses itself, and what groups are expected to want to know what the Mishnah has to say, are matters which never come to full expression.

Yet there can be no doubt of the answer to the question. The building block of Mishnaic discourse, the circumstance addressed whenever the issues of concrete society and material transactions are taken up, is the householder and his context. The Mishnah knows about all sorts of economic activities. But for the Mishnah the center and focus of interest lie in the village. The village is made up of households, each a unit of production in farming. The households are constructed by, and around, the householder, father of an extended family, including his sons and their wives and children, his servants, his slaves, the craftsmen to whom he entrusts tasks he does not choose to do. The concerns of householders are in transactions in land. Their measurement of value is expressed in acreage of top, middle, and bottom grade. Through real estate critical transactions are worked out. The marriage settlement depends upon real property. Civil penalties are exacted through payment of real property. The principal transactions to be taken up are those of the householder who owns beasts which do damage or suffer it; who harvests his crops and must set aside and so by his own word and deed sanctify them for use by the castes scheduled from on high; who uses or sells his crops and feeds his family; and who, if he is fortunate, will acquire still more land. It is to householders that the Mishnah is addressed: the pivot of society and its bulwark, the units of which the village is composed, the corporate component of the society of Israel in the limits of the village and the Land. The householder, as I said, is the building block of the house of Israel, of its *economy* in the classic sense of the word.

So, to revert to the metaphor which has served us well, the great proscenium constructed by the Mishnah now looms before us. Its arch is the canopy of heaven. Its stage is the holy Land of Israel. Its actors are the holy people of Israel. Its events are the drama of unfolding time and common transactions, appointed times and holy events. Yet in this grand design we look in vain for the three principal participants: the audience, the actors, and the playwright. So we must ask why.

The reason is not difficult to discover, when we recall that, after all, what the Mishnah really wants is for nothing to happen. The Mishnah presents a tableau, a wax museum, a diorama. It portrays a world fully perfected and so fully at rest. The one thing the Mishnah does not want to tell us is about change, how things come to be what they are. That is why there can be no sustained attention to the priesthood and its rules, the scribal profession and its constitution, the class of householders and its interests. The Mishnah's pretense is that all of these have come to rest. They compose a world in stasis, perfect and complete, made holy because it is complete and perfect. It is an economy—again in the

classic sense of the word—awaiting the divine *act* of sanctification
which, as at the creation of the world, would set the seal of holy rest
upon an again-complete creation, just as in the beginning. There is no
place for the actors when what is besought is no action whatsoever, but
only perfection, which is unchanging. There is room only for a description of how things are: the present tense, the sequence of completed
statements and static problems. All the action lies within, in how these
statements are made. Once they come to full expression, with nothing
left to say, there also is nothing left to do, no need for actors, whether
scribes, priests, or householders.

Since, to begin with, I have taken the position that a kind of Judaism
is to be described through a document of critical importance to that
kind of Judaism, the work before us is clear. We have now to do two
things.

First, we must isolate the principal components of the
"Judaism"—that is, the Mishnaic world view and way of life—before
us. These constituents are social groups. For, as I said in the beginning,
what makes up a world view and way of life are the people who see, or
are supposed to see, the world in one particular way and expected to
live in accord with a way of living congruent with that singular world
view. So the components of the system at the very basis of things are
the social groups to whom the system refers. These groups obviously
are not comparable to one another. As the framers of Kilayim and
Nedarim would notice, they are not three species of the same social
genus. One is a caste; the second, a profession; the third, a class. What
they have in common is, first, that they do form groups; and, second,
that the groups are social in foundation and collective in expression.
That is not a sizable claim. The priesthood is a social group; it
coalesces. Priests see one another as part of a single caste, with whom,
for example, they will want to intermarry. The scribes are a social
group, because they practice a single profession, following a uniform
set of rules. They coalesce in the methods by which they do their work.
The householders are a social group, the basic productive unit of society, around which other economic activity is perceived to function. In
an essentially agricultural economy, it is quite reasonable to regard the
householder, the head of a basic unit of production, as part of a single
class. If, then, we propose to describe the "Judaism" expressed by a
document, the first task is to isolate the setting in material society of
that document, the social components which speak through it. That is
to say, we now describe those sustained elements—themes, agenda of
inquiry—within the document which speak for groups which we may
identify and describe. It is this sort of social description of Judaism
which, in my judgment, the Mishnah both demands and, happily, also
effectuates.

Second, once the work of analysis is complete and the social groups before us are shown in all their specificity and individuality, we have to proceed to the final labor of synthesis. The Mishnah in form, function, and fact is one book, one cogent system. All of its parts interact with all others. That proposition has been the labor and the burden of the sustained account of chapter 4, above. As a single system, the Mishnah reveals the operation of a single principle of selection. That was the argument of chapter 5, in which the autonomy and inner cogency of the Mishnah were demonstrated through the exercise of differentiation made possible by a single point of reference, the relationship to Scripture and its authority. Once we saw that the Mishnah does not fall into place as a secondary expansion of the Scripture, we could perceive clearly that the Mishnah does coalesce and find cogency through its distinctive principle of selection of those Scriptures which were deemed useful and serviceable in the work defined, to begin with, by the framers of the Mishnah themselves. So, as is clear, and as has been asserted from the opening lines of this book, the Mishnah presents a system, distinctive, whole, fully interacting in all of its parts, capable of making a coherent statement. True, that statement expresses the viewpoints of diverse social groups. But it is one statement, made to a single world in behalf of a single world. That is why the Mishnah coalesces. In this chapter I claim to make that statement, both in its form and in its substance.

This also is why the Mishnah would fall to pieces nearly as soon as it did come together. For that world to which the Mishnah spoke was not a single world at all. The social coalition for which, at a single, enchanted moment, the Mishnah spoke, and to which, for an hour of sustained attention, the Mishnah would address its message, would be a heap of ruins before the play (which was to have no action or plot) was over.

Now this second task, subjected to so long an introduction, may be briefly stated. We have to ask how the several perspectives joined in the Mishnah do coalesce. What that single message is which brings them all together, and how that message forms a powerful, if transient, catalyst for the social groups which hold it—these define the final task in portraying the Judaism for which the Mishnah is the whole evidence. Integral to that task, to be sure, is an account of why, for the moment, the catalyst could serve, as it clearly did, to join together diverse agents, to mingle, mix, indeed unite, for a fleeting moment, social elements quite unlike one another, indeed not even capable of serving as analogies for one another.

As we shall see in due course, one of the recurring exercises of the Mishnaic thinkers is to give an account of how things which are different from one another become part of one another, that is, the problem of mixtures. This problem of mixtures will be in many dimensions, involving cases of doubt; cases of shared traits and distinctive ones; cases of confusion of essentially distinct elements and components; and numerous other concrete instances of successful and of unsuccessful, complete and partial catalysis. If I had to choose one prevailing motif of Mishnaic thought, it is this: the joining together of categories which are distinct. The Mishnaic mode of thought is to bring together principles and to show both how they conflict and how the conflict is resolved; the deal with grey areas and to lay down principles for disposing of cases of doubt; to take up the analysis of entities into their component parts and the catalysis of distinct substances into a single entity; to analyze the whole, the synthesize the parts. The motive force behind the Mishnah's intellectual program of cases and examples, the thing theMishnah wants to do with all of the facts it has in its hand, is described within this inquiry into mixtures. Now the reasons for this deeply typical, intellectual concern with confusion and order, I think, are probably to be found here and there and everywhere.

For, after all, the basic mode of thought of the priests who made up the priestly creation legend is that creation is effected through the orderly formation of each thing after its kind and correct location of each in its place. The persistent quest of the Mishnaic subsystems is for stasis, order, the appropriate situation of all things.

A recurrent theme in the philosophical tradition of Greco-Roman antiquity, current in the time of the Mishnah's formative intellectual processes, is the nature of mixtures, the interpenetration of distinct substances and their qualities, the juxtaposition of incomparables (see Sambursky and Neusner, *Purities* XII, pp. 206–9). The types of mixtures were themselves organized in a taxonomy: a mechanical composition, in which the components remain essentially unchanged, a total fusion, in which all particles are changed and lose their individual properties, and, in between, a mixture proper, in which there is a blending. So concern for keeping things straight and in their place is part of the priestly heritage. Perhaps it was also familiar to the philosophical context of scribes; that is far less certain. Householders can well have understood the notion of well-marked borders and stable and dependable frontiers between frontiers between different properties. What was to be fenced in and fenced out hardly requires specification.

And yet, however tradition and circumstance may have dictated this point of interest in mixtures and their properties, in sorting out what is confused and finding a proper place for every thing, I think there is still another reason for the recurrence of a single type of exercise and a uniform mode of thought. It is the social foundation for the intellectual exercise which is the Mishnah and its Judaism. In my view the very condition of Israel, standing, at the end of the second century, at the end of its own history, at the frontiers among diverse peoples, on both sides of every boundary, whether political or cultural or intellectual—it is the condition of Israel itself which attracted attention to this matter of sorting things out. The concern for the catalyst which joins what is originally distinct, the powerful attraction of problems of confusion and chaos, on the one side, and order and form, on the other—these form the generative problematic of the Mishnah as a system because they express in intellectual form the very nature and being of Israel in its social condition. It is therefore the profound congruence of the intellectual program and the social realities taken up and worked out by that intellectual program which both accounts for the power of the Mishnah to define the subsequent history of Judaism and justifies calling the Mishnah an expression and form of Judaism. The joining together of these distinct forces for order—caste, profession, class—forms the final stage in the description and interpretation of the Mishnah's kind of Judaism. That Judaism, at its deepest foundations, is the creation and expression of the catalyst which joins and holds the parts together.

At the end let us dwell on the curious fact that the Mishnah presents viewpoints of three distinct groups, yet is one document, beautifully composed and capable of exerting a powerful sense for the unity of language and thought, beginning to end. We shall not fully appreciate the brilliant contribution of the scribes, if we do not recognize how much they have drawn together, what obstacles of diversity of program and viewpoint they had to, and did, overcome. The fact is that in style and form the Mishnah is an essentially unitary document. Indeed, matters of style and form supply the principal mode of effecting and expressing that unity. For, as I have just now stressed, the emphases and programs of a number of distinct groups stand before us. To show that fact graphically, we review a taxonomy of the Mishnah's tractates, now divided among those groups principally interested in the various subject matters of the respective tractates (see table on next page).

Abodah Zarah does not fit into this scheme. It is not particular to the household but takes up, more than any other point of encounter, matters of trade and commerce with gentiles. The absence of tractates serving the priesthood and the scribal profession once more is striking. A further remarkable omission is a systematic account of the synagogue, its life of public prayer, Torah reading, and the like. Information on relevant topics is scattered elsewhere, e.g., Megillah for synagogal lections, Rosh Hashshanah and Taanit for liturgies. For its part Berakhot concerns prayers essentially incumbent on the individual and said at home or in the fields, or, on episodic occasions, in a congregation, such as the recitation of the *Shema*', the prayer, and the blessings before eating and grace after meals. These do not refer in particular to the life situation of the synagogue. The exegesis of these

Tractates of Principal Concern to Priests: Temple and Cult	Tractates of Principal Concern to Scribes: Courts and Documents	Tractates of Principal Concern to House-holders: Home and Farm
Demai	Ketubot	Peah
Terumot	Nedarim	Kilayim
Maaserot	Nazir	Orlah
Maaser Sheni	Sotah	Shabbat
Hallah	Gittin	Erubin
Bikkurim	Qiddushin	Besah
Pesahim	Baba Qamma	Moed Qatan
Sheqalim	Baba Mesia	Kelim
Yoma	Baba Batra	Tohorot
Sukkah	Sanhedrin	Niddah
Rosh Hashshanah	Makkot	Uqsin
Taanit	Shebuot	Berakhot
Megillah	Horayot	Abodah Zarah
Hagigah		
Yebamot		
Zebahim		
Menahot		
Hullin		
Bekhorot		
Arakhin		
Temurah		
Keritot		
Meilah		
Tamid		
Middot		
Qinnim		
Ohalot		
Negaim		
Parah		
Miqvaot		
Makhshirin		
Zabim		
Tebul Yom		
Yadayim		

topics in the Mishnah in no way supposes that the synagogue is the setting for any of the liturgies. So Berakhot falls comfortably into the framework of home and hearth. As I said, no tractate, let alone Division, takes up the matter of the synagogue, any more than any treats the schoolhouse. The two principal institutions of rabbinic Judaism thus play no formative or definitive role in the Mishnah.

It goes without saying that the tractates which deal with sources of uncleanness and modes of purification pertain as much to the household as to the cult. That, after all, is the basic theory of the system of Purities. But in so far as they deal with their stated topics, they pertain to begin with to the cult, and only secondarily, and by analogy, to the household. Niddah, for its part, is important primarily at home, because of its effects on sexual relations. Sotah concerns a cultic rite, but its context is secure, for reasons already stated.

Now the point of this protracted taxonomy is very simple. We are able to distinguish among the tractates of the Mishnah and to point to the categorical traits of each one. While, as I have just now said, an argument may be made for including a given tractate in more than a single category (e.g., the Babas in the third column), nonetheless the basic picture is clear. We really do confront definitive topics emerging from programs of quite separate social groups, responsive to topics of special interest to one group and not some other. Obviously every topic is important to all groups; that generality hardly requires specification. But the person who wanted to know in particular the rules governing farming in Peah, Kilayim, and Orlah will have found those rules of greater practical import than the ones, which also affected him and which he also will have kept, on how to prepare a marriage contract, a writ of divorce, or a will, or on how to conduct a trial and to adjudicate among conflicting claims and confused transactions. The scribe may also have been a householder, just as the householder also will have been subject to the laws of distinctive concern to the scribe. But tractates formed around questions pressing for the one can have been secondary for the other group. That the same things are to be said of the priests, who may also have been scribes but who most certainly also were householders, is self-evident. The picture therefore is clear.

The Gift of the Scribes

In its principal and definitive categories of organization, the Mishnah as a whole rests upon three distinct social bases. That fact makes all the more important the unitary character of the form and rhetoric of the document as a whole. It is this fact, that, despite its socially diverse foundations and categories of interest, the Mishnah expresses itself in one mode of thought and expression and through one manner of speaking, which we must now consider.

The mode of thought and expression is that of the scribal profession. The Mishnah is a collection of lists, highly organized information. In so far as the definitive trait of a document of trained scribes is the presentation of vast amounts of information in a systematic and orderly way, e.g., through the making of lists, the Mishnah is in prevailing form and fundamental structure a scribal document, an exercise in *Listenwissenschaft*. The systematic and orderly exposition of ideas through lists, moreover, in no way exhausts the successful program of *Listenwissenschaft* achieved in this document. Whole tractates consist in the systematic and logical exposition of an announced theme or problem, from point to point, beginning to end. Indeed, some tractates, e.g., Negaim, appear to have little more to do than to systematize information in a perfectly orderly way (see M. Neg. 3:3–8:10). A striking sample of the Mishnah's framers' capacity to gather and organize in a neat and easily memorized construction a vast amount of information is presented at M. Zeb. 5 (Neusner, *Holy Things* I, pp. 91–104). A quite standard exercise is the composition of a catalogue of various subgroups of a given group, e.g., a requirement and those wholly, partially, and not at all liable to its observance. An example of this sort of systematic organization of information is the exercise which goes over the ground of those who do not bring first fruits at all, those who bring first fruits but do not recite the Scriptural formula specified at Deut. 26:1–11, and those who bring first fruits and execute the required recitation (M. Bik. 1:1–11). Another instance, among many, of the Mishnah's capacity to organize a large amount of information in a neat scheme works out four possible relationships between women, their husbands, and their levirs: permitted to one, prohibited to the other, vice versa, permitted to both, prohibited to both (M. Yeb. 9:1–2). Still another instance of the systematic organization of information is on offerings which require (1) bringing near but not waving, (2) waving but not bringing near, (3) both, and (4) neither (M. Men. 5:5–6). Finally, the artful organization of masses of information is seen in the list of things which impart corpse uncleanness or interpose against it, impart but do not interpose, interpose but do not impart, and do neither (M. Oh. 8:1–2).

But the formalization of language in the Mishnah, and the use of formalized and patterned language to facilitate the learning and memorization of vast amounts of information, are in no way exhausted by these instances of the neat categorizing of possibilities. On the contrary, there is a constant interplay between form and theme. This interplay is at the deepest levels of meaning. It reveals the philosophical and aesthetic genius of philosophers, not merely scribal listmakers. Specifically, when the theme of discourse shifts, the pattern of language shifts with it. There is, therefore, a particular, recurrent formal pattern, in accord with which sentences are constructed and also by which a particular and distinct theme is worked out. Then, when a new theme commences, a fresh formal pattern will be used. There will be a recurrent pattern of sentence structure repeated time and again within the unit and a shifting at the commencement of the next theme. Each point at which the recurrent pattern commences marks the beginning of a new cognitive unit, that is, the smallest complete unit of thought or discourse. In general, an intermediate division of discourse will contain a carefully enumerated sequence of exempla of cognitive units, in the established formal pattern, in groups of three or five or multiples of three or five.

The cognitive units resort to a remarkably limited repertoire of formal and formulary patterns. The Mishnah manages to say whatever it wants in one of the following: 1. the simple declarative sentence, in which the subject, verb, and predicate are syntactically tightly joined to one another, e.g., *He who does so and so is such and such;* 2. the duplicated subject, in which the subject of the sentence is stated twice, e.g., *He who does so and so, lo, he is such and such;* 3. mild apocopation, in which the subject of the sentence is cut off from the verb, which refers to its own subject, and not the one with which the sentence commences, e.g., *He who does so and so . . ., it* [the thing he has done] *is such and such;* 4. extreme apocopation, in which a series of clauses is presented, none of them tightly joined to what precedes or follows, and all of them cut off from the predicate of the sentence, e.g., *he who does so and so . . ., it* [the thing he has done] *is such and such . . ., it is a matter of doubt whether . . . or whether . . ., lo, it* [referring to nothing in the antecedent, apocopated clauses of the subject of the sentence] *is so and so. . . .* In addition to these formulary patterns, in which the distinctive formulary traits are effected through variations in the relationship between the subject and the predicate of the sentence, or in which the subject itself is given a distinctive development, there is yet a fifth. In this last one we have a contrastive complex predicate, in which case we may have two sentences, independent of one another, yet clearly formulated so as to stand in acute balance with one another in the predicate, thus, *He who does . . . is unclean, and he who does not . . . is clean.*

By itself, a tightly constructed sentence consisting of subject, verb, and complement in which the verb refers to the subject, and the complement to the verb, hardly exhibits traits of particular formal interest. Yet a sequence of such sentences, built along the same gross grammatical lines, exhibits a clear-cut and distinctive pattern. The important point of differentiation, particularly for the simple declarative sentence, appears in the intermediate unit. It is there that we see a single pattern recurring in a long sequence of sentences, e.g., *the X which has lost its Y is unclean because of its Z. The Z which has lost its Y is unclean because of its X.* Another pattern will be a long sequence of highly developed sentences, laden with relative clauses and other explanatory matter, in which a single syntactical pattern will govern the articulation of three or six or nine exempla. That sequence will be followed by one repeated terse sentence, e.g., *X is so and so, Y is such and such, Z is thus and so.* The former pattern will treat one principle or theme, the latter some other. There can be no doubt that the pattern of recurrent declarative sentences in its way is just as carefully formalized as a sequence of severely apocopated sentences or of contrastive predicates or duplicated subjects.

There is no reason to doubt that, if we asked the tradental-redactional authorities behind the Mishnah the immediate purpose of their formalization, their answer would be to facilitate memorization. For that is the proximate effect of the acute formalization of their document. Much in its character can be seen as mnemonic. The Mishnah was meant to be memorized by a distinctive group of people for an extraordinary purpose. The formal aspects of the Mishnaic rhetoric are empty of content, which is proved by the fact that pretty much all themes and conceptions can be reduced to these same few formal patterns of syntax. These patterns, moreover, are established by syntactical recurrences, as distinct from recurrence of sounds. Long sequences of patterned and disciplined sentences fail to repeat the same words—that is, syllabic balance, rhythm, or sound—yet they do establish a powerful claim to order and formulary sophistication and perfection. That is why we name a pattern, *he who . . . it is . . .* apocopation: the arrangement of the words, in set grammatical relationships, not their substance, is indicative of pattern. Accordingly, while we have a document composed along what clearly are mnemonic lines, the Mishnah's susceptibility to memorization rests principally upon the utter abstraction of recurrent syntactical patterns, rather than on the concrete repetition of particular words, rhythms, syllabic counts, or sounds.

It therefore appears that a sense for the deep, inner logic of word patterns, of grammar and syntax, rather than for their external similarities, governs the Mishnaic mnemonic. Even though the Mishnah is to be memorized and handed on orally, it expresses a mode of thought attuned to abstract relationships, rather than concrete and substantive forms. The formulaic, not the formal, character of the Mishnaic rhetoric yields a picture of a group which speaks of immaterial and not material things. In this group the relationship, rather than the thing or person which is related, is primary and constitutes the principle of reality. The thing itself is less than the thing in cathexis with other things, so too the person. The repetition of form creates form. But what here is repeated is not external or superficial, but formulary patterns deep in the structure of cognition, effected through persistent grammatical or syntactical relationships, and affecting an infinite range of diverse objects and topics. Form and structure emerge not from concrete, formal things but from abstract and unstated, but ubiquitous and powerful, relationships.

This fact—the creation of pattern through relationship of syntactical elements, rather than through concrete sounds—tells us that the scribes who memorized conceptions reduced to these particular forms were capable of extraordinarily abstract perception. Hearing peculiarities of word order in diverse cognitive contexts, their ears and minds perceived regularities of grammatical arrangement, repeated functional variations of utilization of diverse words. They grasped from such subtleties syntactical patterns not expressed by recurrent external phenomena and autonomous of particular meanings. What they heard, it is clear, were not only abstract relationships but also principles conveyed along with and through these relationships. For what in fact was memorized was a recurrent and fundamental notion, expressed in diverse examples but in recurrent rhetorical-syntactical patterns. Accordingly, what they could and did hear was what lay far beneath the surface of the rule: the unstated principle, the unsounded pattern. This means that their mode of thought was attuned to what lay beneath the surface. Their minds and their ears perceived what was not said behind what was said and how it was said. They besought that ineffable and metaphysical reality concealed within, but conveyed through spoken and palpable material reality. Social interrelationships within the community of Israel are left behind in the ritual speech of the Mishnah, just as, within the laws, natural realities are made to give form and expression to supernatural or metaphysical regularities. The Mishnah speaks of Israel, but the speakers are a group apart. The Mishnah talks of this-worldly things, but the things stand for and speak of another world entirely.

The style of the Mishnah thus serves to exemplify, but rarely actually to spell out, a deep principle (see M. Kel. 24:1–15 or M. Oh. 10:1–7). That is what makes difficult the description and interpretation of the Mishnah's cogent system, its "Judaism." The Mishnah's mode of discourse rarely wishes to announce what it proposes to say. Its main points are subordinated to details and expressed through details. The framers of the Mishnah compose their document and express its ideas in accord with an aesthetic theory which favors reticence and indirection over explicit statements. This is so in style and in substance. So the language of the Mishnah and its formalized grammatical rhetoric create a world of discourse quite separate from the concrete realities of a given time, place, or society. The exceedingly limited repertoire of grammatical patterns by which all things on all matters are said gives symbolic expression to the notion that beneath the accidents of life are a few comprehensive relationships. Unchanging and enduring patterns lie deep in the inner structure of reality and impose structure upon the accidents of the world. This means, as I said, that reality for the Mishnaic rhetoric consists in the grammar and syntax of language: consistent and enduring patterns of relationship among diverse and changing concrete things or persons. What lasts is not the concrete thing but the abstract interplay governing any and all sorts of concrete things. There is, therefore, a congruence between rhetorical patterns of speech, on the one side, and the framework of discourse established by these same patterns, on the other. Just as we accomplish memorization by perceiving not what is said but how it is said and is persistently arranged, so we undertake to address and describe a world in which what is concrete and material is secondary. But how things are said about what is concrete and material in diverse ways and contexts is principal. The Mishnah is silent about the context of its speech because context is trivial. Principle, beginning in syntactical principles by which all words are arranged in a severely limited repertoire of grammatical sentences ubiquitously pertinent but rarely made explicit, is at the center.

The homogenization of thought and its expression in a limited and uniform rhetorical pattern impose the conception that the norms are axiomatic for, and expose the logic of, all situations in general, but pertain to none in particular. This again brings to the surface the notion, implicit in the way the Mishnah says things, that it describes how things are, whether or not material reality conforms. The absence of reference to a speaker and his role reenforces the conception that this-worldly details of identified teachers, with circumscribed and concrete authority, are not pertinent. The reason is that what comes under description does not depend upon the details of this-worldly institutions. That is why the document is so strikingly indifferent to the differentiation of rhetoric. Diverse ideational materials invariably are reduced to a single rhetoric (tractate Abot is the sole exception). The various contexts to which what is said is applicable are never given definition in the choice of words or rhetorical patterns. In the profoundly conventional discourse of the Mishnah, the one thing left untouched by the effect of convention is the concrete world, which is to conform, whether in fact it does or does not conform.

The scribes behind the Mishnah's language take for granted that the language of the Mishnah will be understood; its nuances appreciated; its points of stress and emphasis grasped. Our discussion of the cathetically neutral and indifferent style of the Mishnah, its failure to speak to some distinct audience in behalf of some defined speaker, does not obscure the simple fact that the Mishnah is not gibberish. It forms a corpus of formed and intensely meaningful statements, the medium of which is meant to bear deep meaning. Accordingly, the gnomic sayings of the Mishnah, corresponding in their deep, universal grammar to the subterranean character of an imagined reality, permit the inference that the reality so described is to be grasped and understood by people of mind. Given the unarticulated points at which stress occurs, the level of grammar autonomous of discrete statements and concrete rulings, moreover, we must conclude that the framers of the

Mishnah expected to be understood by remarkably keen ears and active minds. Conveying what is fundamental at the level of grammar autonomous of meaning, they manifest confidence that the listener will put many things together and draw the important conclusions for himself. That means, as I said, that the Mishnah assumes an active intellect, capable of perceiving inferred convention, and vividly participating audience capable of following what was said with intense concentration. This demands, first, memorizing the message on the surface, and, second, perceiving the subtle and unarticulated message of the medium of syntax and grammar. The hearer, third, is assumed to be capable of putting the two together into the still further insight that the pattern exhibited by diverse statements preserves a substantive cogency among those diverse and delimited statements. Superficially various rules, stated in sentences unlike one another on the surface and made up of unlike word choices, in fact say a single thing. None of this possible, it goes without saying, without anticipating that exegesis of the fixed text will be undertaken by the audience. The Mishnah demands commentary. It takes for granted that the audience is capable of exegesis and proposes to undertake the work. The Mishnah commands a sophisticated and engaged sociointellectual context within the Israelite world. The Mishnah's lack of specificity on this point should not obscure its quite precise expectation. The thing it does not tell us which we have to know is that the Mishnah will be understood. The process of understanding, the character of the Mishnah's language testifies, is complex and difficult. The Mishnah is a document which compliments its audience.

So there are these two striking traits of mind reflected within the Mishnaic rhetoric: first, the perception of order and balance; second, the perception of the mind's centrality in the construction of order and balance, i.e., the imposition of wholeness, upon discrete cases in the case of the routine declarative sentence, and upon discrete phrases in the case of the apocopated one. Both order and balance are contained from within and are imposed from without. The relationships revealed by grammatical consistencies internal to a sentence and the implicit regularities revealed by the congruence and cogency of cases rarely are stated but always are to be discerned. Accordingly, the one thing which the Mishnah invariably does not make explicit but which always is necessary to know is, I stress, the presence of the active intellect, the participant who is the hearer. It is the hearer who ultimately makes sense of, perceives the sense in, the Mishnah. Once more we are impressed by the Mishnah's expectation of high sophistication and profound sensitivity to order and to form on the part of its audience. In assigning this remarkable achievement of intellect to the profession of the scribes, I claim that the intellectual experience and cognitive traditions of an ancient profession alone can have come to such full and complete development as the Mishnah reveals. That scribes make lists, and that people who make lists are scribes—these statements, in gross form, express the sum and substance of my reason to assign the aesthetic and formal achievement of the Mishnah to those scribes who participated in the process of making the Mishnah. The gift of the scribes is the Mishnah's rhetorical power.

The Gift of the Priests

Since I already have presented a full and detailed account of the priests' viewpoint, beginning to end, and of the tractates which express that viewpoint by their choice of topic (see above, especially pp. 225–29, 230–31, and 240–41), it remains only to point to certain passages in the Mishnah, expressive of priestly topics, which diverge from the standard formal and analytical style described in the preceding section. These passages have in common one thing: to describe cultic procedures, they resort to narrative style, telling what someone does or did, with a minimum of interruption for the familiar exercises of analytic and problem solving. There is no effort to phrase all laws on the conduct of the cult in the form of a narrative. But discussions of precisely what is done in a particular rite, e.g., one of sacrifice, or of any Temple liturgy, take the form of a tale. While, for example, we have ample discussion on the costs of the various pilgrim offerings, the whole discussion is in analytical discourse (M. Hag. 1:1ff). The actual killing and disposition of the animals—what the priest and sacrificer really do—are not dealt with. That is why at the point we do not find the mode of discourse shifting into tale-telling. By contrast, when the Mishnah wishes to tell us about how a Passover offering is killed, or how the high priest carries out the laborious liturgy of the Day of Atonement, the document's framers resort solely to the narrative mode.

A catalogue of those passages in the Mishnah which shift from analysis and problem solving to narrative and storytelling follows. First come the stories of the conduct of the cult every day, that is, the daily whole offering and how it is prepared, as well as on special occasions. The narrative of how the daily whole offering is prepared and dealt with at tractate Tamid covers the ground of tractates Zebahim and Menahot and explains why, in those tractates, we do not have a counterpart, for the meat and meal offerings, to tractate Menahot's attractive story of how the priests deal with the show bread from week to week. The collection and expenditure of the *sheqel,* a poll tax in support of the public offerings of the Temple and of the upkeep of the building and its personnel, are worked out through an extended narrative (M. Sheq. 3:1–4:9). The administrators of the Temple are named, and the procedures are related, all in the storytelling style (M. Sheq. 5:1–7:8).

The conduct of the Temple rites involving the high priest on the Day of Atonement is presented wholly in narrative style (M. Yoma 1:1–7:5). This narrative clearly depends upon the tale of Lev. 16 for order and meaning. Now all is told in present-tense language and descriptive tale-telling style. The rite of the *lulab* on the Temple mount when the first day of the Festival coincided with the Sabbath is spelled out in narrative style (M. Suk. 4:4). The same is so for the rite of the willow branch at the altar (M. Suk. 4:5–7), the water libation, and the playing of the flute and the celebration of the drawing of water for the water libation (M. Suk. 5:1–5). All of these are described, rather than analyzed, and the description takes the style of telling a story of how things were done.

The law of slaughtering and roasting the Passover offering is worked out in narrative form (M. Pes. 5:5–10). A narrative relates how the first sheaf of wheat is cut for the *omer* offering (M. Men. 10:2–5). The way in which the priests take the bread offering in and out of the sanctum is told as a story (M. Men. 11:7), as I said above. Bikkurim spells out the bringing of first fruits to the Temple priest. It includes a narrative account of how this is done (M. Bik. 3:2–6, 7–9). The conduct of burning the red cow is presented through a sustained narrative. Then, the story told, the same matter is reviewed through the analysis of cases which exemplify principles and their legal expression (M. Par. 3:1–1, 4:1–4). The prayers for rain and the liturgy of the community for a fast day are set forth in essentially narrative style, describing how things are done, with very little analysis, and much emphasis upon tale-telling (M. Ta. 1:1–7, 2:1–5). The involvement of the priestly watch for a given week is specified and narrated.

The second part of this brief catalogue takes up tales of priestly conduct of special rites, not public and sacrificial liturgies but those required for individual cases and necessitating participation of priests, with or without an actual blood rite. The purification rite of one afflicted with *sara'at* is recorded as a narrative (M. Neg. 14:1–3, 8–10). The Temple rite of administering the bitter water to a woman accused of adultery is presented as a story (M. Sot. 1:4, 2:1–3, 3:1–2, 4).

There is only one exception to the rule that resort to narrative style and the telling of a story is distinctive to the conduct of the priests and the cult. Whether or not we regard as narrative the account of the way a trial is conducted and the witnesses cross-examined, when we come to the description of the mode of execution through stoning, we surely must recognize that we have a narrative along the lines of those on the

conduct of the cultic rites (M. San. 4, 5, 6:1–4, 6; cf. M. San. 7:1–3). A
narrative style also is used to convey information on flogging (M. Mak.
3:12–14).

In sum, the priests' contribution of a fairly systematic and wide-
ranging account of the cult, recorded in various stories, is not large.
But it is pretty much complete, treating both everyday and extraordinary rites alike. It does yield a distinctive dimension to the larger
literary-rhetorical character of the Mishnah and its system. It is hardly
necessary to remark that this formal and literary contribution constitutes only the tip of the iceberg of what is priestly in the Mishnah's
Judaism. Nor should we forget the fact that exactly the same names of
authorities after the wars appear in narrative pericopes as in analytical
ones. So even though there is ample evidence to indicate the presence
of a distinct "source," marked off by its own subject matter, which is
remarkably coherent, as well as by its own literary style, the "priestly
source"* is part and parcel of the Mishnah as we know it. Since the
named authorities are the same, the probable reason for telling stories
in the context of presenting facts about the conduct of the cult has
nothing to do with choices made in the distant past, before the beginning of the Mishnah, or in circles other than those everywhere present
in the Mishnah.

The Gift of the Householders

Now when we ask about the social perspectives of the Mishnah, we
also want to know whose problems are taken up and worked out. No
one can fairly impute an essentially unfair or unbalanced set of judgments or solutions to the framing and resolution of those problems. The
Mishnah's weight is at the center, in the middle of an issue. Its deepest
concern is for balance to both sides. It follows that what we wish to
describe is the range of topics deemed to require attention, not the bias
of the document in favor of one social group and against some other.
The fact that the practical agendum of the Mishnaic law derives from a
society of farmers is hardly surprising. That is why, for example, the
focus on damages caused by oxen is hardly probative evidence of the
social perspective of the legal system as a whole (see, for example, M.
B.Q. 1–7). What is of special interest within the obvious datum that
Israel in Palestine was a farming community is different. It is, as I said,

* I do not believe source criticism is feasible for the Mishnah, for the reasons specified
in the text. What we have is a convention, among a range of literary-rhetorical conventions available to the Mishnah's framers. Another such convention is use of the
names of the Houses of Shammai and Hillel to debate issues vivid only in the mid-second
century, as noted above, pp. 20–22).

whose questions are raised to begin with. Here, to be sure, we shall see
a bias of land against capital. But that is no news.

One persistent source of problems for inquiry and solution, as we
know, is the priestly caste. Another is the proprietary class, the householders. These were farmers of their own land, proprietors of the
smallest viable agricultural unit of production. They stood at the center
of a circle of a sizable corps of dependents: wives, sons and
daughters-in-law, children and grandchildren, slaves servants, day-
laborers. At the outer fringes of the Mishnah's household were such
ancillary groups as craftsmen and purveyors of other such specialties,
wagon-drivers; providers of animals and equipment for rent,
moneylenders, shopkeepers, wholesalers of grain and other produce;
scribes and teachers; and, of course, the ultimate dependents: priests,
Levites, and the poor. As principal and head of so sizable a network of
material relationships, the householder could well see himself as a
pivot in the village, the irreducible building block of society. He was
the solid and responsible center of it all. In the corporate community of
the village, there were many components, each with a particular perspective and program of pressing questions. The householder was only
one of these. But he controlled the mode of production and held the
governance of the basic economic unit of the village. The whole held
together, so far as the Mishnah's picture of society in its material
relationships and productive aspect is concerned, through the householder. Who owns something alone may sanctify it: God in heaven, the
householder on earth.

Ownership of land is the key to much else. Transfer of that ownership is carefully examined. One important way of effecting ownership in times as unsettled as those of the first and second centuries
was through mere right of possession. Squatters' rights clearly came
into conflict with ownership established through documents and inheritance. Indeed, the right of possession contravened the rule of law
when the rightful owner could be pushed off his land. That is why the
control of gaining possession of property or possessions through usu-
fruct was carefully controlled and defined. One may lose a deed and
retain ownership of the land. The main point is that only three full years
of unharassed occupancy and use of land sufficed to establish legitimate ownership (M. B.B. 3:1–8). A piece of land, however small, was a
unit of the economy sufficient for supporting a person. If a person
thought he was dying but still held onto a bit of land, all his gifts in
contemplation of death remained valid in the event that he recovers.
That small bit of property kept in reserve sufficed to show that the gifts
were not on the condition that the donor die (M. B.B. 9:6). Land also
was the medium of exchange in marriage settlements and in paying
compensation for torts and damages.

What is striking, indeed probative, is that the Mishnah takes a remarkably unsympathetic view of the holder of liquid capital or trading goods in kind, the trader, the shopkeeper, but, especially, the holder of capital—moneylender and factor. The householder is represented always as the borrower. The lender is persistently treated as an outsider, to be watched and subjected to regulation. The Mishnah never represents householders as lending money to one another. It does know about factors who provide to a householder capital, in the form of animals, to be tended and raised, then sold. Both parties share in the profits. The Mishnah's deepest interest in such a factoring contract then is that the farmer not work for nothing. Obviously, the priestly code's prohibition of interest also will attract attention. Stress on fair and just commercial relationships is equally unsurprising. But the presence of the principle of true value, permitting only a sixth of deviation from that true value; the notion that the value of seed and crops may vary, but that of capital may not vary with theirs; the conception that lending money for investment is not permitted to yield a profit to the capitalist—these express the position of the householder. True value lies in the land and its produce, not in capital. Seed in the ground can be seen to yield a crop. Money invested in maintaining an agricultural community from one crop to the next cannot. So, in sum, there is a powerful bias against not only usury but interest, in favor not only of regulating frauds but also of restricting honest traders and capitalists. There is a true value, as distinct from market value, to objects of trade. If there is a difference of a sixth in price between true value and what is actually paid, fraud has been committed, and the transaction is null (M. B.M. 4:3–4). The same conception applies to a coin (M. B.M. 4:5). In general, one may not adulterate what is sold. But wholesalers have the right to gather grain among various farms and treat the whole as a single batch (M. B.M. 4:11–12).

The Mishnah, as I said, takes for granted that the borrower is the landholder or householder. That is assumed in the phrasing of the rule that one who lends money should not live for free in the borrower's courtyard (M. B.M. 5:2). He also should not rent a place from the borrower for less than the prevailing rate (ibid.) A further case in which it is the farmer who pays interest and the capitalist who collects it, as noted above, involves factoring, that is, the capitalist's handing over animals to a farmer to raise, with the profits to be shared equally. The farmer must be paid something for his labor, or the arrangement is deemed usurious (M. B.M. 5:4, 5). An agreement on the part of the farmer to tend a flock and to share in the profits, but to bear the whole loss, so that the full value of the flock is guaranteed to the capitalist, is usurious (M. B.M. 5:6). A price cannot be settled upon for a crop before the crop is on the market. Once there is a prevailing market, then a price can be struck for a specific deal (M. B.M. 5:7). The contrary procedure involves trading in naked futures, and that too smacks of usury. The focus upon the householder again is expressed in the notion that a man may not lend tenant farmers wheat to be paid in wheat, if it is for food. But he may do so if it is for seed (M. B.M. 5:8–9). The presupposition of this rule is obvious. Transactions in produce also tend to be phrased in terms of the viewpoint of the householder, e.g., he who sells produce to his fellow (M. B.B. 5:7, 8, 6:1).

But the point of the law is not to favor the seller over the buyer of produce. It is to establish the moment at which the transaction is irrevocable and to make certain that the rights of all parties are respected. And this leads to what is critical.

While the Mishnah takes up questions important to householders and expresses their perspective on the value and uses of capital, the Mishnah aims as I have stressed, at a fair adjudication of conflict. In so far as the Mishnah exhibits a bias, it is in favor of a just, reliable, stable order in which what is fair is done to all parties to a dispute, and in which the rights of everyone are protected. But at issue, time and again, are conflicts among householders and the definition and production of the rights of householders in particular. I cannot think of a single passage about the rights of slaves or craftsmen or storekeepers or moneylenders, for example, comparable to the attention paid to the rights of the buyers and sellers of a piece of land or to parties to a transaction in produce.

The conflict of householders is taken up in that rule that where one party owns a cistern wholly surrounded by the land of another, the rights of both have to be specified (M. B.B. 6:5–6). The other rights of jointholders of a courtyard to subdivide the courtyard or to make alterations to their properties are worked out at some length (M. B.B. 1:1–3). Shared responsibilities and costs of maintenance of the condominium are specified as well (M. B.B. 1:4–6). A householder, moreover, must avoid damaging the property of his neighbor, and that obligation extends to his utilization of his own land (M. B.B. 2:1ff). If one creates a nuisance to neighbors on one's own land, the neighbors can prevent the maintenance of that nuisance, e.g., a cistern, smelly oven, and the like. The right of the householder to the view he has always enjoyed cannot be abridged (M. B.B. 2:4). The mutual responsibilities of two householders who share the same building are carefully worked out. Each joint holder to the building is responsible to maintain it, or to rebuild it in the case of a calamity (M. B.M. 10:1–3). Disputes between owners of adjoining property receive a fair amount of attention (M. B.M. 10:4–6).

When real estate is sold, the language used by the seller of the property requires interpretation, e.g., if the landowner specifies that he is selling ground of a given area, whether the statement is taken to mean the inclusion in the measure of crevices or rocks has to be clarified. Otherwise we are not going to know how much land must be delivered (M. B.B. 7:1–4). When one sells property, one may or may not have sold much which goes along with the property. The established principle is that a householder who sells a property sells what is not movable, but is not deemed to have sold what is (M. B.B. 4:1–9, 5:1–5).

The focus of interest in cases of leasing a field is in the right of the lessor to have the field actually worked and properly tended. The lessee has no right to neglect the established obligations in such a relationship. If the lessee does not properly tend the field, the lessor can force him to maintain the property. Even if the field does not yield a crop, the lessee has to tend it (M. B.M. 9:1–4). The rights of the tenant are protected; he cannot be evicted at an unsuitable season. But the rule once more is phrased, He who rents out (M. B.M. 8:6; cf. M. B.M. 8:7ff).

Another point of sustained interest is bailments, with attention to impairments of what is left, failure properly to take care of the bailment, and similar acts of culpability on the part of the bailee (M. B.M. 3). Craftsmen are held to be paid bailees, which means they are fully responsible for the goods entrusted to their care (M. B.M. 6:6). A lender who took a pledge likewise is in that status (M. B.M. 6:7). In both instances the advantage then lies with the householder who gave over the goods or who handed over the pledge. If someone hands over wool to a dyer, and the dye burned the wool, the dyer pays the value of the wool (M. B.Q. 9:4). If someone gave an object to a craftsman to repair, the craftsman is liable to pay compensation for damages caused by him to the object (M. B.Q. 9:3). If one deposits produce with his fellow, the bailee is not penalized for natural depletion (M. B.M. 3:7–8).

The focus in labor relations is on the mutual obligations of employer and employee. But the language, predictably, always takes up the perspective of the employer: he who hires craftsmen (M. B.M. 6:1), or an ass driver, or workers to take his flax out of the steep, and the like. The point to be made in context is that the one who changes the terms of an agreement suffers the consequences. It is the formulation which supposes that the actor is the householder. The subject of the transaction of dealing with day laborers is he who hires; it is the householder who provides a meal (M. B.M. 7:1, 7). The right of the worker to nibble on the crop on which he is working is carefully delineated (M. B.M. 7:4).

No effort is made to do away with the right, but there is no disposition to treat it in a liberal way (cf. M. B.M. 7:5). One may not purchase wool, milk, or kids from herdsmen, or wood or fruit from the watchmen of an orchard. The concern is to prevent pilferage (M. B.Q. 10:9).

This rapid survey shows that the framing of the topics of the Mishnah and the character and definition of the recurrent problems it selects for attention leave little room for doubt about the Mishnah's perspective. It is that of the householder in a courtyard—the subject of most predicates. He is the proprietor of an estate, however modest, owner of land, however little. He also is a landholder in the fields, an employer with a legitimate claim against lazy or unreliable workers; the head of a family; the manager of a small but self-contained farm. He is someone who gives over his property to craftsmen for their skilled labor, but is not a craftsman himself. He also is someone with a keen interest in assessing and collecting damages done to his herds and flocks, or in paying what he must for what his beasts do. The Mishnah speaks for someone who deems thievery to be the paltry, petty thievery ("oh! the servants!") of watchmen of an orchard and herdsmen of a flock, and for a landowner constantly involved in transactions in real property.

The Mishnah's class perspective, described from its topics and problems, is that of the undercapitalized and overextended upper-class farmer, who has no appreciation whatsoever for the interests of those with liquid capital and no understanding of the role of trading in commodity futures. This landed proprietor of an estate of some size sees a bushel of grain as a measure of value. But he does not concede that, in the provision of supplies and sustenance through the year, from one harvest to the next, lies a kind of increase no less productive than the increase of the fields and the herd. The Mishnah is the voice of the head of the household, the pillar of society, the model of the community, the arbiter and mediator of the goods of this world, fair, just, honorable, above all, reliable. The Mishnah therefore is the voice of the Israelite landholding, proprietary class (cf. Solodukho). Its problems are the problems of the landowner, the householder, as I said, the Mishnah's basic and recurrent subject for nearly all predicates. Its sense of what is just and fair expresses his sense of the givenness and cosmic rightness of the present condition of society. Earth matches heaven. The Mishnah's hope for heaven and its claim on earth, to earth, corresponding to the supernatural basis for the natural world, bespeak the imagination of the surviving Israelite burgherdom of the mid-second-century Land of Israel—people deeply tired of war and its dislocation, profoundly distrustful of messiahs and their dangerous promises. These are men of substance and means, however modest, aching for a stable and predictable world in which to tend their crops and herds, feed their

families and workers, keep to the natural rhythms of the seasons and
the lunar cycles, and, in sum, live out their lives within strong and
secure boundaries, on earth and in heaven.

The Nature of Mixtures

The Mishnah presents a homogeneous set of inquiries, consistently
asking the same sorts of questions, about gray areas, doubts, excluded
middles without regard to the subject at hand or the topics of the
material under analysis. In this section we shall examine the Mishnah's
uniform mode of inquiry, in the next, the uniform set of answers, and,
at the end, the social formation for the intellectual construction, mode
of thought and meaning, described here. But first let us stand back and
take note of why these encompassing questions about intellectual style
and substance must be raised. The reason is that now that the
tributaries to the Mishnah have been specified and their tribute as-
sessed, we realize that the Mishnah far transcends these gifts. So we
have to turn to those traits of intellectual style and substance in which
the Mishnah vastly exceeds the flood of its tributaries, becomes far
more than the sum of its parts. For up to now, in fact, we have not
come close to the points of central interest and critical tension which
make the Mishnah what it is. And the Mishnah in no way presents itself
as a document of class, caste, or profession. It is something different.
The difference comes to complete statement in the two dimensions
which mark the measure of any work of intellect: style and substance,
medium of expression, mode of thought, and message. These have now
to be specified with full attention to recurrent patterns among the
myriad of detailed rules, problems, and exercises, of which the Mishnah is composed.

Let us take up, first of all, the matter of style: the things the Mishnah
wants to *do* with the points of interest, topics of concern, and, above
all, sheer volume of facts which flow into the Mishnah from the Scriptures chosen for exegesis and from diverse other sources, literary and
societal. In the next unit we take up that perspective on all things which
corresponds to this distinctive style: the things the Mishnah wants to
say about the facts, the message the Mishnah frames through the
medium of facts and the exegesis of them. This medium and message,
corresponding to one another, we shall see, define what is particular to
the Mishnah, distinct from any one of its components' messages. The
Mishnah adds up to much more than the sum of its three principal
parts. There are both a mode of thought and a particular message which
make the Mishnah coherent and distinctive, not merely the construct

of priests, scribes, or householders. The former is now to be described and catalogued.

Gray Areas of the Law

Nearly all disputes which dominate and characterize the rhetoric of the Mishnah derive from bringing diverse legal principles into juxtaposition and conflict. So we may say that the Mishnah as a whole is an exercise in the application to a given case, through practical and applied reason, of several distinct principles of law. In this context, it follows, the Mishnah is a protracted inquiry into the intersection of principles; it maps out the gray areas of the law delimitated by such confused borders. An example of this type of "mixture" of legal principles comes in the conflict of two distinct bodies of the law, for instance, the requirement to circumscribe on the eighth day, even when this is the Sabbath (M. Shab. 19:1ff.), the requirement to kill and roast the Passover offering on the fourteenth of Nisan, even when this is the Sabbath (M. Pes. 6:1ff.), and the like. Yet another conflict of rules demanding resolution is a case in which a high priest and a Nazirite, both of them prohibited from contracting corpse uncleanness, come upon a neglected corpse, which one of them must bury (M. Naz. 7:1).

But gray areas are discerned not only through mechanical juxtaposition, through making up a conundrum of distinct principles of law. On the contrary, the Mishnaic philosophers are at their best when they force into conflict laws which, to begin with, scarcely intersect. This they do, for example, by inventing cases in which the secondary implications of one law are brought into conflict with the secondary implications of some other. An excellent example of the Mishnah's power on its own to discern (or invent) a gray area of law and to explore its logic is to be located in the issue of the effect of removing heave offering from produce which the householder is not yet obliged to tithe. Normally, we know, heave offering is removed from produce which is forbidden for use until the heave offering is taken out. But this produce under discussion is not yet forbidden. That is, it has not yet entered that status in which use is not allowed until heave offering is removed. The produce presently is exempt from the law. So the issue is whether the act of removing the heave offering from said produce imposes upon the produce a status which otherwise it would not receive (M. Ma. 2:4). Another instance of an inventive approach involves the produce of a tree in its first three years of growth. This produce is prohibited. What if one takes an old tree and replants it? Then the farmers of the Mishnah will want to know whether transplanting the old tree imposes the status of a new planting and so subjects the tree to liability to the prohibition of use of the fruit for three years (M. Orl. 1:3–5).

Along these same lines, the notion that one must build a fence to protect the basic requirements of the law creates new categories, which are subjected to a law not because of their own traits but because of the implications of a law to begin with not applicable. An example is the addition to the sabbatical year of prohibitions affecting the months before and after the year itself. The particular problem is that agricultural work done in the months before the sabbatical year may serve to benefit crops grown in the sabbatical year itself, with the consequence that the work is tantamount to labor in the sabbatical year. Likewise crops illicitly tended during the sabbatical year may come to fruition thereafter, and if the farmer may use them, then he gains benefit from that illicit labor. That is why these two appendages to the sabbatical year gain sustained attention (M. Sheb. 1:1ff.).

An example of the protracted interest in gray areas of the law is the matter of saying blessings for produce of trees and produce of the earth. The former are deemed to fall into the category of the latter, so that if one said a blessing for the latter before eating the former, one has carried out one's obligation. But in the reverse case, one has not, since produce of the ground is not covered by a blessing for produce of the tree. So the fruit of a tree is a species of the genus, produce of the earth, but the contrary, obviously, is not the case. There is a blessing which is suitable for both as well as for many other things (M. Ber. 6:2). This same sort of exercise in sorting out the species of a genus and showing the relationship of the species to one another and to their common genus fills up vast tracts of Mishnaic discourse (see the whole tractate Kilayim and much of Nedarim, not to mention Tebul Yom). The interest in distinguishing what is primary from what is secondary to be subsumed under what is primary, is expressed in the case of blessing a relish and a loaf. The relish is the principal part of the meal, the loaf is secondary. If one says a blessing for the relish, the loaf is deemed properly blessed for the relish, the loaf is deemed properly blessed as well. If one blesses a primary food, a secondary food served along with it thus does not require a blessing of its own (M. Ber. 6:7).

Finally, nothing will so instantly trigger the imagination of the Mishnah's exegetical minds as matters of ambiguity. The delineation of the status of various plots of vegetables in a single field is one such ambiguous circumstance.

The setting of boundaries for the definition of a field subject to the tax of the corner of the field occupies a fair amount of attention. Knowing what constitutes a field also determines liability to the tax. Things which mark off a boundary are specified (M. Pe. 2:1–4). A given kind of produce is deemed a field unto itself. Plots separated by another crop are deemed distinct (M. Pe. 2:5, 3:1). Still another gray area is cultic property or material which is not subject to the laws of sacrilege, but which also is not available for common, secular use (M. Me. 3:1–8). A third is defined by the effectiveness of a euphemism or a substitute for accepted formularies (M. Ned. 1:1; M. Naz. 1:1, etc.).

Excluded Middles

A species of the genus of gray areas of the law is the excluded middle, that is, that creature or substance which appears to fall between two distinct and definitive categories. The Mishnah's framers time and again allude to or even invent such an entity, because it forms the excluded middle which inevitably will attract attention and demand categorization. There are types of recurrent middles among both human beings and animals as well as vegetables. Indeed, the obsession with the excluded middle leads the Mishnah to invent its own examples, which have then to be analyzed into their definitive components and situated in their appropriate category. What this does is to leave no area lacking in an appropriate location, none to yield irresolvable doubt. An example of the exercise of making up a problem for solution and then solving it is the townsman who goes to a village, or villager who goes to a town. Each is subject to his own rule, e.g., for the date of reading the Scroll of Esther, and what each is to do when in another location has to be properly settled (M. Meg. 2:3).

A more substantial example of the effort to define and dispose of an excluded middle is the subject matter of Erubin. This is the status of a domain which is neither wholly private nor completely public, that is, the courtyard or alleyway subject to multiple owners. It is the peculiarity of that domain which generates the tractate's principle exegetical program. Another point of interest because of the possibility of ruling in one way or another is in the two courtyards which, because of the way in which they come together, for the purposes of the Sabbath may be deemed either a single courtyard or two distinct ones. This is another type of problem which will attract protracted exercises (M. Er. 7:1–5). Still another favorite example of an excluded middle is a tree with roots in one domain but branches in some other (M. Ma. 3:10). An ideal sort of ambiguity is presented by the roofs of a town, which, in the customary manner of building, were contiguous. The possible positions are that they constitute a single domain for purposes of the Sabbath, or they constitute multiple private domains, or for some purposes they are deemed the one, and for some, the other. That, of course, is what is provided (M. Er. 9:1).

The purpose of identifying the excluded middle, of course, is to allow the lawyers to sort out distinct rules, on the one side, and to demonstrate how they intersect without generating intolerable uncertainty, on the other. For example, to explore the theory that an object can serve as either a utensil or a tent, that is, a place capable of spreading the uncleanness of a corpse under its roof, the framers of the Mishnah invent a hive. This is sufficiently large so that it can be imagined to be either a utensil or a tent. When it is whole, it is the former, and if it is broken, it is the latter. The location of the object, e.g., on the ground, off the ground, in a doorway, against a wall, and so on, will further shape the rules governing the cases (M. Oh. 9:1–14; cf. M. Kel. 8:1ff). Again, to indicate the ambiguities lying at the frontiers, the topic of the status of Syria will come under repeated discussion. Syria is deemed not wholly sanctified, as is the Land of Israel, but also not wholly outside of the frame of holy Land, as are all other countries. That is why to Syria apply some rules applicable to holy Land, some rules applicable to secular land. In consequence, numerous points of ambiguity will be uncovered and explored (see M. Sheb. 6:1–6). One example is this: if a field in Syria is adjacent to the Land of Israel and can be reached without contamination, it is deemed part of the Land. If not, it is deemed unclean but is still liable to the laws of tithes and the seventh year (M. Oh. 18:7).

Yet beyond the requirements of the exercise of intersecting principles met through taking up invented instances of an excluded middle, there are numerous actual cases which demanded attention in their own terms. And, in the program of the Mishnah, we can be absolutely certain that they time and again would get attention. The simplest example of the excluded middle is the person who is half-slave and half-free, thus subject to two completely different sets of rules of personal status (M. Git. 4:5). Another excluded middle with which the Mishnah wishes to deal is the "wild man," who is regarded as a wild animal. Yet, some hold, the corpse of a "wild man" imparts uncleanness in a tent, that is, is deemed in this regard to be like a human being (M. Kil. 8:5). Since Scripture itself carefully distinguishes wild from domesticated animals, it is no wonder that for the Mishnah, the categorization of various types of beasts will be of sustained interest (M. Kil. 8:6). Another legal anomaly is the boy nine years and one day old, who is no longer a child but not yet a man. His act of sexual relations (!) is not null but also not wholly consequential (M. Yeb. 10:6–9). Still another source of ambiguity is one who has power to act, but not power to form effective intention, e.g., a deaf-mute, imbecile, or minor. These sorts of people are deemed able, when properly supervised, to do a suitable deed. But they cannot impart to that deed the status lent by appropriate intention, because they are assumed to be unable either to express or even to formulate it. It will follow that they will generate problems of various kinds, e.g., by consummating a marriage, by slaughtering an animal, and the like (M. Hul. 6:3).

An instance among animals of those interstitial creatures is the *koy*, an animal deemed partially domesticated and partially wild. In some ways the *koy* is subject to rules applicable to a wild animal, in some, to those which apply to a domesticated animal, in some, to rules applicable to neither, and in some, to both (M. Bik. 2:8–11). One of those vegetable species generative of problems is arum, which produces produce only after three years of growth. In the first three years, then, if one were to sow on top of them, no appearance of diverse kinds would result (M. Kil. 2:5; Mandelbaum, p. 129). So, on the one side, the seeds are in the ground, and if one sows on top of them, one creates a situation of diverse kinds. On the other hand, there is no appearance of diverse kinds. If the plants are not visible, it is not because they have died. They will sprout again, but have not yet sprouted again. Thus arum is an ideal species for generating special cases and problems. Arum recurs in the context of the seventh year. Covering it up with earth may be done so long as the arum will not sprout. In that case, since the arum yields a crop later on, the person will not have cultivated the crop within the sabbatical year (M. Sheb. 5:2–5). Fenugreek and vetches are other sorts of produce which attract attention. The reason is that, when either one of these is in the stage of sprouting and is tender, it is eaten, so has the status of food. When it is fully ripe, it is too hard for eating and is used for cattle or for other purposes (M. M.S. 2:2–4). These kinds of produce therefore generate the predictable problems. Vetches are a food of an ambiguous type. They may be eaten by humans, and therefore are liable to the separation of heave offering and tithes. More normally, however, they are not eaten by people, but, rather, are used as fodder for cattle. In light of this customary usage, even if they have the status of heave offering, vetches can be fed to the priest's animals (M. Ter. 11:9; Peck, p. 719). If the growth of grain extends over two years, then the point at which its liability to tithes, e.g., second tithe or poor man's tithe, is going to be ambiguous, so too the applicability of the seventh year's taboos (M. Sheb. 2:7–9).

Types of Mixtures

Gray areas of the law in general, and the excluded middle in particular, cover the surface of the law. They fill up nearly every chapter of the Mishnah. But underneath the surface is an inquiry of profound and far-reaching range. It is into the metaphysical or philosophical issues of how things join together and how they do not, of synthesis and analysis, of fusion and union, connection, division, and disintegration. What we have in the recurrent study of the nature of mixtures, broadly construed, is a sustained philosophical treatise in the guise of an episodic exercise in ad hoc problem solving. It is as if the cultic agendum laid forth by the priests, the social agendum defined by the confusing status and condition of Israel, and the program for right categorization of persons and things set forth for the scribes to carry out—all were taken over and subsumed by philosophers who proposed to talk abstractly about what they deemed urgent, while using the concrete language and syntax of other sorts of minds. To put it differently, the framers of the Mishnah, in their reflection on the nature of mixtures in their various potentialities for formation and dissolution, shape the topics provided by others into hidden discourse on an encompassing philosophical-physical problem of their own choosing.

In so doing, as we shall see in the final sections, they phrased the critical question demanding attention and response, the question at once social, political, metaphysical, cultural, and even linguistic, but above all, historical: the question of Israel standing at the outer boundaries of a long history now decisively done with. That same question of acculturation and assimilation, alienation and exile, which had confronted the priests of old is raised once more. Now it is framed in terms of mechanical composition, fusion, and something in between, mixture. But it is phrased in incredible terms of a wildly irrelevant world of unseen things, of how we define the place of the stem in the entity of the apple, the effect of the gravy upon the meat, and the definitive power of a bit of linen in a fabric of wool. In concrete form, the issues are close to comic. In abstract form, the answers speak of nothing of workaday meaning. In reality, at issue is Israel in its Land, once the lines of structure which had emanated from the Temple had been blurred and obliterated.

To begin with, there are certain general propositions governing all cases of mixtures. These may be expressed through particulars of the law, but appear throughout the law. For example, the theory of mixtures distinguishes between mixtures of the same species and those of different ones. When the same species are mixed, they are assumed to be fully uniform. When different species are mixed, there must be some evidence that one kind has imparted its traits to the other kind, before the status of the former is deemed to affect that of the latter (M. A.Z. 5:8). The notion that the categories of creation must be kept orderly and distinct is expressed in the principle that one may not separate heave offering from one batch of produce in behalf of a batch of produce of a different sort. Diverse species of produce must be kept distinct from one another (M. Ter. 2:4). On the other hand, if there is a large batch of produce of a single kind, then one may separate the part of that produce which is of the highest quality to cover the whole batch of produce. Whether or not diverse substances join together to form the volume requisite to constitute a violation of the law is a repeated exercise in the theory of mixtures. This same matter of joining together also is affected by deeds. If we have an improper intention to do one thing to half of the requisite volume of a substance, and an improper intention to do some other thing with the other half of the requisite volume, that is null, "for eating and offering up do not join together" (M. Zeb. 6:7). Where we have two fabrics, one in one category of susceptibility to uncleanness, another in a different category (e.g., one deemed susceptible at a small size, another at a larger size), then the degree of susceptibility applicable to the more stringent of the two pieces is the one which applies. If the material added is subject to greater restriction, then that restriction applies to the whole (M. Kel. 27:3).

The basic possibilities are two. One substance may be deemed fully to join together with, and form an integral part of, another. Or two substances may be deemed essentially separate from one another. Now these two possibilities may be shown to inhere not only in substances, but also in deeds, among persons, and in all manner of social circumstances. For example, we may take up a mixture of actions and ask whether they all constitute a single, extended deed, culpable only on one count, or many discrete deeds, each of them subject to punishment. The ambiguity of determining when an action is single and complete, and when it forms part of a sequence of actions, all of them deemed to constitute a single action for the purpose of the law, is frequently explored. One instance is whether one has to cover up one time or many times the blood of a hundred beasts which one has slaughtered in a single location. Another treats bringing one offering for many sinful acts, or many offerings for one sinful act (M. Hul. 6:4; M. Ker. 1:7, 2:3–6, 3:2–3, 4–6, etc.).

The issue of combining groups or distinguishing groups from one another, when either procedure is possible, is taken up at the discussion on separating people who ate in one place for purposes of forming more than a single quorum for saying the grace after meals. Again, if groups eat separately but in the same house, if they can see one another, they are deemed to be joined for the present purpose. But if not, they are deemed distinct groups and say the grace after meals, each in its own quorum (M. Ber. 7:5). If five "associations," or eating clubs, kept the Sabbath in a single hall, they pose the issue of whether they are deemed one group, because they are in a demarcated space together, or five groups, because they are separate in their activity and function (M. Er. 6:6; M. Pes. 7:13).

But while the sort of mixture constituted by actions which may or may not be deemed to constitute a single protracted deed may draw for analogical purposes upon the concept of mixture, the Mishnah does not deem a mixture to be essentially an analogy. On the contrary, extended exercises will take up the two sides of the same coin: when what is joined is deemed to be distinct, when what is separate is regarded as joined together or wholly connected. The analysis of mixtures requires us to effect differentiations among parts of what appears to be a single mass, e.g., of skin and flesh, bones and sinews, and the like. Establishing what is deemed connected with, therefore part of a single mass with, something else is important for a range of purposes. It allows us to detect the spread of uncleanness from one part of a mixture to some other part. It permits determining whether or not a given mass constitutes a sufficient volume to meet a legal requirement. It tells us whether someone who has touched part of a mass is unclean because of the status of a part of the mass he has not touched. It informs us about the status of hanging parts of a mass, handles, extrusions, and the like. In all of these ways the interest in connections between one part and another of a single mass of material forms a critical core of the larger exercise in the analysis of mixtures (see M. Hul. 9:1–8). Along these same lines, all forms of refuse, remnant, carrion, and creeping things, respectively, are deemed to join together in their several categories (M. Me. 4:3; cf. M. Ar. 4:1–6). The remove of uncleanness affecting solid food made unclean and then joined together has also to be determined in the study of mixtures (M. Toh. 1:5–6). It is understood that all liquids are going to combine fully and fuse, and so enter a single remove of uncleanness. The problem thus will concern solids more than liquids. The mixture of blood and wine, or blood and water, may be adjudicated. If the mixture looks like blood, it is in the status thereof. If blood is mixed with wine, it is null (M. Hul. 6:5; M. Miq. 7:3–5; M. Zeb. 8:6, etc.). Likewise, it is to be determined whether corpse matter of blood from two different corpses will join together to form the volume requisite for imparting corpse uncleanness (M. Oh. 2:2, 3:5). If we divide a bone originally of sufficient size, the status of the two parts requires attention (M. Oh. 2:7). Here the paired questions get at the heart of the matter. Do we deem blood to be a genus, uniting the species of bloods deriving from diverse corpses? If that is the case, then the blood of two different corpses will form the requisite volume to impart corpse uncleanness. The reverse side of the question is phrased in terms of splitting up a bone into two parts. Do we take account of the single point of origin, or do we invoke as the governing criterion the present condition of the bone? True, these formulations of the issue of the one and the many, of mixtures and the decomposition of mixtures into their component parts, are not going to characterize philosophy in an accessible form. But it is how the Mishnah chooses to frame the question. Indeed, there are few questions which recur more predictably than those typified in the present odd topic.

Along these same lines, the parts of a mixture are deemed by diverse criteria to be part of the whole. For example, if an object has extrusions, we have to know the extent to which these connected but still discrete entities are deemed part of the basic object, and the extent to which they are deemed separate, so that what affects them may or may not affect the object to which they are attached. The problems of connection and joining together are taken up, for food, in discussions on the status of stems and inedible parts of edibles. The issue will be whether these form part of the produce to which they are attached, so that, if the one is made unclean, so too is the other, and so that, in addition, they contribute to forming the requisite bulk for uncleanness. The status of handles and husks as to susceptibility and joining together is extensively worked out (M. Uqs. 1:1–2:4). So too there is significant attention to connection between distinct parts of a piece of food, e.g., the shell of an egg and the roasted egg inside (M. Uqs. 2:5–10). We have numerous lists of objects and the length of threads, handles, or other extensions of those objects regarded as connected to the primary utensil and therefore susceptible to the uncleanness affecting the utensil of which they are an accessory. The basic principle is that what is essential to using the object is deemed connected to it. The part of the handle or accessory used when the object is in service will be regarded as integral (M. Kel. 29:1–9). The issue of connection also affects the division of utensils, not only of natural matter, e.g., the parts of a loom (M. Kel. 21:1). An object which serves with, but is not integral to, another object will generate a problem. At issue will be the applicability to the appendage of the rule pertinent to the base object (M. Kel. 2:8).

The issue of connection is important in regard to someone who has immersed on that selfsame day. The person is not yet fully clean, but also is not so unclean as he was before immersion. If such a person touches items which are loosely connected, those items may or may not be wholly unclean. That is, the connection may or may not be effective in the case of the uncleanness imparted by this kind of interstitially unclean person (M. T.Y. 1:1–3:5). The basic point at issue is whether or not the one who has immersed on that selfsame day is deemed essentially clean (M. T.Y. 3:6–4:7). The main theory is that in the case of this particular source of uncleanness, we distinguish a primary substance from what is secondary and additional to it. If one who is unclean in this diminished state touches what is primary, what is secondary is made unfit. But if he touches what is attached or secondary, what is basic is not made unfit. All of this explores a problem of connection of an unusually subtle order.

The foregoing considerations of what is deemed essentially a single uniform mixture and what is deemed a juxtaposition of essentially discrete and unchanged items present many concrete applications and examples. If we deem a mixture to be uniform, then its volume may be such as to neutralize a small component therein. What this means is that produce in the status of heave offering, for example, which is fully joined together and mixed with a much larger volume of ordinary produce, may be deemed null by reason of its negligible part in the whole. The basic traits of this type of mixture account for the possibility of nullification. A problem of mixtures thus concerns the confusion of a hundred parts of untithed produce and one hundred parts of tithed produce. If one wishes to separate heave offering of the tithe from the mixture to cover its untithed part, one takes one hundred and one parts (M. Dem. 7:7; Sarason, *Demai,* pp. 260–67). Interest in mixtures involves the confusion of permitted produce and produce prohibited because it is the yield of the first three years of a tree's growth (M. Orl. 2:1–4). This then involves the possibility of neutralization when the produce which is prohibited is of a negligible volume. A further problem of mixtures involves use of an item subject to the prohibition of fruit in the first three years in the making of a permitted item. Any item which is separate and distinct cannot be deemed neutralized in a mixture. Mixtures of liable and exempt produce are taboo with regard only to the percentage which is liable to tithes (M. Ma. 5:6). In cases involving doubt about a mixture a heave offering and unconsecrated produce, if we do not know into which of several batches of unconsecrated produce heave offering has fallen, all of the produce is deemed to join together to neutralize the small volume of heave offering in one of them. That is, we extend the limits of mixture to the extreme possibility of fusion (M. Ter. 4:12–13).

This same notion, that a mixture may be uniform so that the traits of all the parts are deemed mingled, will yield a contrary conclusion as well. A type of mixture which attracts sustained attention in diverse contexts is one of heave offering which is mixed with other produce. If, for example, heave offering of the tithe taken from *demai* produce fell back into the produce from which it was taken up and which had been fully tithed, the whole mixture is deemed in the status of a mixture prohibited to the nonpriest (M. Dem. 4:1; Sarason, *Demai,* pp. 152–57). Only a priest may eat such a mixture, because we cannot distinguish the parts permissible to a nonpriest from those forbidden to him. Here we have the opposite of fusion.

When, finally, we have a mixture which produces total confusion, we must take account of all possibilities. This sort of mixture forms the bridge to the principles of the resolution of doubts, since, we observe, where we do not know the traits of the components of a mixture and therefore cannot be sure whether the status of one component has or has not affected that of others, we have to treat the mixture as a matter of doubt. For example, if a person convicted of murder is confused with others, all are exempt from the death penalty. If various people convicted of the death penalty are confused, so that the form of the death penalty appropriate to this one cannot be distinguished from the form of the death penalty applying to some other, the most lenient mode of execution is applied to all of them (M. San. 9:3). If animals are designated for various sacrifices, the power of the act of designation is taken for granted; so too is the force of the law governing a given sacrifice. If therefore one designates an animal for a sacrifice, and that animal, in fact, cannot serve for the specified sacrificial purpose, the status of the animal has to be worked out (M. Pes. 9:7). Still more interesting is the case in which an animal is designated for a given sacrifice but then becomes confused with other animals. The status of the whole herd or flock then has to be adjudicated (M. Pes. 9:8, among many instances, and see the whole tractate of Qinnim). These are examples of the way in which cases of irreconcilable doubt are formed. We now turn to principles for disposing of such cases.

The Resolution of Doubt

Cases of genuine doubt about the facts of the matter, as distinct from those in which we are not sure about the operative category to dispose of settled facts, derive from a number of quite practical circumstances. A major area of doubts has to do with retroactive contamination, e.g., of a woman before she realizes that her period is under way (M. Nid. 1:1–2:4). Another has to do with vaginal excretions, the status of which is uncertain (M. Nid. 6:13–9:10). Another unfailing source of doubt and unclarity, awaiting repair, is simultaneity of events of contradictory, or mutually exclusive, character, e.g., a man betroths a mother and daughter at the same moment (M. Ket. 2:7). Doubt is often the result of twilight, e.g., the appearance of a mark of uncleanness at a time which may be assigned to one day or another (M. Zab. 1:6). Another case of doubt is presented by a coin found between two collection points, which may have been intended for one or another of those two points and therefore governed by the rules pertinent thereto (M. Sheq. 7:1–8:3).

A rich source of doubts is generated by the requirement to devote or redeem the firstborn of beasts and human beings. There are points of ambiguity, e.g., beasts born of a Caesarean section. There are many possibilities of confusion, e.g., of infants (M. Bekh. 2:9–32, 8:6). Important cases of confusion, already noted, involve animals set aside for diverse sacrifices which are confused with one another and of collections of blood deriving from diverse sacrifices which are mixed up (M. Zeb. 8:1–5, 6–12; M. Tem. 6:1–3). The principles expressed in these exercises are not particular to their problem and are applicable throughout the law (M. Hul. 8:10; M. Ter. 8:8–11).

Various principles on how we resolve questions of doubt, with attention to the case when it is uncovered, the circumstances of the case, and the like, are spelled out (M. Toh. 3:5–6:8). In matters of doubt concerning uncleanness of the hands and whether they have been rendered clean, they are deemed to be clean (M. Yad. 2:4). If we have a case of doubt, we attribute impairment in status to that which already is impaired. If, for example, a quantity of heave offering has fallen either into a bin of heave offering or into a bin of unconsecrated produce, we assume it has fallen into the latter (M. Ter. 7:5–7).

Finally, a topic generated by an interest in cases of doubt is that of tractate Demai, which tells us how to settle such cases. What is subject to doubt is whether or not produce has been fully, or merely partially, tithed. We assume that heave offering is separated from produce at the threshing floor. What we do not know is whether heave offering of the tithe, which belongs to the priest, also has been set apart, as well as some other tithes.

Conclusion

The Mishnah above all presents a protracted exercise in problems of practical logic and their solutions, applying conflicting principles. The Mishnah as a document is made up of studies in the potentialities of applied and practical reason. The Mishnah therefore accomplishes far more than merely providing well-organized information about topics important to the priests, transactions critical to the householders, and procedures and modes of expression of the scribes. As I have now shown through extensive allusions to all Divisions and topics of the Mishnah, the Mishnah has its own method of analysis; its generative problematic far transcends the topics of interest to its several distinct tributaries. It is in this method of sorting out confused things that the Mishnah becomes truly Mishnaic, distinct from modes of thought and perspective to be assigned to groups represented in the document.

To interpret the meaning of the facts just now described, we must once again recall that the priestly code makes the point that a well-ordered society on earth, with its center and point of reference at the Temple altar, corresponds to a well-ordered canopy of heaven. Creation comes its climax at the perfect rest marked by completion and signifying perfection and sanctification. Indeed, the creation myth represents as the occasion for sanctification a perfected world at rest, with all things in their rightful place. Now the Mishnah takes up this conviction, which is located at the deepest structures of the metaphysic of the framers of the priestly code and, therefore, of their earliest continuators and imitators in the Mishnaic code (see above, pp. 225–29 and 248–50). But the Mishnah frames the conviction that in order is salvation, not through a myth of creation and a description of a cult of precise and perfect order. True, the Mishnah imposes order upon the world through lines of structure emanating from the cult. The Scripture selected as authoritative leaves no alternative. Yet, as we have now seen, the Mishnah at its deepest layers, taking up the raw materials of concern of priests and farmers and scribes, phrases that concern after the manner of philosophers. That is to say, the framers of the Mishnah speak of the physics of mixtures, conflicts of principles which must be sorted out, areas of doubt generated by confusion. The detritus of a world seeking order but suffering chaos now is reduced to the construction of intellect.

If, therefore, we wish to characterize the Mishnah when it is cogent and distinctive, and not merely the artifact of perspectives of distinct groups, we must point to this persistent and pervasive mode of thought. For the Mishnah takes up a vast corpus of facts and treats these facts, so to speak, "Mishnaically," that is, in a way distinctive to the Mishnah, predictable and typical of the Mishnah. That is what I mean when I refer to the style of the Mishnah: its manner of exegesis of a topic, its mode of thought about any subject, the sorts of perplexities which will precipitate the Mishnah's fertilizing flood of problem-making ingenuity. Confusion and conflict will trigger the Mishnah's power to control conflict by showing its limits, and, thus, the range of shared conviction too.

For by treating facts "Mishnaically," the Mishnah establishes boundaries around, and pathways through, confusion. It lays out roads to guide people by ranges of doubt. Consequently, the Mishnah's mode of control over the chaos of conflicting principles, the confusion of doubt, the improbabilities of a world out of alignment is to delimit and demarcate. By exploring the range of interstitial conflict through its ubiquitous disputes, the Mishnah keeps conflict under control. It so preserves that larger range of agreement, that pervasive and shared conviction, which is never expressed, which is always instantiated, and which, above all, is forever taken for granted. The Mishnah's deepest convictions about what lies beyond confusion and conflict are never spelled out; they lie in the preliminary, unstated exercise prior to the commencement of a sustained exercise of inquiry, a tractate. They are the things we know before we take up that exercise and study that tractate.*

Now all of this vast complex of methods and styles, some of them intellectual, some of them literary and formal, may be captured in the

---

* Since the Mishnah rarely bothers to spell out what we know, it makes studying a tractate rather difficult. Still harder is to study a tractate with a proper prologue, e.g., Kelim, Negaim, Ohalot, Baba Qamma, Miqvaot, Shabbat, and even Besah. Here the stated principles are often out of phase with what follows—a bad prologue indeed.

Mishnah's treatment of its own, self-generated conflicts of principles, its search for gray areas of the law. It also may be clearly discerned in the Mishnah's sustained interest in those excluded middles it makes up for the purpose of showing the limits of the law, the confluence and conflict of laws. It further may be perceived in the Mishnah's recurrent exercise in the study of types of mixtures, the ways distinct components of an entity may be joined together, may be deemed separate from one another, may be shown to be fused, or may be shown to share some traits and not others. Finally, the Mishnah's power to sort out matters of confusion will be clearly visible in its repeated statement of the principles by which cases of doubt are to be resolved. A survey of these four modes of thought thus shows us one side of the distinctive and typical character of the Mishnah, when the Mishnah transcends the program of facts, forms, and favored perspectives of its tributaries. We now turn to the side of the substance. What causes and resolves confusion and chaos is the power of the Israelite's will. As is said in the context of measurements for minimum quantities to be subject to uncleanness, "All accords with the measure of the man" (M. Kel. 17:11).

The Catalyst: Sanctification and Man's Will

The Mishnah's principal message, which makes the Judaism of this document and of its social components distinctive and cogent, is that man* is at the center of creation, the head of all creatures upon earth, corresponding to God in heaven, in whose image man is made. The way in which the Mishnah makes this simple and fundamental statement is to impute power to man to inaugurate and initiate those corresponding processes, sanctification and uncleanness, which play so critical a role in the Mishnah's account of reality. The will of man, expressed through the deed of man, is the active power in the world. Will and deed constitute those actors of creation which work upon neutral realms, subject to either sanctification or uncleanness: the Temple and table, the field and family, the altar and hearth, woman, time, space, transactions in the material world and in the world above as well. An object, a substance, a transaction, even a phrase or a sentence is inert but may be made holy, when the interplay of the will and deed of man arouses or generates its potential to be sanctified. Each may be treated as ordinary or (where relevant) made unclean by the neglect of the will and inattentive act of man. Just as the entire system of uncleanness and holiness awaits the intervention of man,

---

* The patriarchal character of the Mishnaic system requires this usage and no other. It would be misrepresented if I were to speak of men and women, even though for certain purposes women are actors and participants.

which imparts the capacity to become unclean upon what was formerly inert, or which removes the capacity to impart cleanness from what was formerly in its natural and puissant condition, so in the other ranges of reality, man is at the center on earth, just as is God in heaven. Man is counterpart and partner and creation, in that, like God he has power over the status and condition of creation, putting everything in its proper place, calling everything by its rightful name.

So, stated briefly, the question taken up by the Mishnah is, What can a man do? And the answer laid down by the Mishnah is, Man, through will and deed, is master of this world, the measure of all things. Since when the Mishnah thinks of man, it means the Israelite, who is the subject and actor of its system, the statement is clear. This man is Israel, who can do what he wills. In the aftermath of the two wars, the message of the Mishnah cannot have proved more pertinent—or poignant and tragic.

Now these statements of generalities take on meaning only when fully illustrated and exemplified in the details of the Mishnaic law. For, as we now know full well, while the Mishnah takes up a dense program of philosophical convictions, and while both in form and in substance the Mishnah assumes a position on a vast range of perennial issues of the mind, still, the Mishnah also, and always, is little more than a mass of specific problems, a morass of concrete details, exercises of logic, and facts. So it is not possible to repeat what the Mishnah wishes to say without confronting the message in the Mishnah's own mode of formulation and expression. Through the medium of law the Mishnah says what it wants to say to its age and about its world. That is why, as has been the case up to now, we turn to the myriad of instances in which a single thing is said.

Reflection on the Nature of Intention

The principal message of the Mishnah is that the will of man affects the material reality of the world and governs the working of those forces, visible or not, which express and effect the sanctification of creation and of Israel alike. This message comes to the surface in countless ways. At the outset a simple example of the supernatural power of man's intention suffices to show the basic power of the Israelite's will to change concrete, tangible facts.

The power of the human will is nowhere more effective than in the cult, where, under certain circumstances, what a person is thinking is more important than what he does. The basic point is that if an animal is designated for a given purpose, but the priest prepares the animal with the thought in mind that the beast serves some other sacrificial purpose, then, in some instances, in particular involving a sin offering and a Passover on the fourteenth of Nisan, the sacrifice is ruined. In this matter of preparation of the animal, moreover, are involved the deeds of slaughtering the beast, collecting, conveying, and tossing the blood on the altar, that is, the principal priestly deeds of sacrifice. Again, if the priest has in mind, when doing these deeds, to offer up the parts to be offered up on the altar, or to eat the parts to be eaten by the priest, in some location other than the proper one (the altar, the court-yard, respectively), or at some time other than the requisite one (the next few hours), the rite is spoiled, the meat must be thrown out. Now that is the case, even if the priest did not do what he was thinking of doing. Here again we have a testimony to the fundamental importance imputed to what a person is thinking, even over what he actually does, in critical aspects of the holy life (see M. Zeb. 1:1–4:6; M. Men. 1:1–4:5; Neusner, *Holy Things* I, pp. 12–90, II, pp. 9–76).

The power of a person to impose the status of sanctity upon an object also is best illustrated in the case of the cult. If a person sets aside an animal for a given sacrifice, the animal becomes holy and is subject to the rules governing that sacrifice for which it is designated. This exercise of the will, therefore, has a material effect upon the status and disposition of the animal. That principle circulates throughout all the laws governing the sacrificial process and is illustrated in countless problems (see M. Pes. 9:7, 8; M. Zeb. 1:1ff., etc.). The critical role of human attentiveness in forming a context of cultic cleanness, moreover, is expressed in the notion that if the person who has to bring the pure water to be used with the ash of the red cow for the making of purification water diverts his attention from his task in any way what-soever, then the water is no longer suitable. That means that if he performs a single action not pertinent to the task of bringing the water, the water is automatically invalid. If, further, he should sit or lie on any object, even if the object is clean, he is deemed unclean for the present purpose. So he must be ever on the move, must not sit down or lie down, from the moment he gets the water to the time at which he mixes it with the ash (M. Par. 5:1–11:6). Truly is it said that attentiveness is the precondition of cleanness (M. Sot. 9:15). The water used for the purification rite must be drawn deliberately, by human action, with a utensil made by a human being (M. Par. 5:1ff). Any act of labor extra-neous to the work of drawing the water and mixing the water with the cow ash is going to invalidate the entire procedure (M. Par. 7:1–4).

Another instance in which the attitude of a person affects the mate-rial reality of the law concerns the use of the immersion pool. All of the flesh must be in contact with the water. If there is some sort of dirt or other object adhering to one's flesh, then it is deemed to interpose only if a person is fastidious about that dirt. If it is not something about which one might be concerned, then it also is deemed to be null, as if it were not there to begin with (M. Pes. 3:2; M. Miq.).

The definitive transfer of ownership of property takes place when the original owner has either willingly given over that object or despaired ever of regaining it. If, therefore, someone saves an object from a flood, if the owner has given up hope of getting the object back, the object belongs to the finder (M. B.Q. 10:2). If the owner still has hope of regaining it, or if the finder has reason to believe that that is the case, then transfer of ownership does not take place (see M. B.M. 2:1–2, 5, 6). So attitude is everything. Despair determines the cessation of rights of ownership.

A piece of wood carved in a form is not deemed an idol until it actually has been worshiped. One belonging to a gentile is deemed prohibited forthwith, since it is assumed to be venerated. But one belonging to an Israelite is forbidden only after the Israelite will have worshiped the object. So the expression of the Israelite's will transforms the inert object into an idol (M. A.Z. 4:4–6).

One current of thought in tractate Kilayim maintains that more important at the foundations of the taboo of mixed seeds is a prohibition of mere appearances, not of actual material confusion, of diverse kinds. If members of a pair belong to two different kinds but are similar in appearance, they will not be considered diverse kinds with one another. So it is necessary that a field not *appear* to be sown with diverse kinds, whether or not it is actually sown with seeds of a different genus. The contrary view is that if two kinds are not similar, but if they belong to one kind, they are not considered to be diverse kinds (see Mandelbaum, p. 4). Here is a fine example of how man is the measure of all things, and man's attitude is decisive over the facts of nature.

Given the power imputed to the human will or intention, we should expect that some sustained attention will focus upon the nature of will. True, we cannot expect the philosophers of the Mishnah to phrase their thought in terms readily accessible to us. Nor is it possible to claim that they undertook a sustained program of inquiry into this, to them critical, matter of the nature of the will. Still, we do find something akin to abstract thought on the subject albeit, 'as always, in the predictable grossly material costume. The inquiry into the nature of the human will is expressed in the question of whether we deem intention to be divisible or indivisible. That is, if one wants something at one time but not at some other, is that an effective act of will? Again, if one wants something with regard to some part of a mixture but not with regard to some other part, the rule has to be defined (M. Makh. 1:1–6). The basic point for imparting susceptibility to uncleanness, that water must be deliberately, that is, intentionally, applied to foodstuffs before they are deemed susceptible, thus generates numerous problems involving the

assessment of the human will (M. Makh. 2:1–11). For instance, if water
is used for one purpose, its status as to a secondary purpose has to be
worked out. If one wets down a house to keep the dust down and wheat
was put into the house and got damp, the purposive use of the water for
one thing renders the water capable of imparting susceptibility to the
grain too (M. Makh. 3:4–5:8). The available positions will maintain, in
general, these views: First, what one does defines what one's intention
was to begin with. What actually happens defines what one originally
thought of doing. The opposite view is that not only action, but intention independent thereof, is determinative. There is a balance to be
found between what one ultimately does and what to begin with one
wanted to do.

Insight into the character of thought about the nature of human intention derives from diverse, concrete rules. One recurrent issue is
whether we take account of what one wishes to do, or only what one
actually has done, to confirm one's stated intention. Another is whether
we trust a person's deed if the deed is reversible, or whether we deem a
person's intention not confirmed until a deed has been done which
cannot again be revised. This notion is expressed in the usual, quite
odd settings (see, for example, M. Kel. 20:6). The issue of whether
intention unratified by actual deed is effective is worked out, for example, in terms of purification water. If someone forms the intention to
drink such water, even without doing so, by mere intent, in the opinion
of some, he has invalidated the water. Others hold the water is made
unfit only when the man actually picks up the cup to drink the water.
But this still is before a physical action has affected the water (M. Par.
9:4). Intention to use an object renders it susceptible to uncleanness as
soon as the object is ready for use. That is the case, even though the
object has not yet actually been used. This will account for the difference between hides belonging to householders, deemed ready for
use even before completely tanned, and those belonging to a tanner,
which are not fully processed. The former are susceptible as soon as
the householder decides to make use of them, even if he has done
nothing to them (M. Kel. 26:8; cf. M. Kel. 26:7).

The notion that a statement of the will of a person bears material
consequences in the status of a thing is limited by the parallel notion
that a person's will has bearing only on what falls within that person's
domain (M. Ar. 1:1–2).* Similarly, it is held that the altar sanctifies what
is appropriate to it, and does not sanctify what is not appropriate to it.
This is without regard to what man wills. The altar does not work
automatically to impart sanctity to whatever touches it. There is a

---

* In effect, this means the householder, who is owner of pretty much everything under
discussion, is principal actor in inaugurating the matched systems of holiness and uncleanness.

necessary congruity between a human act of sanctification and what is sanctified (M. Zeb. 9:1ff.). A further limitation on the power of the will, even of the centrality of right intention in doing a deed, is the position that the one who brings a sin offering must know precisely why he must do so, that is, for what sin or category of sin (M. Ker. 4:2–3). From these rather theoretical remarks, we turn to concrete exemplifications, in the detail of the law, of what intention or will or attitude can and cannot do.

The Positive Power of Intention

Once man wants something, a system of the law begins to function. Intention has the power, in particular, to initiate the processes of sanctification. So the moment at which something becomes sacred and so falls under a range of severe penalties for misappropriation or requires a range of strict modes of attentiveness and protection for the preservation of cleanness is defined by the human will. Stated simply: at the center of the Mishnaic system is the notion that man has the power to inaugurate the work of sanctification, and the Mishnaic system states and restates that power.

This assessment of the positive power of the human will begins with the matter of uncleanness, the antonym, we recall, of sanctification or holiness. Man alone has the power to inaugurate the system of uncleanness. One striking example of that fact is that water in its natural state, not subjected to human intervention and therefore will, not only effects purification but, in requisite volume, is simply not susceptible to uncleanness at all. This means that water is susceptible only when a human being has so acted as to make it susceptible. That fact is congruent with the thesis that things which are not wet down by human action are not susceptible to uncleanness. What is dry is insusceptible. What is wet is susceptible *only* if a human being has made it wet. So at the foundations of the movement from cleanness to uncleanness and back is the intervention of purposeful human deed. What is a source of uncleanness comes from nature, is natural and not caused by human action. But what is susceptible is so, first, because it is useful to a human being, and, second, because it has been wet down by a human being (M. Makh. 1:1–6:3). To be deemed food and therefore to become subject to uncleanness, produce must be regarded by human beings as food. There are things which may or may not be food, with the result that, if people do not regard them as edible, they are not susceptible at all (M. Uqs. 3:1–3, 9). This affects market towns in which only Israelites shop; there forbidden items are not deemed food, because no one will imagine eating them.

From the power of man to introduce an object or substance into the processes of uncleanness, we turn to the corresponding power of man to sanctify an object or a substance. This is a much more subtle matter, but it also is more striking. It is the act of designation by a human being which "activates" that holiness inherent in crops from which no tithes have yet been set aside and removed. Once the human being has designated what is holy within the larger crop, then that designated portion of the crop gathers within itself the formerly diffused holiness and becomes holy, set aside for the use and benefit of the priest to whom it is given. So it is the interplay between the will of the farmer, who owns the crop, and the sanctity inherent in the whole batch of the crop itself which is required for the processes of sanctification to work themselves out. That is why, for example, the question of who has the power to set aside heave offering from a crop will receive sustained attention (see M. Ter. 1:1ff.). The principal point about the obligation to tithe a crop is that the crop must be ripe. God claims the produce when it is ripe, and man must satisfy that claim before he has a right to dispose of the remainder of the crop (M. Ma. 1:3; Jaffee, p. 2). The crop may be tithed when it is ripe. But the point at which it must be tithed comes only at a later time. The obligation to tithe is imposed by the farmer's own acts. He becomes obligated to separate tithes at that point at which the crop has been harvested and processed for storage. That is when the owner's intention to store the produce for use in food is fully ratified in deed. Since the owner has laid claim to the produce as his own and now plans to use it for a meal, he may not proceed with his now fully revealed plan until he has tithed the produce. In establishing his claim to the produce, thus in exposing his intention, he has imposed upon the produce the sanctity which also and concomitantly arouses the divine claim to what belongs to God (M. Ma. 1:5; Jaffee, p. 3). So the point at which the crop must be tithed corresponds to the moment at which the farmer's intentions are fully in effect. Once more we see that is the human will which activates or precipitates the actualization of the sanctity which inheres in the crop. Once a householder has decided to make use of a batch of produce for a meal, the produce may not be used as a snack unless it is first tithed. The intention to make a meal of the produce is determinative. All subsequent acts of eating carry out that original intention. The produce therefore must be tithed before it is eaten (M. Ma. 4). To be sure, actions therefore guide our interpretation of a householder's intentions and so determine whether the obligation to tithe applies. But the main point is that the formulation of the intention affects the liability of the produce, independent of anything the householder actually does (Jaffee, p. 233).

In addition to the power to initiate the process of sanctification and the system of uncleanness and cleanness, man has the power, through the working of his will, to differentiate one thing from another. The fundamental category into which an entity, which may be this or that, is to be placed is decided by the human will for that entity. Man exercises the power of categorization, so ends confusion. The consequence will be that, what man decides, heaven ratifies. Once man determines that something falls in one category and not another, the interest of heaven is provoked. Then misuse of that thing invokes heavenly penalties. So man's will has the capacity so to work as to engage the ratifying power of heaven.

Let us take up first of all the most striking example, the deed itself. It would be difficult to doubt that what one does determines the effect of what one does. But that position is rejected. The very valence and result of a deed depend, to begin with, on one's prior intent. The intent which leads a person to do a deed governs the culpability of the deed. There is no intrinsic weight to the deed itself. For example, one is not supposed to put out a fire on the Sabbath. If one puts out a lamp because one is afraid of gentiles, thugs, or an evil spirit, one is not culpable. If one did so to save the oil, lamp, or wick, one is liable. These latter actions are done for their own sake; the others, for an extrinsic consideration. An act of labor done for a motive which is not culpable, itself is not culpable (M. Shab. 2:5). If a person intended in doing an act to violate the law of the Sabbath but did not actually succeed in doing so, he is not culpable (M. Shab. 10:4, 11:6). For example, if he planned to carry an object in the normal way, which would then be culpable, but carried it in an unusual way, which is not culpable, he is not liable. If he performed a forbidden act of labor for some purpose other than the commission of that act of labor itself, he is not culpable (M. Shab. 10:5).

A related conception is this. A person is liable for transporting an object from one domain to the other on the Sabbath—but that is so only if the object is of worth. If the object is inconsequential, then there is no purpose in moving it about, and a person is not liable on that account (M. Shab. 7:3, 4, 8:1–7, 9:5–7, 10:1). If people would not store away such an object, they also are exempt from liability if they carry it about on the Sabbath.

From the power of will over deed, we turn to the capacity of the human will to determine the status of a substance or an object. One instance is simple to grasp. If an object is useful, it is susceptible to uncleanness. If it is useless, it is deemed broken and therfore clean. The criterion of usefulness is expressed fully in accord with human convenience. A three-legged table which has lost a leg is insusceptible, so too if it loses a second leg. It will tip over. But if it loses a third leg, it is deemed a tray and useful once more. But at that point, the suscepti- bility of the tray, in the view of some, is made to rest upon whether it is automatically useful, or whether a person has to give thought to use the former three-legged table as a tray. The prior issue is whether the maker of the three-legged table had in mind more than that potential use. If we decide that, to begin with, the craftsman imagined that the surface of the table also might serve as a tray, then when the legs are removed, the surface automatically takes up the new purpose, foreseen by the craftsman, and is susceptible. Clearly, much thought on the nature and working of human purpose and intention has gone into the formulation of these problems and their numerous parallels (M. Kel. 22:2; cf. M. Kel. 25:9). Further distinction is made between primary and secondary purpose (M. Kel. 22:7). If there is a rag which may or may not be useful, then, if it is kept in readiness for a particular purpose, it is susceptible to uncleanness, and if not, it is not susceptible. The difference is that in the former case, the rag serves some purpose useful to human need or intention, and that is signified by its being set aside for a given use (M. Kel. 28:5).

When utensils are broken, they are deemed no longer unclean, or (if they were not unclean to begin with) insusceptible to uncleanness. As I said, the criterion for breakage is uselessness. Once a utensil serves no purpose relevant to the needs of a human being, it is deemed useless and insusceptible. In consequence, there will be long lists of functions served by various utensils, with the notion that, so long as said utensils are sufficiently whole to serve these minimal functions, they are susceptible. All of these functions are relative to human need, measured by human estimation, and, immediately as well as ultimately, subject to the criterion of human purpose (see M. Kel. 14:1, 17:1–15).

Human will not only is definitive. It also provides the criterion for differentiation in cases of uncertainty or doubt. This is an overriding fact. That is why I insisted earlier that the principal range of questions addressed by the Mishnah—areas of doubt and uncertainty about status or taxonomy—provokes an encompassing response. This response, it now is clear, is the deep conviction of the Mishnaic law, present at the deepest structures of the law, that what man wills or thinks decides all issues of taxonomy. This claim on my part requires ample instantiation. It is the center of my thesis.

Where we have a gray area, the farmer's intention settles all issues. There are crops which may serve either for seed or for herbs. If the farmer sows the seed intending to produce a new crop, that is, to collect seed for future sowing, then even edible leaves which come up are not subject to the requirement of tithing; the plant is intended as other than food. If the farmer sows to harvest the crop for its leaves, even the seeds must be tithed. The seeds can be eaten and share the status of the leaves, for which the farmer planted the crop to begin with (M. Ma. 4:5–6). There are different removes of uncleanness, e.g., what is used for a utensil is susceptible to corpse uncleanness, while what is used for lying or sitting is susceptible to uncleanness imparted by the pressure or weight of certain unclean persons. Now a given object may serve for one or the other purpose, e.g., a head wrap, which may be used for an article of clothing or for a seat. The shift in human purpose for such an object will govern the remove of uncleanness to which it is susceptible (M. Kel. 24:1–15, 28:5).

Intention as a point of differentiation further occurs in the distinction between wearing garments of diverse kinds because one intends to sell them, which is permitted, and doing so in order to derive benefit or make use of them, which is prohibited. Thus clothes dealers may carry garments of diverse kinds on their backs, so long as the intention is not to protect themselves from the hot sun or the rain. Tailors may sew garments on their laps, so long as they do not do so with the intention of protecting themselves from the sun or rain (M. Kil. 9:5–6). A small hole not made purposefully by man does not serve to allow for the passage of corpse uncleanness. If a hole is very small, but serves a human purpose, e.g., to admit air, then it will permit the passage of uncleanness (M. Oh. 13:2–3). So even the minimum physical dimensions requisite for the present purpose are set aside when human intention enters the situation. A related issue is whether it is man's conception of an item in its natural state which determines whether it is a distinct item, and hence not neutralized in a mixture, or whether that distinctness inheres in the object itself (M. Orl. 3:7).

It is in this context that we can take up the place of "the heart" or attitude and intention in matters of prayer and cultic liturgy. Without knowledge of the context just now reviewed, we might have deemed to be "natural" the importance imputed in the setting of divine service to right thinking. We now realize that that importance in the present case is in fact characteristic of the system which makes judgments such as these on the definitive and differentiating power of the human will or intention. If one was reading from the Torah those passages which contain the words of the *Shema'* at the very moment at which the obligation to say the *Shema'* pertained, one's reading of the passages may or may not be deemed to carry out that obligation. What makes the difference is whether or not the person intends his act of reading the words to constitute the recitation of the *Shema'* to which he is liable (M. Ber. 2:1). If a person merely believes that he is fit to serve as a priest at the altar, then his acts of service are valid. Once he discovers that he in fact is not fit to serve at the altar, any further acts of service will be invalid. So the person's own attitude toward himself governs the substantive value of what he has done at the altar (M. Ter. 8:1). One is supposed to pray facing the Temple. If one cannot do so, it suffices if one "directs one's heart" in that direction (M. Ber. 4:5–6).

At the same time, this power of sanctification through man's will itself will be regulated. Merely willing something is null, if, to begin with, one has not got the right to form an intention for a given thing. If one wills what is contrary to fact, one's intention is not effective. There must be a correspondence between what one wills and what one actually does, where a deed is required to ratify the stated intention. In these and other ways, when the householder wishes to separate heave offering, he must both form the appropriate intention to do so and orally announce that intention, designating the portion of the crop to be deemed holy (M. Ter. 3:8). Without both proper intention and proper deed, nothing has been done.

As in the case of the altar, nothing is automatically sanctified (see above, p. 206). Only if the act of sanctification expresses the purpose and will of one who has the power of sanctification of a given object is that object deemed consecrated. If, for example, someone sowed a vineyard in the seventh year, the owner of the vineyard does not forfeit the plants in punishment for having violated the laws of diverse kinds in a vineyard and those of the seventh year. The other party had no right to do what he did, and the mere physical act is null. This is so also if a natural force caused a violation of the law (M. Kil. 7:7)

The Negative Power of Intention

The power of intention is not only positive, in inaugurating the working of the Mishnah's system. It also is negative, and this is in four aspects.

First of all, if people regard an entity as null, useless, or without value, then the object plays no role in the law at all. So man's will has the power to remove an object or a substance from the system entirely, as we have already noted in a different context (see above, p. 159f.). Something deemed useless or null by people is not going to be taken into account by the law. That applies, for example, tᴄ herbs or weeds which people do not cultivate. Whatever is not subject to the will and purpose of a human being is deemed to be of no effect (M. Sheb. 9:1). Mixtures of heave offering and unconsecrated produce take up a fair amount of attention (M. Ter. 4 and 5). When the heave offering is of a minute and negligible quantity, then it is deemed null and loses its power to impose prohibitions on the mixture of which it is a part (M. Ter. 4:7). If a transaction involving the redemption of produce in the status of second tithe is carried out unintentionally, it is null, and there has been no transfer of sanctity (M. M.S. 1:5–6). Vows made under constraint or in error are null. Merely uttering the formulary of a vow is not binding, without an appropriate intent's being expressed by that formulary (M. Ned. 3:3, 4; M. Naz. 5:1–7). If a person intends to say one thing but says another, what he has said is null. Words are of effect only when they express what the person intended to say (M. Ter. 3:8).

Second, the absence of human intervention is just as critical as its presence. When the law wishes to restore conditions to their natural state, it requires nature, without man's participation, for the work. That is why water to be used for an immersion pool cannot be gathered, that is, may not be subjected to human intention and will. It must gather on its own, flow naturally (M. Miq. 2:4–5:6). When he uses an immersion pool, those bodily adherences or excretions about which a person is fastidious are deemed to interpose. If a person does not take them into account, then they will not be taken into account in the system of cleanness (M. Miq. 9:1–7).

Third, we take account of someone's power to form an effective intention. Only the owner of a batch of produce may validly separate heave offering from that batch. It is he alone who, through his ownership, has power of will over that batch of produce (M. Ter. 1:1, 3:3–4; see also above, p. 131).

Finally, the issue of appearances, and with it, the concern that a person so act as to indicate a valid intention are expressed in the rule that a farmer may stockpile manure in the sabbatical year only in such wise as to show it will be used in the eighth year. He cannot fertilize the field in the sabbatical year or even appear to do so. His deed, that is, his mode of doing the work, must be done so that there can be no ambiguity about his purpose (M. Sheb. 3:1–4; cf. M. Sheb. 3:5–10).

One cannot make oneself unclean. The flux must be natural, not willful (M. Zab. 2:2).

Conclusion

The characteristic mode of thought of the Mishnah is to try to sort things out, exploring the limits of conflict and the range of consensus. The one thing which the Mishnah's framers predictably want to know concerns what falls between two established categories or rules, the gray area of the law, the excluded middle among entities, whether persons, places, or things. This obsession with the liminal or marginal comes to its climax and fulfillment in the remarkably wide-ranging inquiry into the nature of mixtures, whether these are mixtures of substances in a concrete framework or of principles and rules in an abstract one. So the question is fully phrased by both the style of the Mishnaic discourse and its rhetoric. It then is fully answered. The question of how we know what something is, the way in which we assign to its proper frame and category what crosses the lines between categories, is settled by what the Israelite man wants, thinks, hopes, believes, and how he so acts as to indicate his attitude. With the question properly phrased in the style and mode of Mishnaic thought and discourse, the answer is not difficult to express. What makes the difference, what sets things into their proper category and resolves those gray areas of confusion and conflict formed when simple principles intersect and produce dispute, is man's will; Israel's despair or hope is the definitive and differentiating criterion.

Now the definition of what we mean when we speak of will, let alone attitude, intention, purpose, hope, and despair, should not be thought obvious or easy to locate. For it is not. In fact I have spoken of a number of distinct, if interrelated, matters: intellect and heart, a mixture of mind and feeling, a confusion of attitude and desire. Indeed, what is confusing in the Mishnah's understanding of the power of the human will is its capacity to deem as one entity mixtures of mind and heart, intellect and emotion, attitude and expectation. None of these is ever fully sorted out. Perhaps it is the Mishnah's founders' deepest conviction that they should not be sorted out. At any rate, I cannot try. So far as I can see, what the Mishnah wishes to say by a range of words, such as *kawwanah* (intention); *rasson* (will or desire); the very common word choice, *mahshabah* (thought, attitude, or intention)—these are references to diverse sides of a very large but single thing: mind and heart. Perhaps in other times and other places our description might demand that we call this thing the soul. But for our purposes, the work is done when we show the single place and a single function of mind and will and demonstrate, as I have, that in the Mishnaic system man's feelings and powers to reflect bear power over the material world. This power, it turns out, is what sustains the entire structure and moves and motivates the working of the cogent system conceived by the framers of the Mishnah. The single word, intention, thus is made, only for convenience's sake, to cover multiple modes by which the human will comes to full expression and reaches its richest range of power.

The Mishnah's evidence presents a Judaism which at its foundations and through all of its parts deals with a single fundamental question: What can a man do? The evidence of the Mishnah points to a Judaism which answers that question simply: Man, like God, makes the world work. If man wills it, nothing is impossible. When man wills it, all things fall subject to that web of intangible status and incorporeal reality, with a right place for all things, each after its kind, all bearing their proper names, described by the simple word, sanctification. The world is inert and neutral. Man by his word and will initiates the processes which force things to find their rightful place on one side or the other of the frontier, the definitive category, holiness. That is the substance of the Judaism of the Mishnah.

So the Mishnah's style sets the question, and the substance of the

Mishnah's laws answers it. The Mishnah's mode of thought and its manner of exegesis of its topics lay out the issues. Through its message the Mishnah disposes of those issues by introducing the critical and decisive role of the human disposition. This will of man is what differentiates. This intention of man has the power of taxonomy. The Mishnah's Judaism is a system built to celebrate that power of man to form intention, willfully to make the world with full deliberation, in entire awareness, through decision and articulated intent. So does the Mishnah assess the condition of Israel, defeated and helpless, yet in its Land: without power, yet holy; lacking all focus, in no particular place, certainly without Jerusalem, yet set apart from the nations. This message of the Mishnah clashes with a reality itself cacophonous, full of dissonance and disorder. The evidence of the Mishnah points to a Judaism defiant of the human condition of Israel, triumphant over the circumstance of subjugation and humiliation, thus surpassing all reality. All of this is to be through the act of Israel's own mind and heart.

Appendixes

APPENDIX 1

The Division of Agriculture
before the Wars

In the body of the book I refer to certain materials assigned by the redactors of the Mishnah to authorities before 70 and neglect others. The reason for regarding some attributions to the period before 70 as valid, and others as unproven, is spelled out for the five divisions on which I have completed the historical work (Neusner, *Purities* III, V, VIII, X, XII, XIV, XVI, XVII, XVIII, XIX, and XX; *Holy Things* VI; *Women* V; *Appointed Times* V, and *Damages* V). But for Agriculture the required exercise has not been printed. In order to clarify why principles in various pericopes assigned to figures before 70—in particular, to the Houses of Shammai and Hillel—are deemed either to belong to the period before 70 or to be more suitably placed in the second century, I have added this appendix. In this way argumentation not given elsewhere may be examined here.

Demai

1. In the matter of doubtfully tithed produce and its disposition, the Houses treat the status of spiced oil. Unspiced, the oil may be used for food. Spiced, it is an unguent. This then is one of the items standing on border between one category and another, of which the Houses commonly are asked to dispose. In the context of doubtfully tithed produce the rule is slightly different, but the basis for the dispute remains the same. Tosefta (T) materials suggest that this rather subtle issue is formulated in response to Ushan thinking and therefore dates from the second century.

The House of Shammai at M. Dem. 3:1 advise on how to distribute produce to the poor. Charity collectors should give what is tithed to one who does not tithe and vice versa, so as to protect the poor and assure that everyone will eat what has been fully tithed. Sages do not hold charity collectors responsible in this instance. T shows that the issue is live, and undeveloped, at Usha. The same issue, transmuted into the context of guarding one's produce and not selling it to unreliable people, is repeated at M. Dem. 6:6. None of this can be shown to belong to the period before 70.

Kilayim

IRVING MANDELBAUM

The disputes assigned to the Houses in the Mishnah tractate of Kilayim yield some evidence concerning the state of the law of diverse kinds before 70. Four such disputes appear in Mishnah Kilayim (M. Kil. 2:6, 4:1, 4:5, and 6:1) and one, of doubtful authenticity, in the corresponding tractate of Tosefta (T. 4:11). In all of the Mishnah's cases the Houses are concerned with the definition of some specific area or structure.

1. The Houses dispute concerning the minimum size which an area must be, if it is to be considered autonomous of its surroundings, a "field" unto itself. This question is considered both in relation to adjacent beds which are to be planted with different kinds (M. Kil. 2:6), and in connection with bare areas in and around a vineyard which are to be planted with grain or vegetables (M. Kil. 4:1, attested by Judah at M. Kil. 4:3).

2. The Houses discuss at M. Kil. 4:5 the minimum size of a vineyard (i.e., one row of vines vs. two) and the practical consequence of the issue, viz., how many rows of vines must be destroyed when crops are sown in a vineyard. This issue is carried forward (anonymously) at M. Kil. 4:6–7.

3. The dispute at M. Kil. 6:1 concerns the espalier, a row of vines trained upon a fence. At issue in this dispute is whether the vines or the fence constitutes the principal part of the structure as a whole, and so marks the spot from which grain or vegetables are to be distanced by four *amot*. (The dispute is glossed and opposed by Yohanan b. Nuri in the same pericope.) Both in this dispute and in that of M. Kil. 4:5 the Houses attest the concept of the area of tillage, i.e., the distance which must separate climbing plants from plants of other kinds. It appears, then, that two major conceptions of the tractate, the autonomous "field" and the area of tillage, were known to the Houses, and so may originate before 70. It is equally important to remember, however, that the Houses are generally concerned with fundamental definitions of areas or structures involved in the planting of different kinds. It is clear, then, that the Houses stood near the very beginning of the development of the Mishnah's law of diverse kinds.

4. The dispute at T 4:11 (cited by Simeon b. Gamaliel) concerns the minimum amount of earth which must cover a sunken vine before one may sow grain or vegetables above the vine (cf. M. Kil. 7:1). Although the Houses here again are portrayed as discussing a problem of definition, this issue appears to be current in Ushan times, for similar opinions are attributed to Ushan authorities (Meir and Yosé in T; cf. also the view attributed to Eleazar b. Sadoq, who may also be an Ushan, at M. Kil. 7:2). It is likely, therefore, that later authorities attributed to the Houses the opinions of the dispute. It is noteworthy, however, that these later authorities had the Houses dispute concerning the type of issue which the Houses indeed discuss elsewhere. What is said in the name of the Houses thus remains with the limits set by the Houses themselves.

Shebiit

LEONARD GORDON

M. Shebiit contains eight pericopes with material attributed to the period before 70. Of these, seven are disputes between the Houses (M. Sheb. 1:1, 4:2, 4, 10, 5:5, 8, and 8:3), and one is a statement concerning Hillel (M. Sheb. 10:3). As will be shown below, one of these attributions may be shown to be clearly pseudepigraphic (M. Sheb. 1:1), while four others are either unattested or are first attested by Ushan authorities (M. Sheb. 4:2, 10, 5:3, and 8:3). Only in three cases (M. Sheb. 4:4, 5G4, and 10:3) are issues attributed to pre-70 figures discussed by authorities after 70, that is, even in these instances, however, the Yavnean authorities do not build upon specific principles or ideas developed by the Houses. Consequently, none of the pericopes to be discussed below can be definitively assigned to the period before 70.

1. In M. Sheb. 1:1 the Houses dispute over how long into the sixth year plowing is permitted in a tree-planted field. According to the House of Shammai, farmers may plow their fields as long as the work aids the crop grown during the sixth year, and is not intended to prepare the ground for a new planting during the sabbatical year, when such work is prohibited. The Hillelites give a set date (the late spring festival of Pentecost) when plowing in such a field must cease. Their position is explained by Simeon (in M. Sheb. 2:1): If agricultural conditions, and not a set date, provide the basis for the law, then each farmer will set his own timetable for stopping fieldwork. Such a situation would allow farmers who intend to sow a new crop during the sabbatical year to claim that their work is intended to aid the crop of the sixth year.

M. Sheb. 2:1 presents a reprise of the debate of M. Sheb. 1:1, though
the Hillelite position is now given in the name of Simeon (an Ushan),
and that of the Shammaites is stated anonymously. The fact that this
issue is moot in the time of Simeon necessarily casts doubt on the
attribution of M. Sheb. 1:1 to the Houses. Furthermore, no Yavneans
attest the issue of the extention of sabbatical year prohibitions into the
sixth year. From these facts it is possible to conclude that the pericope
is an Ushan pseudepigraph.

2. M. Sheb. 4:2 contains two Houses disputes, both dealing with the
prohibition against deriving benefit from forbidden field labor performed during the sabbatical year. For example, the Shammaites hold
that if a farmer plows his field during the seventh year, he may not eat
produce which is already growing in the field. In this way, the farmer is
penalized for his forbidden work. The Hillelites would qualify this
position, by stating that only if the forbidden action has a tangible
effect on produce need the farmer be penalized. Thus, since the produce was already growing before the forbidden work was done, they
deem it to have grown without cultivation, and permit the farmer to
consume it. While this question is dealt with only in this pericope, it is
attested to Usha by a gloss of Judah.

3. M. Sheb. 4:4 deals with methods of cutting wood for a permitted
purpose during the sabbatical year. Only those methods are permitted
which neither prune the tree, nor clear new land for cultivation, since
both of these actions are forbidden. According to the Shammaites, a
farmer must therefore leave the roots intact when he chops down a tree
so that the ground is not cleared. The Hillelites, on the other hand,
permit a farmer to uproot trees as long as he does not, in the process,
clear a space of ground large enough to be cultivated. The problem of
how one may do a permitted act without thereby preparing the ground
for illegal cultivation is also discussed in pericopae attributed to Yavneans (M. Sheb. 4:6) and Ushans (M. Sheb. 4:5). No single principle is
carried through these pericopes, and it is therefore impossible to judge
whether this dispute originates with the historical Houses. (Note: Y.
Sheb. 4:2 has Tarfon follow the position of the House of Shammai).

4. At issue in M. Sheb 4:10 is the point at which a tree is considered
to have borne fruit, so that cutting it, even for its wood, is prohibited.
This is because produce grown during the sabbatical year must be
consumed in the usual manner and may not be destroyed (cf. M. Sheb
8:1). The Shammaites hold that as soon as the fruit begins to develop
the tree may not be cut. The Hillelites agree with this general rule, but
also give separate rulings for three specific fruit trees which may not be
cut down from a time just before the fruit appears. While the pericope
is a singleton, the dispute is glossed by Simeon b. Gamaliel, thus at-
testing it to Usha.

5. The Houses dispute at M. Sheb. 5:4 is part of a large block of materials dealing with arum, a crop whose growth extends over three years (M. Sheb. 5:2–5). The Houses dispute the case of arum that ripened during the sixth year but is harvested during the sabbatical year. According to the Shammaites, one must harvest such produce with a utensil other than the usual one, so that it will not appear that the farmer is working the land. The Hillelites permit the farmer to harvest the arum in the usual manner since they are concerned with the farmer's intentions, not with appearances. This principle is debated elsewhere by the Houses (in M. Sheb. 8:3), and the specific discussion of arum includes pericopes attributed to Yavneans (Eliezer and Joshua in M. Sheb. 5:3) and to Ushans (Meir in M. Sheb. 5:2 and Judah in M. Sheb. 5:4). None of these pericopes, however, develops the discussion of intention versus appearance, which lies behind the Houses dispute. It is therefore impossible to verify or falsify the attribution.

6. M. Sheb. 5:8 is in the middle of a unit on selling animals and tools during the sabbatical year (M. Sheb. 5:6–9). The problem throughout this unit is the sale of items which may be used by others to perform forbidden fieldwork during the sabbatical year. The Mishnah's operative principle is that if the animal or tool can be used only to perform forbidden types of labor it may not be sold (M. Sheb. 5:6). If the animal or tool can be used either for a forbidden or a permitted purpose, we may assume that the purchaser intends to use it for a permitted task, and therefore it is permissible to sell him the item. The Houses dispute the specific case of the sale of a heifer which is normally used for plowing. The Shammaites forbid its sale, while the Hillelites permit it since such an animal may be brought for slaughter. The Hillelite position then is in accord with the principle upon which the other pericopes in the unit are based. The other pericopes are, however, anonymous.

7. In M. Sheb. 8:3, as in M. Sheb. 5:4, the Shammaites rule that, during the sabbatical year, one may not perform permitted types of field labor in the normal manner, lest it appear as though the farmer is preparing his field for cultivation. The case under discussion is how a farmer may package for sale produce grown during the sabbatical year. This is the only pericope which discusses how such produce may be sold.

8. The final pre-70 attribution is the claim made in M. Sheb. 10:3 that Hillel instituted the *prozbul* (i.e., the document which permits a lender to collect debts owed him even after the sabbatical year, which, according to Deut. 15:2, releases all debts). The concept of the *prozbul* itself is attested to Yavneh by the statements of Chutzpith (M. Sheb. 10:6) and Eliezer (M. Sheb. 10:7). The specific historical claim made in M. Sheb. 10:3 is, however, impossible to verify (see Neusner, *Pharisees* I, pp. 217–24).

Terumot

ALAN PECK

The names of the Houses of Hillel and Shammai occur in three pericopes of Terumot, M. Ter. 1:4, 4:3, and 5:4. As the following survey will show, in the case of two of these pericopes, M. Ter. 1:4 and 5:4, we are on firm ground in stating that the attributions are pseudepigraphic. In both of these cases, the issues assigned to the Houses are shown elsewhere in the Mishnah and Tosetta to be live and under dispute at Yavneh and Usha. Only in the case of M. Ter. 4:3 is there evidence that the issue stated in the name of the Houses indeed may have been of concern before A.D. 70. In this case, the Houses seem to have laid a foundation of law which was taken up and built upon both the authorities of Yavneh and of Usha.

1. In M. Ter. 1:4, the Houses dispute the problem of the validity of heave offering separated from produce of one type for produce of a different type. This problem seems to be Ushan, as is indicated both by Ushan concern elsewhere with the question of the homogeneity of different types of produce for purposes of the separation of heave offering (T. Ter. 4:1b–4), and by clear Ushan interest in the formulation of Houses disputes on this problem. In three Tosefta pericopes (T. Ter. 3:14, 16, and 25), Ushans cite Houses disputes parallel to anonymous statements of law, consistently placing the Hillelites in agreement with the anonymous law. In this same way, the position of the House of Hillel at M. Ter. 1:4 is given later in the chapter, M. Ter. 1:10, as an anonymous statement of law. It thus appears that in all of these cases, the names of the Houses are used by Ushans as tools for the statement of issues which are under dispute in their own time. In particular, they seem to wish to authenticate with the name of the House of Hillel what they advance as normative law.

2. The issue at M. Ter. 4:3 is the percentage of his crop which an individual is required to separate as a priestly gift, certainly a most basic issue for a tractate on heave offering. The pericope has the House of Shammai dispute an anonymous opinion as to the correct proportion. T. Ter. 5:3 states the pericope in a more complete and simple form. It omits what clearly are late glosses in the Mishnah, and indicates the anonymous Mishnah authority to be the House of Hillel. Thus as at M. Ter. 1:4, the Hillelite view is shown to be normative. Unlike at M. Ter. 1:4, however, in this case there is reason to believe that the problem of law assigned to the Houses does in fact originate early in the development of the tractate. Besides the essentially basic character of the issue, which I already have noted, is the fact that the

discussion of how much heave offering is to be separated is carried forward both at Yavneh and Usha. M. Ter. 4:5 has Eliezer, Ishmael, Tarfon, and Aqiba dispute the question of how great a percentage of a batch of produce has the potential, upon the designation of the householder, of taking on the status of heave offering. Ushans, M. Ter. 4:3M and T. Ter. 5:5–6a, want to know the consequences of an individual's separating more or less than the amount established by the House of Hillel. At Yavneh and Usha, however, the specific figure established by the Hillelites is not the subject of controversy. In sum, then, we have no reason to question the authenticity of the assignment of this issue to the Houses, and, in the logical unfolding of the law, do have evidence of its validity.

3. At M. Ter. 5:4, the Houses dispute and debate an issue of law secondary to and dependent upon the laws of neutralization, which hold that if a batch of unconsecrated produce contains an insignificant quantity of heave offering, that heave offering can be ignored, such that the whole batch is permitted for consumption by a nonpriest. The Houses dispute is decidedly Pseudepigraphic, for the whole notion of neutralization has its origins of Yavneh, in particular with Eliezer and Joshua, M. Ter. 4:7 and importantly, M. Ter. 5:2–4. Thus the Houses dispute of M. Ter. 5:4 occurs within a Yavnean legal construction, with its same problem in fact rehearsed by Eliezer and sages (M. Ter. 5:4 O–P). That the Houses tradition may have been modeled on this Yavnean dispute is evidenced at T. Ter. 5:13, which presents the Hillelite position as an anonymous statement of law, attested, however, by Yosé (T. Ter. 5:13E–F). While the interpretation of T. Ter. 5:14 is difficult, it is likely that here also an Ushan, Judah, attests this same issue, offering additional support to the claim that what the Mishnah assigns to the Houses actually has its provenance as late as Usha.

Maaserot

MARTIN JAFFEE

M. Maaserot contains a single attribution to authorities presumed to have been intellectually active before the destruction of the Temple in A.D. 70. This attribution is to the Houses of Shammai and Hillel, who engage in the following dispute: "A basket [of fruit designated during the week to be eaten on] the Sabbath—the House of Shammai declare it to be exempt [from the removal of tithes], but the House of Hillel declare it liable [to the removal of tithes]" (M. Ma. 4:2). At issue is whether the fruit, which must be tithed before it may be used in the meal for which it is designated, need be tithed as well if it is consumed as a snack prior to the time appointed for the meal. Fundamentally, the Houses are divided concerning the role of a person's intentions in determining his obligation to tithe what he eats. For the Shammaites, the intention to consume the produce at a specific meal, e.g., on the Sabbath, is operative only at that time. For this reason, they argue that any consumption of the produce prior to the Sabbath must be deemed a snack. Since untithed produce may be eaten as a snack (M. Ma. 1:5), the House of Shammai permit the owner of the produce to snack during the week without tithing. The Hillelites, to the contrary, hold that the person's intention is operative from the moment it is made known, in this case, when the basket is set aside for the Sabbath meal. Now that it has been set aside for a meal, the Hillelites assume that it shall be used in a meal regardless of whether or not that meal is the one for which the produce is orginally designated. Any produce eaten from that basket in the course of the week is therefore deemed to be consumed for the purpose of a meal and, it follows, must first be tithed.

This dispute concerning the effect of the householder's intention upon the liability of his produce to the removal of tithes plays a central role in M. Ma. 4, the only chapter of that tractate in which a person's intention is the major subject of discussion. In the following argument I claim that the dispute is formulated no earlier than the general problem of the chapter as a whole, and in fact represents concerns first raised by that chapter's formulator-redactors. The dispute, in other words, does not reflect an early stage in the development of M. Maaserot's law, but is rather an Ushan Pseudepigraph, constructed to illustrate an issue of concern to that group of legal philosophers who, after the Bar Kokhba rebellion, continued and brought to completion the construction of the Mishnah. It appears, furthermore, that the dispute has been created by circles associated with Judah bar Ilai, whose position on the issue of intention underlies that attributed to the Hillelites.

Two sorts of evidence are central to my argument. The first is supplied by Yavnean discussions of the issue of intention. The second is the content and redactional location of a ruling attributed to Judah. Let us begin with the former evidence, the issue of intention as formulated in pericopes reliably attested to Yavneh. Discussion of this issue seems scarce at Yavnah and, where attested to a Yavnean authority, appears rather primitive. The sole Yavnean given a ruling on the subject is Eliezer b. Hyrcanus (M. Ma. 4:3), who is certain that a person intending to make a meal of untithed produce must first tithe it. This assumption, of course, is shared by the Houses as well. Eliezer's sole interest in the matter, however, is whether or not, at the time a person takes a batch of untithed produce from a bin, he intends to make a meal of it. If he intends such a meal, he must tithe the produce before eating it. Notice, however, that Eliezer, who succeeds the Houses by a generation, is oblivious to the matter which troubles them, i.e., whether the effects of a particular intention endure the passage of time and the intervention of subsequent actions. Eliezer is concerned with the effects of the intention at the time it is to be implemented.

Thus far we can say no more than the simple fact that Yavnean Eliezer seems unaware of the issue disputed by the Houses a generation before him. Evidence from Usha, however, suggests that that ruling of Eliezer is indeed the presupposition of a line of thought which is picked up at Usha by Judah and, ultimately, associated with the Hillelites of M. Ma. 4:2. Eliezer, in other words, is unaware of the issue before the Houses, because he initiates the thinking which results in the dispute in their name. To demonstrate, we must turn to the thought of Judah, who glosses the Houses' dispute with the following ruling: "Also: one who gathers a basket [of fruit] to send to his fellow [for the Sabbath] shall not eat [the fruit] unless he tithes." If we disregard for the moment the redactional "also" (*'p*) which links Judah's lemma to the dispute, we have a simple ruling which claims that a person who intends his gift for Sabbath use is himself prevented from making a snack of it before he sends it, unless he tithes. Judah carries matters far beyond Eliezer's interest in the effects of intention at the time and place at which it is to be implemented. For Judah, once the intention to use the produce in a meal has been formulated, the agent must tithe what he eats even if he intends the produce for someone else's use at a future time. Judah's innovation, then, is to show that a person's intentions are immediately and permanently effective, even when the produce is destined for another's use.

If we return now to our Houses dispute, we make two important discoveries. First, the position attributed to the Hillelites is identical to that of Judah. That is, once produce is designated for use on the Sabbath, it is forbidden for use as a snack prior to the Sabbath unless it is tithed. Second, and more important, the issue disputed by the Houses offers a far more sophisticated view of matters than that held by Judah. For Judah, the intention to use the produce on the Sabbath renders it forbidden without further ado. For the Houses, however, the real problem is how to interpret actions subsequent to the declaration of intention. The Shammaites, we have seen, are given the view that in light of the intention to eat the produce on the Sabbath, consumption of the produce prior to the Sabbath must be understood as a snack. The Hillelites, however, are given a much firmer position. Since the produce is intended for a meal, any use of it is deemed for that purpose, even if the appointed time for the meal has not yet arrived. Neither position, however, is conceivable apart from the basic proposition of Judah who, as we have seen, continues a set of reflections attested, at its earliest, to Eliezer at Yavneh.

Maaser Sheni

PETER HAAS

Mishnah tractate Maaser Sheni contains a number of laws which are attributed to authorities who lived before 70 C.E. We cannot automatically assume, however, that because the Mishnah assigns a law to an early authority, that law in fact was conceived before A.D. 70. We do find cases, for example, in which issues under dispute by the Houses appear to be the subject of disagreement also at Yavneh or Usha. Since it is unlikely that Yavneans or Ushans would reopen debates already resolved a generation or two earlier, we can conclude that positions taken by later authorities were at times put into the mouths of earlier masters. Before accepting as genuinely early a law attributed to pre-70 figures, then, we need some corroborating evidence. This we have if the law which is claimed to be pre-70 is also conceptually prior to laws assigned to post-70 authorities. That is, we will assume that a Houses dispute is genuinely pre-70, for example, if it is carried forward or refined by a law attributed to Yavneh. On the other hand, a law assigned to an early master but which is not the subject of refinement by later figures we must deem to be undatable.

In tractate Maaser Sheni, we find some nine units of law attributed to pre-70 figures: one assigned to Yohanan the High Priest, and the remaining eight invoking the Houses of Shammai and Hillel. We shall review each of these in turn, asking first whether or not its precise issue is also under dispute by Yavneans or Ushans. If it is, then we probably have a later dispute. If we have no evidence that the dispute is late, we will try to determine whether or not it is conceptually prior to laws assigned to later authorities. As we shall see, only one of the disputes (M. M.S. 2:7) can be shown in this way to be logically prior to other laws in the tractate. This pericope alone, then, can be taken to reflect the laws of second tithe before 70.

1. The Houses appear first in the tractate at M. M.S. 2:3–4. In these parallel pericopes, they disagree as to when fenugreek (M. M.S. 2:3) and vetches (M. M.S. 2:4) are deemed to be food and when they are not. These disputes are appended to Mishnah's rule that produce declared to be second tithe must be used as food. M. M.S. 2:4 has both Shammai and Aqiba join in the debate. It thus appears that the unit is

an artificial construction reflecting an issue moot at Yavneh. This impression is strengthened by T. M.S. 2:1, which has Judah and Meir dispute what the correct version of the Hillelite opinion should be.

2. A series of Houses disputes appears in M. M.S. 2:7–9. This is the one occasion in the tractate in which a position ascribed to one of the Houses is shown to be presupposed by later authorities. Under discussion is whether or not the status of second tithe may be transferred from one batch of coins to another batch of coins. Such a transaction would help a farmer who has a large number of coins to take to Jerusalem and would like to exchange these for a lesser number of coins of higher denomination. The House of Hillel in M. M.S. 2:7 declare that the farmer may exchange his coins in this way, provided that he receives coins of better metal, such as gold, for coins of baser metal, such as silver. The Hillelite position also appears as the view of Aqiba, who claims that he exchanges coins in this way. It is not clear from Aqiba's statement whether he presupposes the Hillelite position or whether he is taking a stand on an issue alive at his time. His statement thus does not help us in establishing the date of the issue. Evidence of the priority of the Hillelite view, however, is provided by the next two pericopes. M. M.S. 2:8–9 have Yavneans dispute a question that grows out of the Hillelite position. Everyone now agrees that coins of baser metal may be exchanged for coins of more precious metal. At issue is whether all the coins the farmer gives in exchange must be of baser metal or whether this need be true of only some of the coins he gives over. The issue is debated by the Houses in M. M.S. 2:8A–C, by Meir and sages in M. M.S. 2:8D–E, and, in slightly different form, by the Houses and a series of Yavneans in M. M.S. 2:9. Since the basic Hillelite position in M. M.S. 2:7 is presupposed, and even carried forward, in laws ascribed to Yavneans, we assume that the dispute at M. M.S. 2:7 accurately reflects an issue in the law before 70.

3. The Houses disputes at M. M.S. 3:6 and 3:9 are surely post-70. Both apply to new situations, the anonymous law of M. M.S. 3:5, which states that once produce in the status of second tithe is brought into Jerusalem, it may no longer be taken out and sold. This rule is rejected by the Yavnean, Simeon b. Gamaliel. The Houses' secondary interest as to whether or not this applies as well to unprocessed produce (M. M.S. 3:6) or unclean produce (M. M.S. 3:9) must be later. This impression is strengthened by the fact that the correct version of both is in fact a matter of doubt among Ushans (cf. T. M.S. 2:11 and 16).

4. M. M.S. 3:7 is concerned with an issue secondary to the theme of our tractate. The issue is to determine the legal location of items located across the boundary of a holy precinct, over the city wall of Jerusalem or on the wall of the Temple courtyard, for example. T has

Ushans disagree over other instantiations of the same question, so the issue seems to be alive at Usha.

5. M. M.S. 3:12 states that a farmer who buys a sealed jug of wine with consecrated money sanctifies both the wine and the jug. The appended Houses dispute (M. M.S. 3:13) concerns what the merchant must do to signal his intention to sell only the wine and not the jug. Although similar discussions concerning the sale of wine jugs occur elsewhere in the tractate, these always occur anonymously. We therefore have no basis for evaluating the reliability of this attribution.

6. In M. M.S. 4:8 the farmer is spending consecrated coins in Jerusalem. The point of the law is that the value of money fluctuates and that the farmer must therefore be sure to spend consecrated money at current values. A Houses dispute is appended, apparently allowing the farmer to leave some small portion of the money unspent since its value is in any case not fixed. The exact sense of the Houses' positions is unclear, however, because of the elliptical nature of the text. It is therefore impossible to judge whether or not the law given in their names is carried forward elsewhere in the tractate. We have no way, consequently, of testing this attribution.

7. The issue under dispute by the Houses in M. M.S. 5:3 is whether or not produce of a tree or vine's fourth year is deemed analogous to produce in the status of second tithe. The question arises since produce of the fourth year is eaten in Jerusalem, as is food designated as second tithe. All authorities named in this discussion (M. M.S. 5:1–5) assume the analogy to hold as the Hillelites argue. Yet T. 5:14–20 portrays the matter as far from settled in the minds of Ushans. It appears, then, that the question of whether produce of the fourth year is like produce in the status of second tithe is Ushan.

8. The final Houses dispute in our tractate occurs in M. M.S. 5:6. The theme here is the law of removal (Deut. 26:12–15) which states that by Passover of the fourth and seventh years of the sabbatical cycle all consecrated produce in the farmer's domain must be properly distributed or destroyed. The Shammaites reject the Hillelites' view that cooking food is equivalent, for the purposes of the law, to destroying it. Since this issue is nowhere else discussed in our tractate, we cannot be certain of its date.

9. The concluding pericope gives a series of laws which allegedly were enacted the time of Yohanan the High Priest. Only the first, his abolition of the recitation of the confession, is relevant to our tractate at all. The Mishnah and Tosefta both devote attention to the text of this confession, however, and M. M.S. 5:10 states explicitly that it is to be said. The point of the pericope is thus ignored by the rest of the tractate. It follows that we have no way of testing the attribution to Yohanan.

Hallah

ABRAHAM HAVIVI

The Mishnaic laws of dough offering begin their development at Yavneh. Only one pericope out of M. Hal. 1 and 2, the only two of the four chapters of tractate Hallah considered here, is attributed to pre-70 authorities, and it is difficult to say whether or not the attribution is reliable. At M. Hal. 1:6, the Houses dispute the liability of dumplings to the separation of dough offering. Two disputes are recorded, but it is likely that one is simply a corrupt version of the other. The attribution of the dispute to the Houses is suspect for two reasons. First, the double dispute is glossed by a late Ushan, Ishmael b. Yosé, at T. Hal. 1:1–2. It seems unlikely that the dispute would derive from pre-70 times but would draw no comment for a hundred years. Second, at the heart of the dispute lies the question of the role of human intention as made manifest by action. In this specific case, what is discussed is how the preparation of dough comes into play as a factor in determining liability to or exemption from offering. Since the philosophical question of intention and action is taken up at Yavneh and thoroughly explored only at Usha, it seems likely that the Houses dispute is pseudepigraphic, deriving from the post-70 era.

One possible line of reasoning supports the authenticity of the Houses dispute. It seems likely that by late Ushan times, the tradition of the dispute was corrupt and no longer fully understood. This is made clear by Ishmael b. Yosé's gloss at T. Hal. 1:1–2 and his dispute there with sages regarding the true import of the Houses' rulings. This confusion concerning the dispute could be adduced as supporting its antiquity.

Clearly, the evidence in favor of the inauthenticity of the Houses dispute is more persuasive than the opposing evidence. This single pre-70 attribution therefore cannot be used as evidence for any claim regarding the development of the law of dough offering before 70. If any such development did, in fact, take place, we have no evidence as to what the nature of that development might have been.

Orlah

The Houses debate about the definition of the volume of a substance sufficient to impart uncleanness to a mixture. The established rule is that what is of the volume of an egg's bulk imparts uncleanness to that with which it is mixed. In the case of something which leavens or imparts flavor, however, the House of Shammai maintain that even less than the stated volume suffices to impart uncleanness. The theory attributed to the Shammaites presumably is that, since that small volume suffices to leaven a mixture or to impart a flavor, it so changes the character of that with which it is mixed as also to impart uncleanness. The House of Hillel deem these several processes—leavening, flavoring, imparting uncleanness—to be distinct, so M. Orl. 2:5. There is no further evidence that the issue of mixtures is systematically worked out before 70. The context of this problem otherwise is wholly Ushan.

APPENDIX 2

Scripture and Tradition in Judaism

Since progress has been made in tracing the history of the Judaic stories and comments on traditions of the ancient Scriptures, we now are able to situate some of those legends at particular times in the history of Judaism. The reason for this success over the past quarter-century may be discerned in the principal statement of the traditions-historical method of comparative Midrash by its founder, Geza Vermes, in *Scripture and Tradition in Judaism*. It follows that, when we propose to describe varieties of Judaism in the first and second centuries, we must take full account of tales and exegeses which first surface in much later rabbinic collections, or in Targums, as well as in writings of the Church Fathers, but which can be shown to have circulated in the period under discussion. The position taken in this book is that the way to describe Judaism in the early centuries is to take up one sizable corpus of evidence clearly to be located in the centuries under discussion and to attempt both to relate the unfolding of ideas and to describe the social groups which stand behind those ideas in the period under study.

This position has now to be brought into alignment with that of Vermes in his great work. For no one can neglect the claim, successfully brought home by Vermes, that our knowledge of Judaism in the early centuries is enriched by information found, under rabbinic auspices, only in documents of much later periods. My program in this appendix is briefly to explain why, for the present purpose, I have taken a position of distance from that quite valid claim. That is, I have insisted upon describing the Judaism portrayed within the Mishnah and that document alone, even though "traditions history" through comparative Midrash, as developed by Vermes and his colleagues, has conclusively demonstrated that we have access to stories and other expressions of ideas and viewpoints which circulated in this same period.

When Vermes speaks of "tradition," he means various stories told about biblical figures or themes. These are meanings imputed to the Scripture's materials by later exegetes. The study of traditions is the study of the history of various ideas—Midrashic ideas. It is an effort to consider the history of those ideas in their original and later settings. So it is traditions which are to be classified and dated. In this context, which, of course, is completely legitimate, "tradition" is best replaced by "traditions." The comparison of stories and exegeses (comparative Midrash) tells us the story of Scripture and later traditions precipitated by Scripture.

Vermes two decades ago carried the matter to a sophisticated level, never surpassed, by raising the questions of the origin and development of exegetical symbolism, the structure and purpose of the rewriting of the Bible, the historical bond between the Bible and its interpretation, and the impact of theology on exegesis and vice versa. The result of this sort of history of ideas is to tell us when a given set of ideas circulated. Traditions history tells us the state of traditions vis-à-vis Scripture at various points in the history of Judaism. The means by which this altogether laudable result is to be attained are to ignore the lines of particular documents. Those who work on what is called "comparative Midrash," that is to say, the comparison and history of traditions vis-à-vis Scripture, shake out the contents of the various books of ancient Judaism and Christianity. They create a jumble of puzzle pieces, reconstructing the original puzzle, the puzzle broken by the framers of documents as much as by the scholars who disintegrate the documents into their smallest cognitive components, that is, complete thoughts.

Renée Bloch thus proposed to classify and date traditions through the established historical and philological criteria, and yet through two others (see Vermes, *Scripture,* pp. 7ff.). First, external, second, internal, comparison would make possible the reconstruction of the whole out of the scattered parts.

This notion of "the whole" then refers to the story, and "the scattered parts" are diverse versions of the story, thus the various books in which the tale makes an appearance. As I shall argue in a moment, this approach to the history of traditions in relationship to Scripture answers important questions about the intellectual and formal history of traditions, while rendering impertinent other important questions about the social history of traditions and of the institutions built upon them, in relationship to Scripture. Vermes describes this process of external comparison with the usual clarity: "In her [Bloch's] view, external comparison consists in confronting Rabbinic writings recording undated traditions with non-Rabbinic Jewish texts which are at least approximately dated." The result will be that we can show that a story ("a tradition") found in a late rabbinic document circulated much earlier than the point at which that late document came to closure. As to the other: "Internal comparison . . . follows the development of a tradition within the boundaries of Rabbinic literature itself." The valuable result is the tracing of the history of traditions, as they surface in one place, then in another. Certainly the most successful and persuasive results are those of Vermes, typified (but only typified, not exhausted by any means) in the brilliant papers on Lebanon, the life of Abraham, the story of Balaam, and the other topics in the book cited above. This radical procedure thus treats stories or ideas independent of their documentary, redactional setting. The advantage is to allow the story or idea itself to come under careful analysis. Its unfolding thus may be traced over a long span and across many frontiers.

But violating the frontiers constituted by the work of redaction, we no longer are able to raise the questions of political and social description and concrete historical, institutional analysis which begin when we ask, To whom was this story important? For telling a story may or may not be an act of politics, a work of social relevance. But redaction, the formation of a book, the declaration of a canon, and the decision to preserve and revere a book and what is in it—there invariably constitute an act of politics and a statement of an enduring group, a socially and institutionally consequential deed. That is why traditions history by itself makes extremely parlous the social history of ideas and motifs. Even when we know with some measure of certainty at what time a particular conception circulated, we do not then know who held that idea.

The exclusion of said idea, story or motif, from its particular redactional setting, furthermore, means that the story is not going to be interpreted as part of a whole and cogent system. On the contrary, the traditions must be considered independent of the documentary systems to which, at various times and for various purposes, the tales and ideas proved useful and expressive. So traditions history produces historical results essentially useless for social description.

The relationship between Scripture and tradition depicted by traditions history is solely intellectual, therefore formal and abstract. Nothing is explained; everything is merely described. The pressing issues on social and institutional description involved in answering the questions of this book are reduced to a set of descriptions of the transfer of motifs and the development and circulation of themes. Or we may be told, without analysis, what irritant in Scripture triggered the formation of a particular pearl of Midrash. That is yet another exercise in formalism. People made books and preserved and revered them for social purposes. The contents of books, removed from the bonds of their covers, float out of reach when who told a story and why are questions deemed not to be asked. It is as if in archeology the site were ignored, the objects displayed in a museum with other objects from somewhere else—and yet we wished to know something about the material culture and the concrete context of that material culture.

"Traditions" in the sense of stories or tales or interpretations of Scriptural figures or motifs do travel from one group to another. For a moment let us dwell on the implications of fact, which Vermes and other scholars of traditions history in Judaism have amply demonstrated and explained. We sometimes notice that a story may occur in a Hellenistic-Jewish documentary framework redacted early, and in a rabbinic text redacted much later. Then if the story is early, it cannot be originally rabbinic (still less Pharisaic). If it is originally rabbinic (Pharisaic), then it cannot be early. According to traditions history, occurrence in a Hellenistic provenance tells us that the point and purpose of the story, whoever told the story, whatever its origins, cannot be deemed quintessentially rabbinic. The tradition thus cannot tell us about the conceptions (e.g., of Scripture) held in the formative circles of rabbinism, that is, among the people who gave the rabbinic Judaism its distinctive modes of reading Scripture and its particular conceptions of the place and meaning of Scripture in their version of Judaism. On the contrary, it seems to me that the historical question to be asked in the context of discovery that a story is early is what the later entry into the rabbinic system of such a quintessentially nonrabbinic story tells us about the *later* history of the rabbinic system itself. We must reckon with the point at which the story was found authoritative. We then may speculate on those traits of the story which were found attractive, therefore (self-evidently) authoritative. Consequently, we learn much about the unfolding and development not only of the kind of Judaism which made up the story but also of that kind of Judaism which received the story and discerned its authenticity to its already-defined world view and way of life.

So the history of traditions shown to be early and, let us say, Essenic, located in Pseudepigraphic apocalypse, originally found in Pseudo-Philo, Philo, Hellenistic Jewish philosophy and historiography, patristic writings, or Targums—the history of such traditions tells us that we may not speak about the place of those stories in rabbinical circles which made them up. For in fact they were made up elsewhere. It follows that, about the authority and role of Scripture in those adoptive circles, the stories tell us nothing. What we know is that simple banality: Scripture was important and authoritative. No important insight follows. The reason is that there are no points of social differentiation, therefore no important questions or generative and encompassing tensions to be discerned. This is the result noted earlier in our inquiry into Scripture's relationships to the Mishnah.

In this setting I need hardly dwell on the fact that we are equally paralyzed before the other questions critical to an understanding of the relationship of Scripture and tradition in Judaism such as are taken up in chapter 5, above. We cannot speak of the character of Scriptural authority in the traditions when they are viewed as discrete stories. We cannot describe the relationship between Scripture and authoritative structures of the adoptive community. The reason, to repeat, is that, by breaking up "tradition" into "traditions," we no longer are able to speak of a community which receives whole and integrated a given corpus of traditions and deems the whole to constitute its tradition. To be concrete, we cannot describe a community which shaped its life around the authority of the Targums. All the more so are we unable to trace the principal characteristics, whether social or doctrinal, of a community behind, e.g., the understanding of the word *Lebanon* as the Temple, as Vermes brilliantly traces it.

This does not mean that there is no historical insight in the noteworthy historical successes of Vermes and others in comparative Midrash. Vermes furnishes rich historical insight. We learn how earth-shaking events came to full expression through Scriptural exegesis. The fact that, in the aftermath of the destruction of the second Temple, the word *Lebanon* took on weighty meanings associated with the destruction, surely is a major insight into the formation of the tradition on the word *Lebanon*. But it then is the tradition which is the object of study. Its history is what we learn. So when "tradition" means "traditions," then history is the history of traditions. The history of traditions tells us about ideas held in the sectors of the Jewish world in which the history of the traditions took shape. But these are not cogent or even identifiably concrete social groups.

Finally, I want explicitly to dismiss the notion that knowing the technology of tradition making, that is, the *how* of exegesis, we learn anything compelling or suggestive about the history of traditions. One of the many strengths in Verme's work is his reticence to "explain" merely on the basis of some trait of a verse subject to exegesis how an exegete reached a particular conclusion. Those who conceive that, by showing the formal bases of a meaning imputed to Scripture, they have accounted for the formation of that meaning, seem to me to stand altogether too much within the tradition of formal exegesis to make a contribution to historical study. When we can discern that formal trait which triggered a substantive comment, we answer the question of the role of Scripture in a purely formal way. Scripture then becomes a set of discrete grammatical and syntactical problems. And so it became— but only after the decision had been reached to accord to those problems that generative focus which allows them to yield their insight into how conclusions were reached. The authority of Scripture is prior to the exegesis of its formal, as much as of its substantive, traits. If we can explain what it is in Scripture which stands behind a particular tradition, if we can point to the '*et* or *raq* or the '*akh* which supposedly served to exclude or to include, we gain nothing but a renewed expression of the simple banality: Scripture is important and authoritative. But we do not know why, how, or for whom, any more than we did before we discovered the '*et* or the '*akh* and concluded that, indeed, Aqiba and Nahum of Gimzu were "right."

One of the marks of scholarly greatness is reticence, the presence of informed silence. In this regard Vermes is a model. He is not a participant in the formal mode of exegesis recommended at certain points in the history of Judaism. He is a scholar of what was done within that mode, as of what was done with much else. He never asks us to believe, therefore, that the given "tradition" is natural, right, authentic, or, therefore, normative, because it states what Scripture "really" says and means. That apologetic is not part of his repertoire, or, in consequence, part of the repertoire of the present, flourishing generation of traditions historians trained by Vermes.

APPENDIX 3

Story and Tradition in Judaism

To the Mishnah's authorities are attributed not only a vast corpus of legal sayings but also a sizable one of stories. These narratives of things sages said and did "on that day" or at one specific time are taken to report historical events, things which a specific person really said or did on one particular day. If that claim of how to interpret the stories about sages be granted, then this account of the evidence of the Mishnah should be much longer than it is (see above, p. 14–22), for even if we restrict our consideration of evidence in that presented by the Mishnah, we should come to grips with evidence pertinent to the lives and acts of the authorities of the Mishnah. At the very least, I should undertake to explain why I do not adduce in evidence for the Judaism of the first and second centuries stories appearing (to be sure) in the later Talmudic literature about important authorities of that time. I ought to argue about historical kernals, fabulous husks. Instead, I have been quite silent about those stories.

In this appendix I wish to explain why I believe that the issue of whether things really happened on one particular occasion in the way in which a story says they happened is not the correct one. To do so, I must state the problem in a wider context than that of the Mishnah, or, indeed, of the study of ancient Judaism and its principal sources. For the governing criterion on how we read a given corpus of stories derives from the prevalent hermeneutic. That is what generates questions to be addressed to the artifacts of diverse cultures and draws the answers together into statements of meaning and significance. When, therefore, we take for granted that the appropriate question is the historical one, it is because of an unarticulated assumption. It is that history as an account of one-time events, of things which really happened and gain significance from their noteworthy, that is, eventful, character, defines significance, provokes meaning. Now, to return to the original question, if we approach the Talmuds' stories about Mishnaic sages with the historical question, then we must take up the historical exercise of forming criteria (e.g., "they must have had a tradition") for an opinion on whether these stories tell us things which people really said and did "on that one day." But if we have another generative question in mind, then we shall not find significant whether or not things really happened. We shall see the stories under an aspect other than that of history, in all its specificity of happening and meaning. In this appendix, I shall confront that larger question in a broader context, then narrow the frame of reference to the limited one of this study.

The Problem

What I wish to do is to show how we may discover questions appropriate to historical facts in our hands. I present an exercise in exemplifying the discovery of correct questions to be addressed to stories about sages.

To state matters rapidly, if superficially: modern culture rejects the claims of history. The scholarly aspect of culture—that is, culture as nurtured in universities—today works itself out essentially independent of the past and, it must follow, independent, too, of the material and social reality of history (by contrast to chapter 6, above). That is why architecture, music, philosophy, literature, and the reading of texts work out their programs of study without regard to the history of architecture, music, philosophy, literature, let alone the history of the study of these subjects. As Carl Schorske states, "The modern mind has been growing indifferent to history because history, conceived as a continuous nourishing tradition, has become useless to it" (pp. xvii–xxii). Evidence for this fact is drawn by Schorske from developments in diverse fields of learning. New critics in literature, he points out, replace literary historicism with "an a-temporal, internalistic, formal analysis." Traditional political philosophy gives way to "the a-historical and politically neutralizing reign of the behaviorists." In philosophy, as Schorske says, "a discipline previously marked by a high consciousness of its own historical character and continuity, the analytic school challenged the validity of the traditional questions that had concerned philosophers since antiquity. In the interest of a restricted and purer functioning in the areas of language and logic, the new philosophy broke the ties both to history . . . and to the discipline's own past."

What is important is that the new methods of analysis in the humanistic fields, which stress internal traits and autonomous, enduring characteristics of structure and style, make the break from history as a primary hermeneutic. That is, once it is recognized that creations of literature and art adhere to canons of logic unbound by context but expressive of a universal and timeless "logic," whether of language or of morphology, then history as the story of where things come from and what they mean because of where they come from no longer explains very much. And, as Schorske says, "the historian could ignore [these autonomous characteristics of structure and style] only at the risk of misreading the historical meaning of his material." Let me now cite Schorske's fine statement of the problem, before turning to the exemplification of the problem in the study of stories told by ancient rabbis in the Talmud:

> The historian will not share to the full the aim of the humanistic textual analyst. The latter aims at the greatest possible illumination of a cultural product, relativizing all principles of analysis to its particular content. The historian seeks rather to locate and interpret the artifact temporally in a field where two lines intersect. One line is vertical, or diachronic, by which he establishes the relation of a text or a system of thought to previous expressions in the same branch of cultural activity. . . . The other is horizontal or synchronic; by it [the historian] assesses the relation of the content of the intellectual object to what is appearing in other branches or aspects of a culture at the same time. [Pp. xxi–xxii]

Let me now restate the problem as I wish to confront it. For a long time, from the beginning of the nineteenth century, history was deemed to provide the principal road into the interpretation of artifacts of culture, whether literary or philosophical or political or religious. The means of description and of explanation were one and the same: this is what happened, so this is what it meant. Consequently, when confronted with the need to describe a religion, people took for granted that the issue was an essentially historical one. Explanation followed from the mode of description. The facts adduced in a given order and by a given program carry with them the explanation induced by that order and demanded by that program. Explanation and interpretation then became subdivisions of history, and meaning emerged from explanation. So what happened in the past was deemed to bear within itself its own claim upon the present. Theories of society emerged from histories of society, and so in the other fields of learning. Since, in the nature of things, learning shapes culture, and culture governs society and its material reality, it would follow that what had happened imparted meaning to what was happening. History became doctrine, "historicism" viewed from the perspective of values.

Attacks on an essentially historical, hence traditional, view of culture seemed to come only from barbarians like Henry Ford, who said, "History is bunk." The citadel of historicism would not fall before mechanics. The point at which the historical reading and explanation of the artifacts of culture proved vulnerable lay outside of the citadel entirely. The great theories never collapse; people simply walk away from them. In the case of historicism, moreover, we deal with a variety of specific versions of the matter, consequently with a sequence of settings in which an other-than-historicist theory of explanation and interpretation would replace the established one. In one setting, it would be a philosophical attack. In another, the discovery of enduring structures of mind, beyond time and circumstance, would call into question the developmental and orderly description which then passed for interpretation. In still a third, the logic embodied in the genetic fallacy would be overturned, so that origins no longer were found adequately to explain even themselves. In a fourth, the end of the fallacy that beginnings explain all carried in its wake the collapse of the notion that historical description contains any explanation at all. And so it would go. In the end matters were as Schorske sets them forth: history seemed bankrupt, to everyone but historians.

The issue is now to be drawn more concretely. To ask the question as simply as I can: How shall we read a story or a text? What do we think is important about that story? So at the outset the matter of history as against ahistory concerns the very purpose of learning, the context of interpretation. Once we determine that our interests are other than in history—history in the sense of the story of one-time events, of narrative—it is obvious that we shall interpret texts from an other-than-historical perspective. We shall want to know different things, so we shall observe different traits. The challenge to a historical reading of stories and texts comes from a simple fact. Historians do not deem important, or even notice, traits of literary structure which call into question whether stories to begin with ever were meant to contain history at all. There are structural traits pointing to the original meaning and purpose of making up and telling a story. These in their nature simply preclude the pertinence of simple analysis of historical, including philological traits. History and philology are interesting but not urgent. The reason is that to ancient fables and tales, including those of a historical character, they present the wrong questions. So their results prove beside the point. That is one position of that structuralism to which Schorske alludes.

In what follows, I shall review three positions: examples of (1) a historicist reading of two Jewish tales of ancient times, (2) a structuralist reading of these same stories, and then, at the end, (3) a poststructuralist reversion to questions of a fundamentally historical character. But these are different ones from those asked at the outset. From asking what really happened "behind" a story (the kernel of truth), I move to questions of what is happening in a given social setting through the principal didactic message of a story. For before us is obviously not an account of one-time events, history in the old sense. Rather, revealed are persistent traits of social culture and of mind, history in a mode congruent to the character and purposes of the evidence. That is the structure of this appendix.

The Problem Exemplified in Ancient Judaism: Story and History

These rather general remarks demand concrete and specific exemplification. For that purpose, I take up two stories found in ancient rabbinic writings and show how they have been used for historical purposes. By attending to the structural traits of these stories, I then shall show that the use of such stories for history misses and so misinterprets the obvious purposes of the tellers of those stories. This I shall do by demonstrating on the basis of the structural traits of those stories just what the storytellers wished to accomplish. In this way we shall see why historicism misreads the historical meaning of these materials. The reason is that asking what really happened, or assuming that what the story says happened really did happen, misses the point of the story. The original and generative purpose of telling the story is on the surface, accessible to us because it is revealed by the basic, blatant structure of the story, its emphases, organization, points of conflict and the resolution of conflict. Stories are not history in so simple a sense as is assumed by a narrowly historical reading of stories. The reason is that they do not contain evidence of one-time events but clearly propose to speak of enduring social truths—a different sort of history.

Let us first of all take up the two stories about Mishnah's sages, then rapidly draw upon a part of the record of what has been said about and done with them by people to whom historical description, interpretation, and explanation constitute a single and simultaneous act: historians in search of a narrative of events. The first story deals with a miracle worker and what he did (''one time''); the second, with a rabbi and what he did (''on that day''). These are two distinct types of historical person in the rabbinic literature, the former, as the name states, capable of affecting nature, the latter the principal heroic type of the rabbinic kind of Judaism. At the outset let us simply see the stories as they appear, in English translation, in their original settings.

The first hero is Honi, the circle drawer, and how he made rain.

A. They said to Honi, the circle drawer, ''Pray for rain.''
He said to them, ''Go and take in the clay ovens used for Passover, so that they do not soften [in the rain that is coming].'' He prayed, but it did not rain.

What did he do? He drew a circle and stood in the middle of it and said before Him, "Lord of the world! Your children have turned to me, for before You, I am like a member of the family. I swear by Your great name—I'm simply not moving from here until you take pity on your children!" It began to rain drop by drop.

B. He said, "This is not what I wanted, but rain for filling up cisterns, pits, and caverns." It began to rain violently.

C. He said, "This is not what I wanted, but rain of good will, blessing, and graciousness." Now it rained the right way, until Israelites had to flee from Jerusalem up to the Temple Mount because of the rain.

D. Now they came and said to him, "Just as you prayed for it to rain, now pray for it to go away." He said to them, "Go, see whether the stone of the strayers is disappeared."

E. Simeon b. Shatah sent [a message] to him, "If you were not Honi, I should decree a ban of excommunication against you. But what am I going to do to you? For you make demands before the Omnipresent so he does what you want, like a son who makes demands on his father so he does what he wants. Concerning you Scripture says, *Let your father and mother be glad, and let her that bore you rejoice* (Prov. 23:25).

[M. Ta. 3:8]

For the present, it suffices to note that the principal action of the story is in a sequence of three events (B, C, D), rain drop by drop, violent rain, and the right kind of rain—but for too long. The story trails off, and Honi ceases to be the chief actor, at D. The message of Simeon, at E, is totally without preparation. It appears to be tacked on, and the saying stands outside of the narrative materials, to which it does not make reference.

The second story is of a more obviously historical character. This story deals with the destruction of the Temple in Jerusalem in A.D. 70 and establishes a link of continuity between that Temple and a schoolhouse of Judaism located in Yabneh (Jamnia), a town just off the southern coast of the Land of Israel. The second hero is Yohanan b. Zakkai, who (as this story tells us) is the one who effected the movement from the doomed Temple to the nascent schoolhouse, from cult to learning, from priest to rabbi, and from independent state to subordinated, autonomous holy nation. (But this view of the focus of the story is wrong, as I shall suggest in a moment.)

A. When Vespasian came to destroy Jerusalem, he said to the inhabitants, "Fools, why do you seek to destroy this city, and why do you seek to burn the Temple? For what do I ask of you but that you send me one bow or one arrow, and I shall leave you?" They said to him, "Even as we went forth against the first two who were here before thee and slew them, so shall we go forth against thee and slay thee."

B. When Rabban Yohanan ben Zakkai heard this, he sent for the men of Jerusalem and said to them, "My children, why do you destroy this city, and why do you seek to burn the Temple? For what is it that he asks of you? He asks of you one bow or one arrow, and he will go off from you." They said to him, "Even as we went forth against the two before him and slew them, so shall we go forth against him and slay him."

C. Vespasian had men stationed near the walls of Jerusalem. Every word which they overheard they would write down, attach [the message] to an arrow and shoot it over the wall, saying the Rabban Yohanan ben Zakkai was one of the Emperor's supporters. Now, after Rabban Yohanan ben Zakkai had spoken to them one day, two days and three days, and they still would not listen to him, he sent for his disciples, for Rabbi Eliezer and Rabbi Joshua. "My sons," he said to them, "arise and take me out of here. Make a coffin for me that I might lie in it." Rabbi Eliezer took the head end of it, Rabbi Joshua took hold of the foot; and they began carrying him as the sun set, until they reached the gates of Jerusalem. "Who is this?" the gateskeepers demanded. "It's a dead man," they replied. "Do you not know that the dead may not be held overnight in Jerusalem?" "If it's a dead man," the gateskeepers said to them, "take him out." They continued carrying him until they reached Vespasian.

D. They opened the coffin and [Rabban Yohanan ben Zakkai] stood up before him. "Are you Rabban Yohanan ben Zakkai?" [Vespasian] inquired; "Tell me, what may I give you?" "I ask of you only Yabneh, where I might go and teach my disciples and there establish a prayer [house] and preform all the commandments." "Go," Vespasian said to him, "and whatever you wish to do, do."

E. Said [Rabban Yohanan] to him, "By your leave, may I say something to you?" "Speak," [Vespasian] said to him. Said [Rabban Yohanan] to him, "Lo, you [already] stand as royalty." "How do you know this?" [Vespasian asked]. [Rabban Yohanan] replied, "This has been handed down to us, that the Temple will not be surrendered to a commoner, but to a king; as it is said, 'And he shall cut down the thickets of the forest with iron, and Lebanon shall fall by a mighty one' (Is. 10:34)." It was said: no more than a day, or two or three days, passed before a pair of men reached him from his city [announcing] that the emperor was dead and that he had been elected to succeed as king.

[Abot de Rabbi Nathan, chapter 4]

This story is in five parts, two before the escape from Jerusalem, the escape itself, then two parts after the escape. The focus of interest in the protagonists runs from Vespasian to Yohanan, then, at the other

end, from Yohanan and what he wants to Vespasian and what he
wants. We shall not be detained by the problem of chronology or by
trying to correlate the tale with the chronicle of Josephus concerning
the war against Rome (Neusner, *Life,* pp. 145–73). To do so would
foreclose discussion of what is important about this story, that is, what
question to begin with is to come to bear upon it.

Beyond Historicism

The two tales before us have performed long and honorable service for
historians. Both of them march through all historical accounts of the
history of the Jewish people in the Land of Israel. Honi everywhere
appears as a miracle worker. Yohanan b. Zakkai figures in all accounts
of the destruction of the Temple. So the events depicted are things that
really happened, at the time at which storyteller says they happened, to
real people: one-time events. The sayings attributed to the participants
in the story really were said, by the people to whom they are assigned,
at some one time, and for some one purpose. History is particular. It
tells not about the ongoing struggles and values of a social group. It
reveals not enduring traits of culture. Reality is specific, and, as I said,
it happens once for all time. True, a certain skepticism about obvious
miracles will figure. It is conventional to avoid total gullibility about
Honi's power. But that skepticism serves a limited purpose. Concerning the story about Yohanan and Vespasian there are no reservations
whatsoever. When we have accomplished the proper exegesis of the
story, with stress on philology, lo and behold, we have history. So the
methodology of history governs the interpretation of these stories. In
this context it is appropriate to cite the wise observation of William
Dever, " 'Methodology' . . . grows directly out of theory: how you look
at the evidence depends on what you want to know and why you think
it may be important" (Dever, p. 42).

Now let me briefly substantiate this statement of how the two stories
have been used.

First, the story about Honi has routinely served to prove the
character of Jewish magical praxis in the time in which Honi is supposed to have lived, three hundred years before the redaction of the
Mishnah, in which the story first appears and is preserved. To take one
among innumerable examples, Joshua Trachtenberg writes, "One of
the most picturesque of ancient Jewish miracle-workers was Honi
HaMe'agel (first century B.C.E.), whose penchant for standing within a
circle while he called down rain from heaven won him his title, 'the
circle-drawer' " (p. 121). In this sentence we see that the story is
deemed fact, historical fact, about a one-time event and a person who

lived in a particular place. The article on Honi in the *Encyclopaedia Judaica* begins, "Renowned miracle worker in the period of the Second Temple. . . . The Talmud recounts wondrous tales as to the manner in which his prayers for rain were answered." So far as I know, these "tales" in fact add up to the *one* which we considered. To be sure, the story occurs in diverse compilations, from the Mishnah onward. So I suppose we are expected to count each time the story is told as evidence of yet another miracle of rainmaking. Later in the same article, the author states, "Honi appears as a charismatic personality and the people considered him undoubtedly a kind of folk prophet with the ability to work miracles. Even Simeon b. Shetah, despite his displeasure with Honi's self-confidence and his wish to place Honi under a ban, was compelled to give way to those who regarded Honi as a 'son who importunes his father.' " To be sure, this paraphrase reads into the tale more than is there. But what is important in this routine account is the frame of reference. It is entirely historical. The story *is* history: a one-time event, a particular person. Honi is not made to typify or to express an established ideal, value, or philosophy. He does not serve as an expression of social conflict or of a class phenomenon. He is a person. He lived at a given time (first century B.C.E.). He did certain things. He is important because we know who he was and what he did.

The story about Yohanan b. Zakkai's emergence from the dying city of Jerusalem, through a coffin, to a new mode of life in Judaism, invariably yields a history of a concrete event. Let me cite one important instance of how the story is discussed:

> It is the accepted view among scholars regarding the negotiations between Vespasian . . . and Rabban Johanan b. Zakkai that the latter, when he foresaw the destruction of Jerusalem and the burning of the Temple, sought to take preventive measures to avert the collapse of the nation and its Torah by establishing a "spiritual center," which would assure the continued existence of the Jewish people, even when its residual political independence was gone and its homeland destroyed. [Alon, p. 269]

Gedalyahu Alon, who wrote these words, goes on to address this question to the story we read (and some of its parallels): "What prompted Rabban Johanan to go particularly to Jabneh?" The reason the question is to be asked is that Alon assumes the story can answer it. The story takes for granted there was some reason to go to that place, and Alon takes for granted the story tells us what really happened. As it happens, Alon takes Yabneh to be a kind of concentration point for Jews who had surrendered to the Romans or were friendly to begin with: "[They] went to Jabneh not because they particularly desired this place, but because they were sent against their will. . . . Rabban Joha-

nan's main request to Vespasian that he should be allowed 'to study
Torah [at Jabneh] and make fringes and perform there all the other
percepts' simply means that their captors should not make the conditions of their confinement unduly stringent, as they were, apparently,
wont to do with others'' (Alon, pp. 294–95). Now what is important is
on the surface. Alon is certain that he discusses an account of words
really said, of deeds truly done, on some one day, by two concrete,
historical personalities. The story is history. Our work is to interpret
the language and details of the story. Properly interpreted, these will
tell us history: what Yohanan b. Zakkai did and why he did it, what
Vespasian said and why he said it—''on that day.''

So the details of the story to which historians draw our attention
concern what was said, what was done. In fact, as I shall now show,
that is a false perspective on the character of each story. It presupposes
that the story asks one set of questions, serves one set of purposes. But
the story addresses a different purpose from the narrowly historical
one. Each one is didactic. Each is an artifact of social culture and
makes a point which is representative of a social group, a fundamentally theological and secondarily exegetical lesson. The storyteller
makes no pretense at narration of things which really happened. The
reason is that his plan is to create not narrative but drama. He wishes
not to tell a one-time event but to create a paradigm. In fact, as we shall
now see, the story about Honi portrays the relationship between the
sage or rabbi and another type of heroic figure within the Jewish community, and the story about Yohanan b. Zakkai and Vespasian expresses the relationship between the sage or rabbi and another type of
heroic figure among the nations of the world. So in their deepest structure both stories take up the problem of the relationship of a rabbi to
another focus or type of power. As I shall spell out, each story answers
the troubling question of how the rabbi relates to some other, compet-
ing type of powerful social character. The stories express the tension
between rabbi and holy man, rabbi and emperor. They resolve that
tension by explicit claims of priority for the source of the rabbi's
power, knowledge of Scripture. The historical question to each is social. The issue unpacked through examining each is the mediation of
social power (''at some one time,'' ''on that day'' indeed!). Let me now
spell this out.

Story and Structure

The importance of seeking the basic structure of a story is in discover-
ing the essential purpose originally and perpetually served by the story.
However interesting are matters of detail, it is when we can state the

main point of a story that we enter into its meaning to the person who made it up. The beginning of interpretation lies not in explaining a mere detail, for instance, what Yohanan b. Zakkai really asked for, or really got, from Vespasian. The first and determinative step of interpretation is to find out the purpose of a story: the source of its conflict and resolution, the center of its action, the provocation of telling one detail and ignoring some other. These things we see when we uncover the basic, irreducible units through which the story unfolds. The power of a structuralist interpretation of literature is to chop away secondary matter and cut right to the heart. It is to uncover the logic of a story, unbound by context but timelessly revealed so that we, far away and long afterward, can see what the story orginally meant (and may continue to mean). That is why so many find compelling the inquiry into structure and interpretation through canons of timeless logic. Structures by definition are timeless and enduring—the opposite of one-time events.

Now historians take for granted that the purpose of telling the tales before us is to relate things which really happened, one-time events, history as historians write it. We have therefore to ask whether the traits of the stories sustain this view. That is to say, when we look into the way in which the story is told, do we discern an interest in an essentially one-time event? To put matters simply: the point of entry is the focus of concern, the main point made by the story. I shall now show that both stories are so constructed as to do two things.

First, there is the principal purpose, which is didactic. The storyteller wishes to make certain points through *how* he tells the story. He is confident the person who hears or reads the story will grasp these points and so apprehend his purpose.

Second, there is a secondary (but culturally primary) purpose, which is to link persons and events of the present age to those of Scripture. That is, the story not only has a didactic purpose, vis-à-vis the life of the community to which the story is addressed and for which it speaks. It also reveals a deeper, exegetical program, vis-à-vis the hero of the story itself. The true power of the rabbi lies in his knowledge of Scripture—and not in his power to work wonders or to dominate the affairs of nations and governments. Directed within the community of rabbis themselves, the stories project a picture of what a rabbi should be, which is, a master of Scripture and of Torah, and show that through Scripture and Torah the rabbi can dispose of the conflicts of supernature and politics alike.

The inner structure of the story is blatant and expresses a highly conventional program. Only if we ignore that inner structure are we able to maintain that the story speaks once for all time, and not—as in fact it does—through lasting structures of recurrent events of power relationships and enduring patterns of conflict. So the stories are not history, but old history newly reenacted. And, as I shall tentatively propose, Honi emerges as a kind of Balaam, and Yohanan b. Zakkai, as a kind of Jeremiah. So "history" is told about what endures. That is, it is a kind of social science.

The Structure of the Story about Honi

I discern four scenes in the story of Honi, but the critical action takes place in a triad: three kinds of rain, too little, too much, just right but for too long. Everything else serves to set up this sequence of action or to make sense of it. These are the scenes.

(Scene One) They come to Honi and say, "Pray for rain." He boasts: "Go take in the ovens so the clay will not soften in the rain— which I, Honi, will now bring down by my prayers." What happens? Nothing.

(Scene Two) Honi draws a circle and stands in the middle. He reminds God that the Israelites are God's children. Then he underlines who he, Honi, is. He is a child of God more than the others. How so? "Everyone knows that I am like a member of the family before you." Honi swears that he, the child of the family, will punish the head of the family. How? By standing in one spot until the head of the family does what Honi demands. What happens? God plays a joke on Honi: "It began to rain drop by drop."

(Scene Three) Honi complains that this is not the kind of rain that move him outside of his circle. "This is not what I wanted!" So God plays another joke on Honi. God gives so much rain that the rain threatens to wash everything away—like the rain of the Flood in the time of Noah.

(Scene Four) Honi complains again that this, too, is not the kind of rain he wanted. Now he gets what he wants. God's last joke on Honi is that God still makes it rain too much. The people who came to Honi to ask him to make it rain now come and tell him to make it stop raining. Honi tries another boast: "Go see if a certain stone is under water." This is as if to say, "If the stone is now submerged, I'll turn off the rain." What happens? Nothing, just as at the outset. Now the story ends. Honi leaves the action. This ending is extremely sudden. Honi now should do something else. Honi does nothing. Why not? Because the point is clear.

The storyteller now makes a comment on the story. He needs no more evidence about Honi. Honi's true character and power, and God's opinion of Honi, are self-evident. But the storyteller repeats in words the point he already has made in the actions and dialogues he has described. That is why we meet Simeon b. Shatah, a leading sage in the time in which Honi is supposed to have lived. What Simeon says is pretty much what Honi has said about himself. But he draws conclusions from the facts. He says that Honi is indeed special. If anyone else tried Honi's stunt, the sages would drive him away. But Honi is what he says he is: "a spoiled child in the heavenly household." Then the storyteller concludes by citing a verse of Scripture that underlines the special, familial relationship between Honi and heaven.

The relevance of the biblical story of Balaam, prophet of the gentiles, is clear. Balaam enjoys a special relationship to God; he is a prophet. At the same time, Balaam is the object of a joke on the part of heaven. He goes to curse Israel, but ends up blessing them. He is a prophet who cannot even discern what a dumb ass can see. His power turns against him. He is an object of ridicule. He who boasts that he can control heaven is manipulated by heaven—derisively so.

The Structure of the Story about Yohanan b. Zakkai and Vespasian

The first thing we must notice is that at the center and heart this is not a story about Yohanan b. Zakkai's escape from Jerusalem. This is not the source of the story's critical tension. The escape is not what makes the story work. The story is about the contrast between Yohanan b. Zakkai and Vespasian. Therein lies its generative tension. The story is long. But each part of it is needed. In fact, it is a play in five separate acts, two before the climax, which are matched against one another, then two after the climax, also matched against one another. And there is one in the middle—the climax of the whole story. Each scene is complete in itself. But one flows right on the next. These "scenes" are conversations. At each point at which someone new begins to say something, we count a scene.

(Scene One) Vespasian talks to the inhabitants of Jerusalem. He tells them he simply wants them to submit. He will leave them alone. They tell him that they have done it before, and they can do it again.

(Scene Two) Yohanan b. Zakkai talks to the same people. Now he says to them, in the very same words, precisely what Vespasian said. He does make one important change. This shift is so important that the repetition of the same words as Vespasian said is absolutely essential to underline the differences. Vespasian called the people *fools*. Yohanan calls them *My children*. But the storyteller has precisely the same ending for both conversations. The people say the same words to Yohanan that they said to Vespasian. They see no difference between sage and general, life and death. This scene ends with a transition, a bridge between what has just happened and what is going to happen.

Vespasian has "men inside the walls," spies. They write down on a piece of paper and shoot over the wall whatever they think Vespasian would want to hear.

(Scene Three) The next conversation is the climax of the story and makes its main point. People talk to one another in a dialogue. But the main point now is not the conversation but the scene itself. The scene is striking. Yohanan b. Zakkai wants to get out of Jerusalem. The storyteller assumes we know something he has not told, which is that one cannot walk out of the city. He can get out only if he is dead. The reason—again, we are not told—is that the people in control will not let anyone out. Since we already know that, so far as they are concerned, Yohanan b. Zakkai, the great sage, is no different from Vespasian, the Roman general, we are prepared for this fact. Yohanan lies down in the coffin. His students, Eliezer and Joshua, carry out the coffin. The gateskeepers ask who is leaving, and they are told it is a corpse. They are treated like ignorant people, "Do you not know . . ." Once they are told the facts, they let the coffin go through. Now Yohanan b. Zakkai is brought to the Roman camp, right up to Vespasian's tent. Why the Roman soldiers would let the Jewish sages carry a coffin through their camp, and what they thought was happening, we are not told. The storyteller will tell us only what we must know, so that he can make his points through what he says, and through what he does not say. The simple climax is that Yohanan rises from the coffin. The coffin is for the dead. Yohanan has gone down into death. And he has risen again, from the dead. He has left the dying city, the city that soon will be dead and full of corpses. He has come to the heart of the enemies camp. There, in the face of the cause of death, he rises from the dead. It is a stunning set of contrasts, a long list of them. Then we have two further conversations.

(Scene Four) Yohanan and Vespasian talk. In fact, they have two conversations. In the first one, Vespasian speaks first and controls the conversation. In the second, Yohanan speaks first and runs things. In the first conversation, Vespasian recognizes Yohanan without being told. He immediately knows it is Yohanan, which is why he asks whether it is Yohanan. If he did not know it was Yohanan, he would not have known to ask. Then he wants to do something for Yohanan because Yohanan is known as a friend of Vespasian. Yohanan asks for three little things. He wants to go down to a coastal town named Yavneh, which is no longer a battlefield. There he will (1) teach Torah to his disciples. And he also will (2) establish a prayer house. And, finally, he will (3) do all the commandments. In fact, these three things sum up all of Judaism as the sages shape it. Judaism is a religion that involves (1) study of Torah, (2) saying of prayers, and (3) doing all of the commandments. So these "three little requests" to Vespasian are hardly so small as they seem. But to Vespasian they will not appear great. For he is engaged in a great war in the Land of Israel and a great adventure in Rome, as well. He wants to become emperor. He will be an important person. It is easy enough for him to do a little favor for Yohanan.

(Scene Five) At the end, Yohanan reciprocates and does a favor for Vespasian. It is also—in Yohanan's eyes—just as slight a favor for the Roman general as the right to go to Yavneh was in Vespasian's view. The thing that matters most to Yohanan is to go to Yavneh and there to teach his students and establish his prayer house and do the commandments. The thing that matters most to Vespasian is to become emperor. So Yohanan tells Vespasian that in a short time he will be made king. But the reason he will be made king, even though Vespasian does not know it, is Vespasian's position, here and now, before Jerusalem. Yohanan believes Vespasian is going to take Jerusalem. He therefore knows that Vespasian soon will be emperor. How does he know it? Because Yohanan is a master of the Torah. And in the Torah is a verse that says that "Lebanon" will fall by "a mighty one." Now in Yohanan's mind, "Lebanon" refers to the Temple. Perhaps this is because it was built out of cedars cut down in Lebanon and brought to Jerusalem in Solomon's time. Lebanon will fall to a mighty one—that is to say, in Yohanan's understanding of what Isaiah had said a long time ago, to an emperor or a king. So because of Yohanan's mastery of the Torah, he is able to tell Vespasian what is about to happen in faraway Rome. The end of this part of the story is predictable. What Yohanan said would happen, did happen.

Now let us stand back and go over the five scenes of the play:

(Scene One) Vespasian and the men of Jerusalem.

(Scene Two) Yohanan b. Zakkai and the men of Jerusalem.

(Scene Three) Yohanan lies down in a coffin and rises up from the coffin.

(Scene Four) Vespasian does a favor for Yohanan, and gives him what he wants most of all.

(Scene Five) Yohanan b. Zakkai does a favor for Vespasian, and gives him what he wants most of all.

So that is the story—a powerful and beautifully constructed drama. It would not be possible to tell the story more simply, or to say more things in the telling of it. The irony of the story is clear. Vespasian thought that he was going to conquer the Jews. But the Jews came out able to rule themselves. Even though they ultimately gave over that bow and arrow, which meant they accepted Roman rule, "our sages" saved them and organized a government for them. Vespasian thought that he was going to become emperor because he was strong. But Yohanan b. Zakkai told him the truth, which is that he would become emperor only because he had the "merit" of taking Jerusalem and burning the Temple. Yohanan was saying that the conqueror of the Temple was able to do it because of one thing alone. God had permitted it. The storyteller's secondary point comes at the end, when he has Yohanan cite the verse of Isaiah to Vespasian. The storyteller believes that Yohanan b. Zakkai knew what was going to happen because Yohanan knew Scripture.

That brings up a second matter, the biblical passages of which the tale reminds us, without citing them at all. Specifically, in the biblical book of Jeremiah, we see another example of someone who in a time of siege tells the people to surrender. Jeremiah believes that Nebuchadnezzar, king of the Babylonians, is the rod of God's anger. He is going to take Jerusalem and destroy the Temple because God wants to punish the Jews for their sins. Jeremiah predicts that Jerusalem will fall to Babylonia. Jer. 20 shows Jeremiah is at odds with the Jerusalemites of his day. The same is clear in Jer. 21, 22, and elsewhere in the prophecies of Jeremiah. Further, when the Babylonians do take Jerusalem, Jeremiah is well treated (Jer. 39). And there is one final point. Jeremiah makes provision for the future. He buys a piece of ground, even when everyone thought that it was all over for the people of Israel in their Land. He did this to make sure people knew that there was hope and a future for the people and Land of Israel. In the light of these passages in Jeremiah (and many others, which say much the same thing), the story about Yohanan b. Zakkai and his dealings with Vespasian takes on depth. We realize that Yohanan is represented as a kind of Jeremiah, a living Scripture.

After Structuralism

Recognizing the structures of the narrative, perceiving the didactic and polemical purpose served by each one, we stress internal traits. That is how we have located those enduring characteristics of structure and style which show us the logic of the story. So at this point in the argument we find ourselves wholly indifferent to a reading of the story as history. The story is something other than history. Those who read this material as history misread the purpose of the storyteller. Yet those who would abandon the historical dimension in interpreting these stories, who take up the structuralist position on interpreting them and treat them as utterly ahistorical, also err. It is not the naive and childish error of gullibility, such as historians of the old sort commit. It is error of a different order, as I shall now try to explain.

What is wrong with a mode of interpretation based principally upon the recognition of underlying structures of a story and leading to an ahistorical account of how the story works is that it is inadequate. Structuralism asks the right questions. It does not stand still to hear all the answers its questions precipitate. For if we conclude the work of interpretation with an account of the way the story is put together, we omit all reference to what remains critical in the interpretation of the story. To state matters simply: if we do not know who told a story, to whom, and for what purpose, if we cannot account for social context, we do not yet fully understand that story. Structure without context, that is, the social and economic, material context defined by concrete history, is insufficient either for description or for explanation. Hermeneutics remains a social exercise.

Let me elaborate on this point. Internalistic, formal analysis is suggestive, but not exhaustive, of the layers of meanings of the story. Creations of literature express a logic unbound by context—but logic itself always is social and contextual. If we relativize all principles of analysis, we shall simply not fully make sense of the story we claim to interpret. There always are both diachronic and synchronic dimensions of interpretation, just as Schorske says. Nothing exists by itself. Someone tells a story. Someone hears, understands, and preserves it. Someone tells it later on. The very existence of sources for historical study bespeaks a historical process and a social continuum. That is why structuralism is impoverished—as much as is historicism.

We may amply describe a structure within the framework of religions and show how a system is constituted and how it functions. We may notice the fundamental concerns of the stories we have examined and show how the way in which the story is told highlights what the story wishes to tell us. But without careful attention to the historical context in which the story, as part of a system of values, actually functions, we still cannot explain what is important about the story: its paradigm and message. That is, we do not know how to describe and make sense of the system, the world view and way of life, of which the story is a part. What is still more important, through (mere) structuralism we cannot account for changes within the system itself. Literature is part of society, and if we do not know what particular stimulus made it necessary or even inevitable that a story such as the ones before us should be told, we cannot make sense of them.

Those structuralists who wish to provide systematic descriptions and literary analyses essentially outside the context of society and its history and change tell us something remarkably evanescent. They explain the condition of stasis. But ours is a world of change. Structuralism outside of the history of society and the framework of changing culture explains a system as it exists for a single moment. But systems unfold in history. True, the explanation is the thing. Out of structuralism have come compelling explanations, stunning questions.

But what is to be said of the explanation for the character of a system, when in yet a little while the system will change? Surely an explanation offered to account for the character of the system also must change. This means that the evidence of a system must be located, for interpretation, in the changing historical context of the social and material life of the people within the structure, in the present case, the people to whom the stories were told and who retell them.

So the challenge in reckoning with the sorts of tales before us is to move not merely past the ruins of historicism but beyond structuralism. A story of the ruined Temple or of drawing a circle and standing in it is misread when narrowly historical questions define the mode of reading. The field of "Jewish history," consisting as it does in the discovery and recitation of facts (for ancient Judaism, pseudofacts, in my view), is incompetent to deal with the sorts of tales we have read (and much else). But there is no salvation in structural anthropology and history of religions formed outside of a social, material context. That is so, however much we must learn from those joined fields about the interpretation of facts, the description and analysis of systems, and the comparison of systems to systems, and of religions to religions. On the one side, history done by historians consists of accounts of one thing after another. On the other, history of religions yields vapid generalization. It often is helpless in the face of the specificities of facts and texts. Anthropology of religions, not unlike history, provides us with interminable catalogues of trivia on the one side, and compelling and enduring explanations of what are, in fact, fleeting structures, on the other. So we stand between the antiquarian triviality of history and the evanescent taxonomy, divorced from all context, of structuralism.

I think in the end we have to find another way. For each party performs a magic of reductionism. The historical side effects the reduction of constants and structures to details. It utterly misses the general in the search for the particular. Event is made to exclude insight or to yield mere homily. The one-timeness of historical narrative, the particularity and cultural narrowness of historical work, the focus on some few aspects of a world and a system—these guarantee that history in its conventional mode will yield triviality. They assure it will collapse, as it does, into mindless antiquarianism. But the other mode, the antihistorical description and interpretation effected by structuralism, reduces the flesh and blood of reality to neat matchboxes ("grid-group" in the work of Mary Douglas is only a caricature of the matter). Still, if I must choose, let my lot fall with the people who take seriously the ebb and flow of time and society, who explain change and culture. The others essentially are reactionary. For all their talk of deep structure, their taxonomies are profoundly irrelevant to the encounter with the world of material reality and social being. Stories such as those before us emerge from society and serve the purposes of society. They serve the brokerage of power and speak of conflict. That may not be why they were told to begin with; of that we cannot be certain. But it certainly is society—a group of people—which preserved and handed on these stories, and the reason is that society, a particular one of rabbis to be sure, understood and valued these stories.

Story and Tradition: Story as History

The analysis of the structure of the two stories indicates the purpose of the storyteller. It is not to report things which really happened (surely an anachronism for ancient times), but to make important points of a theological-didactic character. Consequently, to adduce these stories in evidence of things which really happened as these stories say they happened is absurd. The reason is that the point of the story is missed, the wrong question asked. To be sure, last-ditch defenders of the historicist hermeneutic will invoke the distinction between the historical kernel of truth and the ahistorical husk of fable. But that distinction, imposed on stories such as these, produces capricious and subjective results. Some people eat the kernel, while others (as in the case of Alon) swallow the husk too. Not only are we left without clear and consistent, systematic modes of reading these fables and tales. As I have shown, we also, and especially, focus on what is unimportant and miss what is important. Reading these stories as narrative history is wildly irrelevant to the point of the stories themselves. And, as I shall now suggest, it also obscures the kind of history the stories may be made to reveal, objectively, systematically, and consistently.

The two stories present history. It is a history of ideas and of religion, the history formed within the creative imagination of a group within Israelite society. If we know when, where, and to whom it was important to make up these two stories, we shall have insight into questions troubling the group which expressed itself through these stories. For what we have are statements of the system and structure of rabbis. The obvious purpose of the story about Honi is to ridicule those whom rabbis envy, whose supernatural power they concede. Wonder workers find no place within the rabbinical framework, for the reason expressed by Simeon b. Shatah's saying. The simple purpose of the story about Yohanan and Vespasian is to draw the contrast between the two sorts of powerful men, sage and emperor. So, as I said, at both sides of the margins of Israel the rabbi is represented as the dominant and critical figure. Within the community he confronts the miracle worker. On the other side of the border he deals with another kind of power. He masters both, because in each case what he wants is what one should want—not the power over supernature enjoyed by Honi, not the power over armies and empires enjoyed by Vespasian, but the power of the Torah which stands above supernature and nature.

Moving from these self-evident didactic purposes to the class or group of Israelite society represented by the stories, however, requires information not readily at hand. If we want accurately and fully to make sense of these stories as history, we have to locate the telling of the stories within history (when?), on the one side, and the preservation and retelling of them within a particular social group (by whom?), on the other. Let me ask some obvious questions to illustrate this point: When were miracle workers a pressing problem to sages, so that a story about one of them would prove important? At what point did the rabbinical estate or movement become so remarkably self-conscious as to seek to locate itself at the limns, at the critical turning, of Israelite history? These two questions suggest what is needed to turn the stories into data for cultural and intellectual history. But it should be clear that the stories constitute not only artifacts of culture. They serve also to testify to social facts, to the material reality of relationships of institutions—rabbinical institutions. The storytellers speak of the exercise of power. Indeed, what makes the stories critical is their focus upon the two kinds of power rabbis in general did not exercise, supernatural and political. The power of the stories is their capacity to explain what kind of power rabbis do enjoy and why that sort of power is the most important sort. Since history is the tale of power and its disposition, these stories must stand as quintessentially historical facts.

Let me offer an example of how we might make use of those facts. It is meant to exemplify not results but modes of thought, ways of putting things together. If we postulate that polemic generally takes up threats near at hand, we must ask ourselves whether from that fact we may reconstruct the context.

In the case of a story about how miracle working is true but undignified, we may wonder whether, within rabbinical circles, there were men who aspired to validate rabbinical teachings through the making of miracles, as people said, for example, that the teacher, Jesus, also was a wonder worker. Since the story surfaces in the Mishnah, toward the end of the second century, we may notice that about second-century sages miracle stories are not told in the Mishnah, a document of that time, except for Honi. But rabbis of the third, and, more so, of the fourth century, are widely portrayed as wonder workers. Stories also are told in the strata of literature of that same later period about how first- and second-century rabbis did miracles.

In the case of a story about the rabbi and the emperor, we may, in like manner, wonder whether, within rabbinical circles, there were men who aspired to vindicate rabbinical teachings through taking up political positions and forming an essentially political movement. Since the story surfaces in Abot de Rabbi Natan, a secondary expansion of Abot ("the sayings of the fathers") generally assigned to the period of the fourth or fifth century, we may notice that at precisely that same time a rapprochement appears to have taken place between the rabbinical estate of Babylonia and the exilarch who ruled the Jews of Babylonia with Iranian recognition. Rabbis of the later fourth and fifth centuries associated themselves with the exilarchate in ways in which those of the third and earlier fourth did not. Stories about hostility between rabbi and exilarch are told about figures of the earlier, not the later, period.*

So one might speculate that both stories address for different periods growing tensions within the rabbinical circles themselves. Both take up positions against directions in which, in fact, the rabbinical movement for a time would move, toward wonder working, toward politics. But both stories express the principal and ubiquitous value of the rabbinical movement, that is to say, the primacy and priority of Torah learning. Both rapidly lose their narrow and polemical cloak. It goes without saying that these are mere suggestions of how to think about the tales in their social and historical context. If the proposed context changes, so will our speculation.

Conclusion

The stories focus upon the relationship of powerful people: rabbis and rainmakers, rabbis and emperors or generals. They mediate between the rabbis' kind of power and other kinds, acknowledged to be equally compelling. Telling these stories is urgent, specifically, in the society of rabbis or sages. The context of the telling and retelling is the larger setting of the life of the community of Israel, in which the rabbis claim, and eventually attain, considerable power of a material and substantial order. The tensions and contrasts, which form the center of the two stories and make them work reveal facts about the social relationships in which those who told and heard the stories located themselves. A power other than supernatural or political, as represented by the rainmaker and the general, infuses the sage or rabbi. That power, the

* My *History of the Jews in Babylonia* presents extensive accounts both of wonder-working stories told about rabbis and also of stories expressive of hostility between exilarchs and rabbis. These are divided by periods (demarcated by the lives of the sages about whom they are told), and there clearly is a rise in the number of wonder-working tales from the third through the fifth century, on the one side, and a decline in the number of stories about hostility between rabbis and exilarchs, over the same period. And, of course, Abot de R. Natan to begin with is generally thought to be Palestinian and not Babylonian (!).

stories underline, derives from mastery of Scripture, of Torah. In so far as history is the story of social conflict and the adjudication and mediation of diverse kinds of, and claims to, power, these stories tell us history. True, it is not, and cannot be, the history of a first-century-B.C. wonder worker or a first-century-A.D. prophetic sage.

The story about Honi surfaces in the Mishnah, redacted, as we assume, at the end of the second century. The one on Yohanan first occurs in a document probably to be located in the fourth or fifth century. Some day, when we know more about Israelite society and its larger setting in these periods, as well as about the unfolding of the literature, institutions, and structures of the rabbinic estate and movement, we shall have access to still deeper layers of meaning, for a given place, time, and social group, contained and expressed in making up and preserving these stories. For these stories do constitute facts of history. If they are not factitious for the history of the period *of* which they speak, then they surely testify to the social relationships and imaginative life—the history—of the (many) period(s) *to* which they speak, including, after all, our own.

Scriptural Verses Important in the Mishnah

The Division of Agriculture before the Wars

Shema', Deut. 6:4–9

Hear, O Israel: The Lord our God is one Lord; and you shall love the Lord your God with all your heart, and with all your soul, and with all your might. And these words which I command you this day shall be upon your heart; and you shall teach them diligently to your children, and shall talk of them when you sit in your house, and when you walk by the way, and when you lie down, and when you rise. And you shall bind them as a sign upon your hand, and they shall be as frontlets between your eyes. And you shall write them on the doorposts of your house and on your gates.

To leave the corner of the field, Lev. 19:9–10

When you reap the harvest of your land, you shall not reap your field to its very border, neither shall you gather the gleanings after your harvest. And you shall not strip your vineyard bare, neither shall you gather the fallen grapes of your vineyard; you shall leave them for the poor and for the sojourner: I am the Lord your God.

The forgotten sheaf, Deut. 24:19–22

When you reap your harvest in your field, and have forgotten a sheaf in the field, you shall not go back to get it; it shall be for the sojourner, the fatherless, and the widow; that the Lord your God may bless you in all the work of your hands. When you beat your olive trees, you shall not go over the boughs again; it shall be for the sojourner, the fatherless, and the widow. When you gather the grapes of your vineyard, you shall not glean it afterward; it shall be for the sojourner, the fatherless, and the widow. You shall remember that you were a slave in the land of Egypt; therefore I command you to do this.

Grapes of a fourth-year vineyard, Lev. 19:23–25

When you come into the land and plant all kinds of trees for food, then you shall count their fruit as forbidden; three years it shall be forbidden to you, it must not be eaten. And in the fourth year all their fruit shall be holy, an offering of praise to the Lord. But in the fifth year you may eat of their fruit, that they may yield more richly for you; I am the Lord your God.

Mixed seeds, Lev. 19:19
You shall keep my statutes. You shall not let your cattle breed with a different kind; you shall not sow your field with two kinds of seed; nor shall there come upon you a garment of cloth made of two kinds of stuff.

Mixed seeds in the vineyard, Deut. 22:9–11
You shall not sow your vineyard with two kinds of seed, lest the whole yield be forfeited to the sanctuary, the crop which you have sown and the yield of the vineyard. You shall not plow with an ox and an ass together. You shall not wear a mingled stuff, wool and linen together.

The seventh year, Ex. 23:10–11
For six years you shall sow your land and gather in its yield; but the seventh year you shall let it rest and lie fallow, that the poor of your people may eat; and what they leave the wild beasts may eat. You shall do likewise with your vineyard, and with your olive orchard.

The seventh year, Lev. 25:1–7
The Lord said to Moses on Mount Sinai, "Say to the people of Israel, When you come into the land which I give you, the land shall keep a Sabbath to the Lord. Six years you shall sow your field, and six years you shall prune your vineyard, and gather in its fruits; but in the seventh year there shall be a Sabbath of solemn rest for the land, a Sabbath to the Lord; you shall not sow your field or prune your vineyard. What grows of itself in your harvest you shall not reap, and the grapes of your undressed vine you shall not gather; it shall be a year of solemn rest for the land. The Sabbath of the land shall provide food for you, for yourself and for your male and female slaves and for your hired servant and the sojourner who lives with you; for your cattle also and for the beasts that are in your land all its yield shall be for food."

The seventh year, Deut. 15:1–3
At the end of every seven years you shall grant a release. And this is the manner of the release: every creditor shall release what he has lent to his neighbor; he shall not exact it of his neighbor, his brother, because the Lord's release has been proclaimed. Of a foreigner you may exact it; but whatever of yours is with your brother your hand shall release.

The priestly gift, Num. 18:8

Then the Lord said to Aaron, "And behold, I have given you whatever is kept of the offerings made to me, all the consecrated things of the people of Israel; I have given them to you as a portion, and to your sons as a perpetual due."

The priestly gift, Num. 18:11–12

This also is yours, the offering of their gift, all the wave offerings of the people of Israel; I have given them to you, and to your sons and daughters with you, as a perpetual due; every one who is clean in your house may eat of it. All the best of the oil, and all the best of the wine and of the grain, the first fruits of what they give to the Lord, I give to you.

Second tithe, Deut. 14:22–27

You shall tithe all the yield of your seed, which comes forth from the field year by year. And before the Lord your God, in the place which he will choose, to make his name dwell there, you shall eat the tithe of your grain, of your wine, and of your oil, and the firstlings of your herd and flock; that you may learn to fear the Lord your God always. And if the way is too long for you, so that you are not able to bring the tithe, when the Lord your God blesses you, because the place is too far from you, which the Lord your God chooses, to set his name there, then you shall turn it into money, and bind up the money in your hand, and go to the place which the Lord your God chooses, and spend the money for whatever you desire, oxen, or sheep, or wine or strong drink, whatever your appetite craves; and you shall eat there before the Lord your God and rejoice, you and your household. And you shall not forsake the Levite who is within your towns, for he has no portion or inheritance with you.

Tithes in general, Lev. 27:30–31

All the tithe of the land, whether of the seed of the land or of the fruit of the trees, is the Lord's; it is holy to the Lord. If a man wishes to redeem any of his tithe, he shall add a fifth to it.

Dough offering, Num. 15:17–21

The Lord said to Moses, "Say to the people of Israel, When you come into the land to which I bring you and when you eat of the food of the land, you shall present an offering to the Lord. Of the first of your coarse meal you shall present a cake as an offering; as an offering from the threshing floor, so shall you present it. Of the first of your coarse meal you shall give to the Lord an offering throughout your generations."

The Division of Appointed Times before the Wars

Not kindling flame on the Sabbath, Ex. 35:3
You shall kindle no fire in all your habitations on the Sabbath day.

No cooking is permitted on the Sabbath, but cooking
is allowed on the festival, Ex. 12:16
On the first day you shall hold a holy assembly, and on the seventh day
a holy assembly; no work shall be done on those days; but what every
one must eat, that only may be prepared by you.

The Division of Women before the Wars

Levirate marriage, the rite of removing
the shoe (*ḥaliṣah*), Deut. 25:5–10
If brothers dwell together, and one of them dies and has no son,
the wife of the dead shall not be married outside the family to a
stranger; her husband's brother shall go in to her, and take her as his
wife, and perform the duty of a husband's brother to her. And the first
son whom she bears shall succeed to the name of his brother who is
dead, that his name may not be blotted out of Israel. And if the man
does not wish to take his brother's wife, then his brother's wife shall go
up to the gate to the elders, and say, "My husband's brother refuses to
perpetuate his brother's name in Israel; he will not perform the duty of
a husband's brother to me." Then the elders of his city shall call him,
and speak to him: and if he persists, saying, "I do not wish to take
her," then his brother's wife shall go up to him in the presence of the
elders, and pull his sandal off his foot, and spit in his face; and she shall
answer and say, "So shall it be done to the man who does not build up
his brother's house." And the name of his house shall be called in
Israel, The house of him that had his sandal pulled off.

Consanguinity, Lev. 18:6
None of you shall approach any one near of kin to him to uncover
nakedness. I am the Lord.

No sisters as cowives, Lev. 18:18
And you shall not take a woman as a rival wife to her sister, uncovering
her nakedness while her sister is yet alive.

The woman accused of infidelity, Num. 5:11–31
And the Lord said to Moses, "Say to the people of Israel, If any man's
wife goes astray and acts unfaithfully against him, if a man lies with her
carnally, and it is hidden from the eyes of her husband, and she is
undetected though she has defiled herself, and there is no witness
against her, since she was not taken in the act; and if the spirit of

jealousy comes upon him, and he is jealous of his wife who has defiled herself; or if the spirit of jealousy comes upon him, and he is jealous of his wife, though she has not defiled herself; then the man shall bring his wife to the priest, and bring the offering required of her, a tenth of an *ephah* of barley meal; he shall pour no oil upon it and put no frankincense on it, for it is a cereal offering of jealousy, a cereal offering of remembrance, bringing iniquity to remembrance.

"And the priest shall bring her near, and set her before the Lord; and the priest shall take holy water in an earthen vessel, and take some of the dust that is on the floor of the tabernacle, and put it into the water. And the priest shall set the woman before the Lord, and unbind the hair of the woman's head, and place in her hands the cereal offering of remembrance, which is the cereal offering of jealousy. And in his hand the priest shall have the water of bitterness that brings the curse. Then the priest shall make her take an oath, saying, 'If no man has lain with you, and if you have not turned aside to uncleanness, while you were under your husband's authority, be free from this water of bitterness that brings the curse. But if you have gone astray, though you are under your husband's authority, and if you have defiled yourself, and some man other than your husband has lain with you, then [let the priest make the woman take the oath of the curse, and say to the woman] "the Lord makes your thigh fall away and your body swell; may this water that brings the curse pass into your bowels and make your body swell and your thigh fall away.' And the woman shall say, 'Amen. Amen.'

"Then the priest shall write these curses on a book, and wash them off into the water of bitterness; and he shall make the woman drink the water of bitterness that brings the curse, and the water that brings the curse shall enter into her and cause bitter pain. And the priest shall take the cereal offering of jealousy out of the woman's hand, and shall wave the cereal offering before the Lord and bring it to the altar; and the priest shall take a handful of the cereal offering, as its memorial portion, and burn it upon the altar, and afterward shall make the woman drink the water. And when he has made her drink the water, then, if she has defiled herself and has acted unfaithfully against her husband, the water that brings the curse shall enter into her and cause bitter pain, and her body shall swell, and her thigh shall fall away, and the woman shall become an execration among her people. But if the woman has not defiled herself and is clean, then she shall be free and shall conceive children.

"This is the law in cases of jealousy, when a wife, though under her husband's authority, goes astray and defiles herself, or when the spirit of jealousy comes upon a man and he is jealous of his wife; then he

shall set the woman before the Lord, and the priest shall execute upon her all this law. The man shall be free from iniquity, but the woman shall bear her iniquity."

The Nazirite, Num. 6:1–21

And the Lord said to Moses, "Say to the people of Israel, When either a man or a woman makes a special vow, the vow of a Nazirite, to separate himself to the Lord, he shall separate himself from wine and strong drink; he shall drink no vinegar made from wine or strong drink, and shall not drink any juice of grapes or eat grapes, fresh or dried. All the days of his separation he shall eat nothing that is produced by the grapevine, not even the seeds or the skins.

"All the days of his vow of separation no razor shall come upon his head; until the time is completed for which he separates himself to the Lord, he shall be holy; he shall let the locks of hair of his head grow long.

"All the days that he separates himself to the Lord he shall not go near a dead body. Neither for his father nor for his mother, nor for brother or sister, if they die, shall he make himself unclean; because his separation to God is upon his head. All the days of his separation he is holy to the Lord.

"And if any man dies very suddenly beside him, and he defiles his consecrated head, then he shall shave his head on the day of his cleansing; on the seventh day he shall shave it. On the eighth day he shall bring two turtledoves or two young pigeons to the priest to the door of the tent of meeting, and the priest shall offer one for a sin offering and the other for a burnt offering, and make atonement for him, because he sinned by reason of the dead body. And he shall consecrate his head that same day, and separate himself to the Lord for the days of his separation, and bring a male lamb a year old for a guilt offering; but the former time shall be void, because his separation was defiled.

"And this is the law for the Nazirite, when the time of his separation has been completed: he shall be brought to the door of the tent of meeting, and he shall offer his gift to the Lord, one male lamb a year old without blemish for a burnt offering, and one ewe lamb a year old without blemish as a sin offering, and one ram without blemish as a peace offering, and a basket of unleavened bread, cakes of fine flour mixed with oil, and unleavened wafers spread with oil, and their cereal offering and their drink offerings. And the priest shall present them before the Lord and offer his sin offering and his burnt offering, and he shall offer the ram as a sacrifice of peace offering to the Lord, with the basket of unleavened bread; the priest shall offer also its cereal offering and its drink offering. And the Nazirite shall shave his consecrated head at the door of the tent of meeting, and shall take the hair from his consecrated head and put it on the fire which is under the sacrifice of the peace offering. And the priest shall take the shoulder of the ram, when it is boiled, and one unleavened cake out of the basket, and one unleavened wafer, and shall put them upon the hands of the Nazirite, after he has shaven the hair of his consecration, and the priest shall wave them for a wave offering before the Lord; they are a holy portion to the priest, together with the breast that is waved and the heave that is offered; and after that the Nazirite may drink wine.

"This is the law for the Nazirite who takes a vow. His offering to the Lord shall be according to his vow as a Nazirite, apart from what else he can afford; in accordance with the vow which he takes, so shall he do according to the law for his separation as a Nazirite."

The Division of Holy Things before the Wars

Firstling, Ex. 13:2

Consecrate to me all the firstborn; whatever is the first to open the womb among the people of Israel, both of man and of beast, is mine.

Firstling, Ex. 13:11–13

And when the Lord brings you into the land of the Canaanites, as he swore to you and your fathers, and shall give it to you, you shall set apart to the Lord all that first opens the womb. All the firstlings of your cattle that are males shall be the Lord's. Every firstling of an ass you shall redeem with a lamb, or if you will not redeem it you shall break its neck. Every firstborn of man among your sons you shall redeem.

First fruits, Deut. 18:4

The first fruits of your grain, of your wine and of your oil, and the first of the fleece of your sheep, you shall give him.

The Division of Purities before the Wars

The woman after childbirth, Lev. 12:1–2

The Lord said to Moses, "Say to the people of Israel, If a woman conceives, and bears a male child, then she shall be unclean seven days; as at the time of her menstruation, she shall be unclean."

The person afflicted with *nega'-ṣara'at,* Lev. 13:2–3

When a man has on the skin of his body a swelling or an eruption or a spot, and it turns into a leprous disease on the skin of his body, then he shall be brought to Aaron the priest or to one of his sons the priests, and the priest shall examine the diseased spot on the skin of his body; and if the hair in the diseased spot has turned white and the disease appears to be deeper than the skin of his body, it is a leprous disease; when the priest has examined him he shall pronounce him unclean.

The *zab*, Lev. 15:1–4

The Lord said to Moses and Aaron, "Say to the people of Israel, When any man has a discharge from his body, his discharge is unclean. And this is the law of his uncleanness for a discharge: whether his body runs with his discharge, or his body is stopped from discharge, it is uncleanness in him. Every bed on which he who has the discharge lies shall be unclean; and everything on which he sits shall be unclean."

The *zabah*, Lev. 15:25–26

If a woman has a discharge of blood for many days, not at the time of her impurity, or if she has a discharge beyond the time of her impurity, all the days of the discharge she shall continue in uncleanness; as in the days of her impurity, she shall be unclean. Every bed on which she lies, all the days of her discharge, shall be to her as the bed of her impurity; and everything on which she sits shall be unclean, as in the uncleanness of her impurity.

The menstruating woman, Lev. 15:19–21

When a woman has a discharge of blood which is her regular discharge from her body, she shall be in her impurity for seven days, and whoever touches her shall be unclean until the evening. And everything upon which she lies during her impurity shall be unclean; everything also upon which she sits shall be unclean. And whoever touches her bed shall wash his clothes, and bathe himself in water, and be unclean until the evening.

Utensils, Lev. 11:33–35

And if any of them [a dead creeping thing] falls into any earthen vessel, all that is in it shall be unclean, and you shall break it. Any food in it which may be eaten, upon which water may come, shall be unclean; and all drink which may be drunk from every such vessel shall be unclean. And everything upon which any part of their carcass falls shall be unclean; whether oven or stove, it shall be broken in pieces; they are unclean, and shall be unclean to you.

Produce which has been wet down, Lev. 11:37–39

And if any part of their carcass falls upon any seed for sowing that is to be sown, it is clean; but if water is put on the seed and any part of their carcass falls on it, it is unclean to you. And if any animal of which you may eat dies, he who touches its carcass shall be unclean until the evening.

A corpse in a tent, Num. 19:14–16

This is the law when a man dies in a tent: every one who comes into the tent, and every one who is in the tent, shall be unclean seven days. And every open vessel, which has no cover fastened upon it, is unclean.

Whoever in the open field touches one who is slain with a sword, or a dead body, or a bone of a man, or a grave, shall be unclean seven days.

(Non-)purification with water (example), Lev. 11:39–41

And if any animal of which you may eat dies, he who touches its carcass shall be unclean until the evening, and he who eats of its carcass shall wash his clothes and be unclean until the evening; he also who carries the carcass shall wash his clothes and be unclean until the evening.

The Division of Agriculture between the Wars

(Second) tithe brought to Jerusalem, Deut. 14:22–27

You shall tithe all the yield of your seed, which comes forth from the field year by year. And before the Lord your God, in the place which he will choose, to make his name dwell there, you shall eat the tithe of your grain, of your wine, and of your oil, and the firstlings of your herd and flock; that you may learn to fear the Lord your God always. And if the way is too long for you, so that you are not able to bring the tithe, when the Lord your God blesses you, because the place is too far from you, which the Lord your God chooses, to set his name there, then you shall turn it into money, and bind up the money in your hand, and go to the place which the Lord your God chooses, and spend the money for whatever you desire, oxen, or sheep, or wine or strong drink, whatever your appetite craves; and you shall eat there before the Lord your God and rejoice, you and your household. And you shall not forsake the Levite who is within your towns, for he has no portion or inheritance with you.

Saying blessings, Deut. 8:10

And you shall eat and be full, and you shall bless the Lord your God for the good Land he has given you.

The Division of Appointed Times between the Wars

Preparing food in advance of the Sabbath for use
on the Sabbath, Ex. 16:22–26

On the sixth day they gathered twice as much bread, two omers apiece; and when all the leaders of the congregation came and told Moses, he said to them, "This is what the Lord has commanded: Tomorrow is a day of solemn rest, a holy Sabbath to the Lord; bake what you will bake and boil what you will boil, and all that is left over lay by to be kept till the morning." So they laid it by till the morning, as Moses bade them; and it did not become foul, and there were no worms in it. Moses said, "Eat it today, for today is a Sabbath to the Lord; today you will not find it in the field. Six days you shall not gather it; but on the seventh day, which is a Sabbath, there will be none."

Avoid violating the Sabbath, Ex. 20:8–11

Remember the Sabbath day, to keep it holy. Six days you shall labor, and do all your work; but the seventh day is a Sabbath to the Lord your God; in it you shall not do any work, you, or your son, or your daughter, your manservant, or your maidservant, or your cattle, or the sojourner who is within your gates; for in six days the Lord made heaven and earth, the sea, and all that is in them, and rested the seventh day; therefore the Lord blessed the Sabbath day and hallowed it.

Remaining in place on the Sabbath, Ex. 16:29–30

See! The Lord has given you the Sabbath, therefore on the sixth day he gives you bread for two days; remain every man of you in his place, let no man go out of his place on the seventh day. So the people rested on the seventh day.

The Division of Women between the Wars

Vows and the father's or the husband's right to
nullify them, Num. 30:2–16

When a man vows a vow to the Lord, or swears an oath to bind himself by a pledge, he shall not break his word; he shall do according to all that proceeds out of his mouth. Or when a woman vows a vow to the Lord, and binds herself by a pledge, while within her father's house, in her youth, and her father hears of her vow and of her pledge by which she has bound herself, and says nothing to her; then all her vows shall stand, and every pledge by which she has bound herself shall stand. But if her father expresses disapproval to her on the day that he hears of it, no vow of hers, no pledge by which she has bound herself shall stand; and the Lord will forgive her, because her father opposed her. And if she is married to a husband, while under her vows or any thoughtless utterance of her lips by which she has bound herself, and her husband hears of it, and says nothing to her on the day that he hears; then her vows shall stand, and her pledges by which she has bound herself shall stand. But if, on the day that her husband comes to hear of it, he expresses disapproval, then he shall make void her vow which was on her, and the thoughtless utterance of her lips, by which she bound herself; and the Lord will forgive her. But any vow of a widow or of a divorced woman, anything by which she has bound herself, shall stand against her. And if she vowed in her husband's house, or bound herself by a pledge with an oath, and her husband heard of it, and said nothing to her, and did not oppose her; then all her vows shall stand, and every pledge by which she bound herself shall stand. But if her husband makes them null and void on the day that he hears them, then whatever proceeds out of her lips concerning her vows, or concerning her pledge of herself, shall not stand: her husband has made them void, and the Lord will forgive her. Any vow and any binding oath to afflict herself, her husband may establish, or her husband may make void. But if her husband says nothing to her from day to day, then he establishes all her vows, or all her pledges, that are upon her; he has established them, because he said nothing to her on the day that he heard of them. But if he makes them null and void after he had heard of them, then he shall bear her iniquity.

These are the statutes which the Lord commanded Moses, as between a man and his wife, and between a father and his daughter while in her youth, within her father's house.

Delivering the writ of divorce, Deut. 24:1–4

When a man takes a wife and marries her, if then she finds no favor in his eyes because he has found some indecency in her, and he writes her a bill of divorce and puts it in her hand and sends her out of his house, and she departs out of his house, and if she goes and becomes another man's wife, and the latter husband dislikes her and writes her a bill of divorce and puts it in her hand and sends her out of his house, or if the latter husband dies, who took her to be his wife, then her former husband, who sent her away, may not take her again to be his wife, after she has been defiled; for that is an abomination before the Lord, and you shall not bring guilt upon the land which the Lord your God gives you for an inheritance.

The Division of Damages between the Wars

Returning the lost beast, Deut. 22:1–4

You shall not see your brother's ox or his sheep go astray and withhold your help from them; you shall take them back to your brother. And if he is not near you, or if you do not know him, you shall bring it home to your house, and it shall be with you until your brother seeks it; then you shall restore it to him. And so you shall do with his ass; so you shall do with his garment; so you shall do with any lost thing of your brother's which he loses and you find; you may not withhold your help. You shall not see your brother's ass or his ox fallen down by the way, and withhold your help from them; you shall help him to lift them up again.

Witnessing to a crime, Deut. 19:15–21

A single witness shall not prevail against a man for any crime or for any wrong in connection with any offense he has committed; only on evidence of two witnesses, or of three witnesses, shall a charge be sustained. If a malicious witness rises against any man to accuse him of wrongdoing, then both parties to the dispute shall appear before the Lord, before the priests, and the judges who are in office in those days;

the judges shall inquire diligently, and if the witness is a false witness and has accused his brother falsely, then you shall do to him as he had meant to do to his brother; so you shall purge the evil from the midst of you. And the rest shall hear, and fear, and shall never again commit any such evil among you. Your eye shall not pity; it shall be life for life, eye for eye, tooth for tooth, hand for hand, foot for foot.

Oaths, Lev. 5:1–13

If any one sins in that he hears a public adjuration to testify and though he is a witness, whether he has seen or come to know the matter, yet does not speak, he shall bear his iniquity. Or if any one touches an unclean thing, whether the carcass of an unclean beast or a carcass of unclean cattle or a carcass of unclean swarming things, and it is hidden from him, and he has become unclean, he shall be guilty. Or if he touches human uncleanness, of whatever sort the uncleanness may be with which one becomes unclean, and it is hidden from him, when he comes to know it he shall be guilty. Or if any one utters with his lips a rash oath to do evil or to do good, any sort of rash oath that men swear, and it is hidden from him, when he comes to know it he shall in any of these be guilty. When a man is guilty in any of these, he shall confess the sin he has committed, and he shall bring his guilt offering to the Lord for the sin which he has committed, a female from the flock, a lamb or a goat, for a sin offering; and the priest shall make atonement for him for his sin.

The Division of Holy Things between the Wars

An act of substitution, Lev. 27:9–10

If it is an animal such as men offer as an offering to the Lord, all of such that any man gives to the Lord is holy. He shall not substitute anything for it or exchange it, a good for a bad, or a bad for a good; and if he makes any exchange of beast for beast, then both it and that for which it is exchanged shall be holy.

Sacrilege, Lev. 5:15–16

If any one commits a breach of faith and sins unwittingly in any of the holy things of the Lord, he shall bring, as his guilt offering to the Lord, a ram without blemish out of the flock, valued by you in shekels of silver, according to the shekel of the sanctuary; it is a guilt offering. He shall also make restitution for what he has done amiss in the holy thing, and shall add a fifth to it and give it to the priest; and the priest shall make atonement for him with the ram of the guilt offering, and he shall be forgiven.

Not eating carrion and *terefah* meat, Ex. 22:31

You shall be men consecrated to me; therefore you shall not eat any flesh that is torn by beasts in the field; you shall cast it to the dogs.

Not eating carrion, Deut. 14:21
You shall not eat anything that dies of itself; you may give it to the alien who is within your towns, that he may eat it, or you may sell it to a foreigner; for you are a people holy to the Lord your God.

The Division of Purities between the Wars

Burning the red cow, Num. 19:1–10
Now the Lord said to Moses and to Aaron, "This is the statute of the law which the Lord has commanded: Tell the people of Israel to bring you a red heifer without defect, in which there is no blemish, and upon which a yoke has never come. And you shall give her to Eleazar the priest, and she shall be taken outside the camp and slaughtered before him; and Eleazar the priest shall take some of her blood with his finger, and sprinkle some of her blood toward the front of the tent of meeting seven times. And the heifer shall be burned in his sight; her skin, her flesh, and her blood, with her dung, shall be burned; and the priest shall take cedarwood and hyssop and scarlet stuff, and cast them into the midst of the burning of the heifer. Then the priest shall wash his clothes and bathe his body in water, and afterwards he shall come into the camp; and the priest shall be unclean until evening. He who burns the heifer shall wash his clothes in water and bathe his body in water, and shall be unclean until evening. And a man who is clean shall gather up the ashes of the heifer, and deposit them outside the camp in a clean place; and they shall be kept for the congregation of the people of Israel for the water for impurity, for the removal of sin. And he who gathers the ashes of the heifer shall wash his clothes, and be unclean until evening. And this shall be to the people of Israel, and to the stranger who sojourns among them, a perpetual statute."

Breaking clay utensils purifies them, Lev. 11:33
And if any of them falls into any earthen vessel, all that is in it shall be unclean, and you shall break it.

The Division of Appointed Times after the Wars

The Passover offering and rites of the festival, Ex. 12:1–28
The Lord said to Moses and Aaron in the Land of Egypt, "This month shall be for you the beginning of months; it shall be the first month of the year for you. Tell all the congregation of Israel that on the tenth day of this month they shall take every man a lamb according to their fathers' houses, a lamb for a household; and if the household is too small for a lamb, then a man and his neighbor next to his house shall take according to the number of persons; according to what each can eat you shall make your count for the lamb. Your lamb shall be without blemish, a male a year old; you shall take it from the sheep or from the

goats; and you shall keep it until the fourteenth day of this month, when the whole assembly of the congregation of Israel shall kill their lambs in the evening. Then they shall take some of the blood, and put it on the two doorposts and the lintel of the houses in which they eat them. They shall eat the flesh that night, roasted; with unleavened bread and bitter herbs they shall eat it. Do not eat any of it raw or boiled with water, but roasted, its head with its legs and its inner parts. And you shall let none of it remain until the morning, anything that remains until the morning you shall burn. In this manner you shall eat it: your loins girded, your sandals on your feet, and your staff in your hand; and you shall eat it in haste. It is the Lord's passover. For I will pass through the land of Egypt that night, and I will smite all the firstborn in the land of Egypt, both man and beast; and on all the gods of Egypt I will execute judgments: I am the Lord. The blood shall be a sign for you, upon the houses where you are; and when I see the blood, I will pass over you, and no plague shall fall upon you to destroy you, when I smite the land of Egypt.

"This day shall be for a memorial day, and you shall keep it as a feast to the Lord; throughout your generations you shall observe it as an ordinance for ever. Seven days you shall eat unleavened bread; on the first day you shall put away leaven out of your houses, for if any one eats what is leavened, from the first day until the seventh day, that person shall be cut off from Israel. On the first day you shall hold a holy assembly, and on the seventh day a holy assembly; no work shall be done on those days; but what every one must eat, that only may be prepared by you. And you shall observe the feast of unleavened bread, for on this day I brought your hosts out of the land of Egypt: therefore you shall observe this day, throughout your generations, as an ordinance for ever. In the first month, on the fourteenth day of the month at evening, you shall eat unleavened bread, and so until the twenty-first day of the month at evening. For seven days no leaven shall be found in your houses; for if any one eats what is leavened, that person shall be cut off from the congregation of Israel, whether he is a sojourner or a native of the land. You shall eat nothing leavened; in all your dwellings you shall eat unleavened bread."

Then Moses called all the elders of Israel, and said to them, "Select lambs for yourselves according to your families, and kill the passover lamb. Take a bunch of hyssop and dip it in the blood which is in the basin, and touch the lintel and the two doorposts with the blood which is in the basin; and none of you shall go out of the door of his house until the morning. For the Lord will pass through to slay the Egyptians; and when he sees the blood on the lintel and on the two doorposts, the Lord will pass over the door, and will not allow the destroyer to enter your houses to slay you. You shall observe this rite as an ordinance for you and your sons for ever. And when you come to the land which the Lord will give you, as he has promised, you shall keep this service. And when your children say to you, 'What do you mean by this service?' you shall say, 'It is the sacrifice of the Lord's passover, for he passed over the houses of the people of Israel in Egypt, when he slew the Egyptians but spared our houses.'' And the people bowed their heads and worshipped. Then the people of Israel went and did so; as the Lord had commanded Moses and Aaron, so they did.

Taking the shekel offering, Ex. 30:11–16

The Lord said to Moses, "When you take the census of the people of Israel, then each shall give a ransom for himself to the Lord when you number them, that there be no plague among them when you number them. Each who is numbered in the census shall give this: half a shekel according to the shekel of the sanctuary (the shekel is twenty gerahs), half a shekel as an offering to the Lord. Every one who is numbered in the census, from twenty years old and upward, shall give the Lord's offering. The rich shall not give more, and the poor shall not give less, than the half shekel, when you give the Lord's offering to make atonement for yourselves. And you shall take the atonement money from the people of Israel, and shall appoint it for the service of the tent of meeting; that it may bring the people of Israel to remembrance before the Lord, so as to make atonement for yourselves."

The rite of the high priest on the Day of Atonement, Lev. 16:1–34

The Lord spoke to Moses, after the death of the two sons of Aaron, when they drew near before the Lord and died; and the Lord said to Moses, "Tell Aaron your brother not to come at all times into the holy place within the veil, before the mercy seat which is upon the ark, lest he die; for I will appear in the cloud upon the mercy seat. But thus shall Aaron come into the holy place: with a young bull for a sin offering and a ram for a burnt offering. He shall put on the holy linen coat, and shall have the linen breeches on his body, be girded with the linen girdle, and wear the linen turban; these are the holy garments. He shall bathe his body in water, and then put them on. And he shall take from the congregation of the people of Israel two male goats for a sin offering, and one ram for a burnt offering.

"And Aaron shall offer the bull as a sin offering for himself, and shall make atonement for himself and for his house. Then he shall take the two goats, and set them before the Lord at the door of the tent of meeting; and Aaron shall cast lots upon the two goats, one lot for the Lord and the other lot for Azazel. And Aaron shall present the goat on which the lot fell for the Lord, and offer it as a sin offering; but the goat on which the lot fell for Azazel shall be presented alive before the Lord to make atonement over it, that it may be sent away into the wilderness to Azazel.

"Aaron shall present the bull as a sin offering for himself, and shall make atonement for himself and for his house; he shall kill the bull as a sin offering for himself. And he shall take a censer full of coals of fire from the altar before the Lord, and two handfuls of sweet incense beaten small; and he shall bring it within the veil and put the incense on the fire before the Lord, that the cloud of the incense may cover the mercy seat which is upon the testimony, lest he die; and he shall take some of the blood of the bull, and sprinkle it with his finger on the front of the mercy seat, and before the mercy seat he shall sprinkle the blood with his finger seven times.

"Then he shall kill the goat of the sin offering which is for the people, and bring its blood within the veil, and do with its blood as he did with the blood of the bull, sprinkling it upon the mercy seat and before the mercy seat; thus he shall make atonement for the holy place, because of the uncleanness of the people of Israel, and because of their transgressions, all their sins; and so he shall do for the tent of meeting, which abides with them in the midst of their uncleanness. There shall be no man in the tent of meeting when he enters to make atonement in the holy place until he comes out and has made atonement for himself and for his house and for all the assembly of Israel. Then he shall go out to the altar which is before the Lord and make atonement for it, and shall take some of the blood of the bull and of the blood of the goat, and put it on the horns of the altar round about. And he shall sprinkle some of the blood upon it with his finger seven times, and cleanse it and hallow it from the uncleanness of the people of Israel.

"And when he has made an end of atoning for the holy place and the tent of meeting and the altar, he shall present the live goat; and Aaron shall lay both his hands upon the head of the live goat, and confess over him all the iniquities of the people of Israel, and all their transgressions, all their sins; and he shall put them upon the head of the goat, and send him away into the wilderness by the hand of a man who is in readiness. The goat shall bear all their iniquities upon him to a solitary land; and he shall let the goat go in the wilderness.

"Then Aaron shall come into the tent of meeting, and shall put off the linen garments which he put on when he went into the holy place, and shall leave them there; and he shall bathe his body in water in a holy place, and put on his garments, and come forth, and offer his burnt offering and the burnt offering of the people, and make atonement for himself and for the people. And the fat of the sin offering he shall burn upon the altar. And he who lets the goat go to Azazel shall wash his clothes and bathe his body in water, and afterward he may come into the camp. And the bull for the sin offering and the goat for the sin offering, whose blood was brought in to make atonement in the holy place, shall be carried forth outside the camp; their skin and their flesh and their dung shall be burned with fire. And he who burns them shall wash his clothes and bathe his body in water, and afterward he may come into the camp.

"And it shall be a statute to you for ever that in the seventh month, on the tenth day of the month, you shall afflict yourselves, and shall do no work, either the native or the stranger who sojourns among you; for on this day shall atonement be made for you, to cleanse you; from all your sins you shall be clean before the Lord. It is a Sabbath of solemn rest to you, and you shall afflict yourselves; it is a statute for ever. And the priest who is anointed and consecrated as priest in his father's place shall make atonement, wearing the holy linen garments; he shall make atonement for the sanctuary, and he shall make atonement for the tent of meeting and for the altar, and he shall make atonement for the priests and for all the people of assembly. And this shall be an everlasting statute for you, that atonement may be made for the people of Israel once in the year because of all their sins." And Moses did as the Lord commanded him.

The rites of the festival (Sukkot, Tabernacles),
Lev. 23:33–43 (see also Num. 29:12–38)

And the Lord said to Moses, "Say to the people of Israel, On the fifteenth day of this seventh month and for seven days is the feast of booths to the Lord. On the first day shall be a holy convocation; you shall do no laborious work. Seven days you shall present offerings by fire to the Lord; on the eighth day you shall hold a holy convocation and present an offering by fire to the Lord; it is a solemn assembly; you shall do no laborious work.

"These are the appointed feasts of the Lord, which you shall proclaim as times of holy convocation, for presenting to the Lord offerings by fire, burnt offerings and cereal offerings, sacrifices and drink offerings, each on its proper day; besides the Sabbaths of the Lord, and besides your gifts, and besides all your votive offerings, and besides all your freewill offerings, which you give to the Lord.

"On the fifteenth day of the seventh month, when you have gathered in the produce of the land, you shall keep the feast of the Lord seven days; on the first day shall be a solemn rest, and on the eighth day shall be a solemn rest. And you shall take on the first day the fruit of goodly trees, branches of palm trees, and boughs of leafy trees, and willows of the brook; and you shall rejoice before the Lord your God seven days. You shall keep it as a feast to the Lord seven days in the year; it is a statute for ever throughout your generations; you shall keep it in the seventh month. You shall dwell in booths for seven days; all that are native in Israel shall dwell in booths, that your generations may know that I made the people of Israel dwell in booths when I brought them out of the land of Egypt: I am the Lord your God."

The rites of the festival, Deut. 16:13–15

You shall keep the feast of booths seven days, when you make your ingathering from your threshing door and your wine press; you shall rejoice in your feast, you and your son and your daughter, your man-servant and your maidservant, the levite, the sojourner, the fatherless, and the widow who are within your towns. For seven days you shall keep the feast to the Lord your God at the place which the Lord will choose; because the Lord your God will bless you in all your produce and in all the work of your hands, so that you will be altogether joyful.

The rites of the New Year, Lev. 23:23–25

And the Lord said to Moses, "Say to the people of Israel, in the seventh month, on the first day of the month, you shall observe a day of solemn rest, a memorial proclaimed with blast of trumpets, a holy convocation. You shall do no laborious work; and you shall present an offering by fire to the Lord."

The rites of the New Year, Num. 29:1–6

On the first day of the seventh month you shall have a holy convocation; you shall do no laborious work. It is a day for you to blow the trumpets, and you shall offer a burnt offering, a pleasing odor to the Lord: one young bull, one ram, seven male lambs a year old without blemish; also their cereal offering of fine flour mixed with oil, three tenths of an ephah for the bull, two tenths for the ram, and one tenth for each of the seven lambs; with one male goat for a sin offering, to make atonement for you; besides the burnt offering of the new moon, and its cereal offering and the continual burnt offering and its cereal offering, and their drink offering, according to the ordinance for them, a pleasing odor, an offering by fire to the Lord.

Sounding the trumpet in time of trouble, Num. 10:9

And when you go to war in your land against the adversary who oppresses you, then you shall sound an alarm with the trumpets, that you may be remembered before the Lord your God, and you shall be saved from your enemies.

A festal offering is required on the pilgrim festivals, Ex. 23:14–18

Three times in the year you shall keep a feast to me. You shall keep the feast of unleavened bread; as I commanded you, you shall eat unleavened bread for seven days at the appointed time in the month of Abib, for in it you came out of Egypt. None shall appear before me empty-handed. You shall keep the feast of harvest, of the first fruits of your labor, of what you sow in the field. You shall keep the feast of ingathering at the end of the year, when you gather in from the field the fruit of your labor. Three times in the year shall all your males appear before the Lord God. You shall not offer the blood of my sacrifice with leavened bread, or let the fat of my feast remain until the morning.

Appearing before the Lord with an offering, Deut. 16:14–17

You shall rejoice in your feast, you and your son and your daughter, your manservant and your maidservant, the Levite, the sojourner, the fatherless, and the widow who are within your towns. For seven days you shall keep the feast to the Lord your God at the place which the Lord will choose; because the Lord your God will bless you in all your produce and in all the work of your hands, so that you will be altogether joyful. Three times a year all your males shall appear before the Lord your God at the place which he will choose: at the feast of unleavened bread, at the feast of weeks, and at the feast of booths. They shall not appear before the Lord empty-handed; every man shall give as he is able, according to the blessing of the Lord your God which he has given you.

The Division of Women after the Wars

Penalties for illicit sexual relations, Deut. 22:28–29

If a man meets a virgin who is not betrothed, and seizes her and lies with her, and they are found, then the man who lay with her shall give to the father of the young woman fifty shekels of silver and she shall be his wife, because he has violated her; he may not put her away all his days.

Penalties for illicit sexual relations, Deut. 22:13–21

If any man takes a wife, and goes in to her, and then spurns her, and charges her with shameful conduct, and brings an evil name upon her, saying, "I took this woman, and when I came near her, I did not find in her the tokens of virginity," then the father of the young woman and her mother shall take and bring out the tokens of her virginity to the elders of the city in the gate; and the father of the young woman shall say to the elders, "I gave my daughter to this man to wife, and he spurns her; and lo, he has made shameful charges against her, saying, 'I did not find in your daughter the tokens of virginity.' And yet these are the tokens of my daughter's virginity." And they shall spread the garment before the elders of the city. Then the elders of that city shall take the man and whip him; and they shall fine him a hundred shekels of silver, and give them to the father of the young woman, because he has brought an evil name upon a virgin of Israel; and she shall be his wife; he may not put her away all his days. But if the thing is true, that the tokens of virginity were not found in the young woman, then they shall bring out the young woman to the door of her father's house, and the men of her city shall stone her to death with stones, because she has wrought folly in Israel by playing the harlot in her father's house; so you shall purge the evil from the midst of you.

The Division of Damages after the Wars

Damages to chattels, Ex. 21:33–34

When a man leaves a pit open, or when a man digs a pit and does not cover it, and an ox or an ass falls into it, the owner of the pit shall make it good; he shall give money to its owner, and the dead beast shall be his.

Damages by chattels, Ex. 21:35–36

When one man's ox hurts another's, so that it dies, then they shall sell the live ox and divide the price of it; and the dead beast also they shall divide. Or if it is known that the ox has been accustomed to gore in the past, and its owner has not kept it in, he shall pay ox for ox, and the dead beast shall be his.

Damages by chattels, the distinction between an ox deemed harmless and one which is an attested danger, Ex. 21:28–32

When an ox gores a man or a woman to death, the ox shall be stoned, and its flesh shall not be eaten; but the owner of the ox shall be clear. But if the ox has been accustomed to gore in the past, and its owner has been warned but has not kept it in, and it kills a man or a woman, the ox shall be stoned, and its owner also shall be put to death. If a ransom is laid on him, then he shall give for the redemption of his life whatever is laid upon him. If it gores a man's son or daughter, he shall be dealt with according to this same rule. If the ox gores a slave, male or female, the owner shall give to their master thirty shekels of silver, and the ox shall be stoned.

Five-fold and four-fold damages, Ex. 22:1

If a man steals an ox or a sheep, and kills it or sells it, he shall pay five oxen for an ox, and four sheep for a sheep.

Responsibilities for bailments, Ex. 22:6–8

When fire breaks out and catches in thorns so that the stacked grain or the standing grain or the field is consumed, he that kindled the fire shall make full restitution. If a man delivers to his neighbor money or goods to keep, and it is stolen out of the man's house, then, if the thief is found, he shall pay double. If the thief is not found, the owner of the house shall come near to God, to show whether or not he has put his hand to his neighbor's goods.

Not taking usurious interest, Lev. 25:35–37

If your brother becomes poor, and cannot maintain himself with you, you shall maintain him; as a stranger and a sojourner he shall live with you. Take no interest from him or increase, but fear your God; that your brother may live beside you. You shall not lend him your money at interest, nor give him your food for profit.

Not taking usurious interest, Deut. 23:19–20

You shall not lend upon interest to your brother, interest on money, interest on victuals, interest on anything that is lent for interest. To a foreigner you may lend upon interest, but to your brother you shall not lend upon interest; that the Lord your God may bless you in all that you undertake in the land which you are entering to take possession of it.

Paying workers on time, Deut. 24:14:15

You shall not oppress a hired servant who is poor and needy, whether he is one of your brethren or one of the sojourners who are in your land within your towns; you shall give him his hire on the day he earns it, before the sun goes down (for he is poor, and sets his heart upon it); lest he cry against you to the Lord, and it be sin in you.

Dividing inheritances, Num. 27:8–11

You shall say to the people of Israel, "If a man dies, and has no son, then you shall cause his inheritance to pass to his daughter. And if he has no daughter, then you shall give his inheritance to his brothers. And if he has no brothers, then you shall give his inheritance to his father's brothers. And if his father has no brothers, then you shall give his inheritance to his kinsmen that is next to him of his family, and he shall possess it. And it shall be to the people of Israel a statute and ordinance, as the Lord comanded Moses."

False witnesses punished, Deut. 19:15–21

A single witness shall not prevail against a man for any crime or for any wrong in connection with any offense that he has committed; only on the evidence of two witnesses, or of three witnesses, shall a charge be sustained. If a malicious witness rises against any man to accuse him of wrongdoing, then both parties to the dispute shall appear before the Lord, before the priests, and the judges who are in office in those days; the judges shall inquire diligently, and if the witness is a false witness and has accused his brother falsely, then you shall do to him as he had meant to do to his brother; so you shall purge the evil from the midst of you. And the rest shall hear, and fear, and shall never again commit any such evil among you. Your eye shall not pity; it shall be life for life, eye for eye, tooth for tooth, hand for hand, foot for foot.

Errors made by a court, Lev. 4:1–5

And the Lord said to Moses, "Say to the people of Israel, If any one sins unwittingly in any of the things which the Lord has commanded not to be done, and does any one of them, if it is the anointed priest who sins, thus bringing guilt on the people, then let him offer for the sin which he has committed a young bull without blemish to the Lord for a sin offering. He shall bring the bull to the door of the tent of meeting before the Lord, and lay his hand on the head of the bull, and kill the bull before the Lord. And, the anointed priest shall take some of the blood of the bull and bring it to the tent of meeting."

Errors made by the people, Lev. 4:13–23

If the whole congregation of Israel commits a sin unwittingly and the thing is hidden from the eyes of the assembly, and they do any one of the things which the Lord has commanded not to be done and are guilty; when the sin which they have committed becomes known, the assembly shall offer a young bull for a sin offering and bring it before the tent of meeting; and the elders of the congregation shall lay their hands upon the head of the bull before the Lord, and the bull shall be killed before the Lord. Then the anointed priest shall bring some of the blood of the bull to the tent of meeting, and the priest shall dip his finger in the blood and sprinkle it seven times before the Lord in front of the veil. And he shall put some of the blood on the horns of the altar which is in the tent of meeting before the Lord; and the rest of the blood he shall pour out at the base of the altar of burnt offering which is at the door of the tent of meeting. And all its fat he shall take from it and burn upon the altar. Thus shall he do with the bull; as he did with the bull of the sin offering, so shall he do with this; and the priest shall make atonement for them, and they shall be forgiven. And he shall carry forth the bull outside the camp, and burn it as he burned the first bull; it is the sin offering for the assembly.

When a ruler sins, doing unwittingly any one of all the things which the Lord his God has commanded not to be done, and is guilty, if the sin which he has committed is made known to him, he shall bring as his offering a goat, a male without blemish.

The Division of Holy Things after the Wars

Not slaughtering a beast and its dam on one day, Lev. 22:28

And whether the mother is a cow or a ewe, you shall not kill both her and her young in one day.

Covering the blood of a beast which is slaughtered, Lev. 17:13–14

Any man also of the people of Israel, or of the strangers that sojourn among them, who takes in hunting any beast or bird that may be eaten shall pour out its blood and cover it with dust. For the life of every creature is the blood of it; therefore I have said to the people of Israel, You shall not eat the blood of any creature, for the life of every creature is its blood; whoever eats it shall be cut off.

Not eating the sinew of the thigh bone, Gen. 32:32
Therefore to this day the Israelites do not eat the sinew of the hip which is upon the hollow of the thigh, because he touched the hollow of Jacob's thigh on the sinew of the hip.

The shoulders and the maw of a slaughtered beast
go to the priest, Deut. 18:3–4
And this shall be the priests' due from the people, from those offering a sacrifice, whether it be ox or sheep: they shall give to the priest the shoulder and the two cheeks and the stomach. The first fruits of your grain, of your wine and of your oil, and the first of the fleece of your sheep, you shall give him.

Not taking the mother and the eggs of a bird, Deut. 22:6–7
If you chance to come upon a bird's nest, in any tree or on the ground, with young ones or eggs and the mother sitting upon the young or upon the eggs, you shall not take the mother with the young; you shall let the mother go, but the young you may take to yourself; that it may go well with you, and that you may live long.

Valuations for the support of the Temple, Lev. 27:1–8
The Lord said to Moses, "Say to the people of Israel, When a man makes a special vow of persons to the Lord at your valuation, then your valuation of a male from twenty years old up to sixty years old shall be fifty shekels of silver, according to the shekel of the sanctuary. If the person is a female, your valuation shall be thirty shekels. If the person is from five years old up to twenty years old, your valuation shall be for a male twenty shekels, and for a female ten shekels. If the person is from a month old up to five years old, your valuation shall be for a male five shekels of silver, and for a female your valuation shall be three shekels of silver. And if the person is sixty years old and upward, then your valuation for a male shall be fifteen shekels, and for a female ten shekels. And if a man is too poor to pay your valuation, then he shall bring the person before the priest, and the priest shall value him; according to the ability of him who vowed the priest shall value him."

The Mishnah as a Whole: A Topical Outline

The Division of Agriculture

Producing Crops in a State of Holiness

*Kilayim**

I. Plants: Growing together different kinds of plants. 1:1–7:8
   A. Plants which are or are not considered diverse kinds with one another. 1:1–6
   B. Grafting one kind of plant onto another. 1:7–9D
   C. Sowing together different kinds of crops. 1:9E–3:7
      1. Sowing together different kinds of crops in the same space. 1:9E–2:5
      2. Sowing together different kinds of crops in adjacent spaces. 2:6–3:3
      3. Sowing together different kinds of crops in adjacent spaces. Special case: Trailing plants. 3:4–7
   D. Sowing crops among vines. 4:1–7:8
      1. Permitted sowing of crops in a vineyard. 4:1–5:4
      2. Prohibited sowing of crops in a vineyard. 5:5–8
      3. Permitted sowing of crops near vines: Special cases. 6:1–7:2
      4. Prohibited sowing of crops near vines: Special cases. 7:3–8
II. Animals: Mating or yoking together animals of different kinds. 8:1–6
III. Fibers: Mingling wool and linen. 9:1–10

*Shebiit***

I. The sixth year of the sabbatical cycle. 1:1–2:10

* Mandelbaum, "Kilayim."
** Gordon, "Shebiit."

A. Field labor during the sixth year, the effects of which are felt during the sabbatical year. 1:1–2:5
B. Produce grown during the sixth year, which matures during the sabbatical year. 2:6–10
II. The sabbatical year. 3:1–9:9
A. Field labor: Permitted and forbidden labors during the sabbatical year. 3:1–6:6
B. Produce: Permitted and forbidden uses of produce grown during the sabbatical year. 7:1–9:9
III. Appendix: The release of debts at the end of the sabbatical year, and the *prozbul* (i.e., the document which allows a lender to collect a debt even after the sabbatical year). 10:1–9

*Orlah**

I. Definition of what constitutes *orlah* fruit. 1:1–9
A. Fruit tree. 1:1–2
B. Planting. 1:3–5
C. Fruit, status of the parts. 1:7–9
II. Mixtures of forbidden and permitted produce. 1:6, 2:1–17
A. An orchard of permitted and forbidden saplings. 1:6
B. Procedure for neutralizing forbidden produce in a mixture. 2:1–3.
C. Mixture not neutralized. 2:4–7
D. Mixtures of forbidden and permitted leaven in dough. 2:8–9, 11–12
E. Different seasonings combine in a mixture. 2:10
F. Vessels greased with clean, then unclean, oil. 2:13
G. Mixtures with three components. 2:14–17
III. Prohibition of use of *orlah* fruit. 3:1–8
A. Forbiddden dyes and weaving. 3:1–3
B. Fire made with coals from *orlah* fruit. 3:4–5
C. Mixtures of items made with *orlah* fruit. 3:6–8
IV. Cases of doubt. 3:9
A. Fruit in a status of doubt vis-à-vis the *orlah* taboo is prohibited in the Land of Israel, permitted elsewhere.
B. Application of the prohibitions to land outside of the holy Land.

Disposing of Crops in a State of Holiness

*Peah***

I. The corner of the field (Lev. 19:9, 23:22), to be left to the poor. 1:1–4:9

* Essner, "Orlah."
** Compare Albeck, *Zeraim,* p. 37.

A. The definition of the field liable to the tax. 1:1–3:8
B. The definition of the produce liable to the tax. 4:1–2.
C. How the poor acquire the produce. 4:3–9
II. Gleanings, to be left to the poor. 4:10–5:6
A. The definition of gleanings. 4:10–5:3
B. Who is permitted to receive gleanings and transactions therein. 5:4–6
III. The forgotten sheaf, to be left to the poor. 5:7–7:2
A. The definition of the forgotten sheaf. 5:7–7:2
IV. Grape gleanings, to be left to the poor (Lev. 19:10). Definition. 7:3
V. Defective grape cluster, to be left to the poor. Definition. 7:4–8
VI. General rules governing gifts to the poor. Poor man's tithe Deut. 14:28f.). 8:1–9
A. When the poor glean. 8:1
B. The claims of the poor to produce. 8:2–4
C. The minimum requirement of poor man's tithe. 8:5–9

*Demai**

I. Items subject/not subject to tithing as *demai;* the handling and use of *demai* produce. 1:1–4, 2:1
II. Commercial and commensal relations between those who are and are not trustworthy in the matter of tithing. 2:2–5, 3:1–6, 4:1–7
A. Definitions: the trustworthy person and the ḥaber. 2:2–3
B. Situations in which one must/need not tithe produce that leaves one's possession. 2:4–5, 3:1–6
C. Situations in which one believes those who ordinarily are not deemed trustworthy in the matter of tithing; credibility. 4:1–7
III. Details of tithing procedure; exemplifications of the principle that tithes must not be separated for produce liable to tithing from produce which is exempt, etc. 5:1–11
IV. Appendix. 6:1–12, 7:1–8
A. Cases of shared ownership: To what extent must one take responsibility for tithing the portion which one gives to the other fellow? 6:1–12
B. Further details of the tithing procedure; further cases involving the principle that one must not separate tithes for produce which is liable to tithing from produce which is exempt (mixtures). 7:1–8

* Sarason, *Demai,* pp. 11–18.

*Terumot**

  I. How heave offering is separated. 1:1–4:6
    A. Valid and invalid designations of produce to be heave offering. 1:1–3:4
    B. The rite of the separation of heave offering. 3:5–4:6
  II. Heave offering which has been separated but still is in the hands of the householder. 4:7–10:12
    A. Heave offering which falls back into the batch from which it was separated: Neutralization. 4:7–5:9
    B. Consumption of heave offering by nonpriest. 6:1–8:3
    C. Nonpriest's responsibility to watch over heave offering for priest. 8:4–12
    D. Heave offering which is planted. 9:1–7
    E. Heave offering cooked or prepared with unconsecrated produce. 10:1–12
  III. The disposition of heave offering in the hands of the priest. 11:1–10
    A. Proper preparation of food in the status of heave offering. 11:1–3
    B. Refuse from food in the status of heave offering. 11:4–8
    C. Heave offering which has use other than as human food. 11:9–10

*Maaserot***

  I. Conditions under which produce becomes subject to the law. 1:–4
    A. General conditions. 1:1
    B. Specific conditions. 1:2–4
  II. Procedures by which harvested produce is rendered liable to the removal of tithes. 1:5–4:5A
    A. Processing and storage of untithed produce. 1:5–8
    B. Acquisition of produce in four modes. 2:1–3:4
      1. Gifts. 2:1–4
      2. Purchases. 2:5–6
      3. Barter. 2:7–3:3
      4. Lost produce. 3:4
    C. Bringing produce into the courtyard or home. 3:5–10
    D. Preparation of produce for use in a meal. 4:1–5A
  III. Unmet conditions and incomplete procedures: Cases of doubt. 4:5B–5:8
    A. Unmet conditions: Edibility. 4:5B–6

* Peck, "Terumot."
** Jaffee, "Maaserot."

    B. Incomplete procedures: Harvest. 5:1–2
    C. Unmet conditions: Edibility. 5:3–5
    D. Incomplete procedures: Processing. 5:6–7
    E. Unmet conditions. 5:8
        1. The Land of Israel.
        2. Edibility.

*Maaser Sheni**

  I. Eating second tithe in Jerusalem. 1:1–2:4
    A. Other prohibited uses. 1:1–2
    B. Disposition of inedible items. 1:3–7
    C. Proper use of edible items. 2:1–4
  II. Transferring the status of second tithe. 2:5–4:12
    A. From coins to coins. 2:5–9
    B. From coins to produce. 2:10–3:4
    C. From produce to coins. 3:5–4:8
    D. Produce and coins, the status of which is in doubt. 4:9–12
  III. Special topics. 5:1–15
    A. Produce of a planting's fourth year. 5:1–5
    B. The law of removal. 5:6–9
    C. The confession. 5:10–15

*Hallah***

  I. The substrate of dough offering: Definition of bread dough that is liable. 1:1–2:2
    A. Must be capable of being leavened. 1:1–4C
    B. Must be prepared in way in which bread normally is prepared. 1:4D–6F
    C. Owner, not baker, is obliged to separate offering (an insertion placed here because of formal affinities with surrounding material). 1:6G–7
    D. Must be fit for human consumption. 1:8
    E. Appendix: Similar degree of consecration of dough offering and heave offering. 1:9
    D. Two unusual cases. 2:1–2
  II. The process of separating dough offering. 2:3–9
    A. Unusual cases. 2:3–5
    B. Measurements. 2:6–7
    C. A further case concerning uncleanness. 2:9
  III. The point at which liability to dough offering takes effect. 3:1–6
  IV. Liability to dough offering of various mixtures. 3:7–4:6
  V. Liability of dough outside Israel. 4:7–11

* Haas, "Maaser Sheni."
** Havivi, "Hallah."

*Bikkurim**

I. The obligation to bring first fruits and to make the stated recitation. 1:1–11
   A. Those who do not bring first fruits at all. 1:1–3
   B. Those who bring first fruits but do not make the recitation. 1:4–9
   C. Those who bring and recite. 1:10–11
II. Comparisons between various agricultural gifts and tithes. Human blood and that of a domesticated animal or reptile. A *koy* and a wild or a domesticated animal. 2:1–11
   A. A comparison of the laws governing first fruits, heave offering, and second tithe. 2:1–4
   B. Ways in which heave offering of the tithe is like first fruits or heave offering. Ways in which the citron tree is like a tree or a vegetable. 2:5–6
   C. Other comparisons. 2:7–11
III. The rules of setting first fruits apart and bringing them to Jerusalem. A narrative of the rite. 3:1–12
   A. Setting first fruits apart. 3:1
   B. Bringing first fruits to Jerusalem. 3:2–4
   C. Presenting the first fruits to the priest. 3:5–8
   D. Miscellanies. 3:9–12

*Berakhot***

I. Reciting the *Shema'*. 1:1–3:8
   A. The time for saying the *Shema'*, evening and morning. 1:1–3
   B. The liturgy of saying the *Shema'* and the text of the *Shema'* itself. 1:4–2:3
   C. Special cases in which the requirement to say the *Shema'* is suspended or does not apply. 2:4–3:8
II. Reciting the prayer. 4:1–5:5
   A. The time for reciting the prayer. 4:1–2
   B. The liturgy of the prayer. 4:3–4
   C. Special cases in which the requirement to say the prayer is suspended or does not apply. 4:5–5:1
   D. Additions to the prayer. 5:2–5
III. Blessings for food and for meals. 6:1–8:8
   A. Categories of foods and saying a blessing before eating them. 6:1–7
   B. The grace after meals and its protocol. 6:8–7:5
   C. Special rules regarding blessings at meals and other rites connected with meals. 8:1–8

* Rubenstein, "Bikkurim."
** Cf. Zahavy, "Berakhot."

IV. Other kinds of blessings and private prayers. 9:1–5

The Division of Appointed Times

Appointed Times and the Village

Shabbat

I. General principles of Sabbath observance. 1:1–11
II. Preparing for the Sabbath: Light, food, clothing. 2:1–6:11
   A. The Sabbath lamp. 2:1–7
   B. Food for the Sabbath. 3:1–4:2
   C. Ornaments for animals, clothing for persons, on the Sabbath. 5:1–6:10
III. Prohibited acts of labor on the Sabbath. 7:1–15:3
   A. Generalizations: Prohibited acts of labor. 7:1–2
   B. Transporting an object from one domain to another. 7:3–9:7
   C. Fundamental principles on carrying from one domain to another. 10:1–5(+ 6)
   D. Transporting an object. Throwing something from one domain to another. 11:1–6
   E. Other prohibited acts of labor. 12:1–14:2
   F. Healing on the Sabbath. 14:3–4
   G. Knot tying. Clothing and beds. 15:1–3
IV. Other Sabbath taboos. 16:1–24:5
   A. Saving objects from a fire on the Sabbath. The taboo against using or handling fire. 16:1–8
   B. Handling diverse objects in private domain, so long as the purpose for which the objects is handled is allowed on the Sabbath. 17:1–18:3
   C. Circumcision on the Sabbath. 19:1–6
   D. Preparing food for humans and beasts. Permitted procedures. 20:1–22:6
   E. Seemly behavior on the Sabbath. Permitted and prohibited deeds. 23:1–24:5

Erubin

I. The delineation of a limited domain. 1:1–2:5
   A. Forming an alleyway into a single domain. 1:1–7
   B. Forming an area occupied by a caravan at rest for the Sabbath into a single domain. 1:8–10
   C. A well in public domain. 2:1–4
   D. A large field. 2:5
II. The *erub* and the Sabbath limit of a town. 3:1–5:9

    A. The *erub:* A symbolic meal for establishing joint ownership of a courtyard or for establishing symbolic residence for purposes of legitimate travel on the Sabbath. 3:1–9

    B. The *erub* and violating the Sabbath limit. 4:1–11

    C. Defining the Sabbath limit of a town. 5:1–9

III. The *erub* and commingling ownership of a courtyard or alleyway. 6:1–9:4

    A. The *erub* and the courtyard. 6:1–10

    B. Areas which may be deemed either distinct from one another or as a commingled domain, so that residents have the choice of preparing a joint *erub* or two separate ones. 7:1–5

    C. The *shittuf* (also a symbolic joint meal) and the alleyway. 7:6–8:2

    D. Neglecting the *erub* for a courtyard and the consequences thereof. 8:3–5

    E. An *erub* for more than one courtyard. 8:6–8:11

    F. An *erub* and the area of roofs. 9:1–4

IV. The public domain in general. 10:1–10(+ 11–15)

Besah

    I. The Houses and other authorities. 1:1–3:1

    II. Designating food before the festival for use on the festival. 3:2–8

    III. Doing actions connected with preparing food on a festival day in a manner different from ordinary days. Other restrictions. 4:1–5:2

    IV. Appendix. 5:3–7

Moed Qatan

    I. Labor on the intermediate days of a festival. 1:1–10, 2:1–3

    A. In the fields. 1:1–4

    B. Miscellanies. 1:5–7

    C. Cases of emergency and grievous loss of property. 2:1–3

    II. Commerce on the intermediate days of a festival. 2:3–3:4

    III. Burial of the dead and mourning on the intermediate days of a festival. 3:5–9

Appointed Times and the Cult

Pesahim

    I. Preparation for Passover. 1:1–4:8

    A. Removing leaven. 1:1–2:4

    B. Removing and avoiding what ferments. 2:5–3:8

C. Other requirements for 14 Nissan. 4:1–8
II. The Passover offering on the night of 14 Nissan. Slaying and eating it. 5:1–9:11
    A. General rules on slaughtering the Passover offering. 5:1–10
    B. Special rules for the Sabbath which coincides with 14 Nissan. 6:1–6
    C. Roasting and eating the Passover offerings. 7:1–4
    D. Special rules for the Passover offering. 7:5–9:5
      1. Uncleanness. 7:5–10
      2. Not breaking the bone of the Passover offerings. 7:11–12
      3. Eating the offering in a group. 7:13–8:8
      4. The second Passover. 9:1–5
    E. A special case: An animal designated for use for a Passover offering which was lost, or for which a substitute was designated, and how one deals with such cases. 9:6–11
III. The Passover *seder*. 10:1–9

Sheqalim

I. Collecting the *sheqel*. 1:1–2:5
    A. Imposing the obligation to pay. 1:1–7
    B. Transporting the *sheqel*. Sacrilege. 2:1–5
II. Using the *sheqel* for Temple offerings for the altar. 3:1–4:9
    A. Taking up the *sheqel* for the public offerings. 3:1–4
    B. Disposing of the *sheqel* for various offerings. 4:1–9
III. The Temple administration and its procedures. 5:1–8:8
    A. The administration. 5:1–2
    B. Procedures for selling drink offerings. 5:3–6
    C. Collecting other funds in the Temple. 5:6–8:8
    D. Disposing of money and objects found in the Temple and in Jerusalem. 7:1–8:3
    E. Miscellanies. 8:4–8

Yoma

I. The conduct of the Temple rites on the Day of Atonement. 1:1–7:5
    A. Preparing the high priest for the Day of Atonement. 1:1–7
    B. Clearing the ashes off the altar. 1:8–2:6
    C. The narrative resumes: The daily whole offering on the Day of Atonement. 2:5–3:4
    D. The narrative continues: The high priest's personal offering for the Day of Atonement. 3:6–8
    E. The narrative continues: The two goats and other offerings on the Day of Atonement. 3:9–5:7
    F. The scapegoat and its rule. 6:1–8

G. The rite concludes with Torah reading and prayer. 7:1–5
II. The laws of the Day of Atonement. 8:1–7
    A. Not eating, not drinking. 8:1–7
    B. Atonement. 8:8–9

Sukkah

I. Objects used in celebrating the Festival. 1:1–3:15
    A. The *sukkah* and its roof. 1:1–2:3
    B. Dwelling in the *sukkah*. 2:4–9
    C. The *lulab* and the *etrog*. 3:1–15
II. The rites and offerings of the Festival. 4:1–5:8
    A. The Festival rites carried out on the successive festival days. 4:1–5:4
    B. The offerings on the altar. 5:5–8

Rosh Hashshanah

I. The designation of the new month through the year. 1:1–3:1
    A. Prologue: The four new years. 1:1–2
    B. The new moon. Receiving testimony of the appearance of the new month. 1:3–3:1
II. The *shofar*. 3:2–4:9
    A. Rules of the *shofar*. 3:2–4:4
    B. The liturgy of the New Year. 4:5–6
    C. Sounding the *shofar* in the liturgy. 4:7–9

Taanit

I. Fasts called in order to bring rain. 1:1–2:10, 3:1–9
    A. The sequence of fasts for rain. 1:1–7
    B. The liturgy of the community for a fast day. 2:1–5
    C. Other rules about public fasts. 2:8–10
    D. Other uses of the *shofar* as an alarm, besides for fasts. 3:1–9
II. The delegation (*ma'amad*): Israelite participation in the cult. Various special occasions. 4:1–8
    A. The delegation. 4:1–4
    B. Other occasions. 4:5
    C. Sad days. 4:6–8

Megillah

I. The rules of reading the Scroll of Esther. 1:1–2:6
II. The laws of synagogue property and liturgy. 3:1–4:9
    A. Disposition of synagogue property. 3:1–3
    B. Rules for reading the Scriptures in synagogue worship. 4:1–5
    C. Conduct in the synagogue: Reading the Torah, blessing the congregation, leading the prayers. 4:6–8

Hagigah

I. The appearance offering, festal offering, and peace offering of
   rejoicing. 1:1–2:4
   A. Liability to these offerings. The cost of them. 1:1–2:1
   B. The festal offering and the Sabbath. 2:2–4
II. The rules of uncleanness as they affect ordinary folk and holy
    things of the cult on festivals. 2:5–3:8
    A. Gradations of strictness of rules of uncleanness, with the
       strictest rules affecting the cult. 2:5–3:3
    B. Holy things and the festival. 3:4–8

The Division of Women

The Beginning of Marriage

Qiddushin

I. Betrothals. 1:1–3:11
   A. Rules of acquisition. 1:1–10
   B. Procedures of betrothal: Agency, value, stipulations.
      2:1–5
   C. Impaired betrothal. 2:6–3:1
   D. Stipulations. 3:2–6
   E. Doubts. 3:7–11
II. Castes for the purposes of marriage. 3:12–4:11
    A. The status of the offspring of impaired marriages.
       3:12–13
    B. Castes and intermarriage. 4:1–7
    C. Miscellany. 4:8–11
III. Homiletical conclusion. 4:12–14

Ketubot

I. Formation of the marriage: The material rights of the
   parties to the marital union. 1:1–5:1
   A. The wife. 1:1–2:10
      1. The virgin and her marriage contract. 1:1–4
      2. Conflicting claims for a marriage contract for a vir-
         gin. 1:5–2:3
      3. Miscellanies on testimony. 2:3–2:10
   B. The father and the husband (cf. Deut. 22:15–29). 3:1–5:1
      1. The fine paid to the father (Deut. 21:22) for rape or
         seduction. 3:1–4:1
      2. The father. 4:2(+ 3)

      3. The father and the husband. 4:4–6

      4. The husband. 4:7–5:1

II. The duration of the marriage: Reciprocal responsibilities and rights of husband and wife. 5:2–9:1

  A. The wife's duties to the husband. 5:2–5

  B. The husband's marital rights and duties to the wife. 5:6–6:1

  C. The dowry. 6:2–7

  D. The marital rights and duties of the wife. 7:1–10

  E. The property rights of the wife. 8:1–9:1

III. Cessation of the marriage: the collection of the marriage contract. 9:2–12:4(+ 13:1–9)

  A. Imposing an oath. 9:2–9

  B. Multiple claims on an estate. 10:1–6

  C. Support of the widow. 11:1–5

  D. Rights to and collection of a marriage contract: Special cases. 11:6–12:4

  E. Two casebooks. 13:1–9

IV. Conclusion. 13:10–11

The Duration of a Marriage

Nedarim

I. The language of vows. 1:1–3:11

  A. Euphemisms. 1:1–2:5

  B. Language of no effect. 3:1–4(+ 5)

  C. Language of limited effect. 3:6–11

II. The binding effects of vows. 4:1–8:6

  A. Vows not to derive benefit. 4:1–5:6

  B. Vows not to eat certain food. 6:1–7:2

  C. Vows not to use certain objects. 7:3–5

  D. The temporal limitation in vows. 7:6–8:6

III. The absolution of vows. 8:6–11:12

  A. Grounds for the absolution of vows. 8:6–9:10

  B. The annulment of the vows of a daughter. 10:1–4

  C. The annulment of the vows of a wife. 10:5–8

  D. The husband's power to annul the wife's vows: Special rules. 11:1–8

  E. Vows of a woman not subject to abrogation. 11:9–10

  F. Redactional conclusion. 11:12

Nazir

I. Becoming a Nazirite: The vow. 1:1–4:3

  A. The language of the vow to be a Nazirite. 1:1–7

B. Stipulations and the Nazirite vow. 2:1–10
C. The duration of the vow. 3:1–7
D. Annulling the vow. 4:1–3
II. The Nazirite's offerings. 4:4–5:7
    A. Designation and disposition of the offerings. 4:4–5:4
    B. Concluding conundrum. 5:5–7
III. Restrictions on the Nazirite. 6:1–8:2(+ 9:1–5)
    A. The grape. 6:1–4
    B. Transition. 6:5
    C. Cutting hair. 6:6–11
    D. Corpse uncleanness. 7:1–4
    E. Doubt in the case of the Nazir. 8:1–9:2(+ 3–5)

Sotah

I. Invoking the ordeal. 1:1–3
II. Narrative of the ordeal. 1:4–3:5(+ 3:6–8)
III. Rules of the ordeal. 4:1–6:4
    A. Exemptions and applicability. 4:1–5:1(+ 2–5)
    B. Testimony and exemptions from the ordeal. 6:1–4
IV. Rites conducted in Hebrew. 7:1–9:15
    A. A catalogue. 7:1–8
    B. The anointed for battle and the draft exemptions (cf. Deut. 20:1–9). 8:1–7
    C. The rite of the heifer (cf. Deut. 21:1–9). 9:1–9(+ 10–15)

The End of a Marriage

Yebamot

I. Establishing the marital bond. 1:1–5:6
    A. Neither levirate marriage nor *ḥaliṣah:* Consanguinity. 1:1–2:10
    B. *Ḥaliṣah* but no levirate marriage. 3:1–3:10
    C. Levirate marriage. 4:1–4:13
    D. Reprise: Marriage, divorce, levirate marriage. *Ḥaliṣah.* 5:1–6
II. The special marital bond: Marriage into the priesthood. 6:1–9:6
    A. When a woman may eat heave offering. 6:1–6
    B. Who may eat heave offering. 7:1–8:2
    C. Miscellany. 8:3
    D. The eunuch. 8:4–6
    E. Concluding construction for units I and II. 9:1–6
III. Severing the marital bond. 10:1–16:7
    A. Marital ties subject to doubt. 10:1–11:7
    B. Severing the marital bond of the deceased childless bro-

ther's widow. The rite of *haliṣah* and how it is performed.
12:1–6
C. Severing the marital bond of the minor. Exercising the right
of refusal. 13:1–13
D. The infirm marital bond of the deaf mute. 14:1–4
E. Severing the marital bond through the death of the husband.
15:1–16:7
1. The woman's testimony. 15:1–16:2
2. Identifying a corpse. 16:3–7

Gittin

I. Delivering and preparing a writ of divorce. 1:1–3:8
A. Delivering a writ of divorce. 1:1–2:1
B. Preparing a writ of divorce. 2:2–3:3
C. Confirming the prevailing supposition. 3:4–8
II. Fifteen rulings made for the good order of the world. 4:1–5:9
III. The law of agency in writs of divorce. 6:1–7:2
A. Receiving the writ of divorce. 6:1–4
B. Appointing agents to prepare and deliver a writ of divorce.
6:5–7:2
IV. Stipulations in writs of divorce. 7:3–7:9
V. Invalid writs of divorce. 8:1–9:10
A. Improper delivery. 8:4–10
B. Improper preparation of the writ. 8:4–10
C. Improper stipulations. 9:1–2
D. Improper witnesses. 9:4–9:8
E. Conclusion. 9:9–10

The Division of Women

Civil Law

Baba Qamma

I. Damages done by chattels. 1:1–6:6
A. The fundamental rules of assessing damages when the cause
is one's property, animate and inanimate. The ox. 1:1–2:6
B. Damages done in the public domain. 3:1–7
C. Exercises and illustrations on the ox. 3:8–4:4
D. The ransom and the death penalty for the ox. 4:5–5:4
E. Damages done by the pit (M. 1:1). 5:5–7
F. Crop-destroying beast (M. 1:1). 6:1–3
G. Damages done by fire (M. 1:1). 6:4–6
II. Damages done by persons. Theft. 7:1–10:10

A. Penalties for the theft of an ox or a sheep (cf. Ex. 22:1–4). 7:1–7
B. Penalties for assault. 8:1–7
C. Penalties for damages to property. Restoring what is stolen. 9:1–10:10

Baba Mesia

III. The disposition of other people's possessions. 1:1–3:12
    A. Conflicting claims on lost objects. 1:1–4
    B. Returning an object to the original owner. 1:5–2:1
    C. Rules of bailment in cases of damages. 3:1–12
IV. Illicit commercial transactions. 4:1–5:11
    A. Overcharge and misrepresentation. 4:1–12
    B. Usury. 5:1–11
 V. Licit transactions. B.M. 6:1–10:6; B.B. 1:1–7:4
    A. Hiring workers. Rentals and bailments. 6:1–8:3
        1. The mutual obligations of worker and employer. 6:1–2
        2. Rentals. 6:3–5
        3. Bailments under normal circumstances. 6:6–8
        4. The mutual obligations of worker and employer. 7:1–7
        5. Bailments. 7:8–8:3
    B. Real estate. B.M. 8:4–10:6; B.B. 1:1–5:5
        1. Prologue. 8:4–5
        2. Landlord-tenant relationships. 8:6–9
        3. The landlord's relationships with a tenant farmer and sharecropper. 9:1–10
        4. Miscellanies: Paying laborers promptly. Taking a pledge. 9:11–13

Baba Batra

        5. Joint holders of a common property. B.M. 10:1–6; B.B. 1:1–6
        6. Not infringing the property rights of others. 2:1–4
        7. Establishing title to a field through usucaption. 3:1–8
        8. Transferring real estate (and movables) through sale. 4:1–5:5
    C. Commercial dealings. 5:6–7:4
        1. Conditions of irrevocable transfer of goods. 5:6–11
        2. Unstated stipulations in commercial transactions. 6:1–7:4
VI. Inheritances and wills. Other commercial and legal documents. 8:1–10:8
    A. Inheritance. 8:1–9:10

B. The preparation and confirmation of commercial documents, e.g., writs of debt. 10:1–6
C. Concluding miscellanies. 10:7–8

Abodah Zarah

I. Commercial relationships with gentiles. 1:1–2:7
  A. Festivals and fairs. 1:1–4
  B. Objects prohibited even in commerce with gentiles. 1:5–2:2
  C. Objects prohibited for use but permitted in commerce with gentiles. 2:3–7
II. Idols. 3:1–4:7
  A. General principles. 3:1–6
  B. The *asherah*. 3:7–10
  C. The *Merkolis*. 4:1–2
  D. Nullifying an idol. 4:3–7
III. Libation wine. 4:8–5:12

The Courts and Administration

Sanhedrin

I. The court system. 1:1–5:5
  A. Various kinds of courts and their jurisdiction: Civil, criminal, and political. 1:1–6
  B. Heads of the Israelite nation and court system. High priest and king. 2:1–5
  C. Procedures of the court system. 3:1–5:5
    1. Commercial cases. 3:1–8
    2. Capital cases. 4:1–5:5
II. The death penalty. 6:1–11:6
  A. Stoning. 6:1–6
  B. Four modes of execution and how they are administered. 7:1–3
  C. Those put to death by stoning. 7:4–8:7
  D. Those put to death by burning or decapitation. 9:1–10:6
  E. Those put to death through strangulation. 11:1–6

Makkot

III. Perjury and its penalties. 1:1–10
IV. The penalty of exile (banishment). 2:1–8
  A. Those subjected to banishment. 2:1–3
  B. The cities of banishment. 2:4–8
V. The penalty of flogging. 3:1–14
  A. Those subjected to flogging. 3:1–9

B. The procedure of flogging. 3:10–14
VI. Concluding homilies. 3:15–16

Shebuot

I. Uncleanness of the cult and its holy things and the guilt offering.
1:1–2:5
A. General introduction. 1:1
B. Uncleanness and the cult. 1:2–2:5
II. Oaths. 3:1–8:6
A. Oaths in general. 3:1–6
B. The rash oath. The vain oath. 3:7–11
C. The oath of testimony. 4:1–13
D. The oath of bailment. 5:1–5
E. The oath imposed by judges. 6:1–7:8
F. Oaths and bailments. Concluding exercise. 8:1–6

Horayot

I. The offering brought because of an erroneous decision by a
court. 1:1–5
II. The offering brought by the high priest who has unwittingly
done what is contrary to the commandments of the Torah. The
ruler. 2:1–5
III. The individual, anointed priest, and community. 2:5–3:8

The Division of Holy Things

Rules of the Cult

Zebahim

I. Improper intention and invalidating the act of sacrifice. 1:1–4:6
II. The rules for sacrifice of animals and fowl. 5:1–7:6
A. Animals. 5:1–6:1
B. Fowl. 6:2–7:6
III. Rules of the altar. 8:1–12:4
A. Rules for disposing of sacrificial portions or blood which
derive from diverse sacrifices and have been confused.
8:1–12
B. The altar sanctifies what is appropriate to it. 9:1–7
C. Precedence in use of the altar. 10:1–7+8
D. Blood of a sin offering which spurts onto a garment (Exposi-
tion of Lev. 6:27–28). 11:1–8
E. The division of the meat and hides of sacrificial animals

among the eligible priests. 12:1–4(+ 5–6)
IV. The proper location of the altar and the act of sacrifice. 13:1–14:10

Menahot

I. Reprise for meal offerings of the principles of animal offerings of M. Zebahim. Improper intention and invalidating the meal offerings. 1:1–4:5
   A. Reprise of Zebahim. 1:1–3:1
   B. Other rules of invalidation. 3:2–4:5
II. The proper preparation of meal offerings. 5:1–9:9
   A. General rules. 5:1–6:7
   B. The meal offering accompanying the thank offering. 7:1–6
   C. Sources of flour, oil, and wine used for the offering. 8:1–7
   D. Measuring the materials used for the offering. 9:1–5
   E. Conclusion. General rules. 9:6–9
III. Special meal offerings. 10:1–11:9
   A. The *'omer*. 10:1–9
   B. The two loaves of Pentecost and the show bread. 11:1–9
IV. Vows in connection with meal offerings. 12:1–13:10

Hullin

I. Rules of slaughtering unconsecrated animals for use at home or in the Temple. 1:1–4:7
   A. General rules. 1:1–4(+ 5–7)
   B. Specific regulations. *Terefah* rules. 2:1–6
   C. Slaughter and illicit sacrifice. 2:7–10
   D. *Terefah* and valid carcasses. 3:1–7
   E. The effect of valid slaughter on the parts of a beast's body, e.g., on the foetus. 4:1–7
II. Other rules on the preparation of food, principally for use at home. 5:1–12:5
   A. *It and its young* (Lev. 22:28). 5:1–5
   B. The requirement to cover up the blood (Lev. 17:13–14) 6:1–7
   C. The prohibition of the sciatic nerve (Gen. 32:32). 7:1–6
   D. Milk and meat (Ex. 23:19, 34:26; Deut. 12:21). 8:1–6
   E. Connection. 9:1–8
   F. The shoulder, two cheeks, and maw, which are given to the priest (Deut. 18:4). 10:1–4
   G. First fleece goes to the priest (Deut. 18:4). 11:1–2
   H. The law of letting the dam go from the nest when taking the young (Deut. 22:6–7) 12:1–5

Keritot

    I. The sin offering (Lev. 5:17–19). 1:1–2:2
   II. A single sin offering and multiple sins. 2:3–3:10
  III. The suspensive guilt offering. 4:1–6:8

Tamid

     I. The priests arise in the morning. Clearing the altar of ashes. 1:1–4, 2:1–5
    II. Selecting the lamb for the daily burnt offering. 3:1–5
   III. Clearing the ashes. 3:6–9
   IV. Slaughtering the lamb. 4:1–3
    V. The priests bless the congregation. The limbs are brought to the altar. 5:1–4
   VI. Clearing the ashes. 5:5–6:2(+ 3)
  VII. Conclusion of rite. The limbs are tossed on the altar.

Qinnim

These exercises are summarized, not outlined, as follows:

1:1   The blood of the sin offering of fowl is sprinkled below, that of beast, above, the red line. The blood of burnt offering of fowl is sprinkled above, of beast, below. The proper rite of a pair of birds: a pair brought in fulfillment of an obligation is deemed to include one as a sin offering and one as a burnt offering; a pair brought as a vow or freewill offering is deemed to be only burnt offerings.

1:2   A sin offering which was confused with a burnt offering or a burnt offering with a sin offering. A bird designated as a sin offering confused with birds which were not designated but brought in fulfillment of an obligation.

1:3   Under what circumstances [do the rules of 1:1–2 apply]? In the case of confusion of an offering brought in fulfillment of an obligation with one designated as a freewill offering.

1:4   Continuation of 1:3

2:1   An unassigned pair of birds from which one flew off into the air—let the owner purchase a mate for the second.

2:2   Continuation of 2:1

2:3   Continuation of 2:1

2:4   A pair of birds which had not been designated and a pair of birds which had been designated—a bird flew from one to the other. Continuation of 2:1

2:5   A pair of birds for a sin offering at one side, a pair for a burnt offering at the other, and an unassigned pair in the middle—if one of the unassigned ones flew from the middle to the sides, it has caused no loss. Completion of 2:4

3:1–2 Under what circumstances [do the rules of 1:1–2 apply]? In the case of a priest who makes an inquiry. But if he does not, so that a *post facto* decision is required—1:3 now cited and spelled out.

3:3–5 1:2 cited and spelled out, once more for a *post facto* decision.

3:6 A woman who said, "Lo, I pledge myself to bring a pair of birds if I bear a male child," if she has a boy, brings two pairs, one for the vow, one for the obligation. Reconsideration of the problem of 2:5J–N.

Rules for Providing Animals for Daily Sacrifices
and for the Upkeep of the Altar and Temple Buildings
and Support of the Priestly Staff

Bekhorot

   I. The firstborn of animals. General rules. 1:1–4:2
      A. The firstborn of the ass. 1:1–7
      B. The firstborn of the cow. Reprise of M. Bekh. 1. 2:1–8
      C. Further matters of doubt. 2:9–3:2
      D. Not shearing the firstling (Deut. 15:19). 3:3–4
      E. The requirement to tend to the firstling before handing it over to the priest. 4:1–2
  II. Slaughtering a firstling by reason of blemishes. 4:3–6:12
      A. Examining a firstling to see whether or not it is blemished. 4:3–10
      B. Further rules of slaughtering the firstling. 5:1–6
      C. Blemishes. 6:1–7:7
         1. In animals. 6:1–6:12
         2. In priests. 7:1–7
 III. Firstborn of man. 8:1–9
  IV. The tithe of cattle. 9:1–8

Arakhin

   I. Valuations and vows for the benefit of the Temple. (Lev. 27: 1–8). 1:1–6:5
      A. Basic rules. 1:1–4
      B. Two formal constructions. 2:1–6, 3:1–5
      C. Ability to pay in vows. 4:1–4
      D. The difference between pledging a valuation and vowing the worth, or price, of someone or something. 5:1–5
      E. Collecting valuations. 5:6–6:5
  II. The dedication and redemption of a field which is received as

an inheritance (Lev. 27:16–25). 7:1–8:3
III. The devoted thing [*herem*] (Lev. 27:28–29). 8:4–7
IV. The sale and redemption of a field received as an inheritance and of a dwelling house in a walled city (Lev. 25:25–34). 9:1–8

Temurah

I. The rules of substitution: Who may do so, and to what (Lev. 27:14). 1:1–2:3
   A. Liability to the law of substitution. 1:1–2
   B. Exemptions from the law of substitution. 1:3–6
   C. Formal appendix. 2:1–3
II. The status of the offspring of substitutes. 3:1–4:1(+ 2–4)
   A. Diverse sacrifices and their substitutes and offspring. 3:1–5
   B. Appendix on the supererogatory sin offering. 4:1–4
II. The language used in effecting an act of substitution. 5:5–6 (+ 1–4)
   A. Formal prologue. 5:1–4
   B. The effective formula. 5:5–6
IV. Formal appendix. 6:1–7:6

Meilah

I. Sacrilege of sacrifices in particular (Lev. 5:15–16). 1:1–3:8
   A. When the laws of sacrilege apply to a sacrifice. 1:1–4
   B. Stages in the status of an offering. 2:1–9
   C. Cultic property which is not subject to sacrilege but which also is not to be used for noncultic purposes. 3:1–8
II. Sacrilege of Temple property in general. 4:1–6:6
   A. Sacrilege has been committed only when the value of a *perutah* of Temple property has been used for secular purposes. The joining together of diverse objects for the purpose of reaching the *perutah*'s value. 4:1–2(+ 3–6)
   B. Sacrilege is defined by the one who does it, or by the thing to which it is done. 5:1–2
   C. Sacrilege effects the secularization of sacred property. 5:3–5
   D. Agency in effecting an act of sacrilege. 6:1–5(+ 6)

Middot

I. Watch posts and gates. 1:1–9
II. The layout of the Temple mount. 2:1–6
III. The altar and porch. 3:1–8
IV. The sanctuary and courtyard. 4:1–7, 5:1–4

The Division of Purities

Sources of Uncleanness

Ohalot

   I. Proems. 1:1–8

  II. Modes of imparting uncleanness, sources of uncleanness. 2:1–3:5

     A. Basic definitions. 2:1–5

     B. Dividing sources of uncleanness. 2:6–3:5

 III. Tents. 3:6–16:2E

     A. An opening of a squared handbreadth suffices for the passage of uncleanness. 3:6–7

     B. The subdivisions of a tent, if of requisite space, constitute tents on their own. 4:1–3, 5:1–4

     C. Utensils afford protection with the walls of tents. 5:5–7

     D. Men and utensils serve as tents to contaminate but not to afford protection. 6:1–2

     E. Walls serving more than one house and how they are subdivided. 6:3–7:2

     F. Miscellanies. 7:3–6

     G. Substances which interpose and bring uncleanness. 8:1–6

     H. Rules of interposition and overshadowing. 9:1–12:8

        1. The hive. 9:1–14

        2. Further cases. 9:15–16

        3. The hatchway. 10:1–7

        4. Other problems. 11:1–12:8

     I. Apertures through which corpse uncleanness exudes. 13:1–6

     J. Projections which serve to overshadow. 14:1–7

     K. Miscellanies and conclusion. 15:1–16:2E

 IV. Sources of uncleanness analogous to corpse matter. 16:2F–18:10

Negaim (Lev. 13–14)

   I. The proem. 1:1–6

  II. Plagues in general. Miscellanies. 2:1–5, 3:1–2

 III. The prologue. 3:3–8

 IV. The bright spot. 4:1–8:10

     A. Tokens of uncleanness in the bright spot. 4:1–3

     B. Miscellanies on white hair. 4:4

     C. Fifteen problems involving the bright spot. 4:4–4:11

     D. Doubts in matters of plagues are resolved in favor of cleanness. 5:1–5

E. Places on the human being which are not susceptible to uncleanness. 6:7–7:2
   1. Because of the appearance of a bright spot containing quick flesh.
   2. Because of the appearance of a bright spot.
   3. Bright spots which are not susceptible to uncleanness no matter where they occur.
F. Removing the symptoms of uncleanness. 7:3–5
G. Breaking forth over the entire body. 8:1–10
V. The boil and the burning. 9:1–3
VI. Scalls. 10:1–9
VII. The baldspot on forehead and temple. 10:10
VIII. Garments. 11:1–12
IX. Houses. 12:1–7, 13:1–13
X. Process of purification of the leper. 14:1–13

Niddah

I. Retroactive contamination. 1:1–2:4
II. Unclean excretions. 2:5–5:2
   A. The unclean blood. 2:5–7
   B. Status of abortions as to uncleanness. 3:1–7
   C. Samaritan, Sadducees, and gentile women. 4:1–3
   D. Status of blood produced in labor. 4:4–6
   E. Status of blood in *zibah* period. 4:7
   F. Blood produced in birth by Caesarean section. 5:1A–D
   G. Point at which unclean fluid imparts uncleanness. 5:11E–G (+ 5:2)
III. Rules applicable at various ages (and attached apophthegmatic construction). 5:3–6:12
IV. Doubts in connection with unclean excretions. 6:13–9:10
   A. Bloodstains and other matters of doubt. 6:13–14
   B. Blood of menstruating woman, flesh of corpse, etc. 7:1
   C. Doubts about creeping thing, bloodstain. 7:2
   D. Bloodstains (= doubtfully unclean blood) of Israelites, gentiles, and Samaritans. 7:3–5
   E. Doubts about bloodstain and drops of blood. 8:1–9:7
   F. The fixed period. 9:8–10
V. Concluding miscellanies (Houses). 9:11–10:8
   A. Nature of female excretions. 9:11–10:1
   B. Doubts of cleanness re failure to examine. 10:2–3
   C. Uncleanness of *zab*, menstruating woman. 10:4–5
   D. Status of woman in period of purifying after childbirth. 10:6–7

    E. She who sees blood on eleventh day of *zibah* period. 10:8

Makhshirin

  I. Intention: Divisible or indivisible. 1:1–6
  II. Water capable of imparting susceptibility mixed with water incapable of imparting susceptibility. 2:1–3(+ 2:4–11)
  III. Absorption of water. 3:1–3
  IV. Water used for one purpose—status as to a secondary purpose. 3:4–5:8
  V. Stream as connector. 5:9–11I
  VI. Liquids not used intentionally are insusceptible. 5:11J–M, 6:1–3
  VII. Liquids which impart susceptibility to uncleanness. 6:4–8

Zabim

  I. Becoming a *zab*. 1:1–6, 2:1–3
  II. Transferring the *zab's* uncleanness. 2:4, 3:1–3, 5:1–12
    A. Pressure. 2:4, 3:1–3
    B. Generalizations. 5:1–12

Tebul Yom

  I. Connection in the case of the *tebul yom*. 1:1–3:5
    A. The principle. 1:1–5
    B. Liquids and connection in the case of the *tebul yom*. 2:1–8
    C. Solid food and connection in the case of the *tebul yom*. 3:1–5
  II. The uncleanness of the *tebul yom*. 3:6, 4:1–4(+ 4:5–7)

Loci of Uncleanness

Kelim

  I. Proems. 1:1–9
  II. Earthenware utensils. 2:1–10:8
    A. Prologue. 2:1
    B. Susceptibility and insusceptibility of earthenware utensils. 2:2–3:4
    C. Connection and materials used for repairing clay utensils. 3:5–4:4
    D. Baking ovens. 5:1–7:6
    E. Contamination of baking ovens. 8:1–9:7
    F. The tightly stopped up cover in the tent of the corpse. 10:1–8
  III. Metal utensils. 11:1–14:8
  IV. Other materials (wood, leather, etc.). 15:1–18:2
    A. Proem. 15:1A–E

  B. Wooden utensils and their susceptibility. 15:1F–16:3
  C. Leather utensils. 16:4–8
  D. The measure of breakage to render an object insusceptible.
   17:1–12
  E. General traits of utensils as to susceptibility: Materials,
   receptacles. Miscellanies. 17:13–18:3E
 V. The wooden bed and its ropes. 18:3F–19:6
 VI. Susceptibility of utensils to various kinds of uncleanness, and
  the end of susceptibility. Connection. 19:7–24:17
  A. Pressure uncleanness (*midras*) and corpse uncleanness.
   19:7–20:2
  B. Connection. 20:3
  C. Changes in the status as to susceptibility of diverse objects.
   20:4–7
  D. Connection. 21:1–3
  E. Susceptibility to *midras* or corpse uncleanness of tables and
   chairs and other objects. 22:1–23:5
  F. Susceptibility to *midras* and corpse uncleanness. 24:1–17
 VII. Principle of susceptibility: The parts of an object. 25:1–9
 VIII. Leather objects. 26:1–9
 IX. Woven materials and fabrics. 27:1–28:10
 X. Connectors. 29:1–8
 XI. Glass utensils. 30:1–4

Tohorot

 I. Proems. 1:1–8
 II. Susceptibility to uncleanness of holy things, heave offering,
  and unconsecrated food. 1:9, 2:1–8, 3:1–4
 III. Doubts in matters of uncleanness. 3:5–8, 4:1–13, 5:1–9, 6:1–9
 IV. The observant (*ḥaber*) and the nonobservant (*'am ha'ares*) Is-
  raelite. 7:1–9, 8:1–5
 V. Concluding miscellanies: Uncleanness of foods and liquids.
  Connection. 8:6–9
 VI. Special liquids: Olive oil and wine. Reprise of II–IV. 9:1–9,
  10:1–8

Uqsin

 I. Food: Handles, husks. 1:1–2:4
  A. Susceptibility to uncleanness. 1:1–6
  B. Joining together. 2:1–4
 II. Food: Connection. 2:1–8(+ 2:9–10)
 III. Food: Susceptibility to uncleanness. 3:1–11

Modes of Purification

Parah

I. The red cow defined. 1:1–2:5
  A. Age, origin. 1:1A–C
  B. Blemishes. 2:2–5
II. The conduct of the rite. A narrative. 3:1–11
  A. Purification of the priest. 3:1–4
  B. Purification rite must be performed with intent specifically for the rite in hand. Preparations for one slaughter do not serve for some other.
  C. Intruded detail, the collected ashes of previously burned cows (3:1B) now explained. Who burned cows?
  D. Moving cow and priests (3:1–2) from Temple Mount to Mount of Olives
  E. Priest then made unclean.
  F. The pyre.
  G. The slaughter.
  H. Cedar, hyssop, scarlet wool thrown into cow.
  I. Preparation and disposition of ash.
III. The conduct of the rite. Laws. 4:1–4
  A. The cow is (or is not) subject to the laws of the sanctuary.
  B. It must be burned in its pit.
  C. Sprinking the blood.
  D. Burning the cow.
  E. Flaying the cow.
  F. Slaughter with wrong intention (= A).
  G. Acts of extraneous labor. Contamination.
  H. General rules on the rite.
  I. Reprise of A.
IV. The purity of utensils used in the rite. 5:1–4
  A. The utensil must be guarded even from the time before it is susceptible to uncleanness.
  B. Immersing a utensil used for the purification rite.
  C. The reed used for collecting ashes.
V. Utensils used in the rite. 5:5–9
  A. The mixing of ashes into the water takes place in a whole utensil.
  B. Trough used for mixing.
VI. Mixing the ash and the water. 6:1–3
  A. The mixing of the ash into the water must be intentional.
  B. Retrieving ash for further use.

    C. Water-and-ash mixture is presumed to enter a narrow-mouthed flask.

VII. Drawing the water. 6:3–8:1

    A. Water must come from a utensil, not be squeezed out of a sponge.

    B. Water must be drawn by hand into a utensil.

    C. Drawing of water followed by mixing of ashes into the water must not be interrupted by an act of labor extraneous to the rite (= 4:4). If it is, the water is spoiled.

    D. If the water is guarded by two men, so long as one is a suitable watchman, the water is acceptably guarded.

VIII. Extraneous matter. 8:2–8

    A. The one who mixes ashes into water should not wear a sandal, because if liquid falls on the sandal, the sandal is made unclean and it makes the man unclean.

    B. All seas are like a pool, Meir. Judah: The Mediterranean alone is like a pool. Yosé: Seas when running are like springs but cannot be used for the cow.

IX. Water used for the rite. 8:9–11, 9:1–6 + 9:7

    A. Spring water is to be used. It must be sweet, flow regularly, not be mixed.

    B. If unfit water fell into fit water, it can be removed, so Eliezer. Sages: It cannot.

    C. If an insect fell into water and burst or imparted a color to the water, it is unfit.

    D. If an animal left spittle in the water, it is unfit.

    E. An unacceptable intention does (does not) spoil the water.

    F. Unfit water and its disposition.

    G. Protection of water and ash.

    H. Mixture of suitable and unsuitable ash.

X. Uncleanness and the purification rite. 9:8–9, 10:1–6, 11:1–6

    A. Capacity of unfit water, ash, to convey uncleanness.

    B. What can contact *midras* uncleanness is regarded as unclean with *maddaf* uncleanness so far as the purification rite is concerned.

    C. The water must be kept in a clean place.

    D. Joshua's view, illustrated in seven cases.

    E. Doubts in cleanness of the purification rite.

    F. Heave offering which fell into purification water.

    G. An extraneous unit.

XI. Hyssop for sprinkling. 11:7–9, 12:1

    A. What sort of hyssop is used.

    B. What part of hyssop is used in sprinkling.

    C. Uncleanness and the hyssop.

    D. Hyssop defined: three stalks, three buds, etc.

    E. If hyssop is too short to dip into the water.

XII. The rules of sprinkling. 12:2–11

    A. Doubts as to sprinkling are resolved strictly.

    B. Sprinkling requires the proper intent of the one who does the sprinkling.

    C. Doubts as to sprinkling in the public domain are solved leniently; in the private domain, strictly.

    D. Purification water which has carried out its proper function, having been sprinkled, no longer conveys uncleanness.

    E. Sprinkling with an unclean hyssop.

    F. We do not reckon degrees of uncleanness in the purification rite.

    G. Connection for uncleanness and for sprinkling.

    H. Who may sprinkle?

    I. When sprinkling may take place.

Miqvaot

    I. Proem: Six grades of gatherings of water. 1:1–8

    II. Doubts about immersion and immersion pools. 2:1–3

    III. Diverse sorts of water. 2:4–10D, 3:1–4, 4:1–5, 5:1–6

    IV. The union of pools to form the requisite volume of water. 5:6, 6:1–11

    V. Miscellanies: Water and wine. Mud. Water in various locales. 7:1–5(+ 10:6–8), 7:6–7, 8:1–4

    VI. The use of the pool: Interposition. 8:5, 9:1–7, 10:1–5, 6–8

Yadayim

    I. Washing hands. 1:1–2:4

    A. Repertoire of rules. 1:1–5

    B. The status and condition of the water, first and second rinsing. 2:1–4

    II. The status of uncleanness imputed to hands. 3:1–2

    III. The uncleanness of sacred Scriptures. 3:3–5, 4:5–6

    IV. Appendix. Traditions on "On that Day." 4:1–4

    V. Appendix. Traditions on "We complain against you." 4:7–8

Abbreviations and References

Agassi
   Joseph Agassi. "Conventions of Knowledge in Talmudic Law." In Jackson, *Studies*. Pp. 16–34.
Ah. Ahilot
Albeck, *Moed*
   Hanokh Albeck. *Seder Mo'ed*. Jerusalem and Tel Aviv, 1954.
Albeck, *Nashim*
   Hanokh Albeck. *Seder Nashim*. Jerusalem and Tel Aviv, 1954.
Albeck, *Neziqin*
   Hanokh Albeck. *Seder Neziqin*. Jerusalem and Tel Aviv, 1959.
Albeck, *Qodoshim*
   Hanokh Albeck. *Seder Qodoshim*. Jerusalem and Tel Aviv, 1959.
Albeck, *Tohorot*
   Hanokh Albeck. *Seder Tohorot*. Jerusalem and Tel Aviv, 1958.
Albeck, *Zeraim*
   Hanokh Albeck, *Seder Zera'im*. Jerusalem and Tel Aviv, 1957.
Alon, Gedalyahu Alon. *Jews, Judaism, and the Classical World*. Jerusalem: Hebrew University, Magnes Press, 1977.
ANRW
   Aufstieg und Niedergang der römischen Welt: Geschichte und Kultur Roms im Spiegel der neueren Forschung. Vol. 1: ed. Hildegard Temporini. Vol 2: ed. Wolfgang Haase. Berlin and New York: De Gruyter, 1972–.
Ar. Arakhin
A.Z. Abodah Zarah
B. Babylonian Talmud
Bammel
   Ernst Bammel. "Die Blutgerichtsbarkeit in der römischen Provinz Judäa vor dem ersten jüdischen Aufstand." In Jackson, *Studies*. Pp. 35–49.

381

Bartels
  R. A. Bartels. "Law and Sin in 4 Esdras and St. Paul." *Lutheran Quarterly* 1 (1949): 319–29.
B.B. Baba Batra
Bekh. Bekhorot
Ber. Berakhot
Bewer, *Moore*
  J. A. Bewer. Review of Moore, *Judaism. N.Y. Herald Tribune* (Books), 12 June 1927. P. 2.
Bik. Bikkurim
Bloch
  J. Bloch. "Ezra Apocalypse: Was It Written in Hebrew, Greek or Aramaic?" *Jewish Quarterly Review* n.s. 48 (1958): 279–94.
Bloch
  J. Bloch. "Ezra Apocalypse: Was It Written in Hebrew, Greek or Aramaic?" *Jewish Quarterly Review* n.s. 48 (1958): 279–94.
Bloch, *Ezra*
  J. Bloch. "Some Christological Interpolations in the Ezra-Apocalypse." *Harvard Theological Review* 51 (1958): 87–94.
B.M. Baba Mesia
Boelter
  Francis W. Boelter. "Sepphoris, Seat of the Galilean Sanhedrin." *Explor* 3 (1977): 36–43.
Bogaert
  P. M. Bogaert. *Apocalypse du Baruch: Introduction, traduction du Syriaque et commentaire.* Paris, 1969. Vols. 1 and 2.
Bogaert, *Apocalypses*
  P. M. Bogaert. "La Ruine de Jérusalem et les apocalypses juives après 70." In *Apocalypses et théologie de l'espérance: Congrès de Toulouse (1975).* Paris: Les Éditions du Cerf, 1977. Pp. 124–41.
Bogaert, *Baruch*
  P. M. Bogaert. "Le Nom de Baruch dans la littérature pseudépigraphique: L'Apocalypse syriaque et le livre deutérocanonique." In *Unnik: La Littérature juive.* Leiden, 1974. Pp. 56–72.
Bokser
  Baruch M. Bokser. "An Annotated Bibliographical Guide to the Study of the Palestinian Talmud." *ANRW.* Pp. 139–256.
Bokser, *Commentary*
  Baruch M. Bokser. "Samuel's Commentary on the Mishnah: Its Nature, Forms, and Content." In AJS *Newsletter,* 16 February 1976.
Bokser, *Form Criticism*
  Baruch M. Bokser. "Talmudic Form Criticism." *Journal of Jewish Studies,* 1980.

Bokser, *Mishnah*
    Baruch M. Bokser. "Jacob N. Epstein's *Introduction to the Text of the Mishnah*," "Jacob N. Epstein on the formation of the Mishnah," and "Y. I. Halevy." In Neusner, *Modern Study*. Pp. 13–36, 37–55, 135–54.
Bokser, *Philo*
    Baruch M. Bokser. "Philo's Description of Jewish Practices." Center for Hermeneutical Studies in Hellenistic and Modern Culture. Protocol of the Thirtieth Colloquy. Ed. Wilhelm Wuellner. Berkeley, 1977.
Bokser, *Reflections*
    Baruch M. Bokser. "Reflections from Jewish Sources on the Religious Crisis of the Third Century" [= a "Response"]. In Peter Brown, *A Social Context to the Religious Crisis of the Third Century A.D.* Center for Hermeneutical Studies in Hellenistic and Modern Culture. Protocol of the Fourteenth Colloquy: Feb. 9, 1975. Ed. Wilhelm Wuellner. Berkeley, 1975. Pp. 19–24.
Bokser, *Samuel*
    Baruch M. Bokser. *Samuel's Commentary on the Mishnah: Its Nature, Forms, and Content.* Pt. 1. *Samuel in Berakhot.* Leiden: E. J. Brill, 1975.
Bokser, *Traditions*
    Baruch M. Bokser. "Two Traditions of Samuel: Evaluating Alternative Versions." In Jacob Neusner, *Christianity*. 4:46–55.
Box, George Herbert Box. *The Ezra Apocalypse.* 1912.
Boyarin
    D. Boyarin. "Penitential Liturgy in 4 Ezra." *Journal for the Study of Judaism* 3 (1972): 30–4.
Breech
    E. Breech. "These Fragments I Have Shored against My Ruins: The Form and Function of 4 Ezra." *Journal of Biblical Literature* 92 (1973): 267–74.
B.Q. Baba Qamma
Brendel
    Otto J. Brendel. *Prolegomena to the Study of Roman Art.* New Haven and London: Yale University Press, 1979.
Brown
    Peter Brown. "Understanding Islam." *New York Review of Books,* 22 February 1979.
Burkitt
    F. C. Burkitt. "Baruch, Apocalypse of." In J. Hastings, ed., *Dictionary of the Apostolic Church.* 1915–18. 1:142–44.
1 Chr. 1 Chronicles
2 Chr. 2 Chronicles

Case, *Moore*
S. J. Case. Review of Moore, *Judaism. Nation*, 24 August 1927.
Chandler
Karen Chandler. "History of Religions in Gnostic Studies." Unpublished MS., 1979.
Charles
R. H. Charles and W. O. E. Oesterley. *The Apocalypse of Baruch*. London, 1929.
Charlesworth, *Enoch*
James H. Charlesworth. "Seminar Report: The SNTS Pseudepigrapha Seminars at Tübingen and Paris on the Books of Enoch." *New Testament Studies* 25:315–23.
Charlesworth, *Ode*
James H. Charlesworth. "Haplography and Philology: A Study of Ode of Solomon 16:8." *New Testament Studies* 25:221–27.
Charlesworth, *Research*
James H. Charlesworth. *The Pseudepigrapha and Modern Research*. Missoula: Scholars Press, 1980.
Charlesworth, *Testaments*
James H. Charlesworth. "Seminar Report. Reflections on the SNTS Pseudepigrapha Seminar at Duke on the Testaments of the Twelve Patriarchs." *New Testament Studies* 23:296–304.
Charlesworth *re* Thompson
James H. Charlesworth. Review of Alden Lloyd Thompson, *Responsibility for Evil in the Theodicy of IV Ezra. JBL* 98 (1979): 465–67.
Chesnut
Glenn F. Chesnut. *The First Christian Histories: Eusebius, Socrates, Sozomen, Theodoret, and Evagrius*. Paris: Éditions Beauchesne, 1977. Théologie Historique 46.
Coggins
R. J. Coggins and M. A. Knibb. *The First and Second Books of Esdras*. Cambridge, 1979.
Cohen, *Moore*
B. Cohen. Review of Moore, *Judaism. World Tomorrow* 10 (December 1927): 521.
Colafemmina, *Ipogeo*
Cesare Colafemmina. "Un nuovo ipogeo cristiano a Venosa." *Rivista de Teologia Ecumenico Patristica* 3 (1975): 159–68.
Colofemmina, *Iscrizioni*
Cesare Colafemmina. "Iscrizioni paleocristiane di Venosa." *Vetera Christianorum* 13 (1976): 149–65.
Colafemmina, *Scoperte*
Cesare Colafemmina. "Nuove scoperte nella catacomba ebraica

di Venosa." *Vetera Christianorum* 15 (1978): 369–81.

Colafemmina, *Studi*
Cesare Colafemmina, ed. *Studi storici.* Molfetta, 1974.

Colafemmina, *Venosa*
Cesare Colafemmina. "Un 'iscrizione venosina inedita dell' 822." *Rassegna Mensile d'Israel* 43 (1977): 261–63.

Dautzenberg
G. Dautzenberg. "Das Bild der Prophetie im 4 Esra und im Syr. Bar." *Urchristliche Prophetie: Ihre Erforschung, ihre Voraussetzungen im Judentum und ihre Struktur im ersten Korintherbrief.* BWANT Folge 6. Heft 4. Stuttgart, 1975. Pp. 90–98.

Dem. Demai

Denis, Albert-Marie Denis. *Introduction aux pseudépigraphes grecs d'Ancien Testament.* Leiden, 1970. Studia in Veteris Testamenti Pseudepigrapha. Vol. 1.

Deut. Deuteronomy

Dever, William Dever. In *Biblical Archaeologist* 43, no. 1 (1980).

Dombrowski
Bruno W. Dombrowski. "*Hayyahad* and *To Koinón:* An Instance of Early Greek and Jewish Synthesis." *Harvard Theological Review* 59 (1966): 293–307.

Duff, A. M. Duff. *Freedmen in the Early Roman Empire.* 2d ed. Oxford, 1958.

Duncan-Jones
Richard Duncan-Jones. *The Economy of the Roman Empire.* Cambridge, 1974.

Ed. Eduyyot

Eddy, Samuel K. Eddy. *The King is Dead: Studies in the Near Eastern Resistance to Hellenism, 334–31 B.C.* Lincoln: University of Nebraska Press, 1961.

EJ Encyclopaedia Judaica. Jerusalem, 1971.

Erub. Erubin

Essner, "Orlah"
Howard Essner. "Orlah: A Commentary." In Green, *Approaches* III.

Ex. Exodus

Ezek. Ezekiel

Fábrega
V. Fàbrega. *Das Endgericht in der syrischen Baruchapokalypse.* Innsbruck, 1969.

Ferch
Arthur Ferch. "The Two Eons and the Messiah in Pseudo-Philo, 4 Ezra, and 2 Baruch." *Andrews University Seminary Studies* 15 (1977): 135–52.

Finley
    M. I. Finley. *The Ancient Economy*. Berkeley and Los Angeles:
    University of California Press, 1973.
Gen. Genesis
Gereboff, *Frankel*
    Joel D. Gereboff. "The Pioneer: Zecharias Frankel," "Hirsch
    Mendel Pineles: The First Critical Exegete," "Joachim Op-
    penheim." In Neusner, *Modern Study*. Pp. 59–75, 90–104,
    155–66, 180–96.
Gereboff, *Tarfon*
    Joel D. Gereboff. *Rabbi Tarfon: The Tradition, the Man, and
    Early Rabbinic Judaism*. Missoula: Scholars Press, 1979.
Gero, S. Gero. "'My Son the Messiah': A Note on 4 Esra 28–29."
    Zeitschrift für die Neutesamentliche Wissenschaft 66 (1975):
    264–67.
Git. Gittin
Goldenberg, *Axis*
    Robert Goldenberg. "The Broken Axis: Rabbinic Judaism and
    the Fall of Jerusalem." *Journal of the American Academy of
    Religion. Supplement*. 45 (1977): 869–82.
Goldenberg, *Commandment*
    Robert Goldenberg. "Commandment and Consciousness in Tal-
    mudic Thought." *Harvard Theological Review* 68 (1975): 261–71.
Goldenberg, *Gamaliel*
    Robert Goldenberg. "The Deposition of Rabban Gamaliel II."
    Journal of Jewish Studies 23 (1972): 167–90.
Goldenberg, *Jewish Law*
    Robert Goldenberg. "The Historical Study of Jewish Law." AJS
    Newsletter 22 (1978): 13–14, 19.
Goldenberg, *Meir*
    Robert Goldenberg. *The Sabbath-Law of Rabbi Meir*. Missoula:
    Scholars Press, 1979.
Goldenberg, *Niebuhr*
    Robert Goldenberg. "The Ethical Categories of Reinhold
    Niebuhr." *Conservative Judaism* 22 (1967): 67–74.
Goldenberg, *Sabbath*
    Robert Goldenberg. "The Jewish Sabbath in the Roman World."
    ANRW. II.19.1.
Goldenberg, *Talmud*
    Robert Goldenberg. "B. M. Lewin and the Saboraic Element,"
    "Jacob B. Epstein," and "David Weiss Halivni, *Meqorot
    uMesorot: Ketuvot*." In Neusner, *Formation*. Pp. 51–60, 75–86,
    134–147.

Goodblatt, *Beruriah*
    David Goodblatt. "The Beruriah Traditions." *Journal of Jewish Studies* 26 (1975): 58–85.
Goodblatt, *Bibliography*
    David Goodblatt. "Bibliography on Rabbinic Judaism." In Jacob Neusner, ed., *Understanding Rabbinic Judaism: From Talmudic to Modern Times.* New York: KTAV, 1974. Pp. 383–402.
Goodblatt, *Historiography*
    David Goodblatt. "Historiography in the Service of Text Criticism." AJS *Newsletter* 24 (1979): 17.
Goodblatt, *Instruction*
    David Goodblatt. *Rabbinic Instruction in Sasanian Babylonia.* Leiden: E. J. Brill, 1974.
Goodblatt, *Origins*
    David Goodblatt. "The Origins of Roman Recognition of the Palestinian Patriarchate." *Studies in the History of the Jewish People and the Land of Israel.* Vol. 4. Haifa, 1978. Pp. 89–102.
Goodblatt, *Reader*
    David Goodblatt. *Reader on the History of the Jews in Parthian and Sassanian Mesopotamia.* Haifa: University of Haifa Student Union, 1976.
Goodblatt, *Sects*
    David Goodblatt. *Reader on Jewish Sects in Late Antiquity.* Haifa: University of Haifa Student Union, 1974.
Goodblatt, *Sources*
    David Goodblatt. "The Talmudic Sources on the Origins of Organized Jewish Education." *Studies in the History of the Jewish People and the Land of Israel.* Vol. 5. Haifa, forthcoming.
Goodblatt, *Talmud*
    David Goodblatt. "The Babylonian Talmud." *ANRW.* Pp. 257–336.
Goodblatt, *Talmud-Formation*
    David Goodblatt. "Y. I. Halevy," "Abraham Weiss: The Search for Literary Forms," and "David Weiss Halivni, *Meqorot uMesorot: Gittin.*" In Neusner, *Formation.* Pp. 246–47, 95–103, 164–74.
Goodblatt, *Tax*
    David Goodblatt. "The Poll Tax in Sassanian Babylonia: The Talmudic Evidence." *Journal for the Economic and Social History of the Orient,* in press.
Goodblatt, *Traditions*
    David Goodblatt. "Local Traditions in the Babylonian Talmud." *Hebrew Union College Annual* 98 (1977): 60–90.

Gordon, "Shebiit"
> Leonard Gordon. "Shebiit: A Commentary." Unpublished Ms.

Green, *ANRW*
> William S. Green. "Palestinian Holy Men: Charismatic Leadership and Rabbinic Tradition." *ANRW.* Pp. 619–47.

Green, *Approaches* I
> William S. Green, ed. *Approaches to Ancient Judaism.* Missoula: Scholars Press, 1978.

Green, *Approaches* II
> William S. Green, ed. *Approaches to Ancient Judaism.* Vol. 2. Missoula: Scholars Press, 1980

Green, *Approaches* III
> William S. Green, ed. *Approaches to Ancient Judaism.* Vol 3. Chicago: Scholars Press, 1981.

Green, *Bloch*
> William S. Green, trans. (with W. J. Sullivan). Renée Bloch, "Methodological Note for the Study of Rabbinic Literature." In Green, *Appoaches* I. Pp. 29–50.

Green, *Context*
> William S. Green. "Context and Meaning in Rabbinic Biography." In Green, *Approaches* II.

Green, *Joshua*
> William S. Green. *The Traditions of Joshua ben Hananiah.* Part 1: *The Early Traditions.* Leiden: E. J. Brill, 1981.

Green, *Mishnah*
> William S. Green. "The Talmudic Historians: N. Krochmal, H. Graetz, I. H. Weiss, and Z. Jawits," "J. S. Zuri," and "Abraham Goldberg." In Neusner, *Modern Study.* Pp. 107–21, 169–79, 225–41.

Green, *Name*
> William S. Green. "What's in a Name—The Problematic of Rabbinic 'Biography.'" In Green, *Approaches* I.

Green, *Persons*
> William S. Green, ed. *Persons and Institutions in Early Rabbinic Judaism.* Missoula: Scholars Press, 1977.

Grintz
> Joshua M. Grintz. "Baruch, Apocalypse of." *EJ* 4:270–72.

Groh, Dennis Groh. "Galilee and the Eastern Roman Empire in Late Antiquity." *Explor* 3 (1977): 78–92.

Gry, Léon Gry. *Les Dires Prophétiques d'Esdras (IVe d'Esdras).* Vols. 1 and 2, Paris, 1938.

Gry, *Mort*
> Léon Gry. "La 'Mort du Messie' en IV Esdras, VII, 29 [III, v. 4]." *Mémorial Lagrange.* Paris, 1940. Pp. 133–39.

Haas, "Maaser Sheni"
    Peter Haas. "Maaser Sheni: A Commentary." Unpublished Ms.
Hadfield
    P. Hadfield. "Resurrection Body." *Church Quarterly Review* 158
    (1957): 296–305.
Hadot, *Baruch*
    J. Hadot. "Le Problème de l'Apocalypse syriaque de Baruch
    d'après un ouvrage récent." *Semitica* 20 (1970): 59–76.
Hadot, *Datation*
    J. Hadot. "La Datation de l'Apocalypse syriaque de Baruch."
    Semitica 15 (1965): 79–95.
Hag. Hagigah
Hal. Hallah
Hallo, William W. Hallo. "New Moons and Sabbaths: A Case-Study in
    the Contrastive Approach." *Hebrew Union College Annual* 48
    (1977): 1–18.
Harnisch
    Wolfgang Harnisch. *Verhängnis und Verheissung der Geschichte:
    Untersuchungen zum Zeit- und Geschichtsverständnis im 4. Buch
    Esra und in der Syr Baruchapokalypse.* Göttingen, 1969.
Harrington
    Daniel J. Harrington and Maurya P. Horgan. "Palestinian Adap-
    tations of Biblical Narratives and Prophecies." Unpublished Ms.
Havivi, "Hallah I-II"
    Abraham Havivi, "Hallah Chapters 1 and 2: A Commentary." In
    Green, *Approaches* III.
Hayman
    A. P. Hayman. "The Problem of Pseudanonymity in the Ezra
    Apocalypse." *Journal for the Study of Judaism* 6 (1975): 47–56.
Heinemann
    Joseph Heinemann. "Early *Halakhah* in the Palestinian Tar-
    gumim." In Jackson, *Studies.* Pp. 114–22.
Hengel
    Martin Hengel. *Acts and the History of Earliest Christianity.*
    Trans. John Bowden. London: SCM Press, 1979.
Hertzberg
    A. Hertzberg, ed. *Judaism.* New York, 1963.
Homer, *Moore*
    Sidney Homer. Review of Moore, *Judaism. Boston Transcript,*
    16 April 1927.
Hor. Horayot
Hul. Hullin
Humphreys
    W. Lee Humphreys. *Crisis and Story: Introduction to the Old*

Testament. Palo Alto: Mayfield, 1979.
Is. Isaiah
Jackson, *Fence-Breaker*
Bernard S. Jackson. "The Fence-Breaker and the *actio de pastu pecoris* in Early Jewish Law. In Jackson, *Studies*. Pp. 123–36.
Jackson, *History*
Bernard S. Jackson. "History, Dogmatics, and Halakhah." Unpublished Ms., 1979.
Jackson, *Roman Influence*
Bernard S. Jackson. "On the Problem of Roman Influence on the *Halakhah* and Normative Self-Definition in Judaism." Unpublished Ms., 1979.
Jackson, *Structuralism*
Bernard S. Jackson, *Structuralism and Legal Theory*. Liverpool: Liverpool Polytechnic Department of Law, 1979. Occasional Paper 20.
Jackson, *Studies*
Bernard S. Jackson. *Studies in Jewish Legal History in Honour of David Daube. Journal of Jewish Studies* 25 (February 1974).
Jackson, *Stratification*
J. A. Jackson, ed. *Social Stratification*. London, 1968.
Jacobson
Howard Jacobson. "Note on the Greek Apocalypse of Baruch." *Journal for the Study of Judaism* 7 (1976): 201–3.
Jaffee, "Maaserot"
Martin Jaffee. "Maaserot: A Commentary." Unpublished Ms.
Jer. Jeremiah
Kallen, *Moore*
Horace M. Kallen. "A Contradiction in Terms." [Review of Moore, *Judaism*] *Menorah Journal* 13 (1927): 479–86.
Kaminka
Armand Kaminka. "Beiträge zur Erklärung der Esra-Apokalypse und zur Rekonstruktion ihres hebräischen Urtextes." *Monatsschrift für Geschichte und Wissenschaft des Judentums* 76 (1932): 121–38, 206–12, 494–511, 604–7; 77 (1933): 339–55.
Kanter, *Gamaliel*
Shamai Kanter. "I. H. Weiss and J. S. Zuri," "Abraham Weiss: Source Criticism," and "David Weiss Halivni, *Meqorot uMesorot:* Qiddushin." In Neusner, *Formation*. Pp. 11–25, 87–94, 148–63.
Kaufman, *Structure*
Steven A. Kaufman. "The Structure of the Deuteronomic Law." *Maarav* 1 (1978–79): 105–58.
Kel. Kelim

Kelly, J. M. Kelly. *Roman Litigation*. Oxford, 1966.

Ker. Keritot

Ket. Ketubot

Kil. Kilayim

Klijn, *Sources*

> A. F. J. Klijn. "Sources and the Redaction of the Syriac Apocalypse of Baruch." *Journal for the Study of Judaism* 1 (1970): 65–76.

Kolenkow

> A. C. B. Kolenkow. "Introduction to II Baruch 53:56–74: Structure and Substance." *Harvard Theological Review* 65 (1972): 597–98.

Kraabel, *Synagogue*

> A. T. Kraabel. "The Diaspora Synagogue: Achaeological and Epigraphic Evidence since Sukenik." *ANRW*. II.19.1. Pp. 477–510.

Kraabel, *Systems*

> A. T. Kraabel. "Social Systems of Six Diaspora Synagogues (with one plan)." Prepared for the SBL/AAR section, "Art and the Bible," under the theme "Ancient Synagogues: The Current State of Research." Unpublished Ms., 1979.

Lee, G. M. Lee. "Apocryphal Cats: Baruch 6." *Vetus Testamentum* 21 (1971): 111–12.

Lev. Leviticus

Levine

> Baruch A. Levine. *In the Presence of the Lord*. Leiden: E. J. Brill, 1974.

Licht, J. S. Licht. "Ezra, 4 Ezra, Apocalypse of Ezra." *Encyclopedia Miqra'ith* (1971) 6:155–60.

Licht, *Ezra*

> J. S. Licht. *The Book of the Apocalypse of Ezra*. Jerusalem, 1968.

Lightstone, *Canon*

> Jack N. Lightstone. "The Development of the Biblical Canon in Late Antique Judaism: Prolegomenon toward a Reassessment." *Studies in Religion*, 1979.

Lightstone, *History*

> Jack N. Lightstone. "Yosé the Galilean in Mishnah-Tosefta and the History of Early Rabbinic Judaism." *Journal of Jewish Studies*, 1979.

Lightstone, *Judaism*

> Jack N. Lightstone. "Judaism of the Second Commonwealth: Toward the Reform of the Scholarly Tradition." In H. Joseph, J. Lightstone, M. Oppenheim, eds., *Essays in Judaism and Religion for Rabbi Solomon Frank at 80*, forthcoming.

Lightstone, *Oral Torah*
    Jack N. Lightstone. "Oral Torah in the Eyes of the Midrashists:
    Toward an Understanding of the Method and Message of the
    Halakic Midrashim." *Studies in Religion,* 1980.
Lightstone, *Problems*
    Jack N. Lightstone. "Problems and New Perspectives in the
    Study of Early Rabbinic Ethics." In Charles Davis, ed., *Essays
    on Religious Ethics.* Waterloo: Wilfred Laurier Press, forthcom-
    ing.
Lightstone, *Sadducees*
    Jack N. Lightstone. "Sadducees versus Pharisees: The Tannaitic
    Sources." In Neusner, *Christianity.* 3:206–17.
Lightstone, *Sadoq*
    Jack N. Lightstone. "R. Ṣadoq." In W. S. Green, ed., *Persons
    and Institutions in Early Rabbinic Judaism.* Missoula: Scholars
    Press, 1977. Pp. 49–148.
Lightstone, *Yosé*
    Jack N. Lightstone. *Yosé the Galilean: I. Traditions in
    Mishnah-Tosefta.* Leiden, E. J. Brill, 1979.
Loewe
    Raphael Loewe. "Rabbi Joshua ben Ḥananiah: LL.D. or D.
    Litt.?" In Jackson, *Studies.* Pp. 137–54.
Luck, Ulrich Luck. "Das Weltverständnis in der jüdischen Apokalyp-
    tik. Dargestellt am Äthiopischen Henoch und am 4 Esra." *Zeit-
    schrift für Theologie und Kirche* 73 (1976): 283–305.
M. Mishnah
Ma. Maaserot
MacMullen, *Relations*
    Ramsay MacMullen. *Roman Social Relations. 50 B.C. to A.D. 284.*
    New Haven, 1974.
Mak. Makkot
Makh. Makhshirin
Mandelbaum, *Kilaim*
    Irving Mandelbaum. "Kilaim: A Commentary." Unpublished
    Ms.
Marshall
    T. H. Marshall. *Citizenship and Social Class and Other Essays.*
    Cambridge, 1950.
MacHardy
    W. D. MacHardy, et. al. "The Second Book of Esdras." *The
    New English Bible with the Apocrypha.* New York, 1971. Pp.
    19–53.
Me. Meilah

Meeks and Wilken
> Wayne A. Meeks and Robert L. Wilken. *Jews and Christians in Antioch in the First Four Centuries of the Common Era.* Missoula: Scholars Press, 1978.

Meg. Megillah

Men. Menahot

Meshorer, *Sepphoris*
> Y. Meshorer. "Sepphoris and Rome." In *Greek Numismatics and Archaeology: Essays in Honor of Margaret Thompson.* Wetteren, Belgium, 1979. Pp. 159–71 and plates.

Metzger
> Bruce M. Metzger. "Lost Section of II Esdras; i.e., IV Ezra." *Journal of Biblical Literature* (1957): 153–56.

Metzger, *Pseudepigrapha*
> Bruce M. Metzger. "The Fourth Book of Ezra and 2 Baruch." In "The Pseudepigrapha of the Old Testament," ed. J. H. Charlesworth. Unpublished Ms.

Meyers, *Archaeology*
> Eric M. Meyers, A. T. Kraabel, and J. F. Strange. "Archaeology and Rabbinic Tradition at Khirbet Shema: 1970 and 1971 Campaigns." *Biblical Archaeologist* 35 (1972): 2–31.

Meyers, *Burial*
> Eric M. Meyers. "The Theological Implication of an Ancient Jewish Burial Custom." *Jewish Quarterly Review* 72 (1971): 95–119.

Meyers, *Galilee*
> Eric M. Meyers. "Galilean Regionalism as a Factor in Historical Reconstruction." *Bulletin of the American School of Oriental Research* 221 (1976): 93–101.

Meyers, *Meiron*
> Eric M. Meyers, et al. "The Meiron Excavation Project: Archaeological Survey in Galilee and Golan, 1976." *Bulletin of the American School of Oriental Research* 230 (1978): 1–22.

Meyers, *Meiron* III-IV
> Eric M. Meyers, C. Meyers, and J. F. Strange. *Report on the Excavations at Ancient Meiron, 1971–77.* Vols. 3–4 of Meiron Excavation Project Series, 1980.

Meyers, *Report*
> Eric M. Meyers, et al. "Preliminary Report on the 1977 and 1978 Seasons at Gush Halav (el Jish)." *Bulletin of the American School of Oriental Research* 233 (1979): 33–58.

Meyers, *Setting*
> Eric M. Meyers. "The Cultural Setting of Galilee: The Case of Regionalism and Early Judaism." *ANRW* II. 19.1. Pp. 687–702.

Meyers, *Shema*
> Eric M. Meyers, A. T. Kraabel, and J. F. Strange. *Synagogue Excavations at Khirbet Shema'*. Duke University Press and Annual of the American School of Oriental Research No. 42. Durham, 1976.

Meyers, *Survey*
> Eric M. Meyers and J. F. Strange. "Survey in Galilee: 1976." *Explor* 3 (1977): 7–17.

Meyers, *Synagogue*
> Eric M. Meyers. "Galilean Synagogues and the Eastern Diaspora." Unpublished Ms., 1979.

Meyers and Strange
> Eric M. Meyers and J. F. Strange. *Archaeology, the Rabbis, and the New Testament*. Nashville: Abingdon, 1980.

Mid. Middot

Miq. Miqvaot

Moe, Dean L. Moe. "The Cross and the Menorah." *Archaeology* 30 (1977): 148–57.

Moore
> George Foot Moore. *Judaism in the First Centuries of the Christian Era: The Age of the Tannaim*. Vols. 1–3. Cambridge, Mass.: Harvard University Press, 1954. Orig. pub. 1927.

Moore, *Baruch*
> C. A. Moore. "Toward the Dating of the Book of Baruch." *Catholic Biblical Quarterly* 36 (1974): 312–20.

M.Q. Moed Qatan

M.S. Maaser Sheni

Nag Hammadi
> *The Nag Hammadi Library in English*. Translated by members of the Coptic Gnostic Library Project of the Institute for Antiquity and Christianity, James M. Robinson, director. San Francisco, 1977.

Naz. Nazir

Ned. Nedarim

Neg. Negaim

Neusner, *Academic Study*
> Jacob Neusner. *The Academic Study of Judaism*. Vols. 1–3. N.Y., 1975, 1977, 1980.

Neusner, *ANRW*
> Jacob Neusner. "The Formation of Rabbinic Judaism: Yavneh (Jamnia) from A.D. 70 to 100." *ANRW*. Pp. 3–42.

Neusner, *Aphrahat*
> Jacob Neusner. *Aphrahat and Judaism: The Christian-Jewish Argument in Fourth Century Iran*. Leiden, 1971.

Neusner, *Appointed Times*
Jacob Neusner. *A History of the Mishnaic Law of Appointed Times*. Vols. 1–5. Leiden, 1981–82.
Neusner, *Christianity*
Jacob Neusner, ed. *Christianity, Judaism, and Other Greco-Roman Cults: Studies for Morton Smith at Sixty*. Leiden: E. J. Brill, 1975.
Neusner, "Comparing Judaisms"
Jacob Neusner. "Comparing Judaisms: Essay-Review of *Paul and Palestinean Judaism* by E. P. Sanders." *History of Religions* 18 (1978): 177–91.
Neusner, *Damages*
Jacob Neusner. *A History of the Mishnaic Law of Damages*. Vols. 1–5. Leiden, 1982.
Neusner, *Development*
Jacob Neusner. *Development of a Legend: Studies in the Traditions Concerning Yohanan ben Zakkai*. Leiden, 1970.
Neusner, *Eliezer*
Jacob Neusner. *Eliezer ben Hyrcanus: The Tradition and the Man*. Vols. 1–3. Leiden, 1973.
Neusner, *Form-Analysis*
Jacob Neusner. *Form-Analysis and Exegesis: A Fresh Approach to the Interpretation of Mishnah* (Minneapolis, 1980).
Neusner, *Formation*
Jacob Neusner, ed. *The Formation of the Babylonian Talmud*. Leiden, 1970.
Neusner, *History*
Jacob Neusner. *A History of the Jews in Babylonia*. Vols. 1–5. Leiden, 1965–70.
Neusner, *Holy Things*
Jacob Neusner. *A History of the Mishnaic Law of Holy Things*. Vols. 1–6. Leiden, 1978–79.
Neusner, *Life*
Jacob Neusner. *A Life of Yohanan ben Zakkai*. Leiden, 1970. Orig. pub. 1962.
Neusner, "Maddaf"
Jacob Neusner. "From Scripture to Mishnah: The Exegetical Origins of Maddaf." Fiftieth Anniversary Festschrift of the American Academy for Jewish Research. *Proceedings of the AAJR* (1979), pp. 99–111.
Neusner, *Method and Meaning*
Jacob Neusner. *Method and Meaning in Ancient Judaism: Essays on System and Order*. Missoula, 1979. Second Series: Chicago, 1980. Third Series: 1981.

Neusner, *Modern Study*.
Jacob Neusner. *The Modern Study of the Mishnah*. Leiden, 1973.
Neusner, "Niddah"
Jacob Neusner. "From Scripture to Mishnah: The Case of Niddah." *Journal of Jewish Studies* 29 (1978): 135–48.
Neusner, *Pharisees*
Jacob Neusner. *The Rabbinic Traditions about the Pharisees before 70*. Vols. 1–3. Leiden, 1971.
Neusner, *Purity*
Jacob Neusner. *The Idea of Purity in Ancient Judaism: The 1972–73 Haskell Lectures*. Leiden, 1973.
Neusner, *Purities*
Jacob Neusner. *A History of the Mishnaic Law of Purities*. Vols. 1–22. Leiden, 1974–77.
Neusner, "The Sages"
Jacob Neusner. Review of *The Sages: Beliefs and Opinions*, by Ephraim E. Urbach. *Journal of Jewish Studies* 27 (1976): 23–35.
Neusner, *Story*
Jacob Neusner. *After Historicism, beyond Structuralism: Story as History in Ancient Judaism*. Brunswick, Me.: Bowdoin College, 1980. The Spindel Memorial Lecture.
Neusner, *Tosefta*
Jacob Neusner. *The Tosefta: Translated from the Hebrew*. Vols. 2–6. New York, 1977–81.
Neusner, *Way*
Jacob Neusner. *Way of Torah: An Introduction to Judaism*. 3d. ed. Belmont, 1979.
Neusner, *Women*
Jacob Neusner. *A History of the Mishnaic Law of Women*. Vols. 1–5. Leiden, 1979–80.
Nickelsburg
G. W. E. Nickelsburg. "Narrative Traditions in the Paralipomena of Jeremiah and 2 Baruch." *Catholic Biblical Quarterly* 35 (1973): 60–68.
Nid. Niddah
Nock, Arthur Darby Nock. *Essays on Religion and the Ancient World*. Selected and edited, with an introduction, bibliography of Nock's writings, and indexes, by Zeph Stewart. Vols. 1–2. Oxford: Clarendon Press, 1972.
Num. Numbers
Oh. Ohalot
Oppenheimer
Aharon Oppenheimer. "Jewish Settlement in Galilee in the

Period of Yabneh and the Revolt of Bar Kokhba." *Qatedrah letoledot eres yisra'el veyishubah.* Jerusalem, 1977. 4:52–83.

Or. Orlah

Ossowski

    S. Ossowski. *Class Structure in the Social Consciousness.* London, 1963.

Pagels

    Elaine Pagels. *The Gnostic Gospels.* New York: Random House, 1979.

Par. Parah

Pe. Peah

Pes. Pesahim

Peck, *Terumot*

    Alan Peck. "Terumot: A Commentary." Unpublished Ms.

Pesch

    W. Pesch. "Die Abhängigkeit des II. salomonischen Psalms vom letzten Kapitel des Buches Baruch." *Zeitschrift für die alttestamentliche Wissenschaft* 67, nos. 3–4 (1955): 251–63.

Philonenko

    M. Philonenko. "L'Âme à l'étroit." In *Hommages à A. Dupont-Sommer.* Paris, 1971. Pp. 421–28.

Picard, J. C. Picard. "Observations sur l'Apocalypse grecque de Baruch." *Semitica* 20 (2970): 77–103.

Porter, *Moore*

    F. C. Porter. Review of Moore, *Judaism. Journal of Religion* 8 (January, 1928): 30–62.

Porton, *Dispute*

    Gary G. Porton. "The Artificial Dispute: Ishmael and Aqiba." In Neusner, *Christianity.* 4:18–29.

Porton, *Form*

    Gary G. Porton. "According to Rabbi Y: A Palestinian Amoraic Form." In Green, *Approaches* I. Pp. 173–88.

Porton, *Ishmael*

    Gary G. Porton. *The Traditions of Rabbi Ishmael.* Pt. 1: *Non-Exegetical Materials.* Leiden: E. J. Brill, 1976.

Porton, *Ishmael, II*

    Gary G. Porton. *The Traditions of Rabbi Ishmael.* Pt. 2: *Exegetical Comments in Tannaitic Collections.* Leiden: E. J. Brill, 1977.

Porton, *Ishmael III*

    Gary G. Porton. *The Traditions of Rabbi Ishmael.* Pt. 3: *Exegetical Comments in Amoraic Collections.* Leiden: E. J. Brill, 1979.

Porton, *Midrash*

    Gary G. Porton. "Midrash: Palestinian Jews and the Hebrew Bible in the Greco-Roman Period." *ANRW.* Pp. 103–38.

Porton, *Mishnah*
    Gary G. Porton. "Jacob Brüll: The Mishnah as a Law-code," and "Hanokh Albeck on the Mishnah." In Neusner, *Modern Study*. Pp. 76–89, 209–24.
Porton, *Talmud*
    Gary G. Porton. "Hanokh Albeck on the Talmudic Sugya." In Neusner, *Formation*. Pp. 127–133.
Pr. Proverbs
Ps. Psalms
Primus, *Aqiva*
    Charles Primus. *Aqiva's Contribution to Law of Zera'im.* Leiden: E. J. Brill, 1977.
Primus, *Mishnah*
    Charles Primus. "David Hoffman's 'The First Mishnah,'" "Abraham Weiss," and "Benjamin DeVries." In Neusner, *Modern Study.* Pp. 122–34, 197–208, 242–55.
Primus, *Visions*
    Charles Primus, ed. *Visions of the Land: Aspects of the Land of Israel in Jewish Tradition.* Notre Dame: Notre Dame University Press, forthcoming.
Qin. Qinnim
Radin, *Moore*
    Paul Radin. Review of Moore, *Judaism. New York Evening Post,* 23 April 1927. P. 5.
R.H. Rosh Hashshanah
Rist, M. Rist. "Baruch, Apocalypse of." *International Dictionary of the Bible.* 1:361f.
Rivkin
    Ellis Rivkin. *A Hidden Revolution: The Pharisees' Search for the Kingdom Within.* Nashville: Abingdon, 1978.
Rosenthal
    Ferdinand Rosenthal. *Vier apokryphische Bücher aus der Zeit und Schule R. Akiba's: Assumptio Mosis, Das vierte Buch Esra, Die Apokalypse Baruch, Das Buch Tobi.* Leipzig, 1885.
Rubenstein, *Bikkurim* I–II
    Margaret Wenig Rubenstein. "Bikkurim: A Commentary." In Green, *Approaches* III.
Russell
    D. S. Russell. *The Method and Message of Jewish Apocalyptic.* London, 1964.
Ryssel
    V. Ryssel. "Die syrische Baruchapokalypse." In E. Kautsch, *Die Apokryphen und Pseudepigraphen des Alten Testaments.* 1900. 2:406–446.

San. Sanhedrin

Sanders

E. P. Sanders. *Paul and Palestinian Judaism*. London: SCM Press, 1977.

Sarason, *Demai*

Richard Sarason. *A History of the Mishnaic Law of Agriculture: Section 3: A Study of Tractate Demai*. Part 1: *Commentary*. Leiden: E. J. Brill, 1979.

Sarason, *Liturgy*

Richard S. Sarason. "On the Use of Method in the Modern Study of Jewish Liturgy." In Green, *Approaches* I. *Theory and Practice*. Pp. 97–172.

Sarason, *Midrash*

Richard S. Sarason. "Toward a New Agendum for the Study of Rabbinic Midrashic Literature." In Jakob J. Petuchowski and Ezra Fleischer, eds., *Joseph Heinemann Memorial Volume*. Cincinnati and Jerusalem: HUC Press and Magnes Press, forthcoming.

Sarason, "Mishnah"

Richard Sarason, "Mishnah and Scripture: Preliminary Observations on the Law of Tithing in *Seder Zera'im*," in Green, *Approaches* II.

Sarason, *Modern Study*

Richard S. Sarason, ed. *The Modern Study of Midrash*. In progress.

Sarason, *Prayer*

Joseph Heinemann. *Prayer in the Talmud: Forms and Patterns*. Trans. Richard S. Sarason. Berlin: de Gruyter, 1977.

Saunders

Ernest W. Saunders. "Christian Synagogues and Jewish Christianity in Galilee." *Explor* 3 (1977): 70–77.

Schäfer

P. Schäfer. "Die Flucht Johanan b. Zakkais aus Jerusalem und die Gründung des 'Lehrhauses' in Jabne." *ANRW*. Pp. 43–101.

Schiffman

Larry H. Schiffman. "Communal Meals at Qumran." *Revue de Qumran* 10 (1979): 45–56.

Schmid

H. Schmid, "Baruch und ihm zugeschriebene Apokryphe und pseudepigraphische Literatur." *Judaica* 30 (1974): 54–70.

Schorske

Carl E. Schorske. *Fin-de-Siècle Vienna: Politics and Culture*. New York: Knopf, 1980.

Schulman, *Moore*
Samuel Schulman. Review of Moore, *Judaism*. *Jewish Quarterly Review* 18 (1927–1928): 339–55.

Schürer
Emil Schürer. *A History of the Jewish People in the Time of Jesus Christ*. Second Division. III: *The Internal Condition of Palestine, and of the Jewish People, in the Time of Jesus Christ*. Trans. Sophia Tayler and Peter Christie. Edinburgh, 1886.

Schwartz
J. Schwartz. "Sur la date de IV Esdras." In *Mélanges Andres Neher*, pp. 191–96.

Scroggs
Robin Scroggs. "The Sociological Interpretation of the New Testament: The Present State of Research." *New Testament Studies* 26 (1980): 164–79.

Shab. Shabbat
Shebu. Shebuot
Sheb. Shebiit
Sheq. Sheqalim
Smertenko, *Moore*
Johan Smertenko. Review of Moore, *Judaism*. *New York Times*, 19 June 1927. P. 5.

Smith
Jonathan Z. Smith. *Map Is Not Territory*. Leiden: E. J. Brill, 1977.

Smith, *Jesus*
Morton Smith. *Jesus the Magician*. New York: Harper and Row, 1978.

Smith, *Palestinian Parties*
Morton Smith, *Palestinian Parties and Politics That Shaped the Old Testament*. New York: Columbia University Press, 1971.

Solodukho
Y. A. Solodukho. *Soviet Views of Talmudic Judaism. Five Papers by Yu. A. Solodukho*. Ed. Jacob Neusner. Leiden: E. J. Brill, 1973.

Sot. Sotah
Stanton
G. N. Stanton. "5 Ezra and Matthean Christianity in the Second Century." *Journal of Theological Studies* 28 (1977): 67–83.

Steck, Odil Steck. "Die Aufnahme von Genesis I in Jubiläen 2 und 4 Esra 6." *Journal for the Study of Judaism* 8 (1977): 154–82.

Stoderl
Wenzel Stoderl. *Zur Echtheitsfrage von Baruch I–III*. Vol. 8. Münster, 1922.

Stone, Michael E. Stone. "The Concept of the Messiah in IV Ezra." In *Religions in Antiquity: Essays in Memory of Erwin Ramsdell Goodenough*, ed. Jacob Neusner. Leiden, 1968. Pp. 295–314.

Stone, *Baruch*
Michael E. Stone. "Baruch, Book of." *EJ* 4:272–73.

Stone, *Ezra*
Michael E. Stone. "Ezra, Apocalypse of." *EJ* 6:1108–9.

Stone, *Features*
Michael E. Stone. *Features of the Eschatology of IV Ezra*. Ph.D. Dissertation, Harvard University, 1965.

Stone, *Remarks*
Michael E. Stone. "Some Remarks on the Textual Criticism of IV Ezra." *Harvard Theological Review* 60 (1967): 107–15.

Suk. Sukkah

T. Tosefta

Ta. Taanit

Tam. Tamid

Tem. Temurah

Ter. Terumot

Thackeray
Henry St. John Thackeray. *The Septuagint and Jewish Worship*. London, 1923. Pp. 80–111.

Thoma
C. Thoma. "Jüdische Apokalyptik am Ende des ersten nach-christlichen Jahrhunderts: Religionsgeschichtliche Bemerkungen zur syrischen Baruchapokalypse und zum vierten Esrabuch." *Kairos* 11 (1969): 134–44.

Thompson
A. L. Thompson. *Responsibility for Evil in the Theodicy of IV Ezra: A Study Illustrating the Significance of Form and Structure for the Meaning of the Book*. (SBLDS 29). Missoula: Scholars Press, 1977.

Toh. Tohorot

Trachtenberg
Joshua Trachtenberg. *Jewish Magic and Superstition*. Philadelphia, 1961. Jewish Publication Society of America.

Turdeanu
E. Turdeanu. "L'Apocalypse de Baruch en slave." *Revue des etudes slaves* 48 (1969): 23–48.

T.Y. Tebul Yom

Urbach
E. E. Urbach. *The Sages: Their Concepts and Beliefs*. Trans. Israel Abrahams. Jerusalem: Magnes Press.

Uqs. Uqsin

Vermes, *Halakhah*
    Geza Vermes. "Sectarian Matrimonial Halakhah in the Damascus Rule." In Jackson, *Studies*. Pp. 197–202.
Vermes, *Scripture*
    Geza Vermes. *Scripture and Tradition in Judaism.* Leiden: E. J. Brill, 1961.
Vermes-Schürer
    Emil Schürer. *The History of the Jewish People in the Age of Jesus Christ (175 B.C.–A.D. 135).* Vols. 1–2. Rev. and ed. by Geza Vermes and Fergus Millar. Edinburgh: T. & T. Clark, 1973.
Wächter, *Reinheitsvorschriften*
    Theodor Wächter. *Reinheitsvorschriften im griechischen Kult.* Vol. 9. Giessen, 1910. *Religionsgeschichtliche Versuche und Vorarbeiten.*
Wahl, Otto Wahl, ed. *Apocalypsis Esdrae; Apocalypsis Sedrach; Visio Beati Esdrae.* Leiden, 1977.
Wambacq
    B. N. Wambacq. "L'Unité littéraire de Baruch I–III." *Bibliotheca Ephemeridum Theologicarum Lovaniensium* 12 (1959): 455–60.
Wambacq, *Baruch*
    B. N. Wambacq. "Les Prières de Baruch I:15–II:19, et de Daniel IX:5–19." *Biblica* 40 (1959): 463–475.
Wambacq, *L'Unité*
    B. N. Wambacq, "L'Unité du livre de Baruch." *Biblica* (1966). Pp. 574–76.
Weitzmann
    Kurt Weitzmann, ed. *The Age of Spirituality: Late Antique and Early Christian Art, Third to Seventh Century.* Catalogue of the exhibition at the Metropolitan Museum of Art, November 19, 1977 through February 12, 1978. Princeton: Princeton University Press, 1979.
Wilson
    R. McL. Wilson. *The Gnostic Problem: A Study of the Relations between Hellenistic Judaism and the Gnostic Heresy.* London, 1958.
Y. Yerushalmi. Palestinian Talmud.
Yad. Yadayim
Yeb. Yebamot
Y.T. Yom Tob
Zab, Zabim
Zahavy, "Berakhot"
    Tzvee Zahavy. "Berakhot: A Commentary." Unpublished Ms.

Zahavy, *Eleazar*
    Tzvee Zahavy. *The Traditions of Eleazar ben Azariah*. Missoula: Scholars Press, 1978.
Zeb. Zebahim
Zimmerman
    F. Zimmerman. "Underlying Documents of IV Ezra." *Jewish Quarterly Review* 51 (1960) 107–34.

Index of Biblical and Rabbinic Passages

405

General Index

416

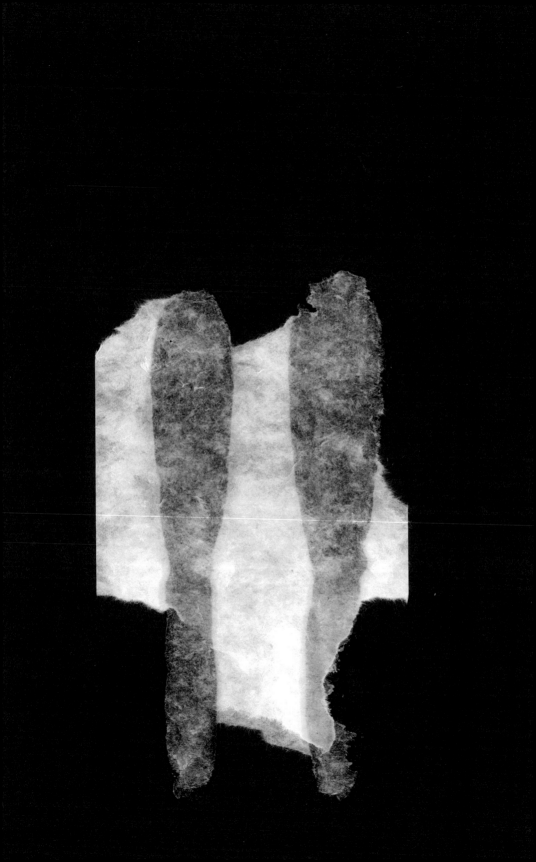